TEACHING HOT TOPICS

JEWISH VALUES, RESOURCES, AND ACTIVITIES

SUSAN FREEMAN

A.R.E. Publishing, Inc.
Denver, Colorado

Pages 13, 14, 282: Selections from *Love and Sex: A Modern Jewish Perspective* by Robert Gordis reprinted with permission.

Page 98: Reprinted from *On the Doorposts of Your House: A Mezuzot Beitcha - Prayers and Ceremonies for the Jewish Home* (pp. 146-147), edited by Chaim Stern, © 1995 CCAR Press.

Pages 280, 286, 288, 307-308: Reprinted from *This Is My Beloved, This Is My Friend* (pp. 27-28, p. 13, pp. 30-36), by Elliot N. Dorff, © 1996, The Rabbinical Assembly.

Pages 32, 37, 299, 307, 319, 321-322, 335, 336: Reprinted from *Matters of Life and Death*, Elliot N. Dorff, 1998 © The Jewish Publication Society with permission of the publisher, The Jewish Publication Society.

Pages 276, 287-288, 292, 300, 308, 336-337: Reprinted from *Does God Belong in the Bedroom*, Michael Gold, 1992 © The Jewish Publication Society with permission of the publisher, The Jewish Publication Society.

Published by:
A.R.E. Publishing, Inc.
Denver, Colorado

Library of Congress Control Number: 2003106052
ISBN 0-86705-083-7

© A.R.E. Publishing, Inc. 2003

Printed in the United States of America
10   9   8   7   6   5   4   3   2   1

DEDICATION

This book is dedicated to my sons,
Benjamin Freeman Graubart and Ilan Freeman Graubart.

ACKNOWLEDGEMENTS

I am blessed with friends and colleagues who graciously agreed to read parts of this book and provide significant feedback. Their insights and expertise challenged me to be more accurate and nuanced in my understanding of very complex issues. I am tremendously appreciative to them for their generosity of time and advice, their thoughtfulness and support. While this book is far stronger with their input, I take full responsibility for any shortcomings that remain.

These individuals are: Steve Arons, attorney and professor of legal studies at the University of Massachusetts, Amherst; Dr. Hal Blumenfeld, M.D./Ph.D. in neurology at Yale University, New Haven, Connecticut; Dr. Michelle Brody, clinical psychologist at the University of Hartford; Dr. Robert Dorit, professor of biology at Smith College; Efraim Eisen, M.F.C.T. and Rosalie Eisen, M.Ed., founders of Basherte, Inc. (a nonprofit organization known for innovative workshops and support services for Jewish singles and couples); Dr. Joyce Freeman, sociologist; Samuel Freeman, attorney and business executive; Rabbi Philip Graubart, novelist and Rabbi of Congregation Beth El, La Jolla, CA; Claudia Levin, filmmaker, whose recent production, the three-part documentary *Only a Teacher* was shown on P.B.S. and elsewhere; Laura Michaels, attorney and Executive Director of the Colorado Psychiatric Society; Dr. Susan Mosler, internist; Dorothy Nemetz, attorney and writer; and Jody Rosenbloom, Education Director at the Jewish Community of Amherst, Massachusetts.

I would also like to thank my publishers at A.R.E. Publishing, Inc.: Steve Brodsky, President; Audrey Friedman Marcus, Senior Editor; and Rabbi Raymond A. Zwerin, Senior Editor and Senior Rabbi at Temple Sinai in Denver, Colorado.

Many others listened to me as I explored ideas out loud, tried out theories, and shared discoveries. They also provided valuable support, and I am grateful to them. They include Pamela Cosman, professor of engineering at the University of California, San Diego; Joel Feldman, attorney; Rabbi Nancy Flam of the Spirituality Institute; Carol Freeman, attorney; Rana Morissey, Jewish educator specializing in teaching seventh graders; Pamela Schwartz, attorney at the National Priorities Project; and Abbie Steiner, teacher and artist.

Besides their professional accomplishments, these individuals are treasured members of their families, active members of their communities, trustworthy friends, and dedicated Jews. I have learned from them in so many ways.

CONTENTS

INTRODUCTION

WHY THIS BOOK?

Life issues are complex. Abortion, euthanasia, animal experimentation, consumerism, the death penalty, sexuality, and war are some of the many issues covered in this book. These "hot topics" raise difficult questions. A search for simple answers will elude us. Yet, to aspire to a moral life, we recognize the need to try to do the right thing.

In ethics we face the challenge of figuring out what exactly *is* the right thing. Priorities and values compete, and we must weigh our decisions carefully. We must judge how the course we take will affect our personal lives, the lives of our loved ones, the members of the larger community, and the environment. In Jewish ethics, we also wrestle with what we believe God wants of us and what our tradition expects of us. Ethics is a central area of Jewish interest. It has been for centuries, really since biblical times — the beginnings of our religion.

The goal of this book is to give learners comprehensive resources and tools for grappling with complex issues. Jewish teachings can help us form worthy responses to the challenges of our time. We may extrapolate from our tradition, but also may need to innovate as we encounter modern lifestyles, civil laws, new technologies, scientific discoveries, and sociological realities. Thus, contemporary factors will color our perspectives and decisions.

Rather than *prescribing* the "right" response to a particular dilemma, this book seeks to *describe* a range of defensible responses. The ideas and material in this book will help learners meaningfully confront some of the most difficult issues of our day. This book provides:

- Facts, general perspectives, and other important information about each issue covered;

- Jewish Perspectives;

- Scenarios, highlighting how issues have changed over the years;

- Text study passages with probing questions;

- Activity suggestions that draw on wide-ranging pedagogical methods;

- Bibliographies for each chapter;

- Glossary of important terms;

- A succinct table summarizing points and counterpoints;

- Related virtues *(middot)* and commandments *(mitzvot)*.

See the "How The Chapters are Organized" section below for more about the content of the chapters.

WHO IS THIS BOOK FOR?

Because of the complex and sometimes mature subject matter of the material, *Teaching Hot Topics* is geared toward those who teach students from middle school through adulthood. However, a teacher who wants to address one or more issues with a younger group will also find useful material and suggestions. One of the beauties of *Teaching Hot Topics* is its flexibility — the entire manual can be used as the central curriculum for an upper grade or Confirmation program, or individual chapters can be implemented as "mini-courses," electives, or one-shot study sessions with middle school students, teens, or adults. The topics are ideal for high school students in youth group and camp settings, or for adults in a retreat or weekly study program.

The book also lends itself to independent study. That is, an individual can take him/herself through a substantial course of study by focusing on the Overview and Text Study sections of each chapter. In self-run study groups, such as in Havurot, auxiliary organizations of congregations, etc., the book may serve as a guide.

HOW THE CHAPTERS ARE ORGANIZED

Specifically, with slight variations, a reader will find these subheadings:

- Overview
- Scenarios
- Text Study
- Related Middot and Mitzvot
- Activities
- Glossary
- Bibliography

Detailed explanations of each of these sections follows.

Overview

The Overview is an orientation to the topic. A brief introduction presents the crux of the issue and the moral challenge. That is, what essential dilemmas and ethical quandaries does the issue pose? Then, background, major considerations, and controversies are presented under the subcategories of General Perspectives and Jewish Perspectives. The Overview concludes with a summary of critical points. Some readers may find it useful to read the Summary of the Overview first, then go back to the beginning of the Overview.

General Perspectives

This section includes some or all of the following: factual information, relevant secular laws, modern attitudes, sociological factors, and ideas and theories drawn from thinkers in the Jewish and non-Jewish world.

To grasp the complexity of the issues as we face them today, we must draw on resources that reach beyond traditional Jewish texts. Some subjects discussed in this book were virtually unknown, or at least rarely broached, until contemporary times. Such issues include school violence, eating disorders, cloning and genetic engineering, and the serious effects of cigarette smoking and alcohol abuse. Other issues look very different now than they did even a few decades ago. Examples include birth control, abortion, animal experimentation, war, and euthanasia. We need a broad understanding of each topic. A firm grasp of *general* perspectives will enhance our ability to find appropriate *Jewish* responses to vital issues.

Jewish Perspectives

This section includes analysis of relevant legal and narrative material drawn from Jewish sacred texts and other historical documents. In addition, this section presents contemporary Jewish views: theories, attitudes, *halachic* (legal) opinions, and ongoing debates.

Ultimately, this book assumes that our goal is to strive to respond to contemporary dilemmas from an authentic Jewish place. Authenticity requires us to engage with our tradition, our heritage, our sacred books. As Jews, we do not draw conclusions solely by reading an article in *The New York Times* or in a prestigious medical journal. We look beyond contemporary media and sociological trends for answers. Conversely, we do not limit our decision making to personal whims, agendas, impressions, or even gut feelings. As significant as our own experiences and circumstances may be, as Jews, we try to support our responses using writings and traditions from our heritage.

A search for moral choices requires study and analysis of the layers of insights in our tradition. In the end, our intent is for our responses to critical issues to reflect Jewish wisdom and moral integrity. By wrestling with Jewish and general perspectives, we accept the awesome responsibility of dealing with life's complexities.

Summary of the Overview

A few short statements summarize the main dilemmas and conclusions presented in the Overview. Some readers may choose to "preview" an issue by skipping to the Summary, and then going back to the chapter beginning for more details. Since the Summary captures the issue's main points, a leader may wish to return to it for review and reinforcement during the course of study. The Summary provides a good check for teachers: "Do my students understand these key points? Have I covered the material sufficiently so that these concluding statements are now obvious to my students? Could my students repeat these ideas back to me?" Also, reviewing the Summary statements will help students reorient to the topic when they revisit it over multiple sessions.

Scenarios

Each chapter includes two or more scenarios. In most chapters, a key objective of the scenarios is to show how things have changed over the years. That is, what gives the issue its particular complexity *now*, as opposed to earlier times? Presenting scenarios in this way highlights the uniqueness of the challenges we face today. Furthermore, scenarios help personalize abstract ideas, making them more immediate and relevant.

Text Study

The Text Study passages are categorized under the subheadings of "On the One Hand . . . " and "On the Other Hand . . . " This division of ideas helps learners focus on the tensions that make each issue so enigmatic or problematic. For example, in the Death Penalty chapter, the first grouping of texts are placed under these two subheadings:

On the One Hand:

It is appropriate to consider capital punishment for the perpetrators of certain crimes.

On the Other Hand:

The death penalty is so severe, so final, that to carry it out should be very difficult, if not impossible.

Beneath each subheading are one or more texts. Under the first "On the One Hand" subheading, the texts are numbered 1A, 1B, 1C, etc. Under the second "On the Other Hand" subheading, the texts are numbered 1a, 1b, 1c, etc.

Studying opposing viewpoints, juxtaposed against each other, intensifies students' awareness of just how complex the issues are. The same "On the One Hand/On the Other Hand" points (without the texts) also can be found in an easily accessible chart format near the beginning of the "Text Study" section of each chapter. This chart succinctly highlights the questions, points, and counterpoints that make each issue so enigmatic. The chart is particularly useful in that it is straightforward, concise, and easy to reproduce (photocopy) for student use. As an example, the first question, point, and counterpoint presented in the chapter on the Death Penalty are reproduced at the top of the next page.

Evaluating the Death Penalty: Questions to Consider

The Question	On the One Hand	On the Other Hand
1. Is the death penalty a legitimate punishment? (see p. 138)	It is appropriate to consider capital punishment for the perpetrator of certain crimes.	The death penalty is so severe, so final that to carry it out should be very difficult, if not impossible.

Probing questions follow each pairing of texts. These questions further students' engagement with the material.

An exception to the Text Study format outlined above is in the chapter on "Harmful Behaviors: Smoking, Drinking, and Over/Undereating." The texts in that chapter are organized in a more straightforward way — according to subtopic rather than according to viewpoints and opposing viewpoints.

Related Middot and Mitzvot

Each chapter includes a comprehensive list of *middot* (virtues) and *mitzvot* (commandments) that relate directly to the topic at hand. These virtues, values, qualities, and actions support and enhance ethical decision making. Moral choices ideally extend beyond a "going-through-the-motions." That is, *how* we do things on a more qualitative level is something to pay attention to, as well. For example, an ethical decision regarding euthanasia should encompass more than *halachic* or legal discussions around "should we or shouldn't we pull the plug." Trustworthiness, compassion, and humility are a few of the additional qualities that a wise decision maker aspires to embody.

Activities that encourage students to reflect upon and develop qualities that support ethical choices are found in the "Activities" section of each chapter, under "Applying *Middot* and *Mitzvot*" (see a description of that section below).

Activities

There are all kinds of ways to learn. This book holds that the most effective learning happens when teachers draw on as many modalities as possible. Teaching texts, facts, and established information is essential. This part of learning is what we might call "transmission."[1] But "transformation" is necessary, too. Transformation requires students to delve deep within themselves to process ideas and dilemmas. To discuss the facts without processing feelings and examining personal experience, or to rely on feelings without the facts shortchanges meaningful understanding of the issues. Along with Text Study and probing questions, most chapters include the six activity sections described below.

A First Look: Key Issues and Ideas

Like Text Study, this section emphasizes "transmission." That is, the objective is transmission of information — helping students grasp facts and established ideas. To analyze dilemmas and come up with ethical responses to them requires mastery of certain basic information — a foundation of knowledge.

Applying Middot and Mitzvot

The activities in this section encourage students to reflect upon and develop qualities that support ethical choices. They relate directly to the virtues, values, qualities, and actions listed in the "Related *Middot* and *Mitzvot*" section of each

---

[1]See Carol K. Ingall's *Transmission and Transformation: A Jewish Perspective on Moral Education,* New York: The Melton Center for Jewish Education, 1999.

chapter (see description above). Also included in this section are additional resources that provide more background information on these important *middot* and *mitzvot*.

Stories: Understanding through Listening

Many issues in this book bring up dilemmas that are out of the range of students' everyday experience. Clearly, students may have had direct exposure to a particular topic, such as smoking, drinking, school violence, or sexuality. Still, listening to the stories of others — vicariously entering the narratives of other people's worlds — adds a dimension of understanding that can be extremely compelling. Stories transform abstract details of laws, rules, history, and scientific facts into something more tangible; the issues take on a heightened level of importance, and even urgency. Listening to others' stories may challenge conclusions we draw when we rely only upon our own personal experiences.

This section provides suggestions and activities for learning by listening to and reflecting on real or potentially real situations.

Action: Getting Out, Getting Involved

These activities seek to move students beyond the theoretical realm and into the practical. The activities respond to such questions as: What does what I'm learning mean outside the classroom? What is the significance of our discussions? How might taking action concerning these issues make the world a better place?

Jewish ethical practice includes learning what our tradition says. It includes struggling with our own consciences. But there is an additional challenge. Comprehensive ethical practice includes *Tikkun Olam*, repairing the world.

The action suggestions in this section guide students to "get out" and "get involved" in the issues that concern them. Through these activities, students are urged to "make a difference."

Wrestling: Engagement with the Issues

This section focuses on the processing that takes place within our minds and hearts as we put all the pieces together. More so than the other activity sections, this one requires students to invest *themselves* in the issues, to engage with the implications of their decisions. The activities challenge learners to grapple with what Jewish tradition says, with what general perspectives teach, and with what their consciences tell them: How to find the right balance; how ultimately to make moral choices.

Drawing on creative writing, art, drama, and other modes of expression, these activities provide an extensive opportunity for students to explore the tensions embedded in the issues.

Empathy

Struggling with critical dilemmas and making choices can be an anguishing process. We may have personal experience with some issues. However, even if we do not, we can empathize with those who confront difficult questions, such as the following:

- I was raped, and now I am pregnant. Should I have an abortion?

- What is an appropriate punishment for the man who murdered my son?

- Should I have my stepfather taken off the life support machinery he has become dependent upon?

- My addiction to alcohol is ruining my life. How can I stop feeling so overwhelmed?

- Should I refuse to participate in animal dissections in my science class?

- Should I sleep with my boyfriend/girlfriend?

- How do I make appropriate and responsible decisions about love and sexuality?

Part of the learning process should include fostering empathy in our students. No matter what the outcome to questions like those above, recognizing and appreciating the challenging and often painful struggles people go through enhances our humanity. Ethics calls upon us to "do the right thing." But *to be a compassionate person doing the right thing* is what "a good Jew" aspires to. Teachers and leaders can nurture compassion by including some activities that emphasize empathy.

Glossary

Chapters may include Hebrew or scientific terms that will be unfamiliar to some teachers and students. Where appropriate, a Glossary is included as a helpful reference for such terms.

Bibliography

Most chapters include an extensive listing of Jewish and general books, web sites, and films for further reference, research, and/or support. Note that while specific sections of the films listed may be valuable for illustrating certain aspects of a particular topic, it may not be appropriate to have students view the entire film. Prescreening is strongly recommended.

A complete Bibliography for the five chapters dealing with issues of sexuality (Chapters 11-15) appears at the end of Chapter 11, "Foundations of Sexual Ethics," on pages 294-296.

HOW TO USE THIS BOOK

Who Should Teach?

Both experienced teachers and novice teachers will find this book valuable. *Teaching Hot Topics* seeks to be a comprehensive resource; thus, interested individuals of any background, including self-guided learners, can effectively draw on the information and ideas presented here.

Effective Learning Environments

The material in this book may be taught in a synagogue classroom, sanctuary, Day School classroom, living room, youth group lounge, senior center, outdoors at a retreat, or at any other appropriate place. A skillful teacher, particularly a classroom teacher, will vary pedagogical approaches to study, discussion, and activities. Possible learning frameworks include:

- The whole group working together

- Learning in pairs or small groups

- Solo work

- Homework

- Field Work (i.e., site visits and/or social action projects outside the classroom)

Defining Goals

What do you want your students to gain by learning about these issues? What do you want them to walk away with? Many reasonable goals exist. Whether you do a whole course on critical issues or just one session, knowing what your goals are will make planning and execution of lessons more coherent and successful. Below are examples of possible goals. As preparation for teaching, a worthwhile exercise is to rank order your goals. You may want to use the goals listed below, perhaps deleting some and/or adding others:

- Teach students what Judaism says about issues they hear about in the popular press and elsewhere.

- Educate students about critical issues in our world today.

- Give students the opportunity to discuss challenging topics in a trusting, safe environment.

- Provide students with skills and methods for addressing ethical dilemmas, which they may apply to circumstances outside the classroom.

- Supervise social activism experiences that relate to these issues — giving students a foundation for lifelong dedication to *Tikkun Olam* ("repairing the world").

- Support students in making difficult decisions in their personal lives.

- Nurture compassion, sensitivity, and tolerance for different views.

- Build group bonding and rapport through study of significant issues.

- Challenge students intellectually.

- Respond to a particular current event.

- Address a specific situation in your community.

Getting Started

How to start a lesson? For some, this is the hardest part of planning. Once you make a decision on how to begin, planning the next steps often is easier. Here are various suggestions for introducing a topic.

- Organize a "whip" — quickly going around the group, giving everyone a chance to say one thing they know (or would like to learn) about the topic at hand.

- Using a lecture style, draw on the chapter's Overview to give students a framework for the issue. Make notes or use a highlighter pen to remind yourself of ideas you want to be sure to cover.

- Have students read all or part of the Overview silently.

- Write the statements from the Summary of the Overview on the board. Then elaborate on each statement, using information provided in the Overview itself. (The Summary of the Overview concludes each chapter's Overview.)

- Begin with Text Study.

- Begin with an Activity.

- Begin with the Scenarios.

- For each student, photocopy the "On the One Hand/On the Other Hand" Table (in each chapter's "Text Study" section). As a whole group or in pairs, read through and discuss the points and counterpoints.

- Bring in a guest to share his/her personal story.

- Go on a field trip to a place that has relevance to the topic.

- Share newspaper and/or magazine articles that address current news and events related to the topic.

Once you get started, the possibilities for grappling with these topics are endless. The material is fascinating and engaging!

Perhaps you will begin a session on the ethics of war by having students listen to the story of a war veteran, continue by studying what Jewish texts say, hold a debate, and conclude by creating a war memorial in remembrance of a particular conflict.

Or, you might begin a session on animal experimentation by studying the points and counterpoints presented in the Table in the "Text Study" section, then elaborate on the controversies by presenting ideas included in the Overview, continue by completing two or more activities, and conclude by taking a field trip to a medical research facility.

Your path of study will lead you to many interesting and challenging places. May this journey of learning support you and your students as you strive to live lives of integrity!

B'Hatzlacha — may you find success in your teaching!

PART I

BODY, HEALTH, MEDICINE

ABORTION

CLONING AND OTHER GENETIC TECHNOLOGIES

EUTHANASIA

HARMFUL BEHAVIORS: SMOKING, DRINKING,
AND OVER/UNDEREATING

CHAPTER I

ABORTION

OVERVIEW

When does life begin? For what reasons might abortion be acceptable? for any reason? under limited circumstances? never? Who decides? Is the decision completely up to the pregnant woman herself? Do others, such as the woman's partner, family members, her religious community, the government, have a legitimate stake in a woman's decision to continue or to terminate a pregnancy? Such questions stir up controversy and impassioned feelings. Responses to these questions form the crux of the debate concerning abortion. In this chapter we will examine opinions on what defines a person, what circumstances may and may not justify abortion, and what role society should play in regulating the personal decisions of the individual.

Jewish Perspectives

Our body of Jewish literature does not offer us one clear-cut position on abortion. Rather, there are matters of more and matters of less consensus. To grasp Jewish opinion on this subject, it is helpful to highlight areas of agreement, and then examine areas in which there is more dissent.

Defining a Person

Our tradition makes a distinction between the status of a fetus as opposed to that of an independent, live human being. An often cited example involves a situation in which two men are scuffling. A pregnant woman standing by gets hit and because of her injury, miscarries. Punishment for damage to the fetus does not result in punishment equal to damage caused to the mother (Exodus 21:22; Text #1d below).

From a Jewish legal point of view, a fetus in the womb is not a person until it is born (*Sanhedrin* 72b). The consensus notion is this: full human life deserves more consideration than "potential life," yet potential life is valued.

What then is potential life? We understand that our tradition attaches value to potential life, even if not to the same degree as full human life. Still, we must be more specific, as our understanding of potential life impacts abortion decisions. Over the years, Jewish sources have attempted to specify various stages of fetal development. For example, until the fortieth day, a pregnancy is said to consist of "mere fluid" (*Yevamot* 69b). Thus, until that day, abortion opinions tend to be more lenient. Other sources consider the fetus to be an organic part of the mother's body (*Chullin* 58a, *Arachin* 7a; Text #1a and #1b below). Wrestling with these and other notions of personhood is an integral part of the Jewish ethical process of assessing whether termination of a pregnancy is justified.

To sum up the Jewish perspective so far: the definition of personhood is a key gray area; our Sages have differing opinions as to when it begins. There is consensus that a fetus does not have the same status as a live human being. There is less agreement, however, about what exactly is the status of a fetus. Divided attitudes toward potential life produce the sometimes contradictory judgments on the permissibility of abortion.

When Is Abortion Acceptable?

Our Sages agree that if we are being "pursued" by someone who would cause us harm, we are allowed to protect ourselves. When a woman's life is in danger due to her pregnancy, the fetus may be considered a "pursuer." A woman is justified in saving her own life from the threat of the pursuer and may terminate the pregnancy. Specifically, if a woman in labor is having a life threatening difficulty, we may dismember the embryo within her, either with drugs or surgery because the fetus is like a pursuer seeking to kill her. The pregnant woman's life takes precedence over fetal life. But once the head or greater part of the fetus has emerged, it is considered a person and cannot be harmed since we do not set aside one life for another (see Text Study #4 a-c below).

Thus, there is consensus in Judaism that abortion is permissible when a woman's life is in imminent, physical danger. The more controversial question is this: What about when a woman's life is not in imminent, physical danger? That is, are there situations when our Rabbis would allow abortion?

Respected opinions express reluctance for terminating a pregnancy that is not a direct threat to a woman's life. Even so, Jewish discussion over the ages devotes serious consideration to a broad range of potentially legitimate reasons for abortion. These include: saving a mother from great pain, severe emotional anguish, or public shame; in cases of rape; and/or when there is medical evidence indicating a deformed or diseased fetus. Taken into account are both traditional *halachic* opinions, and information gleaned from modern knowledge (for example, genetic tests that indicate fatal diseases or serious deformities). The "Text Study" section below includes a wide range of voices concerning permissibility of abortion outside of life threatening cases (see passages under #5 and #6, plus #8B).

While there are perspectives, even in traditional Jewish circles, that reflect a liberal attitude toward abortion, we are not to take such decisions lightly. We also value potential life, and the abundant discussion about abortion reflects our impulse to protect it. The challenge is how to do so appropriately and wisely. This sentiment of caution leads to another area of relative consensus from a Jewish perspective. That is, very few, if any Jewish religious leaders would regard abor-

tion for whatever reason as a legitimate Jewish position. For example, using abortion as a means of selecting the gender of a baby or as a form of birth control is considered unacceptable.

Who Decides?

Generally, Jews would agree on who should *not* make decisions about abortion. That is, we tend to be wary of public officials becoming involved in what may be considered private and/or religious matters. In making decisions about abortion, religious Jews will want to know what *our* tradition has to say regarding their circumstances. They likely will view their situation as very personal and private. Therefore, the widely accepted Jewish view is that abortion decisions do not belong in the domain of government.

Then, where do abortion decisions belong? With no one Jewish position on abortion, a middle ground response would be: abortion decisions belong with the pregnant woman in consultation with supportive and compassionate individuals who have her essential needs and beliefs at heart. To make a *Jewish decision* involves study of Jewish sources. Some women may feel the need to discuss their situation with a Rabbi. Other appropriate support and guidance resources for Jewish women include: Jewish Family Services and Planned Parenthood (some branches of which have Rabbis who are available as "all options counselors").

Is there a Jewish perspective that would advocate for a woman's right to choose, no matter what her extended family or community might desire? We have learned that many Jewish legal sources recognize a woman's emotional pain, anguish, and/or shame as providing sufficient grounds for permitting abortion. Clearly, no one but a woman herself can fully understand her feelings about her pregnancy. No one but she experiences her internal state of being. Allowing for a woman's psychological needs — which a Jewish perspective does — comes close to the notion of a woman's right to choose. Pressing emotional needs can undercut other considerations. In such a circumstance, a woman's feelings about her pregnancy would influence an abortion decision to such an extent that, in effect, the decision could be seen as originating from her, as being *chosen* by her.

The American Jewish community is overwhelmingly supportive of reproductive choice. The Jewish Council for Public Affairs advocates for women's right to choose. However, the Union of Orthodox Jewish Congregations has expressed concerns that the Council's policy usurps a Rabbi's role in deciding each case based on Jewish law. Still, the JCPA continues to fight government efforts to restrict access to safe and legal abortion.

General Perspectives

Defining a Person

There are both secular and non-Jewish religious perspectives that agree with the Jewish position that life begins at birth. But not everyone agrees. The Jewish belief is that a fetus is a full person only once the greater part of its body (or head) has entered the world. In contrast, a belief largely represented in America by the Catholic Church as well as a number of Protestant denominations, is that life begins at conception. Those who maintain this belief consider an embryo a person who has a soul. They may assert that deliberately ending fetal life is a violent crime. Some anti-abortionists equate abortion with murder.

There is a serious belief gap between one group that likens a pregnancy in its early stages to "mere fluid" (*Yevamot* 69b) and another that asserts that an embryo embodies a human soul. The distance between such beliefs is what makes abortion a controversial issue, fraught with emotion. Perhaps the only thing we can say for sure regarding general perspectives defining a person is that there is a range of views. Just as people have different beliefs concerning afterlife, we have different beliefs about the essence of life before birth. At this point in human history, we

have no objective means of determining what a soul is, how it exists, and when it enters the body.

When Is Abortion Acceptable?

Over the years, the United States, as elsewhere, has passed many laws regulating the parameters of what constitutes a legally performed abortion. Generally, various political, medical, ethical, and/or religious groups will look at two key considerations. They are: (1) for what reasons might an abortion be justified, and (2) up until what, if any, stage (i.e., trimester) in the pregnancy may an abortion be performed.

There was a time in the U.S. as recent as the early twentieth century in which birth control was not available to women. Legal mandates were passed prohibiting the dissemination of birth control. As many as one in three pregnancies was terminated through abortion. Though "therapeutic" abortion was allowable in cases where physicians deemed it to be medically necessary, realistically, the procedure was available only to women of means. Many poor women, who had to resort to non-professional or self-induced abortions, died or became mutilated because of botched procedures.

In the decades prior to the 1950s, physicians had a hard time justifying abortions by deeming them medically necessary. With advances in medicine and fewer pregnancies facing complications, physicians increasingly were questioned for labeling abortions "therapeutic." In 1959, the American Law Institute proposed new guidelines that addressed the reasons that an abortion might be justified. The Institute's "Model Penal Code"[1] permitted physicians to terminate a pregnancy:

- if they believed it threatened the life of the pregnant woman or would critically impair her physical or mental condition.

- if the child would be born with a grave physical or mental defect.

[1]*Abortion: An Eternal Social and Moral Issue* by Mei Ling Rein, 8.

- if the pregnancy resulted from rape or incest.

- if the need for abortion was approved by two physicians.

Despite these guidelines, attaining a legal abortion in America nonetheless remained very difficult. In the 1960s, the abortion issue was pushed further. There were two key factors for this: One reason had to do with an unfolding situation in which many pregnant women were bearing infants with birth defects. Thalidomide, a drug given to pregnant women to treat morning sickness, was producing deformities in infants. In addition, pregnant women who had contracted rubella during an epidemic of the illness were delivering children with serious disabilities. The ability to make choices in the face of these health threats was an important factor advancing efforts to liberalize abortion laws. The other important reason was the rise of the civil rights movement that emphasized individual freedoms. Women began to rally around their right to self-determination, including making decisions affecting their bodies, and indeed their whole lives.

In 1973, the Supreme Court made a landmark decision on abortion in *Roe v. Wade*. On the one hand, the Court sought to protect individual privacy and a woman's right to terminate a pregnancy. On the other hand, it recognized the state's interest in protecting the health of pregnant women and the potential for human life. The Court's decision addressed the key issues of: (1) valid reasons for justifying abortions, and (2) stages of pregnancy during which abortion may be performed. It allowed unrestricted abortion in the first trimester, reasonably regulated abortion in relation to the woman's health in the second trimester, and permitted states to prohibit abortion, except when necessary to preserve the woman's life or health, in the third semester.

During the decades following *Roe v. Wade*, there has been a great deal of legislation around abortion issues. In particular, those who oppose abortion have made efforts to impose increasing restrictions on and limit access to the procedure. As long as there are differing views on the definition of a person, the status of the fetus, and the extent of a woman's right to self-determination, the issue will continue to be a volatile one.

Who Decides?

Citizens of a nation are subject to its laws, even as they may try to live by the precepts of their personal beliefs. America is a democratic country that officially upholds such values as:

- separation of church and state.

- civil liberties, including the right to privacy.

- equality of opportunity.

- equality of protection for citizens.

Public officials face the challenge of creating laws that reflect these values.

When abortion laws are liberal, individuals have more latitude in determining if and when termination of a pregnancy is the appropriate choice for them. They may base their decision on personal beliefs, religious affiliation, and health and lifestyle needs. The law remains liberal when it emphasizes values of separation of church and state, civil liberties, and equality of opportunity (e.g., access to health services).

Abortion law becomes more restrictive when lawmakers assert that the value of protecting citizens includes fetuses. They attach a sense of urgency to "protection of the unborn" and feel this protection outweighs other values (such as separation of church and state or civil liberties). Underlying restrictive abortion laws is the belief that fetal life is no different in worth from full human life. Some elected officials and the voters who put them in office assert that the state has an obligation to define personhood, that is, to defend "truth" as they perceive it. To them, this platform includes creating laws that would restrict a woman's choices concerning the course of her pregnancy.

In sum, as to the question of who decides, when the law is liberal, women make their own choices regarding abortion. Women may choose to do so in consultation with individuals such as other family members, clergy, physicians, mental health professionals, teachers, friends, and so on.

In contrast, when the law is restrictive, the choices narrow and potentially disappear. If a woman's desires and needs fall outside current legal regulations, she will face two "choices." One is to break the law by seeking an illegal abortion. This may involve penalties. Furthermore, unregulated abortions can be unsafe and even life threatening. A woman's other "choice" is to carry an unwanted pregnancy to term. Thus, when the law is restrictive, politics and lawmakers have more input, possibly prescribing the course a woman's pregnancy *must* take. What the pregnant woman herself needs or wants regarding her body and her family planning may be ruled irrelevant. Abortion laws at the most restrictive level eliminate from a woman's control the question of "who decides."

Summary of the Overview

The paragraphs below summarize key Jewish considerations regarding abortion as discussed in the overview.

1. An embryo is potential life. Jewish tradition regards potential life respectfully even though we may not equate it in value to full human life.

2. Reasons to abort must be evaluated thoughtfully as a decision to abort is a serious matter. Abortion is a legitimate option when a woman's life is in imminent danger due to her pregnancy. Rabbis and scholars weigh in differently regarding abortion for other reasons, such as: the fetus is deformed or diseased, the pregnancy is causing the woman great emotional anguish, or the pregnancy is a result of an illicit union. On balance, Judaism is on the more liberal side of the spectrum in accepting abortion for reasons other than a life threatening situation.

3. Weighing the possibility of abortion usually begins with the pregnant woman. Her physical condition, her personal situation, and the community in which she lives all may be factored into a decision. A woman may decide on her own or choose to consult with others. She may relinquish the decision to religious authorities. If she lives in a place where abortion laws are restrictive, she may have no choice at all. That is, the law will dictate the course her pregnancy must take given her particular circumstances.

SCENARIOS: JEWS LIVING IN DIFFERENT COMMUNITIES

Below are two imaginary scenarios highlighting the potential effects of religious guidelines and/or secular laws on a woman's reproductive choices. They are intended to raise questions and spark discussion. Read each scenario to or with your students, and engage them in small or large group discussions. Use the "Focus the Discussion" section below to help identify the important issues and facilitate these discussions. Note that additional questions relating to these scenarios are found in the "Stories: Understanding through Listening" section below (pp. 17-18).

Following the discussions, continue on to the "Text Study" section to see what Jewish and other sources have to say on the subject. Finally, you may wish to have students discuss the scenarios a second time, to see if their views have changed.

Scenario I: A Jewish Community in Jerusalem in 1900

Devorah, a 16-year-old, was raped by her uncle. From this violent act, she is pregnant. She feels anguish, shame, and anger regarding her circumstances. Her uncle has been punished for his crime. Meanwhile, Devorah faces an unwanted pregnancy. Chances are reasonable that she would give birth to a healthy infant. However, she cannot bear to go through with the pregnancy and either raise the child or give it up for adoption. She wants an abortion.

While not all Rabbis would feel abortion is appropriate in Devorah's situation, her own Rabbi supports her in her wish to terminate the pregnancy. She is referred to a respected midwife who prescribes herbs for her that induce abortion.

Scenario II: In America in 1900

Debra, a 16-year-old, was raped by her uncle. From this violent act, she is pregnant. She feels anguish, shame, and anger regarding her circumstances. Her uncle has been punished for his crime. Meanwhile, Debra faces an unwanted pregnancy. Chances are reasonable that she would give birth to a healthy infant. However, she cannot bear to go through with the pregnancy and either raise the child or give it up for adoption. She wants an abortion.

However, abortion is illegal. Her Rabbi supports her in her wish to terminate the pregnancy, yet he feels he must caution her against following through with the procedure since it is illegal. Furthermore, because abortion is unregulated, it is potentially dangerous.

Despite the caution, Debra proceeds to arrange for an illegal abortion. From a neighbor she obtains the name of a person who performs abortions. Debra does not realize that the person is unqualified and goes through with the procedure. There are complications that the abortion provider is ill-equipped to handle. Debra barely makes it through. Her reproductive organs are permanently scarred. She will never be able to give birth to children in the future.

Focus the Discussion

Both religious guidelines and secular laws have a tremendous potential to affect a woman's reproductive choices. When guidelines are flexible and take into account a wide range of factors, the outcome of an abortion decision will best reflect the health and well-being of the pregnant woman. When abortion is illegal, as it was in America for many years, women still may seek to exercise control over their future, but will do so at greatly increased risk to themselves.

TEXT STUDY

The questions of defining a person, when abortion should be acceptable, and who should make that decision are difficult and controversial. Jewish textual sources provide many answers, but these answers often highlight the tension between seemingly opposing considerations. The chart on the next page poses the questions and offers two opposing points of view. Text sources supporting each of these points of view follow below.

1. **Should abortion be permitted?**

   On the One Hand:

   Abortion deliberately ends life in its earliest stages. Permitting abortion forces us to wrestle with our sacred obligation to protect life.

   A. I hereby declare today, with heaven and earth as my witnesses, that I have put before you life and death, blessing and curse. Choose life, that you and your descendants may live (Deuteronomy 30:19).

   On the Other Hand:

   A fetus is not equivalent to a full human being; it is *potential* life.

   a. The fetus is as the thigh of its mother (*Chullin* 58a).

   b. . . . for [the fetus] is her body (*Arachin* 7a).

   c. If a woman is pregnant, the semen, until the fortieth day is only a mere fluid (*Yevamot* 69b).

Making an Ethical Decision about Abortion: Questions to Consider

The Question	On the One Hand	On the Other Hand
1. Should abortion be permitted? (see p. 8)	Abortion deliberately ends life in its earliest stages. Permitting abortion forces us to wrestle with our sacred obligation to protect life.	A fetus is not equivalent to a full human being; it is *potential* life.
2. What is our duty to protect an unborn fetus? (see p. 10)	Even *potential* life is to be valued.	Our duty to protect *potential* life differs from our duty to protect living human beings.
3. What status does a fetus have as part of the mother? (see p. 10)	A fetus is an organic part of the mother's body. Aborting it is like wounding oneself, and wounding oneself is prohibited.	When the fetus is not yet fully developed (but "merely fluid"), aborting is not "wounding." There is no established organ to wound.
4. Who has the right to decide life or death? (see p. 11)	God alone pronounces life and death.	When your life is threatened, you are permitted to protect yourself from the danger that "pursues" you.
5. Under what circumstances relating to the health of the mother would abortion be justified? (see p. 11)	One area of leniency for justifying abortion is when the mother's life is in danger.	There are legitimate needs for terminating a pregnancy, other than imminent danger to a mother's physical health, that justify abortion.
6. Under what circumstances relating to the health of the fetus would abortion be justified? (see p. 12)	Justifying abortion to prevent the birth of a defective, retarded, or deformed infant is unacceptable.	Aborting when sufficient medical evidence indicates the infant will be born deformed is permissible.
7. Who should determine the course of an individual human being's life? (see p. 13)	The course of our existence is not solely in our hands.	It is up to individual human beings to steer the course of their lives as best they can determine, including what happens to their bodies.
8. Who should be responsible for setting standards regarding abortion? (see p. 14)	Society has a stake in the life of the fetus.	No objective standard exists for permitting or prohibiting abortion. Abortion is a private issue.

d. [Capital punishment is not imposed on one who, during a scuffle, causes a pregnant woman to miscarry because there is] no form [yet to the fetus] . . . (*Septuagint* translation of Exodus 21:22).

Probing: Ideas and Issues

Do you agree that we have a sacred obligation to protect life? If so, where does this obligation come from? Consider these questions:

- Does the fetus have a soul?

- Is the fetus part of the mother's body?

- Does the status of the fetus change over the course of the pregnancy (e.g., in the first trimester or the first 40 days versus in the last trimester)?

What do you believe about life in the womb and from where do you derive your beliefs?

2. **What is our duty to protect an unborn fetus?**

On the One Hand:

Even potential life is to be valued.

A. When two men scuffle and one deals a blow to a pregnant woman, so that her children abort forth, but (other) harm does not occur, he is to be fined, yes, fined, as the woman's spouse imposes for him, and the matter placed before the judges . . . (Exodus 21:22).

B. He who indulges in marital intercourse on the ninetieth day [of pregnancy, when it was thought to injure the embryo], it is as though he had shed blood (*Niddah* 31a).

C. As the Mishnah states regarding a one day old infant, that capital punishment is prescribed for murdering it, for a one day old infant, but not for a fetus . . . nevertheless with regard to keeping the laws (i.e., of Shabbat) we set them aside for it (i.e., we may break the laws of Shabbat in

order to save a fetus) . . . since the Torah declared "set aside one Sabbath that someone might keep many Sabbaths" (*Halachot Gedolot*).

On the Other Hand:

Our duty to protect potential life differs from our duty to protect living human beings.

a. But if harm should occur [to the pregnant woman herself], then shall you give life for life (Exodus 21:23).

b. It was necessary for the Torah to write "he that smites a man [*ish*] so that he dies shall surely be put to death" [Exodus 21:12]. For had the Torah written only "whoso kills any person [*nefesh*] the murderer shall be slain" [Numbers 35:30], one would have concluded that capital punishment is applied to one who destroys a fetus (*Sanhedrin* 84b).

Probing: Ideas and Issues

The Bible states that a fine is to be imposed on a man who, in the midst of a scuffle with another man, causes a pregnant woman standing by to miscarry. Do you think a fine is the appropriate punishment? Explain.

In Talmudic days, it was thought that engaging in sexual intercourse during certain stages of pregnancy could damage the fetus. Nowadays, in healthy pregnancies, we know this is not a concern. The underlying message, however, is relevant — that potential life has value. How might this message be applied in discussions on the ethics of abortion? How do our obligations to protect potential life differ from our obligations to protect full human life?

3. **What status does a fetus have as part of the mother?**

On the One Hand:

A fetus is an organic part of the mother's body. Aborting it is like wounding oneself, and wounding oneself is prohibited.

A. It is prohibited for people to injure themselves or their peers (Maimonides, *Laws of Injury and Damage* 5:1).

On the Other Hand:

When the fetus is not yet fully developed (but "merely fluid"), aborting is not "wounding." There is no established organ to wound.

a. Once abortion is viewed as the wounding of a limb (in this case of the mother), then prior to the formation of the fetus, which takes place at 40 days, there cannot be any organ to be wounded (Basil F. Herring, contemporary scholar, explaining Rabbi Weinberg's opinion in *Responsa Seridei Ish*, Jerusalem, 1966, vol. 3, no. 127).

Probing: Ideas and Issues

Do you think a reasonable argument against abortion is that it is equivalent to deliberately wounding yourself? Why or why not?

4. **Who has the right to decide life or death?**

On the One Hand:

God alone pronounces life and death.

A. "I [God] will kill and I will make to live" (Deuteronomy 32:39).

On the Other Hand:

When your life is threatened, you are permitted to protect yourself from the danger that "pursues" you.

a. If a woman in labor has a [life threatening] difficulty, one dismembers the embryo within her, removing it limb by limb, for her life takes precedence over its life. But once its greater part [*Tosefta Yevamot* 9: "head"] has emerged, it may

not be harmed, for we do not set aside one life for another (*Ohalot* 7:6).

b. " . . . removing it limb by limb." This is because as long as it has not emerged into the world it is not a human being [*lav nefesh hu*], and therefore it can be killed in order to save its mother (Rashi, *Sanhedrin* 72b).

c. [We are commanded] not to have compassion on the life of the pursuer. The sages ruled that when a woman has difficulty in labor, one may dismember the embryo within her, either with drugs or surgery, because [the fetus] is like a pursuer seeking to kill her. But once the head has emerged, [the fetus] is not to be harmed, for we do not set aside one life for another. This is the natural course of the world (Maimonides, *Mishneh Torah, Hilchot Rotzayach* 1:9).

Probing: Ideas and Issues

Jewish Sages agree that when a woman's life is in danger due to her pregnancy, abortion is an acceptable option. What is their reasoning as described in these texts? Do you feel this reasoning is sound? Imagine someone saying that we should "let nature take its course," not interfere with God's plans, even if the pregnant woman's life is threatened. How would you respond to such an opinion?

5. **Under what circumstances relating to the health of the mother would abortion be justified?**

On the One Hand:

One area of leniency for justifying abortion is when the mother's life is in danger.

A. See #4a and #4c above.

On the Other Hand:

There are legitimate needs for terminating a pregnancy, other than imminent danger to a mother's physical health, that justify abortion (see also #6a, b, and c below).

a. [Abortion is permitted, provided] there is great need, and as labor has not yet begun, even if it is not to save the mother's life but only to save her from evil caused by great pain (*Responsa She'elat Ya'abetz*, Altona, 1739, no. 43).

b. It is clear that abortion is not permitted without reason . . . but for a reason, even if a weak reason, such as to prevent [a woman from] public shame, we have precedent and authority [i.e., *Arachin* 7a] to permit it (*Responsa Mishpetei Uziel, Choshen Mishpat* 3:46, Tel Aviv, 1935).

c. We would therefore permit abortion in the case of Thalidomide babies [whose exposure to that drug likely will result in deformity], cases of rape and the like, not because such a fetus has no right to life but because it constitutes a threat to the health of the mother. This is an area of controversy. Many authorities would disagree and limit abortion to cases in which the threat to the life of the mother is direct. We would not permit abortions that are prompted merely by the desire of the mother not to have another child (Rabbi Isaac Klein, "Abortion and Jewish Tradition," in *Conservative Judaism*, 1970).

Probing: Ideas and Issues

A pregnancy that is causing imminent danger to a woman's life is one reason to induce abortion. What other motivations do these texts mention for seeking abortion? Do you believe some motivations are more acceptable than others? Explain. On what do you base your beliefs concerning acceptable versus unacceptable reasons for abortion — that is, would you say your beliefs express your own personal feelings, that they represent Jewish values, or that they reflect universal truths?

6. **Under what circumstances relating to the health of the fetus would abortion be justified?**

On the One Hand:

Justifying abortion to prevent the birth of a defective, retarded, or deformed infant is unacceptable.

A. No matter how deformed a baby might be, the fact that it is born of a human mother gives it human status, and therefore absolute equality with other humans in its claim to life (Rabbi Eliezer Fleckeles, *Teshuvah me-Ahavah*, 19th c., as explained by Basil F. Herring, *Jewish Ethics and Halachah for Our Time*, p. 42).

B. Abortion . . . is considered actual murder, whether the fetus is pure or illegitimate, [for] regular fetuses or those which are suffering from Tay-Sachs [abortion] is strictly prohibited . . . (Rabbi Moshe Feinstein, *Iggrot Moshe, Choshen Mishpat*, 2, 49).

On the Other Hand:

Aborting when sufficient medical evidence indicates the infant will be born deformed is permissible.

a. [Where there is a possibility of a deformed fetus, abortion may be granted on account that] the possibility is causing severe anguish to the mother (Rabbi David Feldman, *Birth Control in Jewish Law*, New York: 1968, p. 292).

b. If there is good reason to suspect that the baby will be born deformed and experience pain, one can incline to permit an abortion prior to 40 days of pregnancy, and even to permit this as long as three months of pregnancy have not yet passed and there is no fetal movement (Rabbi

Eliezer Waldenberg, *Responsa Tzitz Eliezer*, 9:237).

c. With regard to an abortion because of the Tay Sachs disease . . . in which the consequences are so grave if the pregnancy and childbirth are allowed to continue, it is permissible to terminate the pregnancy until seven months have elapsed . . . [Moreover, according to some scholarly opinion, abortion is permitted] for a Jewish woman whenever that matter was necessary for her health even when her life was not at stake . . . And therefore, ask yourself is there a greater need [that would justify terminating the pregnancy]. Pain and suffering greater than the woman in our case [can bear] . . . will be inflicted upon her if she gives birth to such a creature whose very being is one of pain and suffering. And [the infant's] death is certain within a few years . . . Add to that the pain and suffering of the infant . . . This would seem to be the classic case in which abortion may be permitted, and it doesn't matter what type of pain and suffering is endured, physical or emotional, as emotional pain and suffering is to a large extent much greater than physical pain and suffering (Rabbi Eliezer Waldenberg, *Responsa Tzitz Eliezer*, 13:102; adapted).

Probing: Ideas and Issues

Aborting because the infant may be deformed is a particularly charged subject. What positions do these texts convey on the matter? What is the rationale behind opposing abortion in the case of probable infant deformity? What is the rationale behind permitting abortion in such a case? Do you believe one rationale is more valid than the other? Explain.

7. **Who should determine the course of an individual human being's life?**

On the One Hand:

The course of our existence is not solely in our hands.

A. The alleged right of abortion on demand is generally supported by the argument that a woman has rights over her own body. This is a contention which Judaism, and indeed all high religion, must reject on both theological and ethical grounds as being essentially a pagan doctrine. It is basic Jewish teaching that human beings are not masters of their own bodies, because they did not create themselves; male and female alike have been fashioned by God in God's image (Robert Gordis, *Love & Sex: A Modern Jewish Perspective*, 1977, p. 145; adapted).

On the Other Hand:

It is up to individual human beings to steer the course of their lives as best they can determine, including what happens to their bodies.

a. According to Reform principles . . . every person owns his/her own body, with the ultimate right, consequently, to determine what that body shall do and experience. This being the case, it is a Reform presumption that whatever exists within the confines of a person's body and is physically connected to it is part of that body, and therefore entirely under the authority of the person whose body it is . . . No entity — state, religious institution, or individual — has taken even beginning steps to demonstrate objectively that a fetus is a person or that the entity possesses a moral right to override a woman's authority over her own body (Alvin Reines, "Reform Judaism, Bioethics and Abortion" in *Journal of Reform Judaism*, 1990).

Probing: Ideas and Issues

Which text (#7A or #7a) do you feel makes a more worthy point, and why? Is it possible to accept the ideas in both passages, or do the ideas in one text necessarily cancel out the ideas in the other?

8. Who should be responsible for setting standards regarding abortion?

On the One Hand:

Society has a stake in the life of the fetus.

A. The law on abortion is and should be liberal, to meet genuine cases of hardship and misery that are not soluble in any other way. But society has an obligation to educate its members to ethical standards that rise above the level of abortion on demand. In other words, abortion should be legally available but ethically restricted, to be practiced only for very good reasons. Men and women must be persuaded that though the abortion of a fetus is not equivalent to taking an actual life, it does represent the destruction of potential life and must not be undertaken lightly or flippantly (Robert Gordis, *Love & Sex: A Modern Jewish Perspective*, 1977, p. 147).

B. Under Israeli law, abortion is permitted if carried out in a recognized medical institution, with the woman's approval, and according to one or more of the following criteria: if the birth would endanger the woman's life or injure her physical or emotional health; if it can be determined that the child would be born either physically or mentally handicapped; if the pregnancy was the result of rape, incestuous relations, or intercourse outside of marriage; if the woman is under the age of 16 or over 40 (Robert Gordis, *Love & Sex: A Modern Jewish Perspective*, 1977, p. 147-148; adapted).

On the Other Hand:

No objective standard exists for permitting or prohibiting abortion. Abortion is a private issue.

a. From the testimony of the religious, philosophic, and scientific communities of the world viewed as a whole, it is evident that there is no generally accepted objective standard for determining whether a fetus is a human being or part of the mother in which it exists (Alvin Reines, "Reform Judaism, Bioethics and Abortion" in *Journal of Reform Judaism*, 1990).

b. Abortion is an intensely complex and personal decision, one which raises profound moral and religious questions that the government cannot and should not attempt to answer for every individual (Raymond A. Zwerin and Richard J. Shapiro, *Judaism and Abortion*, Washington, D.C.: Religious Coalition for Abortion Rights).

c. The diversity of religious views in this country, on the sensitive issue of abortion, requires that abortion decisions must remain with the individual, to be made on the basis of conscience and personal religious principles and free from government interference (*Words of Choice*, Washington, D.C., Coalition for Abortion Rights, 1991).

Probing: Ideas and Issues

What are some of the possible ways a society *could* influence and/or dictate abortion decisions (e.g., through laws, education, grassroots organizing, and so on)? How *should* society be involved in abortion decisions, if at all? That is, does society have obligations in terms of regulating, educating about, or guaranteeing equal access to the procedure? Does society have responsibilities for protecting fetal life?

RELATED MIDDOT AND MITZVOT

Practicing these virtues and commandments supports the process of addressing abortion issues in an ethical manner.

Anavah (Humility): In making abortion decisions, humility is in order. No one but the pregnant woman herself experiences the full impact and possibly agony of an abortion decision. We must be conscious of respecting each other's beliefs and refraining from assumptions about the universal rightness of our own personal values.

Eino Samayach BeHora'ah (Not delighting in Rendering Decisions): We are not to take abortion decisions lightly, but rather recognize that terminating a pregnancy is a significant act.

Lo Levayesh (Not Embarrassing Others): Certain pregnancies are the result of circumstances a woman feels a need to keep private. She should not be made to endure public scrutiny and judgment over what may be a painful and sensitive situation.

Lo Ta'amod al Dam Rayecha (Do Not Stand Idly by the Blood of Your Neighbor): When abortions were illegal, women still sought them, sometimes at the cost of their lives (from botched procedures). We must take care not to create a situation that restricts abortion to such an extent that women will endanger their lives in order to terminate a pregnancy.

Pikuach Nefesh (Saving a Life): When a pregnancy endangers a woman's life, the priority is to save her, even though the fetus may have to be aborted.

Rachamim (Compassion): Treating a woman facing an unwanted pregnancy with compassion paves the way for a wise decision concerning her situation.

Yirah (Awe and Reverence): The process of conception, gestation, and birth is mysterious and wondrous. Reverence for God requires us to weigh abortion decisions carefully and responsibly.

ACTIVITIES

A First Look: Key Issues and Ideas

1. To introduce the topic and get a sense of students' attitudes toward and knowledge about abortion, spend a few minutes listening to responses to these questions:

   - What do you know about abortion?

   - Why is abortion so controversial?

   - What are the current laws regarding abortion where you live?

2. Focus on how personhood is defined. Have small groups or the whole group together write a few dictionary-style sentences that they believe express the Jewish sense of personhood. Next, have them write two or three other ways personhood might be defined. Now, look back at the definitions. Ask: How might your attitude toward abortion change depending on which definition of personhood you held?

3. After giving an overview of abortion and engaging in Text Study, have the group go through the following list of possible reasons for which a woman might terminate a pregnancy:

   - The pregnancy endangers the woman's life.

   - The pregnancy may cause significant harm to the woman's physical health.

   - The pregnancy threatens a woman's mental or emotional health.

   - The pregnancy is the result of rape or incest.

- The birth will put an overly burdensome financial strain on the woman and/or her family.

- The pregnant woman is a minor who doesn't have the means or family support to care for a baby.

- The fetus is showing signs of serious deformity or disease.

- The pregnancy is the result of an extra-marital affair or other problematic partnering.

- The pregnant woman doesn't want children at all.

- The pregnant woman doesn't want children at this time in her life.

- The pregnant woman doesn't want any more children than she already has.

- The pregnant woman is over 40 and does not wish to take on the responsibility of raising a child at this stage in her life.

- The pregnant woman is over 40 and does not wish to expose herself to the increased health risks that come with giving birth at her age.

- A prenatal test reveals that the baby would be a boy, but a baby girl is preferred (or vice versa).

Participants rate each reason according to what they believe Jewish tradition would say about it. Assign a number from 1 to 10 to each reason, with "1" being a not very controversial reason and "10" being highly controversial. Students can do the rating exercise individually, in pairs, or as a whole group.

Next, the group discusses whether or not their ratings would be the same if the task had been simply to record their own personal evaluation of the reasons (as opposed to trying to reflect what Judaism says).

4. Making a decision to terminate a pregnancy can be difficult. While the pregnant woman herself may feel the weight of ultimate responsibility for the decision, typically she will look to others for guidance and support as she goes through the decision making process. Depending on current legal regulations, she may have more or less latitude in controlling the outcome of her pregnancy. How might contacts with the following individuals influence (or dictate) a decision concerning a woman's pregnancy?

- the pregnant woman's partner
- other children in the family
- the pregnant woman's parents
- a Rabbi
- a doctor or midwife
- a close friend
- an acquaintance who has had an abortion
- a family planning counselor
- a lawyer or judge

Ask: Where would *you* first turn for counsel in dealing with an unwanted pregnancy, and why? With whom else might you consult, and why? Is there anyone you definitely would not consult or that you feel should not have input in the decision? Explain.

Applying Middot and Mitzvot

1. Refer to the list of "Related *Middot* and *Mitzvot*" above on p. 15. Ask participants to answer these questions and be prepared to explain their responses:

- Are there *middot* or *mitzvot* you would add to this list?

- Are there any you would leave off?

2. Discuss: Suppose a friend is pregnant and comes to you for support and guidance. Your friend is leaning toward making a decision

you really disagree with; perhaps you even feel the decision would be unethical. To what extent are you obliged to be compassionate and humble by keeping your views to yourself? To what extent do you feel you should express your true beliefs? Here are two specific scenarios to consider, or invent your own:

- Your unmarried 17-year-old friend finds she is pregnant and wants to have the baby and raise the child on her own. You feel this is unrealistic, that your friend is not very stable emotionally, and that she will end up in a situation that will overwhelm her and be bad for the child.

- Your friend is 33 years old and has two children. One child is six, the other is three. She is in good health, has a stable marriage, and is financially secure. She would like to terminate the pregnancy because she does not want more children.

3. Films or photos that show the embryo and fetus at various stages of development are tools that anti-abortionists might use to try to convince pregnant women not to have an abortion. Pictures may be shown in order to suggest that the wonder of the developing fetus deserves our utmost awe and reverence, and that abortion should be discouraged to whatever extent possible. Do you feel using film and photos this way is ethical? Do you believe such an effort is Jewishly sound — that it honors the principle of *yirah* or that it degrades it? Explain.

4. For more information and activities on:

   Anavah (Humility): see *Teaching Jewish Virtues* by Susan Freeman, pp. 8-25.

   Lo Levayesh (Not Embarrassing Others): see *Teaching Jewish Virtues* by Susan Freeman, pp. 119-135.

   Lo Ta'amod al Dam Rayecha (Do Not Stand Idly by the Blood of Your Neighbor): see *Teaching Mitzvot* by Barbara Binder Kadden and Bruce Kadden, pp. 181-185.

   Rachamim (Compassion): see *Teaching Jewish Virtues* by Susan Freeman, pp. 55-68.

   Yirah (Awe and Reverence): see *Teaching Jewish Virtues* by Susan Freeman, pp. 332-346.

Stories: Understanding through Listening

1. Read over the imaginary situations in the "Scenarios" section above. Discuss these questions:

   - What was the predicament faced by Devorah and Debra in each of the scenarios?

   - What do you think was going through the minds of these young women when they realized they were pregnant?

   - What was the first step each of the young women took in response to their pregnancies?

   - Were their first steps appropriate?

   - What additional steps might they have taken?

   - How did each of the women eventually deal with their unwanted pregnancies?

   - Would each of their decisions be considered ethical from a Jewish point of view? Explain.

   - Imagine a young woman (or yourself) in such a predicament nowadays. How might you handle the predicament in similar ways to Devorah and Debra? How might you handle things differently?

2. Invite someone from Planned Parenthood, the Jewish Family Service, the Religious Coalition for Reproductive Choice, or another organization that works with women facing unintended or worrisome pregnancies. You may want to ask a Rabbi to join you, as well. Ask the guest(s) to talk about some of the struggles women go through in considering pregnancy options. Prepare a list of questions beforehand. Be sure to include ques-

tions that address how religious beliefs might influence a decision.

3. Discuss the two dilemma stories in *When Life Is in the Balance* by Barry D. Cytron and Earl Schwartz, p. 76-77.

Action: Getting Out, Getting Involved

1. Invite someone from Planned Parenthood, NARAL Pro-Choice America, or the Religious Coalition for Reproductive Choice to talk with your group about current political issues around abortion rights. After the visit, process with the group how they believe Judaism would or should respond to the issues raised. If they believe the issues raised are important, have the group plan ways in which they can become involved in relevant and appropriate activism.

2. Legislation having to do with reproductive options is complicated. There are many considerations, and they go beyond the question of whether abortion should or should not be legal. Here is a sampling of some of the questions with which lawmakers and others have wrestled:

- Should minors be required to inform or get permission from one or both parents (or legal guardians) before obtaining an abortion?

- Should a woman be required to obtain permission for an abortion from the man who is partner in the pregnancy?

- Should women be required to go through a "waiting period" (i.e., 24 hours) between meeting with a clinician to arrange an abortion and actually having the procedure? (Presumably, a "waiting period" gives a woman an extra window of time to change her mind, but is another hurdle to get over, and prolongs an already difficult process.)

- Should there be a prohibition against using public funds to counsel a woman

to have an abortion not necessary to save her life (even in countries where abortion is legal)?

- Should demonstrators opposing abortion be allowed to picket outside a clinic in which abortions are performed? If so, what if any limits should be placed on them — that is, should they be prohibited from coming within a certain number of feet of the clinic, should they be prohibited from showing graphic pictures of aborted fetuses on their signs or displaying aborted fetuses in jars, etc.?

- Should health insurance companies be required to cover abortions as equally as they cover other surgical procedures or drug therapies?

- Should Medicaid (paid by the American government for the poor) cover abortions? What about other government funded health plans — should abortion be covered for military personnel, women in prison, Peace Corps volunteers, public school teachers, or subsidized Native American health programs? Should countries with national health insurance, such as Canada, cover abortions?

- What sort of sex education should there be in public schools? Specifically, what should be taught about birth control, abstinence, and pregnancy options?

- Should birth control be available through schools? Should it be available "no questions asked"? If not, then what questions should be asked?

- Should medical researchers be permitted to use aborted fetal tissue in their experiments? If so, should there be any conditions such as, not charging money for the tissue or obtaining permission from the woman who had the abortion?

Have the group respond to some or all of the above issues. Discuss what they think the

Jewish "answer" would be to the questions. Then, research what current legal regulations are. Good resources: The Center for Reproductive Law and Policy, Planned Parenthood, NARAL Pro-Choice America, and The Religious Coalition for Reproductive Choice (for web site addresses, see the Bibliography below). Also, the latest edition of *Abortion: An Eternal Social and Moral Issue* will include relevant updates.

Encourage students who want to learn more to get involved in influencing the politics on subjects about which they feel strongly. Some possibilities for grassroots activism include letter writing campaigns, petitions, education programs, and becoming active in an established organization (such as one of those mentioned in the previous paragraph).

Wrestling: Engagement with the Issues

1. Have the group create artistic works expressing what they feel the essence of personhood to be. Use collage, painting, drawing, or other preferred medium. These works may include concrete images, abstract ones, or both. The artists may want to begin pondering the meaning of personhood by brainstorming (individually) a list of words that come to mind on the subject. (A sample list might include these words: breath, soul, blood, love, emotion, bones, etc.).

2. Stage a debate. This is the situation:

   A woman is five months pregnant. She has just been diagnosed with a serious illness. The fetus is unaffected by the illness, and results of prenatal tests indicate the fetus is developing normally. Doctors agree that the woman will not be in life threatening danger if she goes through with the pregnancy. However, doctors are in disagreement concerning long-term harm. Some suspect her ongoing health would be damaged. Others feel that any long-term harm would be mild, at most.

   Divide into two groups: One is supportive of the woman having an abortion and the other is opposed. Have the groups prepare for the debate by referring to the "On the One Hand"/"On the Other Hand" points listed in the "Text Study" section above. Arguments should be grounded in Jewish thought.

3. Ask students to take a deeper look at some of the typical reasons for which a woman might elect an abortion. Refer to the list found at the beginning of this activities section in "A First Look: Key Issues and Ideas," #3 on pp. 15-16. Select a few of the reasons. Have students flesh out more of the details of what the circumstances behind the reasons may have been, plus what the woman may have been thinking and feeling. This exercise may be done orally, in writing, or through art or dance.

4. Evaluate the advisability of having laws regulating abortion. Begin by reviewing some of the basic parameters in Israeli law (see Text #8B, p. 14), as well as U.S. or Canadian law (see Overview, General Perspectives, "When Is Abortion Acceptable?", p. 5, and "Who Decides?", p. 6). For further information, an excellent summary of major abortion cases in the United States can be found in *Abortion: An Eternal Social and Moral Issue* by Mei Ling Rein (Wylie, Texas: Information Plus Reference Series, 2000, or later edition), pp. 12-13. Or check the web site for The Center for Repro-ductive Law and Policy at www.crlp.org.

   Next, create two lists. On one list include what the group perceives to be the benefits of creating laws which regulate abortion. On the other list, brainstorm possible drawbacks.

   Continue by dividing into small groups. Each imagines it is a committee of government leaders. Committees are to compose regulations and guidelines concerning abortion. When the small groups have completed their task, have the whole group reassemble. Each smaller group presents its ideas, and then must respond to questions or criticisms posed by the rest of the group. Additionally, during each of the presentations, evaluate the extent to which the regulations and guidelines would be acceptable from a Jewish standpoint.

5. This is an exercise for a mature group that has established trust. In pairs, take turns listening to each other talk about fears, feelings, attitudes, and questions concerning reproduction related issues. These issues may include pregnancy, birth, abortion, and the essence of personhood. Participants may wish to share things they feel sure about as well as what they feel unsure or confused about. The tenor of the listening is all-important. Listeners must be openhearted, non-judgmental, and supportive. In addition, speakers should not interrupt each other, nor offer any comment or reaction. Each speaker should talk for three to five minutes (possibly longer for some groups). After one person has had a turn speaking, switch roles, so that the first speaker now becomes the listener. You can do this as a journal exercise, too — the "listener" being the pages of the journal. After everyone has had an opportunity to "speak" (either to another person or to write in his/her journal), come back together as a group and allow participants to share reactions to this experience.

Empathy

1. Refer to the "Scenarios" section above on pp. 7-8. Have students write several diary entries as if they are Devorah and/or Debra going through the process of making a decision concerning the unwanted pregnancy. Other scenarios that can be used: the one above in "Wrestling: Engagement with the Issues," activity #2, or the dilemma stories in *When Life Is in the Balance* by Barry D. Cytron and Earl Schwartz, pp. 76-77.

   An alternative: Have students invent details of their own imagined scenario, then compose related diary entries.

2. Have participants write a prayer to be recited by a person facing a difficult decision concerning an unwanted or otherwise problematic pregnancy. For an example, see the one published in *On the Doorposts of Your House*, p. 163. An alternative: Have participants create a more extended ritual for someone who has decided to terminate a pregnancy. Several chapters in *Lifecycles Volume 1: Jewish Women on Life Passages and Personal Milestones*, edited by Debra Orenstein, would be helpful with this project.

3. Visit the web site www.aheartbreaking-choice.com. Reading some of the material posted there gives a sense of how difficult and painful an abortion decision can be. With improved awareness of others' experiences, we increase our understanding of how important it is to be compassionate and supportive of those who find themselves facing a "heart-breaking choice."

4. Plan and hold a religious service within your own Jewish community or work with others to create an interfaith service that expresses feelings, prayers, and affirmations regarding reproductive choice. Songs and psalms can be included, as well as prayers composed especially for this occasion. Below are a few samples of prayers included in one such interfaith service. This particular service was called "The Religious Roots of Reproductive Freedom," held on September 25, 1997 in Denver, Colorado, and sponsored by Planned Parenthood of the Rocky Mountains and the Religious Coalition for Reproductive Choice.

Responsive Reading:

Reader: I stand on behalf of women who did not want to bear children, in times of anguish, in circumstances of need, but who had no means and no options.

Reader: I stand on behalf of women who suffered fear and humiliation from illegal abortions.

Reader: I stand on behalf of women injured or killed from unsafe abortions.

All: Let us hear these voices; let us acknowledge this suffering; and let us answer with commitment.

Reader: I stand on behalf of women violated by domestic assault, by rape, by incest.

Reader: I stand on behalf of women who have abused their children out of their own abuse.

Reader: I stand on behalf of near relations and friends who have had to watch beloved women suffer harm from pregnancy or childbirth in circumstances of violence.

All: Let us hear these voices; let us attend to the pain of this violence; and let us answer with compassion and help.

Reader: I stand on behalf of women whose pregnancies have been distressed by risks to their health or the health of developing fetuses, leaving them with painful choices.

Reader: I stand on behalf of those women whose poverty has prevented them from obtaining the care they need to have a healthy pregnancy.

Reader: I stand on behalf of those women left isolated with depression following birth.

All: Let us hear these voices; let us share the weight of these struggles; and let us answer with understanding and support.

Reader: I stand on behalf of women who found within themselves the moral strength to make a decision of conscience and faith about their pregnancy.

Reader: I stand on behalf of women censured and silenced because of the moral decision they made to end or to continue a difficult pregnancy.

Reader: I stand on behalf of those who have challenged extremism and accusation and upheld tolerance and moral choice.

(All Rise)

All: We stand and hear these voices; we recognize moral courage and endurance; and we answer with affirmation and trust.

(Adapted from the General Board of Global Ministries, The United Methodist Church "Briefing on Abortion Rights," 1990.)

Community Prayer:

God of our mothers and fathers, source of all life, we are saddened that we live in a world of brokenness in which hard choices must be made.
Our sisters have made difficult choices.
Let us trust them as moral decision makers in your continuing creation;
Let us affirm them as beloved members of the faith community;
And let us uphold them as they sustain their own lives
and those surrounding them to whom they are committed.
God of our mothers and fathers, source of all life, hear our prayer.

Amen.

(Adapted from "The Way We Were . . . the Way We Could Be Again," RCAR, New York Metropolitan Area, 1990.)

Closing Prayer:

O God, you who are to us like a strong mother or a tender father,
we come to you with so many questions:
Why have you made a world with such extravagance,
creating rainbows we barely notice,
raising up mighty mountains we take for granted,
bringing life to abundance in a desert and we miss the miracle?
But most of all, why have you created humans in such reckless diversity and then told us to "love one another"?
And why have you allowed so much hurt and heartache on this speck of star dust,
where too many children are born unwanted,
where too many women are denied freedom of choice,
where men of power lose the capacity for compassion?
Why?
But even amidst the mystery, and the aching silence,

we are grateful that neither partisan politician, nor ecclesiastical authority, nor faceless bureaucrat can finally thwart our freedom.
We are grateful for leaders who run risks, accept burdens, speak their convictions, and carry neither fear nor favor. And who love all life and want new life to be welcomed with tenderness and joy.
We are grateful to be here this day in celebration of these freedoms and of those who defend them with dignity and decency, eschew violence, and refuse to succumb to petty angers or personal malice.
Deliver us all from anger and fear, restrain us in our foolishness, but steady us in our convictions and our courage.
And so may we break bread with gratitude and embrace the mystery, the wonderful mystery, by which you have created us in lavish diversity and told us "to love one another."

Amen.

(Prayer delivered at a Roe v. Wade Luncheon for Planned Parenthood of Central and Northern Arizona, 1996.)

BIBLIOGRAPHY

Books

Abraham, Abraham S. *The Comprehensive Guide To Medical Halachah*. Jerusalem and New York: Feldheim Publishers, 1996.

Cytron, Barry D., and Earl Schwartz. *When Life Is in the Balance*. New York: United Synagogue of America, 1986.

Freeman, Susan. *Teaching Jewish Virtues: Sacred Sources and Arts Activities*. Denver, CO: A.R.E. Publishing, Inc., 1999.

Gordis, Robert. *Love & Sex: A Modern Jewish Perspective*. New York: Farrar Straus Giroux, 1978.

Herring, Basil F. *Jewish Ethics and the Halakhah for Our Time: Sources and Commentary*, Volume I. New York: KTAV Publishing House, Inc. and Yeshiva University Press, 1984.

Kadden, Barbara Binder, and Bruce Kadden. *Teaching Mitzvot: Concepts, Values, and Activities*. Rev. ed. Denver, CO: A.R.E. Publishing, Inc., 2003.

Mackler, Aaron L., ed. *Life & Death Responsibilities in Jewish Biomedical Ethics*. New York: The Jewish Theological Seminary of America, 2000.

Orenstein, Debra, ed. *Lifecycles Volume 1: Jewish Women on Life Passages and Personal Milestones*. Woodstock, VT: Jewish Lights Publishing, 1994.

Rein, Mei Ling. *Abortion: An Eternal Social and Moral Issue*. Wylie, TX: Information Plus Reference Series, 2000.

Religious Coalition for Abortion Rights, "Personhood and the Bible in the Abortion Debate," 1991.

Reiss, Glynis Conyer. "Abortion." In *Where We Stand: Jewish Consciousness on Campus*, edited by Allan L. Smith. New York: UAHC Press, 1997.

Rosner, Fred. *Modern Medicine and Jewish Ethics*. Hoboken, NJ: KTAV Publishing House, Inc. and New York: Yeshiva University Press, 1991.

Stern, Chaim, et al, ed. *On the Doorposts of Your House*. New York: CCAR Press, 1994.

Wahrman, Miriam Z. *Brave New Judaism: When Science and Scripture Collide*. Waltham, MA: Brandeis University, 2002.

Zwerin, Raymond A., and Richard J. Shapiro. *Judaism and Abortion*. Washington, DC: Religious Coalition for Abortion Rights, n.d.

Web Sites

A Heart Breaking Choice: www.aheartbreaking-choice.com

> *A site for parents who have interrupted a wanted pregnancy because of a poor medical diagnosis.*

Center for Reproductive Law and Policy: www.crlp.org

> *A nonprofit legal advocacy organization dedicated to promoting and defending women's reproductive rights worldwide.*

Focus on the Family: www.family.org

> *The web site of Focus on the Family, a conservative Christian organization whose mission is to preserve traditional values and the institution of the family.*

NARAL Pro-Choice America (formerly The National Abortion and Reproductive Rights Action League): www.naral.org

> *NARAL is the political arm of the pro-choice movement and a strong advocate of reproductive freedom and choice.*

National Council of Jewish Women: www.ncjw.org

> *Works to improve the quality of life for women, children and families and strives to ensure individual rights and freedoms for all.*

Planned Parenthood: www.plannedparenthood.org

> *Advocates for reproductive self-determination.*

Religious Coalition for Reproductive Choice: www.rcrc.org

Works to ensure reproductive choice through the moral power of religious communities.

Teenwire from Planned Parenthood Federation of America: www.teenwire.com

The Planned Parenthood Federation of America Web site for young people needing information about all aspects of sexual health.

Films

The following commercial films deal with the issue of abortion in a frank and mature manner. While specific sections may be valuable for illustrating certain ideas about the topic, it may not be appropriate for students to view the entire film. Prescreening is strongly recommended.

The Cider House Rules (1999, 126 minutes, rated PG-13)

A young boy, raised in an orphanage, is trained to be a physician by a compassionate doctor who performs illegal abortions. Available from video stores.

If These Walls Could Talk (1996, 95 minutes, rated R)

A trilogy of stories set in the same house, but with different occupants and spanning over 40 years, deals with various women and moral crisis over unexpected pregnancies and their choice of abortion. Available from video stores, or online from the HBO Store at http://store.hbo.com.

A Private Matter (1992, 89 minutes, rated PG-13)

The true story of Romper Room host "Miss Sherri" Finkbine (played by Sissy Spacek), who, after the devastating effects of Thalidomide were discovered in the early 1960s, sparked a firestorm of controversy with her determination to obtain an abortion. Available from video stores, or online from the HBO Store at http://store.hbo.com.

CHAPTER 2

CLONING AND OTHER GENETIC TECHNOLOGIES

OVERVIEW

Note: A preliminary understanding of the following biotechnological terms is important for understanding this chapter: Cloning, Gene, and Gene Therapy. See the Glossary on pp. 46-47 for definitions of these and other important terms.

Introduction

Two compelling reasons to pursue cloning and other genetic technologies are their therapeutic promise and their potential to address infertility. Current scientific developments are very encouraging regarding these two goals. Who can argue with such laudatory intentions — healing people and helping people to have children? As it happens, there is plenty to argue about.

One critical ethical dilemma rests on this classical question: Do the ends justify the means? In other words, gene therapies may allow a person to overcome an illness or even avoid getting a disease in the first place. That would be the goal or the "ends." But achieving that goal — the "means" — might involve an ethically murky process. The process might involve costly, possibly unsafe procedures. These procedures may need to rely on ethically questionable intermediate steps (for example, the creation of surplus embryos or other partially developed life forms that will be discarded).

A related concern is this: With genetic technologies, we may end up creating more, possibly worse problems than we solve. That is, we may create more harm in the long run. We have to ask if the results we desire will lead to additional or future undesirable results. Thus, another critical ethical dilemma is this: Do the ends justify (all) the ends?

We have mentioned ethical dilemmas involving the technology itself. However, related dilemmas may arise. Possibly only elite (wealthy) members of society will have the means to access the technology. Another concern is that society may neglect important responsibilities as it channels substantial resources to genetic-related health procedures. For example, funds committed to genetics may divert needed money away from schools, environmental protection, or aid to destitute individuals.

Cloning and other genetic technologies may have the potential for great good, but ethical questions loom. These questions present daunting obstacles as research goes ahead. Because many obstacles are so problematic, some recommend putting a stop to this line of scientific inquiry. Others suggest vigilant regulation of genetic technologies. Still others favor only limited regulation, believing scientists and potential beneficiaries should be free to make their own decisions regarding experiments and treatments.

General Perspectives

In 1998, Dr. Avraham Steinberg[1] delivered a paper to the Institute for Jewish Medical Ethics of the Hebrew Academy of San Francisco entitled "Human Cloning — Scientific, Moral and Jewish Perspectives." Besides giving insights into the Jewish repercussions of this issue, he provides a helpful general overview of some positive and negative consequences stemming from genetic technology. The following two sections are adapted from his ideas.

---

[1]Director, Center for Medical Ethics, Hebrew University, Hadassah Medical School, Jerusalem.

Potential Medical Benefits:

- Renewing the activity of damaged cells may improve the prognosis for debilitating illnesses. One procedure exchanges cells that have died with others cloned by genetic techniques. Examples of who might benefit are sufferers of Parkinson's or Alzheimer's Disease. In these two diseases, specialized brain cells have been damaged. To renew or replace damaged cells would require only the cloning technology, not the cloning of full human beings.

- Curbing the proliferation of cancerous cells could lead to cures for certain malignant diseases. This also would require only cloning technology, and not necessarily the cloning of full human beings.

- In theory, humans created with similar immunities could serve as organ donors for each other. For example, one could provide the other with a kidney or be a source for a bone marrow transplant. However, scientists are not really thinking about cloning humans as organ donors, but rather of cloning organs.

- Cloning technologies could be used with certain animals, to serve human needs. The idea is that animals could become potential sources of transplant organs for humans.

- Cloning could solve the problem of infertile couples, for whom other modern, reproductive techniques haven't worked.[2]

Potential Disadvantages and Concerns:

- Already, genetic technologies are vulnerable to eugenics (see Glossary, pp. 46-47). Cloning adds another dimension to the ethics of eugenics. Humans could be replicated because of unique distinction (such as geniuses) or because they have preferred characteristics (such as athletic talents or physical beauty). Or, perhaps diabolical dictators like Hitler would attempt to have themselves cloned. Note that cloning such an individual would not ensure that he/she also would be morally perverse. That is, replicating a person's genes does not replicate the fullness of an individual's personality. Nevertheless, the possibility of the likes of Hitler cloning themselves is unsettling and deserves ethical notice.

- Cloning that leads to creating large groups of people with similar appearance and personality would compromise the individuality of every member. This scenario would challenge our value of respecting people precisely because they are unique individuals. Additionally, there is the possibility of psychological damage to human clones. (Note, however, that genetic composition alone does not determine the nature of a person. Environment, with its physical and psychological components, exerts substantial influence on determining the essence of the individual.)

- The loss of genetic variation among cloned humans could cause genetic inbreeding. The loss of genetic diversity could eventually reduce survival. Human survival is best ensured by the intermixing of genetic material.

- Use of mature cells, enlivened with the potential to develop into whole organisms could introduce problematic consequences. Negative changes that arose in the cell with age could be transferred to the next generations.

- "Black markets" for fetuses could arise. This industry would create fetuses from people of desirable traits, such as geniuses, particularly strong or beautiful people, etc. "Designer" fetuses would be sold to interested potential parents.

- New technologies would alter society's determination and definition of parenthood. For

---

[2]The "Potential Medical Benefits" are adapted from "Human Cloning — Scientific, Moral and Jewish Perspectives," 2.

instance: Suppose a woman contributes genetic material to the baby, bears the child, and raises it. We would say that the woman is the mother. But who is the father? Is the biological father the baby's grandfather (since part of the mother's genetic material comes from her father, i.e., the baby's grandfather)? If no man adopts the baby, does that mean the baby has no father?

- Some worry about upheavals in the international, societal order. People might be created outside of homes and families. They could be produced in a nondomestic, mechanical, indifferent setting, without identifiable parents or love.[3] Though theoretically a concern, no upheaval occurred with the development of other reproductive techniques (such as *in vitro* fertilization). Thus, this problem would not likely occur with cloning either.

Just an Orientation

A discussion of the above potential benefits and disadvantages could fill many chapters. The goal here is simply to orient readers to the complexity of the matters with which we are dealing. We continue by focusing on possible Jewish approaches to our topic.

Jewish Perspectives

Finding traditional Jewish sources that apply neatly to modern genetic science is not easy. We may suggest that Eve was created (cloned?) from Adam's side. But that is a stretch, as is extrapolating useful guidance from the lore originating in Prague that speaks of a golem, a fabricated anthropoid. Primarily, we must look toward overarching Jewish principles to help us respond to the ethical challenges. Besides considerations raised in the "General Perspectives" section above, we add others, as follows.

Reasons to Pursue Genetic Technologies

Pikuach Nefesh (Saving a Life): To save a life is a great accomplishment, equivalent to saving a whole world (*Sanhedrin* 4:5, see Text Study #3B below). Genetic technologies may help save lives. (See "Potential Medical Benefits" in the "General Perspectives" section above for some specific examples.)

Rofeh Cholim (Healing the Sick): This and similar mandates teach of our obligation and duty to heal. Genetic technologies hold great promise in treating and curing disease. (Again, see the "General Perspectives" section above.)

Mechabayd Zeh et Zeh (Honoring One Another): This *middah* requires us to respect the dignity of each individual. In our context here, this value is an extension of *Rofeh Cholim*. Suppose someone suffers from a debilitating disease, such as Parkinson's or Alzheimer's Disease. When afflicted with physical or mental deterioration, maintaining one's dignity can be a constant battle. We honor others when we respond to their suffering. Judaism would teach that we have a responsibility to pursue therapies to improve physical mobility or halt mental decline.

Choosing Life (Deuteronomy 30:19, see Text Study #3A below): This passage suggests that though there may be risks involved (in genetic procedures), we should pursue the most life affirming options.

Be Fruitful and Multiply (Genesis 1:28, see also Text Study #4A below): God commands that we have children. Jewish social traditions reinforce this value. Cloning may allow individuals to have biologically related children when other fertility treatments fail.

Reasons for Caution

Anavah (Humility): This principle would caution us not to overreach in our efforts to be *k'Elohim*,

---

[3]The "Potential Disadvantages and Concerns" are adapted from "Human Cloning — Scientific, Moral and Jewish Perspectives," 2-3.

like God (see Text Study #7b, c, and d below).

HaNeshamah be'kirbee (My Soul is In my Body): This phrase from the morning liturgy teaches that we are integrated, whole beings. Genetic technologies could involve the creation of quasi-life forms as part of manufacturing "spare part" organs. However, "manufacturing" should typify the making of objects, not the creation of human life. We must ask what fragmenting bodies into semi-living pieces does to the sacredness and integrity of human life.

"One may not sacrifice one life to preserve another" (*Mishneh Torah, Hilchot Yesodei Hatorah* 5:7): We must question the legitimacy of creating a person to save another person. An example is parents who decide to have another child, hoping a new sibling will help their sick child regain health. That is, the new child would supply the sick child with compatible, healthy cells or tissue. Now, no one literally "sacrifices" the new child (the forced donations will not kill him/her). Yet, suppose he/she will be "used" as a continual source of therapeutic treatments for the sick individual (see Text Study #6a below). While some might say the new child's role in the world is ennobling, is it fair to force such an obligation on a child?

Another troubling possibility is creating a clone of the sick person, but repairing the genetic abnormality that caused the original person to become sick in the first place. The clone would serve the health needs of the original person, perhaps with a disease-free kidney or other body part.

God intends each human being to be unique: The Torah says to "be fruitful and multiply" through the joining of female and male. The Talmud speaks of three partners in the creation of a human being: God, the father, and the mother (*Niddah* 31a). By means of each one's contribution, a unique person is created.

The Rabbis of the Talmud extol God's ability to make each person an original: "Each individual was created alone . . . to proclaim the greatness of the Holy One. For if a person strikes many coins from one die, they all resemble one another; in fact they are exactly alike. But though the Sovereign of Sovereigns, the Holy One Who Is Blessed, fashioned every person from the die of the first man, not a single one of them is like his/her fellow" (*Sanhedrin* 38a).

Clearly, the Rabbis knew about twins and did not condemn them. Cloned individuals are no more similar (and in fact less similar) than twins. Even so, the Rabbis did not envision the possibility of purposely creating dozens or more "twins." Judaism appreciates individual uniqueness. A practice that deliberately stifles uniqueness calls for caution.

Self-idolization: Self-idolization can be a threat when people replicate themselves through cloning. Combining genes through sexual intercourse or through artificial fertility procedures involves participation of two individuals (egg and sperm). In contrast, cloning essentially is a self-involved act. Although we do not actually attain immortality through a clone, genetic self-perpetuation encourages undue focus on the self.

In a related (though unlikely) possibility, cloning "spare parts" and replacement tissue could conceivably prolong life endlessly. We would turn in worn out or diseased body parts for new ones and renew aging cells with a fresh supply. What becomes of the Psalmist's request of God: "Teach us to number our days so that we may attain a heart of wisdom" (Psalms 90:12, also Text Study #3a below)?

Bal Tashchit (Do Not Waste or Destroy): This important Jewish principle underlies environmental laws. Thus, it is problematic that wasting and destroying occurs in the research and application of genetic therapies. The work requires the use of large amounts of genetic material, including embryos, female eggs, and/or other tissue. Experiments may result in partially and abnormally developed clones that must be destroyed. God took man (Adam) and placed him in the garden of Eden, to "till it and tend it" (Genesis 2:15, see Text Study #5d below). Are the efforts being made in genetic technology consistent with "tilling and tending"?

Additional Considerations

B'tzelem Elohim, in God's Image did God Create Humankind (Genesis 1:27): Some might say that God is the Creator, and that when we engage in cloning, we presume a role that is not legitimately ours. Even so, cloning does not undermine God's ultimate place in the universe. That is, God is responsible for the very origins of Creation. The mysteries of the universe do not disappear just because researchers gain ground in cloning. Mysteries always will remain despite the scientific discoveries that human beings make.

Use of Embryonic Material: Judaism does not equate an embryo with full life. An embryo is called "mere fluid" until the fortieth day from conception (*Yevamot* 69b). Rashi says the soul doesn't enter the body until the majority (or head) of the fetus is born into the world. Still, an embryo is *potential* life. As "life on the way," we value the embryo and treat it with respect.

Just how far to take that respect is the question. If an embryo has properties that may help save or heal someone, and since an embryo is not a full person, can we do what we want with it? Are there any limits? That is, can we use an embryo's cells for our benefit, without being concerned if an embryo (or hundreds of embryos) is destroyed in the process?

Genetic technologies use embryos when they are only a few days old. The cells are cultivated outside the human body. This cluster of cells would not develop into a human baby if left on its own (without being returned to a womb). Thus, while Judaism values potential life, cell clusters in petri dishes may not merit the same status we might ascribe to a normally developing fetus. We reasonably can argue that using embryos in research and therapies is legitimate.

Nevertheless, some Jews — along with others — harbor qualms. They are troubled by the possible disregard for the sanctity of human life, even in its most elemental form. They worry about a factory-type attitude toward embryos. Is it really perfectly fine to manufacture, use, and destroy embryos by the hundreds, perhaps the thousands without a second thought about it? Does it matter if we view human embryo cells no differently from how we would view the cells of a carrot or a blade of grass?

A compromise approach to the use of embryos might incorporate our Jewish notion of *Bal Tashchit* (not wasting or destroying). To use an analogy: Suppose we needed gold or diamonds for use in significant research, such as to find cures for painful illnesses. We would use the gold, and we would use the diamonds. But we would be careful to use only what we truly needed. We would be exceedingly cautious not to waste our precious materials. We would cooperate with other labs to reduce waste.

Most people understand the aura around gold and diamonds. If we would be that careful in using these precious, inorganic materials, all the more so should we use care in our use of human embryos. A moderate position would dictate use of embryos only to the degree that is absolutely necessary for our purposes. Our purposes should be of great importance (i.e., for healing). And we should look for alternatives to the use of embryos (such as, using adult tissue). Developing alternative tissue sources and alternative research methods (not using embryos) is already happening. (Passages in Text Study #2 below relate to use of embryos.)

Use of community resources: Medical care is just one of many services a community must provide. Spending too much in one area can undermine the well-being of others. As long ago as the Talmud, communities understood the need to allocate resources carefully. The Talmud lists ten things a worthy community must provide (see Text Study #5a below). When we consider the merit of genetic technology, we must factor in the expense. At this point, costs are enormous. Some might argue that we might have to spend a lot in the beginning, but that we are investing in the future. The potential benefits to humankind are priceless. Furthermore, how can we put a price tag on alleviating pain?

All this may be so, but difficult financial decisions will need to be made. We might agree to use public money (or pooled health insurance funds) for treating diabetes with more effective therapies. Should we also agree to use our funds to help an infertile couple clone a child? Where do we draw the line? The "line" that emerges from the Talmud is that we must limit our medical expenditures to the degree necessary in order to prevent other important community services from suffering.

Little can be done to stop private efforts in funding genetic technology. Yet, even private expenditures reflect a community's overall values. There is great interest now in cloning cherished pets. Some are willing to spend millions of dollars to make that happen. Dr. Arthur Caplan, a University of Pennsylvania bioethicist, observed: "The commercial future of cloning is absolutely in animals."[4] Those same millions could be directed to research and therapies for debilitating human diseases, or for that matter, for dilapidated schools or environmental problems. Open debate regarding the ethics of spending priorities is worthwhile regardless of where the dollars come from.

Access To Treatments: As mentioned above, genetic therapies can be very expensive. Who should benefit from the technologies? To follow the precedent set by Abba, a healer during Talmudic times, we would not discriminate based on ability to pay. That is, therapies would be available to rich and poor alike (see Text Study #5b below). Because of the high costs of genetic therapies, the wealthy could gain better access to their healing effects. A Jewish perspective would urge us to avoid medical practices that favor the privileged, but leave out specific populations of people.

In Cloning, Who Are the Parents? This question involves complicated scientific details and *halachic* (Jewish legal) rules. An egg may come from one woman, the genetic material might

come from the same woman, a different woman, or a man. The man may be the husband of the egg donor, the gene donor, or the womb provider, or he may not be related to them at all. Once configured, the embryo might be implanted in the womb of the woman who is genetically related to it, or the embryo might be implanted in the womb of another woman. Despite such complex matters, reputable *halachic* scholars believe we can avoid problems of bastardy and effectively resolve questions of paternity and maternity.

A Jewish Approach

With compelling reasons to pursue genetic technology, and chilling reasons to impede such efforts, where should Judaism stand? A moderate and reasonable conclusion would be: proceed, but with great caution. We would base our caution on the many concerns raised above.

Dr. Avraham Steinberg (who was quoted in the "General Perspectives" section above) offers these practical suggestions:[5]

> The Parliaments of the Western world should establish a multi-disciplinary, international committee that will examine the positive and negative aspects of the topic before us . . . Furthermore, this international committee should be given credence to judge all the positive and negative aspects of the genetics of the future. The purpose of this committee will include the following tasks:
>
> • Recommendations for the methods of research and development of these technologies.
>
> • Recommendations for the application of these technologies.
>
> • International supervision on the application and implementation of the use of these technologies, modeled after the supervision over unconventional weapons.

---

[4]"Attack of the Calico Clones" by Maureen Dowd, in *The New York Times*, Week in Review, Sunday, February 17, 2002, 11.

[5]"Human Cloning — Scientific, Moral and Jewish Perspectives," 10.

- Supervision over the allotments for research and application of these technologies.

Summary of the Overview

- Cloning and other genetic technologies have potential benefits in the realms of healing and fertility. They also have potentially worrisome consequences.

- A ban on genetic research and development is not realistic, and may be unwise, as well.

- Judaism shares many of the general moral concerns expressed concerning genetic technologies. In addition, Judaism has concerns that specifically reflect our values and beliefs.

- Because of the ethical issues associated with cloning and other genetic technologies, rigorous regulation and supervision are an absolute necessity. The goal is to nurture scientific advances which enhance humanity, minimize dangerous risks, and avoid destructive mistakes.

SCENARIOS: A FEW POSSIBLE DIRECTIONS IN GENETIC TECHNOLOGIES

Below are three imaginary scenarios related to cloning and genetic technologies, intended to raise questions and spark discussion. Read each scenario to or with your students, and engage them in small or large group discussions. Use the "Focus the Discussion" section below to help identify the important issues and facilitate these discussions. Note that additional activities relating to these scenarios are found in the "Stories: Understanding through Listening" section below (pp. 42-43).

Following the discussions, continue on to the "Text Study" section to see what Jewish and other sources have to say on the subject. Finally, you may wish to have students discuss the scenarios a second time, to see if their views have changed.

Scenario 1

Dave is 70 years old. He is in great physical health, but his mental faculties are declining. A medical exam and some tests confirm what the family fears: Dave is showing the beginning signs of Alzheimer's Disease. Fortunately, he is an excellent candidate to participate in experimental genetic-based treatments.

Medical scientists develop a therapy compatible with Dave's genetic makeup. So far, Dave is responding well. Doctors feel hopeful that Dave will improve. Though these treatments are very expensive, researchers expect they will be able to bring down the costs somewhat as they perfect the procedure.

Scenario 2

David is 70 years old. He has begun to suffer from a degenerative muscle condition. Genetic researchers believe that if they were able to replace some of David's degenerating tissue with healthy tissue, his health could improve greatly. David would like to have himself cloned, with the clone serving as a source for healthy muscle tissue. David's son and daughter-in-law say they are willing to raise the cloned child since David doesn't feel prepared to take that on. David is a wealthy man and cost is no obstacle. He is willing to spend whatever it takes for the chance to overcome his debilitating health problems.

Scenario 3

Same scenario as #2, except "Davey" is a cat with a degenerative muscle disease. The interest in, decisions about, and funding for cloning Davey come from the cat's owners.

Focus the Discussion

Dave, David, and Davey's cases are just three possible directions in which genetic technology could go. People value different things in life, and these values influence their choices and actions. Loose, random judgments about others' actions are neither productive nor meaningful.

For example: "Who are *you* to tell me how I should spend my money . . . " Or, "Why should health insurance pay for *your* pills, but not pay for cloning *my* tissue?"

Yet, because of the ramifications of genetic technology, society must be careful about allowing anything that can scientifically happen to happen. We discuss potential ramifications in some detail in the above sections. The scenarios should only underscore the conclusion we have come to already: how important it is to establish a multi-disciplinary, international committee that will examine the positive and negative aspects of genetic technology, make recommendations about how it should develop, and formulate regulations and procedures for supervision.

TEXT STUDY

Though cloning and genetic engineering are very new technologies, they raise ethical questions with which Judaism has dealt for thousands of years. Jewish sources, both our ancient texts and contemporary writings, provide many answers, but these answers often highlight the tension between seemingly opposing considerations. The chart on the next page poses the questions and offers two opposing points of view. Text sources supporting each of these points of view follow below.

1. **Should genetic research be unrestricted, strictly regulated, or banned entirely?**

On the One Hand:

Banning the development of new scientific ideas (technologies) is unrealistic and possibly unwise. Genetic research will continue to evolve over the next decades.

A. Is it, then, any wonder that [humans] should try to do in [their] own small way what God did in the beginning?

(Gershom Scholem, as quoted in *The Great Jewish Cities of Central and Eastern Europe* by Eli Valley, Jason Aronson Inc., 1999, p. 44).

B. There is no stopping human inquisitiveness, and once we begin to ask questions, it's only a matter of time before we begin to take steps to answer them and then to act on the answers (Alan Meisel, *The Jerusalem Report*, April 16, 1998).

C. The Jewish demand that we do our best to provide healing makes it important that we take advantage of the promise of cloning to aid us in finding cures for a variety of diseases and in overcoming infertility . . . To pretend that human cloning will not take place if it is banned in experiments funded with government money is simply unrealistic; it will happen with private funds in the United States and/or abroad (Rabbi Elliot N. Dorff, *Matters of Life and Death*, pp. 322-323).

On the Other Hand:

We must direct genetic science by regulating who does the research, who supervises the efforts, and who benefits from or receives applications of the research.

a. The dangers of cloning . . . require that it be supervised and restricted. Specifically, cloning should be allowed only for medical research or therapy; clones must be recognized as having full and equal status with other fetuses or human beings, with the equivalent protections; and careful policies must be devised to determine how cloning mistakes will be identified and handled . . . (Rabbi Elliot N. Dorff, *Matters of Life and Death*, pp. 322-323).

b. It is indefensible to initiate uncontrolled experiments with incalculable effects on the balance of nature and the preservation of [humankind's] incomparable spirituality without the most careful evalua-

Ethical Responses to Cloning and Genetic Engineering: Questions to Consider

The Question	On the One Hand	On the Other Hand
1. Should genetic research be unrestricted, strictly regulated, or banned entirely? (see p. 32)	Banning the development of new scientific ideas is unrealistic and possibly unwise. Genetic research will continue to evolve over the next decades.	We must direct genetic science by regulating who does the research, who supervises the efforts, and who benefits from or receives applications of the research.
2. Should the use of embryonic cells and/or tissue be allowed for medical research? (see p. 34)	Promising genetic research and techniques involve use of embryos which essentially are clusters of pre-life cells.	Embryos may not be full human beings with souls, but they embody early stage life. We must question the ethics of meddling in an embryo's natural development.
3. To what extent should healing and preserving life supercede other values? (see p. 35)	If we have the ability to improve the physical quality of human life, we should do so.	Human beings are more than *just bodies*.
4. Should the cloning of human beings for the purpose of helping infertile couples to have children be allowed? (see p. 36)	Cloning will help infertile couples bring children into the world who carry the genetic imprint of one of them.	There are values that transcend passing along our genes.
5. Should the cloning of human beings for the purpose of curing illness and genetic disorders be allowed? (see p. 37)	Cloning and related gene manipulation techniques will help us find cures to devastating illnesses and genetic disorders.	The hurdles for using cloning to find cures are daunting, including: expense, individually tailoring therapies, access (by the wealthy and privileged only?), safety, environmental issues, and unforeseen detrimental genetic consequences affecting future generations.
6. Should the cloning of human beings for the purpose of providing healthy tissue and/or organs be allowed? (see p. 38)	A cloned individual can provide healthy tissue/organs to its ill counterpart without the problems of immune incompatibility. Creating a new organ (without the full body) is another possibility.	Manufacturing some people to serve others is coercive and an abuse of power. In creating an organ, we take risks that it will evolve in abnormal and frightening ways.

(continued on next page)

7. Should cloning or the manipulation of genes for the purpose of producing desirable characteristics in human beings be allowed? (see p. 39)	Cloning will help us as a society to improve the quality of our species by cloning special individuals or isolating favorable genetic qualities to pass on to the next generation.	The practice of eugenics is hubris. That is, manipulating genes for the purpose of producing "desirable" characteristics is sacrilegious arrogance. It turns humans into objects and creates a breeding ground for racism.

tion of the likely consequences beforehand . . . (Rabbi Immanuel Jakobovits, *Jewish Medical Ethics*, p. 261).

c. There are certain inevitabilities in life, and I'm afraid [cloning] is one of them. Passing laws to prohibit the practice won't work. We need to face up to the challenge and try to assure that science and technology work for us rather than sabotaging us. That should be the aim first of public debate and then of law (Alan Meisel, *The Jerusalem Report*, April 16, 1998).

Probing: Ideas and Issues

What might be the consequences of banning research related to cloning? What might be the consequences of encouraging research? Of the six texts above, whose words do you find most compelling and why?

Note: For more detailed Jewish views on the status and nature of the embryo, see Chapter 1, "Abortion" beginning on p. 3. Several passages in that chapter's "Text Study" section are included below, as well.

2. **Should the use of embryonic cells and/or tissue be allowed for medical research?**

On the One Hand:

Promising genetic research and techniques involve use of embryos which essentially are clusters of pre-life cells.

Texts A, B, and C are from traditional Jewish sources, and texts D and E reflect modern science.

A. If a woman is pregnant, the fetus, until the fortieth day is only a mere fluid (*Yevamot* 69b).

B. [Capital punishment is not imposed on one who, during a scuffle, causes a pregnant woman to miscarry because there is] no form [yet to the fetus]. . . (*Septuagint* translation of Exodus 21:22).

C. If a woman in labor has a [life-threatening] difficulty, one dismembers the embryo within her, removing it limb by limb, for her life takes precedence over its life. But once its greater part has emerged, it may not be harmed, for we do not set aside one life for another (*Ohalot* 7:6) . . . [The embryo can be removed "limb by limb"] because, as long as it has not emerged into the world, it is not a human being [*lav nefesh hu*], and therefore it can be killed in order to save its mother (Rashi, *Sanhedrin* 72b).

D. A four to five day old embryo is called a blastocyst. Between six and nine days old, an embryo implants itself on the uterine wall.

Blastocyst: A hollow sphere of some 250 cells that develop four to five days after an egg is fertilized. Inside is a clump of about 30 cells, the inner cell mass, from which the embryo develops. When removed and grown in the lab, cells from the inner cell mass are called embryonic stem cells ("Glossary," *The New York Times, Science Times*, p. D10).

E. Embryonic stem cells . . . have two attributes that make them attractive for regenerative medicine.[6] They are versatile, in that they can be turned into any other type of tissue or cell in the body, at least in theory. And they can be easily multiplied in culture, providing an ample supply of cells (Andrew Pollack, "Scientists Seek Ways to Rebuild the Body, Bypassing the Embryo, *The New York Times, Science Times*, p. D6).

On the Other Hand:

Embryos may not be full human beings with souls, but they embody early stage life. We must question the ethics of meddling in an embryo's natural development.

a. He who indulges in marital intercourse on the ninetieth day [of pregnancy, when it was thought to injure the embryo], it is as though he had shed blood (*Niddah* 31a).

b. From the perspective of an Orthodox Christian reverend and scholar:

> Sometime during the development of a human person, from the moment of conception until birth, that person becomes "ensouled." We will never know when or how that occurs. Once a human zygote forms and begins to develop, it is committed to becoming a human person. Because we do not know when or how that person obtains a soul, we must not interfere with that development in any deleterious way at any time. We must treat the developing embryo with dignity and respect because we do not know when it becomes a person (Rev. Dr.

Demetri Demopulos, "Cloning: Sanctity or Utility," from *Reflections, Newsletter of the Program for Ethics, Science, and the Environment*, Department for Philosophy, Oregon State University, Special Edition, May 1997).

Probing: Ideas and Issues

Judaism does not regard the fetus as a full human life until it is born. It is called "mere fluid" up until 40 days (*Yevamot* 69b). Suppose a scientist wants to conduct his/her research in ways consistent with Judaism. Can the scientist use embryos (under 40 days old) as freely in experiments as he/she might use any other cells (for example, from a carrot or a mouse)? To what extent, if at all, do you believe Jews should heed Rev. Demopulos' words?

3. **To what extent should healing and preserving life supercede other values?**

   On the One Hand:

   If we have the ability to improve the physical quality of human life, we should do so.

   A. I hereby declare today, with heaven and earth as my witnesses, that I have put before you life and death, blessing and curse. Choose life, that you and your descendants may live (Deuteronomy 30:19).

   B. If one destroys a single person, Scripture considers it as if he/she had destroyed the whole population of the world. And if one saves the life of a single person, Scripture considers it as though he/she saves the whole world (*Sanhedrin* 4:5, see also Text #1C above).

---

[6]Regenerative Medicine: Repairing the body by harnessing its own repair mechanisms — stem cells and signaling proteins — to renew damaged tissues and organs. ("Glossary," *The New York Times, Science Times*, D10)

On the Other Hand:

Human beings are more than just bodies.

a. Teach us to number our days so that we may attain a heart of wisdom (Psalms 90:12).

b. Judaism upholds the values of perpetuating life and healing. Still, we may find these thoughts of a Hindu scholar and spiritual leader challenging. He eloquently questions the *degree* of value we should attach to our physical bodies.

"Those who think the Self is the body will lose their way in life . . . It is true that the body is perishable, but within it dwells the imperishable Self . . . " (*Chandogya Upanishad*). The supreme purpose of life is to reveal the divine spark that is latent within every one of us. When we hear about important scientific discoveries like the splitting of the atom or the cloning of a sheep, we can always ask ourselves: "Will this help me in my search for realizing God, who is enshrined in the depths of my consciousness?" (Sri Eknath Easwaran, "Brave New World," *Reflections*, May 1997).

Probing: Ideas and Issues

Do Sri Eknath Easwaran's words contradict the Jewish texts #3A and B? Explain. Judaism also suggests that each of us has a spark of the Divine within us. That is, we, who are created in the Divine image, come to life because God "breathes the soul-breath" into each one of us. Does cloning put undue emphasis on our physical beings?

4. **Should the cloning of human beings for the purpose of helping infertile couples to have children be allowed?**

On the One Hand:

Cloning techniques will help infertile couples bring children into the world who carry the genetic imprint of one of them.

A. Be fruitful and multiply (Genesis 1:28).

B. Show me a young man who is sterile, whose family was obliterated by the Holocaust and who is the last in a genetic line. I would advise cloning him to create a descendant (Rabbi Moshe Tendler, "The Right Situation" [op-ed] *New York Times*, December 12, 1997, A22).

On the Other Hand:

There are values that transcend passing along our genes.

a. If God's goal is to populate the earth with men and women who are exact genetic copies, the commandment ["be fruitful and multiply"] could mean, *"Replicate yourselves,"* and cloning would fit the bill. But look around you — we are clearly not genetic replicas of each other. The diversity of our species suggests that what God has in mind is not replication, but *reproduction*. Children are not genetic replicas of either parent. They are a *product* of their union; genetic heirs of both parents, they are genetically unique (Harvey L. Gordon, M.D., "Human Cloning and the Jewish Tradition, in *Bioethics, Program Guide X: Cloning*, UAHC Department of Family Concerns").

b. Sexual reproduction carries the promise that each individual represents something new, something unique that may enhance the species (Morton D. Prager, Ph.D., "Cloning," in *Bioethics, Program Guide X: Cloning*).

c. In the circumstance where a procedure with unsure consequences and uncertain implications is the only way to produce progeny, liberal Judaism offers several ways to continue to pass one's endowment to future generations — through charitable acts and donations, creations such as books and music that we leave behind, and the memories with which we grace others (Dr. Stephen M. Modell, "Four Cloning Scenarios from the Perspective of Science and the Jewish Tradition," in *Bioethics, Program Guide X: Cloning*).

d. . . . Cloning is less a treatment for infertility than a treatment for vanity. It is a way to produce an exact genetic replica of yourself that will walk the earth years after you're gone (Charles Krauthammer, "Of Headless Mice . . . And Men," *Time Magazine*, January 19, 1998).

Probing: Ideas and Issues

Which "On the One Hand" or "On the Other Hand" position and grouping of texts is stronger (#4A and B or #4a-d)? Explain your response.

5. **Should the cloning of human beings for the purpose of curing illness and genetic disorders be allowed?**

On the One Hand:

Cloning and related gene manipulation techniques will help us find cures to devastating illnesses and genetic disorders.

A. Since the function of medicine, as construed in Jewish sources, is to aid God in the process of healing, research into further ways to accomplish that end finds enthusiastic endorsement within Jewish ideology and law (Rabbi Elliot N. Dorff, *Matters of Life and Death*, p. 310).

On the Other Hand:

The hurdles for using cloning to find cures are daunting, including: expense, individually tailoring therapies, access (by the wealthy/privileged only?), safety, environmental issues, and unforeseen detrimental genetic consequences affecting future generations.

a. A community should not spend so much on medical needs that other needs are compromised. The services of a surgeon is just one of ten things that a worthy community must provide:

> A scholar should not reside in a city where [any] of the following ten things is missing: (1) A court of justice, (2) a charity fund, (3) a synagogue, (4) public baths, (5) toilet facilities, (6) a circumciser (*mohel*), (7) a surgeon, (8) a notary, (9) a slaughterer (*shochet*), and (10) a schoolmaster. Rabbi Akiba [included] several kinds of fruit because they are beneficial for eyesight (*Sanhedrin* 17b).

b. The Talmud sets forth the ideal that everyone in need of healing will have access to it, regardless of their means to pay.

> Abba the blood-letter [an ancient type of medical healer] placed a box outside his office where his fees were to be deposited. Whoever had money put it in, but those who had none could come in without feeling embarrassed. When he saw a person who was in no position to pay, he would offer him some money, saying to him, "Go, strengthen yourself [after the bleeding procedure]" (*Ta'anit* 21b).

c. To what extent should we go to take health and safety risks for the possibility of gaining something useful?

> We are commanded to remove all obstacles and sources of danger from all places in which we live (Maimonides, *The Commandments*, vol. 1, p. 197).

d. For sufficient tissue to use in genetic therapies, scientists must create more tissue than they will use as they develop genetic therapies. The tissue might include embryonic tissue, adult cells, partially developed organs, etc. Surplus and abnormally developed tissue/clones must be destroyed (or preserved in their quasi-living state). The laws of *Bal Tashchit*, instructing us not to be destructive or wasteful, originate in the Torah:

> The Eternal God took the man and placed him in the garden of Eden, to till it and tend it (Genesis 2:15).

e. Germ-line gene therapy (GLGT) manipulates cells involved in reproduction.

> Whatever changes are introduced into the germ line will perpetuate themselves in subsequent generations . . . An error introduced by the procedure will (in an almost a biblical sense) visit itself unto the fourth generation (Exodus 34:7) and beyond (Dr. Stephen M. Modell, "Four Cloning Scenarios from the Perspective of Science and the Jewish Tradition," in *Bioethics, Program Guide X: Cloning*).

f. There is a difference between purely reproductive technologies, such as *in vitro* fertilization (IVF), and genetic technologies, which try to change the shape of future organisms (*The Economist*, "The Politics of Genes: America's Next Ethical War," April 14, 2001, p. 21).

g. "Many of the animal clones that have been produced show serious developmental abnormalities . . . " (Stephen G. Post, quoting a British expert on fertility in "The Judeo-Christian Case against Human Cloning," *Biotechnology*, p. 103).

Probing: Ideas and Issues

The "hurdle" of expense may seem too high to surmount if genetic therapies consumed an overwhelming percentage of society's health expenditures, or society spent more money on genetic therapies than public schools, the arts, environmental protection, or another valued cause. For the following, give examples of when *you* think the hurdle would become so prohibitively high that you could no longer justify potential therapeutic benefits: expense, individually tailoring therapies, access (by the wealthy/privileged only?), safety, environmental issues, and unforeseen detrimental genetic consequences affecting future generations.

6. **Should the cloning of human beings for the purpose of providing healthy tissue and/or organs be allowed?**

On the One Hand:

A cloned individual can provide healthy tissue/organs to its ill counterpart without the problems of immune incompatibility. Creating a new organ (without the full body) is another possibility.

A. Show me a child whose survival depends on transplantation of bone marrow. I would advise cloning to save the child's life. A child produced for this purpose would then be doubly loved (Rabbi Moshe Tendler," The Right Situation" [Op-Ed] *New York Times*, December 12, 1997, A22).

B. Embryonic cells seem less antagonistic to the immune system than are ordinary cells . . . Adult stem cells, if they could be extracted from each patient as need arose, could be used without any risk of immune rejection (Nicholas Wade, "In Tiny Cells, Glimpses of Body's Master Plan," *New York Times*, December 18, 2001, D8).

C. The promise of embryonic stem cells for medicine rests on more than their powers to morph [transform] into any body tissue. In the lab, they exhibit another amazing property — the ability to assemble spontaneously into structures seen in living tissues [e.g., blood vessels, glands, heart muscle] . . . The cells are just engineered to self-assemble, given the right cues and conditions (Nicholas Wade, "In Tiny Cells, Glimpses of Body's Master Plan," *New York Times*, December 18, 2001, D8).

D. It would almost certainly be possible to produce human bodies without a forebrain . . . These human bodies without any semblance of consciousness would not be considered persons, and thus it would be perfectly legal to keep them "alive" as a future source of organs (Lee Silver, Princeton biologist quoted by Charles Krauthammer in "Of Headless Mice . . . And Men," *Time Magazine*, January 19, 1998).

On the Other Hand:

Manufacturing some people to serve others is coercive and an abuse of power. In creating an organ, we take risks that it will evolve in abnormal and frightening ways.

a. It is a cardinal principle of Judaism that one may not sacrifice one life to preserve another . . . (see *Mishneh Torah, Hilchot Yesodei Hatorah* 5:7). One might argue this principle does not apply to the current situation since the donor clone will continue to live after contributing bone marrow. Let us suppose, however, that the cloned person is to be considered a constant source of bone marrow for the original [sibling], which might occur, say, in a case of chronic leukemia . . . This condition is not unlike the relationship between Isaac and his brother Ishmael. There were natural rivalries between Sarah and Hagar (Ishmael's mother) and between Isaac and Ishmael, so that eventually Abraham banished Hagar and Ishmael and ceded patriarchy to Isaac. Who is to say that a child born to service another will not be taken for granted or gain a lesser status in parental eyes if their contribution to a brother or sister is a recurrent necessity? There is also the

question of the emotional impact on the cloned, developing child . . . (Dr. Stephen M. Modell, "Four Cloning Scenarios from the Perspective of Science and the Jewish Tradition," in *Bioethics, Program Guide X: Cloning*).

b. When prominent scientists are prepared to acquiesce in — or indeed encourage — the deliberate creation of deformed and dying quasi-human life [for example, as part of one's "own personal, precisely tissue-matched organ farm"], you know we are facing a bioethical abyss. There is no grosser corruption of biotechnology than creating a human mutant and disemboweling it at our pleasure for spare parts (Charles Krauthammer, "Of Headless Mice . . . And Men," *Time Magazine*, January 19, 1998).

c. Injected into mice, the unchanged [embryonic stem] cells form not an embryo but a grisly tumor full of hair and teeth and known as a "monster cancer" or teratoma (Nicholas Wade, "In Tiny Cells, Glimpses of Body's Master Plan," *New York Times*, December 18, 2001, D8).

Probing: Ideas and Issues

Why might you justify the use of a clone and/or a "manufactured" organ for therapeutic use? Why might you say doing such things is prohibited? Where should Judaism stand on this matter? Explain.

7. **Should cloning or the manipulation of genes for the purpose of producing desirable characteristics in human beings be allowed?**

On the One Hand:

Cloning will help us as a society to improve the quality of our species by cloning special individuals or isolating favorable genetic qualities to pass on to the next generation.

A. Many people now argue that science is allowing a healthier, non-coercive version of eugenics, practiced by caring parents as opposed to a racist state . . . (*The Economist*, "The Politics of Genes: America's Next Ethical War," April 14, 2001, p. 22).

B. An example of pre-birth genetic screening:

> A Jewish committee in New York that is concerned to prevent genetic disease organizes tests to discourage Ashkenzi Jews who carry the Tay-Sachs mutation from marrying each other. But it went further . . . with the specific selection of "Baby Adam," from among 15 healthy embryos, because he had the right bone marrow to help his sister, who had a rare disease (*The Economist*, "The Politics of Genes: America's Next Ethical War," April 14, 2001, p. 22).

On the Other Hand:

The practice of eugenics is hubris. That is, manipulating genes for the purpose of producing "desirable" characteristics is sacrilegious arrogance. It turns humans into objects and creates a breeding ground for racism.

a. The argument (that "cloning will help us as a society to improve the quality of our species . . . ") is often used, but it relies on a flawed understanding of the genetics of populations. If we were to prevent the reproduction of all individuals exhibiting a genetic disease, we would have very little effect on the frequency of the defective gene in the human population. We are not really "improving the species" by pursuing cloning. On the other hand . . . if we can avoid individual suffering by prescreening embryos, are we not obliged to do so? (Robert Dorit, Professor of Biology, Smith College,

February 2002).

b. Cloning is another blow to the necessary sense of humility we should have in dealing with the mysteries of life (Rabbi David Wolpe, quoted by Barbara Trainin Blank in "The Ethics of Cloning," *Hadassah Magazine*, June/July 1997).

c. For many people, the difficulties come when biotechnology leaps from stopping disease to adding advantages — enhancing the genes that make you more intelligent, more musical, or less homosexual (as it may yet do: it can't at present) (*The Economist*, "The Politics of Genes: America's Next Ethical War," April 14, 2001, p. 22).

d. The sex of children is already up for sale. At first, [one] institute helped couples with hereditary diseases that tend to occur in boys. Now it offers "family balancing" to couples who want to choose their next child from "the under-represented gender" (*The Economist*, "The Politics of Genes: America's Next Ethical War," April 14, 2001, p. 22).

Probing: Ideas and Issues

Why might a person argue in favor of eugenics? Why might a person argue against it? Why would Judaism (and other religion-based ethics) prohibit this practice?

RELATED MIDDOT AND MITZVOT

Practicing these virtues supports ethical decision-making regarding cloning and other genetic technologies.

> *Anavah* (Humility): Just because we *can* do something, doesn't mean we *should*. Focusing on healing and cooperating with international regulations will help us maintain

humility as we pursue genetic technologies.

Mechabayd Zeh et Zeh (Honoring the Dignity of Each Individual): Before going ahead with a genetic procedure, we must carefully evaluate how it will affect the dignity of any and all persons involved.

Rofeh Cholim (Healing the Sick): We have a duty to heal suffering in our midst. Genetic technologies may prove to be an important tool in working toward that aim.

Samayach B'Chelko (Contentment with One's Lot): Perhaps this includes contentment with there being one version of our genes in the world (or two if we're an identical twin). Cloning ourselves is reaching beyond what we reasonably should expect to be our life's "portion."

Sho-eyl U'Maysheev (Asking and Answering Questions): Genetic technologies raise many important and difficult questions. We must encourage vibrant discussion and debate about these questions. Hopefully, in doing so, our society's decisions will be well reasoned and will prove as wise as possible.

Yirah (Awe and Reverence): Despite human "advances" in the sciences, we must not lose sight of God's role as the ultimate Source of Mystery in the universe.

ACTIVITIES

A First Look: Key Issues and Ideas

1. To engage intelligently in discussion of this topic, students will need a modest understanding of certain biological terms. Divide students into pairs and assign each pair one term (or two, if necessary because of group size) from the Glossary for this topic, found on pp. 46-47. Each pair designs a glossary poster, in which they illustrate their term(s). When they complete the task, have pairs explain their posters to each other.

Try to limit this introductory exercise to 15 minutes (five minutes to explain/set up exercise, five minutes to work on the posters, and five minutes to explain terms to each other). The goal is to give students some basic vocabulary, not a comprehensive biology lesson.

2. Here is one way to give students a sense of the ethical issues involved with cloning and other genetic technologies. Draw on the material in the Overview, but mix up the order in which you present the pros, cons, and additional considerations for pursuing genetic technologies. After explaining each ethical concern, ask students where the reasoning belongs (as pro, con, or unclear). You may want to keep track of the ratings on a chalk board. Present both the general concerns and the particularly Jewish concerns.

   For example, you might explain the potential healing benefits of genetic technologies. Students would then discuss and likely decide that this reasoning belongs in the "pro" column. Then, you might explain concerns about trying to be *k'Elohim*, "like God" in pursuing this work. Students might decide this concern belongs in the "unclear" column.

3. Refer to the 14 "On the One Hand/On the Other Hand" points listed in the "Text Study" section above (seven points from one side plus seven from the other). Individually, each person rank orders the 14 points from most important to least. Then as a group compare and explain the rankings. Ask: What do your results reflect about your attitude toward cloning and other genetic technologies? What was most challenging about completing this exercise?

4. Discuss the meaning of the "slippery slope" as it applies to cloning and other genetic technologies. First, ask students to come up with two or three examples (or scenarios) which they feel *would justify* the use of genetic technology. Here is one example:

Developing therapies from cloned tissue that could help a paraplegic person with a spinal injury heal enough to be able to walk and move about freely again.

Next, have them come up with two or three examples for which they feel the use of cloning is questionable. Here is an example: Cloning a child for a couple for whom other fertility procedures are not effective. (Not everyone will agree where this example belongs: whether it is permissible, questionable, or prohibited.)

Finally, have students come up with two or three examples of things they feel are clearly unacceptable uses of cloning or other genetic technologies. Here is an example: Offering parents options to choose "desirable" genetic characteristics in an embryo they intend to nurture into development (by implanting the "designer" embryo in the woman).

Now, discuss how a society should judge what belongs on the top and what belongs on the bottom of the slippery slope (the top being completely acceptable, the bottom being unacceptable). Who should make decisions about what should be allowed in genetic technologies? Who should enforce the decisions, and how should they do so?

5. Have your group educate itself on current issues regarding cloning and other genetic technologies by exploring the content in the web sites mentioned in the Bibliography for this chapter, pp. 48-49. Looking at the web sites and referring to some of the links will give students a sense of the many organizations concerned with and interested in this topic.

Applying Middot and Mitzvot

1. Refer to the six *middot* listed in the "Related *Middot* and *Mitzvot*" section above. Have students rank order these from what they consider most to least important in terms of developing a proper attitude toward genetic technologies. Then, have them discuss and explain their ratings.

2. *Sho-eyl U'Maysheev* stresses the importance of asking and answering questions. Have group members imagine they are representatives on a genetic ethics panel. What five questions would they insist a regulation and supervision committee respond to as that committee formulates recommendations for genetic research and development? You may want to have group members first work on questions in pairs, then share their ideas with the whole "panel."

3. For more information and activities on:

   Yirah (Awe and Reverence): see *Teaching Jewish Virtues: Sacred Sources and Arts Activities* by Susan Freeman, pp. 332-346.

   Samayach B'Chelko (Contentment with One's Lot): see *Teaching Jewish Virtues: Sacred Sources and Arts Activities* by Susan Freeman, pp. 211-227 and *The Jewish Moral Virtues* by Eugene B. Borowitz and Frances Weinman Schwartz, pp. 161-172.

   Mechabayd Zeh et Zeh (Honoring the Dignity of Each Individual): see *Teaching Jewish Virtues: Sacred Sources and Arts Activities* by Susan Freeman, pp. 179-194.

   Anavah (Humility): see *Teaching Jewish Virtues: Sacred Sources and Arts Activities* by Susan Freeman, pp. 8-25 and *The Jewish Moral Virtues* by Eugene B. Borowitz and Frances Weinman Schwartz, pp. 137-148.

   Rofeh Cholim (Healing the Sick): see *Teaching Jewish Virtues: Sacred Sources and Arts Activities* by Susan Freeman, pp. 299-317.

Stories: Understanding through Listening

1. Read over the imaginary situations in the "Scenarios" section above. Have the group set up a mock television style panel interview. The "guests" are Dave, Dave's wife, and one of Dave's children; David, David's son and David's daughter-in-law; and Davey the

cat's owners. You'll also need to appoint an interviewer. The interviewer should ask the guests to share their stories. The interviewer may follow up with questions and also solicit questions from the audience.

A variation: Have the group create another "episode" with different guests and other stories to share and discuss.

2. Another TV interview show possibility: Invite two students to act as guests and another to act as interviewer. The guests are clones. Each was created to serve the health needs of his/her chronically sick sibling by providing healthy tissue (through a painless procedure, on an approximately monthly basis). One sibling-clone resents his/her role, and the other is happy to serve. In this show the interviewer and audience members should probe the issues affecting the attitudes and feelings of the guests.

3. Have participants develop a survey to find out about people's feelings about cloning. Here are some sample questions:

   • Do you support cloning? Why or why not?

   • If a therapeutic technique involving cloning some of your tissue would allow you to live to 100, would you want it? What about if the technique would allow you to live until 150?

   • Do you think people should have the goal of living forever? Why or why not?

   • If you couldn't have children because of infertility problems, would you like to have a clone made of yourself?

   • How much (if anything) would you pay to have a beloved pet cloned?

   • Do you think taxpayer money should go to genetic research?

   • Do you think health insurance should cover genetic therapies?

   • Do you believe God approves of cloning?

   • Etc.

Now, have participants plan out how they will conduct the survey (by interviewing students, friends and family, random people on the street?). Also, do they want to do the interviews just with pencil and paper, or with tape recorders or video cameras? After survey data is collected, have group members discuss and process their findings.

Action: Getting Out, Getting Involved

1. Have participants find out what are the latest controversies concerning cloning and other genetic technologies. Have them start their research by checking out these two web sites: National Academy of Sciences (www.nationalacademies.org) and National Institute of Health (www.nih.gov). Search these organizations' databases by using the key term "cloning" or "genetic engineering."

   Is there an issue the researchers feel strongly about? For example, maybe they want to see increased (or decreased) public spending on stem cell research. Encourage students to make specific efforts to get involved in an area that interests them. Perhaps they will write government officials, write a letter to the editor in their local newspaper, start a petition, plan a publicity and education campaign, or volunteer at a genetic research institute.

2. Some day there may be a need for a "Clones' Bill of Rights." Have your group compose a draft of such a document. They may also or instead choose to draft a section on genetic therapy for a "Patients' Bill of Rights."

Wrestling: Engagement with the Issues

1. Organize debate teams to argue one or more of the points presented in "Text Study" section above. Allow time for teams to prepare their arguments and for the debate itself.

For example: Text Study #5 examines "hurdles" to genetic technologies. Have the two teams debate these hurdles. One side's position is: "The Hurdles Are Too High." The other side's position is: "We Can Overcome the Hurdles."

2. One's definition of personhood would influence one's views on cloning and other genetic technologies. Have the group focus on the question of personhood. Assign individuals or pairs to research "defining a person" from two or more different points of view, one of which should be Jewish. Some of the passages in the "Text Study" section above touch on this question (see Text Study #2 and #3). Possible perspectives to research might include those of other religions, philosophical systems, and medical literature. These are some issues to consider:

   - Am I person because I have a mind?

   - Am I person because I have a body?

   - Am I person because I have a soul?

   - Am I person because I have emotions?

   - Does our unique genetic imprint define our personhood?

   - Is personhood defined by brain and/or heart functioning?

   - Does personhood begin with the birth of a child or some time during pregnancy?

   - If a person suffers from a brain injury that radically changes his/her personality, is he/she less of a person?

   - To what extent is someone a person because of his/her relationships with other people (e.g., a mother and child)?

   - If a robot can complete "thinking" functions, does that make it a person?

   - What distinguishes a chimpanzee from a person?

   - If we create a living human-like organ without a brain, is it a person? (If not,

what is it?)

   - How is God like a person? How is God unlike a person?

When participants complete their research, have the whole group reassemble. Researchers present their findings. Group members discuss how the various definitions of personhood would influence views on cloning, genetic research, and genetic therapies.

3. A variation on the above activity: Have participants explore and express definitions of personhood through an art medium.

4. Ethicists may recommend strict regulation of genetic technologies by a multi-disciplinary, international panel of experts. Have your group come up with ten or so regulations they believe should be included in a panel's recommendations.

   To make this exercise more challenging, assign individuals to play specific roles on the panel as it decides on its recommendations. For instance, include:

   - A wheelchair bound person suffering from a spinal injury that might be helped through a genetic therapy.

   - Someone with diabetes who might be helped by a genetic therapy.

   - A Rabbi.

   - A Catholic priest.

   - An infertile woman.

   - A scientist at a lab who wants to clone pets as part of a commercial business.

   - A member of a minority population that worries about eugenics.

   - An environmentalist.

   - An expert on economic injustices in our society.

   - A health safety expert.

   - Etc.

5. Divide the group. Half the participants make up "Clone Court." The other half presents their cases to the court. The court must probe the presenter's wish and motivations, then decide if it will approve the presenter's request. Presenters can come up with their own ideas to bring to the court or use one of these:

- A scientist has discovered genetic material from a dinosaur. She would like permission to try to clone a dinosaur from the preserved cells.

- A certain type of squirrel is in danger of becoming extinct. A zoologist would like to clone 25 new animals. He will need to fund this multimillion dollar effort with taxpayer dollars.

- Parents would like to clone an embryo, and have the two embryos implanted in the woman, who would then give birth to identical twins. The twins could supply each other with "parts" (tissue or organs) if the need were to arise.

- An enterprising scientist would like to establish a "spare parts" bank. A "customer" could pay to have a number of body parts developed and preserved for use down the road (such as a kidney, lung, pancreas, heart muscle tissue, etc.).

- The elite "High I.Q. Society" would like to clone its smartest member. The 75-year-old genius has contributed more to science, scholarship, and the arts than anyone in the world in the last 100 years.

- The NBA (National Basketball Association) would like to clone its most talented player of all time.

- A psychology research organization would like to create a clone from the remains of one of the most evil dictators of all time. Organization members believe that by studying this individual, they will gain important insights as to the origins of evil behavior.

- A paraplegic individual argues that more government funds should be allocated for stem cell research. Such research could provide therapies to treat spinal injuries (which is what the paraplegic suffers from) as well as other painful medical conditions.

- Characters from the situations in the "Scenarios" section above (p. 31) could make up three additional court appearances.

For a follow-up suggestion, see "Empathy," activity #1 below.

6. Have participants create collages which visually capture the complexity of cloning and genetic technologies. Here are some words, phrases, and images that might help trigger artists' own ideas: "'And to heal he shall heal' (Exodus 21:19). From this verse we infer that permission has been given [by God] to the physician to heal" (*Brachot* 60a); "I am the Eternal, your healer" (Exodus 15:26); the duty to save life; relieving suffering; vanity; overreaching or hubris; trying to be *k'Elohim* (like God); discrimination; fear; taking risks; turning humans into objects; manufacturing embryos; honoring humans by caring about their pain; respecting uniqueness; manipulation; isolating "desirable" characteristics.

Empathy

1. By arguing the "Clone Court" cases ("Wrestling" activity #5 above), presenters should feel empathy for their characters. That is, they should try to understand and deeply feel the beliefs of the person they represent. As a follow-up to that activity, have court actors share how they felt as they presented their cases.

2. Refer to the "On the One Hand/On the Other Hand" chart in the "Text Study" section above. Encourage participants to understand how a person could embrace each one of the 14 beliefs. Specifically, ask them to add

one more sentence to each of the points. The sentence should begin with these words, "I believe this point is important because . . . " Even if they don't *really* believe in the merit of the statement, the goal is to try to grasp and verbalize different perspectives.

GLOSSARY

Note: Studying the terms below provides a preliminary foundation of the science we are discussing in this chapter. To begin to address the ethical issues, at least some minimal understanding of the science is necessary.

Adult DNA Cloning:

Cell nuclear replacement, in which an existing animal is replicated. Sheep and other mammals have been cloned using this technique. The scientist removes the nucleus containing the DNA from an embryonic cell and replaces it with the nucleus from an adult animal cell. Next, the embryonic cell undergoes several rounds of cell division. It is then implanted in a surrogate's womb to develop into a new animal. This technique possesses the potential for cloning human beings, that is, producing a twin of an existing person.

Blastocyst:

Four to five days after an egg is fertilized, a hollow sphere of about 250 cells develops. This is the blastocyst. Within is a clump of approximately 30 cells, the inner cell mass. The embryo develops from this inner cell mass. "Embryonic stem cells" is the term used for cells attained from the inner cell mass and grown in a laboratory.

Cloning:

With this technique, a scientist may replicate a single gene, DNA segments, a cell, or an entire organism.

DNA:

DNA, or deoxyribonucleic acid, is a long, double-stranded molecule coiled inside a cell. Nucleotides are subunits of a DNA molecule. They designate specific genetic information.

Embryo Cloning:

This technique produces monozygotic (identical) twins or triplets. It duplicates nature's process of producing twins or triplets. A medical technician removes one or more cells from a fertilized embryo and prompts the cell(s) to develop into one or more duplicate embryos. The result is genetically identical twins or triplets. Scientists have used the technique for many years on various species of animals. Comparable experimentation on humans has been very limited.

Embryonic Stem Cells:

See "Blastocyst" above. These cells seem to be pluripotent. That is, they seem to have the potential to grow into any of the body's 260 or so cell types, though they cannot create a new individual on their own. In contrast, the egg cell is considered totipotent, meaning it can develop into a complete embryo.

Eugenics:

Manipulating embryonic genes to attain preferred characteristics; for example, eye color, sex of the baby, correction of a genetic disease indicator, etc.

Gene:

An ordered string of DNA nucleotides that transmit hereditary characteristics.

Gene Therapy:

New DNA or an entire gene is transferred into an individual. Typically, the goal in replacing a damaged or missing gene is to assist in restoring the gene's intended function. See also the related term, "Therapeutic Cloning."

Parthenogenesis:

An egg develops into an embryo without fertilization. This kind of reproduction does not occur naturally in mammals. Rather, scientists simulate fertilization, using chemicals or electricity to prompt certain animals' eggs to divide. Experiments with human eggs are the next step.

Stem Cells:

Master cells from which the specialized cells of tissues and organs form. Stem cells have the capacity to reproduce indefinitely.

Therapeutic Cloning:

The goal of therapeutic cloning is to produce a healthy copy of a sick person's tissue or organ for transplant. From perhaps a patient's skin cell, a medical technician removes the nucleus. The nucleus is inserted into a donated human egg cell without its own nucleus. The egg cell reprograms the patient's cell nucleus back to its totipotent state. That is, the reformatted patient's cell has regained its potential to form a complete embryo (i.e., any of a number of cells). Embryonic stem cells are cultured from the egg once it becomes a 5-day-old embryo. These new, "flexible" embryonic stem cells are changed into healthy (therapeutic) cells for injection into the patient. Perhaps the new cells will be changed into healthy liver tissue for a patient who has a diseased liver. In the therapeutic cloning process, the embryo dies. This technique has the potential to decrease reliance on other people for organ transplants, to eliminate the need for "waiting lists." Since the transplant would use the sick person's original DNA, taking immunosuppressant drugs would not be necessary. There would be less likelihood that the patient's body would "reject" the new tissue or organ.

BIBLIOGRAPHY

Books and Articles

Angier, Natalie. "Defining the Undefinable: Being Alive." In *The New York Times, Science Times*, December 18, 2001.

Balin, Carole, and Aaron Panken. "Shall We Counsel Germ Cell Gene Therapy?" In *Reform Jewish Ethics and the Halakhah*, edited by Eugene B. Borowitz. West Orange, NJ: Behrman House, Inc., 1988.

Balkin, Jack M. "The Cloning Conundrum." Op-ed, *The New York Times*, January 30, 2002.

Blank, Barbara Trainin. "The Ethics of Cloning." In *Hadassah Magazine,* June/July 1997.

Borowitz, Eugene B., and Frances Weinman Schwartz. *The Jewish Moral Virtues*. Philadelphia, PA: The Jewish Publication Society, 1999.

Brody, Jane E. "Weighing the Rights of the Embryo Against Those of the Sick." In *The New York Times, Science Times*, December 18, 2001.

Dorff, Elliot N. *Matters of Life and Death: A Jewish Approach To Modern Medical Ethics*. Philadelphia, PA: The Jewish Publication Society, 1998.

Duenes, Steve, and Kris Goodfellow. "The Embryonic Journey and Its Milestones." In *The New York Times, Science Times*, December 18, 2001.

Freeman, Susan. *Teaching Jewish Virtues: Sacred Sources and Arts Activities*. Denver, CO: A.R.E. Publishing, Inc., 1999.

"From Cloning To Cures." *The New York Times*, editorial. August 4, 2001.

Hamilton, Michael P., ed. *The New Genetics and the Future of Man*. Grand Rapids, MI: William B. Eerdmans Publishing Company, 1972.

Jakobovits, Immanuel. *Jewish Medical Ethics*. New York: Bloch, 1975.

Kass, Leon R., and Daniel Callahan. "Ban Stand: Cloning's Big Test." *The New Republic*, August 6, 2001.

Kolata, Gina. *Cloning: The Road To Dolly and the Path Ahead*. New York: William Morrow and Company, Inc., 1998.

———. "A Thick Line between Theory and Therapy, as Shown with Mice." *The New York Times, Science Times*, December 18, 2001.

Krauthammer, Charles. "Of Headless Mice . . . And Men." *Time Magazine*, January 19, 1998.

Messina, Lynn, ed. *Biotechnology,* from the series *The Reference Shelf* , Vol. 72, No. 4. New York: The H.W. Wilson Company, 2000.

"The Politics of Genes: America's Next Ethical War." *The Economist*, April 14, 2001.

Pollack, Andrew. "Scientists Seek Ways to Rebuild the Body, Bypassing the Embryos" and "Use of Cloning to Tailor Treatment Has Big Hurdles, Including Cost." *The New York Times, Science Times*, December 18, 2001.

Post, Stephen G. "The Judeo-Christian Case against Human Cloning." *America*, June 21-28, 1997. Included in *Biotechnology*, from the series *The Reference Shelf* , Vol. 72, No. 4, edited by Lynn Messina. New York: The H.W. Wilson Company, 2000.

Reisner, Avram I. "Curiouser and Curiouser: Genetic Engineering of Nonhuman Life." In *Life and Death Responsibilities in Jewish Biomedical Ethics*, edited by Aaron L. Mackler. New York: The Louis Finkelstein Institute of The Jewish Theological Seminary, 2000.

Rosner, Fred. *Modern Medicine and Jewish Ethics*. Hoboken, NJ: KTAV Publishing House, Inc. and New York: Yeshiva University Press, 1991.

Rosner, Fred, and J. David Bleich, eds. *Jewish Bioethics*. New York and London: Sanhedrin Press, 1979.

Steinberg, Avraham. "Human Cloning — Scientific, Moral and Jewish Perspectives." Paper delivered to The Institute for Jewish Medical Ethics of the Hebrew Academy of San Francisco, www.ijme.org/Content/Transcripts/Steinberg/scloning.htm., 1998.

Stolberg, Sheryl Gay. "Controversy Reignites Over Stem Cells and Clones." *The New York Times, Science Times*, December 18, 2001.

Tendler, Moshe. "The Right Situation" (Op-ed) *New York Times*, December 12, 1997, A22.

UAHC Committee of the UAHC Department of Jewish Family Concerns. *Bioethics, Program Guide X: Cloning*. New York: Union of American Hebrew Congregations, Summer, 1998.

Vorspan, Albert, and David Saperstein. *Tough Choices*. New York: UAHC Press, 1992.

Wade, Nicholas. "Apostle of Regenerative Medicine Foresees Longer Health and Life," and "In Tiny Cells, Glimpses of Body's Master Plan." *The New York Times, Science Times*, December 18, 2001.

Web Sites

Advanced Cell Technology, Inc.: www.advanced-cell.com

"Involved in the research and development of technologies of Nuclear Transfer for human therapeutics and animal cloning."

Genetic Savings and Clone: www.savingsand-clone.com

A commercial enterprise with a special interest in cloning pets.

Jewish Law: www.jlaw.com

Articles and commentary examining halachah, Jewish issues, and secular law.

National Academy of Sciences: www.nationalacademies.org

Search the database for "cloning" or "genetic engineering."

National Institute of Health: www.nih.gov

Governmental organization of the United States Department of Health and Human Services. Search the database for "cloning" or "genetic engineering."

Why Biotech?: www.whybiotech.com

Focused on supporting, explaining, and defending genetic research primarily for agricultural purposes.

Films

Specific sections of the following commercial films may be valuable for illustrating certain aspects of the topic of cloning, but it may not be appropriate for students to view the entire film. Prescreening is strongly recommended.

The 6th Day (1999, 123 minutes, rated PG-13)

A futuristic Arnold Shwarzenegger action film about a man who meets a clone of himself and stumbles into a grand conspiracy about clones taking over the world. Available from video stores.

Multiplicity (1996, 117 minutes, rated PG-13)

A comedy about an overworked and overscheduled man who clones himself to make more time for his wife and family. Available from video stores.

CHAPTER 3

EUTHANASIA AND ASSISTED SUICIDE

OVERVIEW

Euthanasia literally means "a good death." Sometimes called "mercy killing," euthanasia is an act of inducing death painlessly. This chapter explores the challenges that come with wanting to honor the sacredness of life, yet feeling conflicted when it seems the best way to end the relentless suffering of those we love is by helping them to die. Over the last 50 years, medical understanding and technological advances have raised questions and concerns never imagined by our ancestors. We will look at the impact of some of these changes. As we delve into this complex subject, the reader will note that not every type of euthanasia is treated in the same way (see the Glossary, p. 70, for definitions of types).

Jewish Perspectives

A number of Jewish principles are relevant to the discussion of euthanasia. For example, Judaism clearly professes that life is sacred and that we must do whatever we can to protect and preserve it. We believe that murder is forbidden, as is "standing idly by" when another is in danger. Injuring another person (Exodus 21) or oneself (*Baba Kama* 8:6-7) is condemned.

Throughout the ages, our tradition stresses the value of compassion for those who are suffering. How might we alleviate pain, how might we comfort those who are ailing? To be a righteous Jew is to keep concerns of loving-kindness at the forefront of our minds, and then to act accordingly.

Beyond general principles such as those mentioned above, the discussion gets more complicated. Sure, Jews can agree that murder is wrong

and that compassion is good. But when talking about euthanasia, making decisions based on these notions doesn't get us very far. Under the justification of compassion, for instance, two physicians could take two different approaches to the same case. One physician might administer an increasingly lethal dose of medication for a patient who is suffering greatly from a terminal illness (which may alleviate pain but hasten death, as in "double effect" — see the Glossary, p. 70). Another physician might refuse to administer any treatment that in any way could hasten a person's death. This second physician would argue that administering quantities of medication known to be lethal is equivalent to murder and can hardly be called "compassionate." Thus, what it means to be compassionate is arguable. What exactly constitutes "murder" is debatable, too.

To remove life support machines from a person who is dead surely is not "murder." If it is determined that a patient has no brain activity (is "brain dead"), disconnecting him/her from a respirator or a heart-lung machine is not especially controversial from a Jewish perspective, as there is a valid argument that the person is dead. But what if some minimal brain activity is discerned, yet the patient's breathing and/or heartbeat cannot be sustained on the patient's own? Then may life support machines be disconnected? What if medical experts agree that this patient will remain in a permanent vegetative state? When cases get more complex, Jewish sources are not in agreement on how to define death.

As described above, there is no consensus about when it is permissible to detach a dying person from a respirator or heart-lung machine. There is more agreement, however, about "routine" treatment. For example, providing food is part of routine treatment, and thus, withholding food from a dying person would be unacceptable. But even the notion of what it means to "provide food" isn't as easily understood as it once was. Providing food through the insertion of feeding tubes might be considered a medical treatment and thus not necessarily routine.[1]

"Hastening a patient's death" is forbidden (see Text Study #8A below), while "removing an impediment" to death is permitted (see Text Study #8a below). Even so, the distinction between these two concepts is not always obvious (see Text Study #8b below). Moreover, some Rabbinic texts actually seem to condone euthanasia (see Text Study #3a and #3b below).

Liberal Jewish perspectives would include individual autonomy as a valid "ingredient" in making decisions (i.e., "I should have the liberty to decide what happens to my own body"). In Israel, where Jewish values and democratic values both complement and compete with each other, a precedent has been set for a more liberal attitude toward those who wish to reject medical treatments. In the 1990s, an individual in the terminal stages of the disease Amyotrophic Lateral Sclerosis (A.L.S., also known as Lou Gehrig's Disease) was allowed by the court to refuse life sustaining treatment, including artificial respiration and artificial feeding, when he ultimately would slip into a persistent vegetative state.

To what extent can we assist a *gosays* (a moribund patient whose death is imminent) through the last stage of life? Some would agree that administering increasing amounts of pain relieving morphine is acceptable, though it likely will hasten death. There is more consensus concerning the removal of an impediment to death. Traditional Jewish texts give the example of silencing the knocking noise of a nearby woodchopper. The noise presumably distracts the

dying person from letting go into death (see Text Study #8a below). While exactly how to deal with a *gosays* is open to dispute, our tradition is more definitive about cases involving a non-*gosays* — someone for whom death is not imminent. That is, say a relatively healthy person is diagnosed with a disease carrying a bleak prognosis, such as multiple sclerosis or a certain psychiatric disorder. Assisting in such a person's suicide would be forbidden.

Some may argue that liberalizing Jewish approaches toward euthanasia is valid. This might include accepting the absence of brain activity as a definition of death, sanctioning double effect (see the Glossary, p. 70), and/or allowing for the removal of life support when a person is in a persistent vegetative state. Even so, the warnings culled from the secular world reinforce the need for caution concerning any adjustments we may want to sanction (see next section).

General Perspectives

In the world at large, there is a great deal of discussion about euthanasia. Whether assisted suicide is ever justified is perhaps the most controversial question. Patients, families, and care providers all have consciences and religious/spiritual commitments that influence end of life decisions.

The foremost rationale given for assisted suicide is release from pain and suffering. Another is that by effecting the time of death, patients are said to retain more control of a situation that might feel frightening and confusing. A third rationale is that by assisting in a patient's suicide, a doctor does not abandon his/her patient in the time of the patient's greatest need even though nothing else medically can be done. Fourth, patients can avoid feeling victimized by certain medical technologies that seem to pro-

---

[1]The Supreme Court (in the Cruzan v. Missouri case) considered the insertion of feeding tubes to be a medical treatment that a competent patient could refuse by living will or proxy decision maker. It is difficult to impose a definitive Jewish posi- tion on whether the insertion of feeding tubes should be considered "routine" or not.

long their suffering.[2]

There are compelling arguments against physician assisted suicide, as well. First, no one can be absolutely certain about the prognosis of a disease, even for so-called terminally ill patients. Second, the impetus to request suicide may be more of a general cry for help to which a doctor could respond in ways that aren't lethal. Third, permitting physician assisted suicide may cause resources to be diverted away from research in palliative or pain relief care. (It is notable that requests for suicide greatly decrease when adequate pain relief is supplied to those suffering from serious illnesses.) Fourth, patients may feel coerced to die (as when a dying patient's wife states to her husband that he can either elect death or be sent to a home for the chronically ill, which, by the way, will wipe out the family's savings). Fifth is the risk that those who are most vulnerable in society will be singled out as candidates for death, i.e., the poor, the disabled, the elderly, and the very young.[3]

In 1997, the Supreme Court of the United States decided a significant case — Vacco v. Quill. Essentially, the plaintiffs made an equal protection argument. They said that since the law guarantees every patient the right to refuse unwanted medical treatment, the patient on life support can "commit suicide" with the doctor's help (e.g., by ordering the doctor to remove a feeding tube or respirator). But the New York law before the court made it illegal for an equally sick patient *not* on life support to "commit suicide" with a doctor's help (e.g., the doctor prescribing a lethal dose of drugs to the patient). Thus, they argued the law treats equally sick people (one on life support, the other not) in an unconstitutionally unequal way. The plaintiff's argument was rejected by the Supreme Court, which upheld New York's law making physician assisted suicide illegal. The Court distinguished between withdrawing life sustaining treatment and assisted suicide. It contended that when a

patient refuses life support, he/she dies because the disease has run its natural course. However, if a patient self-administers lethal drugs, his/her death results from that medication. The Court also distinguished between the physician's intention in both scenarios — ending futile treatment and suffering versus hastening death.

The American Medical Association encourages proactive efforts in medical decision making. It recommends that patients exercise as much control as possible over end of life decisions through:

1. creating living wills

2. appointing durable powers of attorney (to make medical decisions if one is unable to do so)

3. advance directives (making surrogate decision makers aware of one's wishes).

Still, there are important limits on the efficacy of these instruments from one state to another, and on how doctors and hospitals do or don't follow them. Complex issues can arise even if people make out living wills when they are in good health. These instruments can be helpful, but they cannot totally obviate the need to work through the hardest, most painful decisions.

Summary of the Overview

The paragraphs below summarize key considerations regarding euthanasia as discussed in the Overview.

1. Life is precious, a gift from God. The value of life is immeasurable. Human beings should not hasten death in any way, for God bestows life and determines when life should end.

2. Loving another person as yourself (Leviticus 19:18) includes choosing an easy death for him/her (*Sanhedrin* 45a). To prolong the suffering of those who have clearly begun the

---

[2]These categories are described in "Euthanasia, Physician Assisted Suicide and the Dying Patient: Medical Status" by Philippa Newfield, M.D., a paper given at the Institute for Jewish Medical Ethics, 1997, 3-4.

[3]Ibid., 4.

dying process — for whom continued aggressive medical therapy would be futile — may detract from life's sanctity and reduce a person's dignity.[4] We must do whatever we can to help alleviate a person's pain, including accepting a patient's decision to refuse life sustaining treatments.

3. The technological/medical advances of the last 50 years have prolonged life and extended the dying process. Due to improved methods available for supporting respiration and heart function, it has become difficult to recognize when death is imminent. These factors have created a new urgency and difficulty in dealing with the spiritual and moral dimensions of care and decision making at the end of life.

SCENARIOS: HOW THINGS HAVE CHANGED

Below are two imaginary scenarios that illustrate some of the issues of euthanasia that we have raised so far. They are intended to raise questions and spark discussion. Read each scenario to or with your students, and engage them in small or large group discussions. Use the "Focus the Discussion" section below to help identify the important issues and facilitate these discussions. Note that additional questions and activities relating to these scenarios are found in the "Stories: Understanding through Listening" section below (pp. 65-66).

Following the discussions, have students continue on to the "Text Study" section to see what Jewish and other sources have to say on the subject. Finally, you may wish to have students discuss the questions a second time, to see if their views have changed.

Scenario I: 1150 C.E.

Shlomo ben Shlomo had shown a decline in health in recent years, related to a growing weakness in his muscles. One day, Shlomo was bathing in a river. As he emerged from the water, he lost his footing, fell back into the water, and knocked his head on a large rock. Nearby, a fisherman, who had observed this incident, ran to Shlomo's aid. But the damage had been done. The fisherman leaned over Shlomo's face. No breath could be discerned. Shlomo was dead.

Scenario II: Contemporary Times

Sheldon had declined in health in recent years, due to a disease which causes progressive muscle deterioration. One day, Sheldon was walking by the river, two blocks from where Main Street intersects Central Avenue. It was so hot that he decided to wade in and splash his face with some cool water. As he emerged from the water, he lost his footing, fell back, and knocked his head on a large rock. Nearby, a fisherman, who had observed this incident, grabbed his cell phone, immediately dialed 911, and summoned help while running over to Sheldon's aid. The fisherman leaned over Sheldon's face. No breath could be discerned. He began "rescue breathing" — breathing his own breath into Sheldon's lungs. Very shortly, the ambulance appeared, and the emergency medical technicians took over. Sheldon was taken to the hospital. As he was unable to breathe on his own, he was put on a respirator. Within a few hours, his breathing returned to normal. However, because of his underlying illness, doctors decided to keep him at the hospital for a few days in order to monitor his condition. By the end of the week, Sheldon felt well enough to return home.

---

[4]This definition of the dying process id adapted from "Making Sacred Choices at the End of Life" by Rabbi Richard F. Address in *Lifelights*, 4.

Focus the Discussion

There are a number of factors which make euthanasia and assisted suicide particularly complicated in our day. The prolongation of life with artificial life support is one. With the use of sophisticated machinery, the need to define death becomes more pressing. Today, medical technology can accurately determine if there is any brain activity in a person who appears to be in a persistent vegetative state. In contrast, in earlier times the debate was mostly centered around questions of whether life should be defined by breath, heartbeat, and/or physical movement.

Medical advances have deepened our understanding of the prognosis of certain illnesses. Such knowledge gives medical experts increasing confidence in projecting the direction of a disease — whether it be a possibility for full recovery, a likelihood of status quo symptoms, or painful physical deterioration. With the projections of medical experts, the patient may want to consider options that never would have entered into the discussion in a prior age.

There have been improvements in palliative care, in pain relief. The potential for quality care, despite illness, may influence medical decisions of those who are suffering. In addition, providing good psychological support and spiritual counseling may help alleviate patients' suffering enough to nurture their will to live. Even so, there is more research to do and more loving care to offer to those who are in pain.

In determining how to make end of life decisions in the contemporary world, we face the challenge of legally safeguarding individuals from abuses, while honoring a variety of religious and moral approaches. Should the law adopt one position and have sanctions for it, or allow for different beliefs and personal decisions? If one perspective is to be adopted, whose should it be?

TEXT STUDY

As we have seen, the issues of euthanasia and assisted suicide are quite complicated. Jewish sources provide many opinions, yet these often highlight the tension between seemingly opposing considerations. The chart on the next two pages poses a number of questions and offers two opposing points of view for each. Text sources supporting each of these points of view follow below.

1. **Is preserving life always the highest priority in medical settings?**

   On the One Hand:

   Life is sacred. Euthanasia and assisted suicide are murder.

   A. I [God] bring death, bestow life, I wound and I Myself heal (Deuteronomy 32:39).

   B. Behold, all souls are Mine (Ezekiel 18:4).

   C. You shall not murder (Exodus 20:13, see also Genesis 9:6, Exodus 21:14, Leviticus 24:17 and 24:21, Numbers 35:30, and Deuteronomy 5:17).

   D. One who closes the eyes of a dying person while the soul is departing sheds blood (*Shabbat* 151b; see also Text Study #8 below).

   On the Other Hand:

   To sustain forcibly the physical body under all circumstances is a distortion of the definition of life.

   a. And it came to pass in the morning when the wine was gone out of Nabal, that his wife told him these things, and his heart died within him, and he became as a stone. And it came to pass about ten days later, after the Eternal smote Nabal, that he died (I Samuel 25:37).

TEACHING HOT TOPICS

Making an Ethical Decision about Euthanasia/Assisted Suicide: Questions to Consider

The Question	On the One Hand	On the Other Hand
1. Is preserving life always the highest priority in medical settings? (see p. 55)	Life is sacred. Euthanasia and assisted suicide are murder.	To forcibly sustain the physical body under all circumstances is a distortion of the definition of life.
2. What is a physician's primary responsibility? (see p. 57)	Physicians have a responsibility to preserve and protect life.	Physicians have a responsibility to alleviate pain and suffering.
3. Are there traditional Jewish sources sympathetic toward euthanasia and assisted suicide? (see p. 57)	Intentionally causing another person harm is condemned.	Insisting that a person endure unrelenting pain when there is a way out is harmful.
4. To what extent should we rely on medical prognoses? (see p. 58)	There can be errors in diagnosis.	There can be strict guidelines regarding second and third opinions before decisions are made concerning termination of treatment.
5. Do we offer sufficient treatment and care to those who are dying or who are in pain? (see p. 59)	By increasing access to euthanasia, there is less motivation to research pain control medications or to pursue alternative ways of offering comfort and care to the dying (e.g., spiritual or psychological support).	Dying people often express a clear wish to continue or discontinue treatment. We can persist in researching and offering "alternatives," but ultimately the choice of how one's life ends should be up to the patient.
6. Will easing restrictions on euthanasia lead to abuses? (see p. 60)	Those without a strong advocate — the poor, young, elderly, mentally disabled — could be exploited.	Legal scholars could come up with safeguards so that all are protected equally under the law.
7. Isn't choosing euthanasia or assisted suicide an expression of a person's free will? (see p. 61)	Those suffering with illnesses could be coerced to die, either blatantly or subtly. Even mentioning euthanasia to dying patients compromises the notion that they would be choosing to die of their own free will.	It is appropriate to be honest with people who are dying about all of their options.

(continued on next page)

8. How do we compare "hastening a person's death" to "removing an impediment"? (see p. 62)	"Hastening a person's death" is equivalent to murder.	"Removing an impediment" to death is permitted.

Probing: Ideas and Issues

What key reason is stated for the prohibition against taking another's life? If a person becomes a "stone," he/she is not a living organism any longer. Does Text #1a offer a sufficient foundation for developing the case for euthanasia (under specific circumstances)?

2. **What is a physician's primary responsibility?**

On the One Hand:

Physicians have a responsibility to preserve and protect life.

A. The Sages in the school of Rabbi Ishmael taught: "And to heal he shall heal" (Exodus 21:19). From this verse we infer that permission has been given [by God] to the physician to heal (*Brachot* 60a).

On the Other Hand:

Physicians have a responsibility to alleviate pain and suffering.

a. When a person is led out to be executed, the person is given a goblet of wine containing a grain of frankincense in order to numb the person's senses (*Sanhedrin* 43a).

b. Behold Rabbi Nachman said in Rabbah ben Abbuha's name: Scripture says, "Love your neighbor as yourself" — choose an easy death for him/her (*Sanhedrin* 45a).

Probing: Ideas and Issues

What responsibilities do physicians have according to these texts? Do the responsibilities extend beyond physical care? How so?

3. **Are there traditional Jewish sources sympathetic toward euthanasia and assisted suicide?**

On the One Hand:

Intentionally causing another person harm is condemned.

A. One who strikes a person so that the person dies is to be put to death, yes, death (Exodus 21:12).

On the Other Hand:

Insisting that a person endure unrelenting pain when there is a way out is harmful.

a. When [Judah Ha-Nasi] was dying, the Rabbis declared a public fast and offered prayers that God have mercy on him [i.e., spare his life] . . . Rabbi's maid went up to the roof and prayed: "The angels want Rabbi [to join them in heaven] and the people want him to remain with them. May it be God's will that the people overpower the angels." However, when she saw how many times he had to use the bathroom, each time painfully taking off his *tefillin* and putting them on again, she prayed, "May it be God's will that the angels overpower the people." But the Rabbis did not cease imploring God's mercy [to allow Rabbi to live]. She, then, took a vase and threw it off the roof. [The Rabbis] stopped praying [because they were startled by the noise], and the soul of Rabbi departed (*Ketubot* 104a).

b. There is a story of a woman who grew very old. She came before Rabbi Yosi ben Halafta. She said to him, "Rabbi, I have gotten too old. Life is repugnant to me —

I can neither taste food nor drink. I would like to depart from this world." He said to her, "How is it that you have lived so long?" She answered, "Every day, I am accustomed to go early to the synagogue even if I must stop doing something I like." He said to her, "Refrain for three successive days from going to the synagogue." She did this. On the third day, she became ill and died (*Yalkut Shimoni* 2, 943).

Probing: Ideas and Issues

Would you say that Texts #3a and #3b are sufficient proof that Judaism is sympathetic to euthanasia? to assisted suicide? Explain your position.

4. To what extent should we rely on medical prognoses?

On the One Hand:

There can be errors in diagnosis.

A. [Elisha] went in, shut the door behind the two of them and prayed to the Eternal. Then he mounted [the bed] and placed himself over the [seemingly dead] child. He put his mouth on its mouth, his eyes on its eyes, and his hands on its hands, as he bent over. And the body of the child became warm. He stepped down, walked once up and down the room, then mounted and bent over him. Thereupon, the boy sneezed seven times, and the boy opened his eyes (II Kings 4:33-35).

On the Other Hand:

There can be strict guidelines regarding second and third opinions before decisions are made concerning termination of treatment.

a. The following are excerpts from The Oregon Death with Dignity Act (1994, implemented 1997). Under this Act, a mentally competent adult resident of Oregon who is terminally ill (likely to die within six months) may request a prescription for a lethal dose of medication to end his or her life. The practice of a physician prescribing medication to end a patient's life (assisted suicide) departs from what would be acceptable from most Jewish points of view.

Section 3.01: attending physician responsibilities

The attending physician shall:

(1) Make the initial determination of whether a patient has a terminal disease, is capable, and has made the request voluntarily;

(2) Inform the patient of:

(a) his or her medical diagnosis;

(b) his or her prognosis;

(c) the potential risks associated with taking the medication prescribed [to end one's life in a humane and dignified manner];

(d) the probable result of taking the medication to be prescribed;

(e) the feasible alternatives, including, but not limited to, comfort care, hospice care, and pain control.

(3) Refer the patient to a consulting physician for medical confirmation of the diagnosis, and for determination that the patient is capable and acting voluntarily;

(4) Refer the patient for counseling if appropriate pursuant to section 3.03;

(5) Request that the patient notify next of kin;

(6) Inform the patient that he or she has an opportunity to rescind the request

at any time and in any manner, and offer the patient an opportunity to rescind at the end of the 15 day waiting period . . . ;

(7) Verify, immediately prior to writing the prescription for medication under this Act, that the patient is making an informed decision;

(8) Fulfill the medical record documentation requirements . . .

(9) Ensure that all appropriate steps are carried out in accordance with this Act prior to writing a prescription for medication to enable a qualified patient to end his or her life in a humane and dignified manner.

3.02 Consulting Physician Confirmation

Before a patient is qualified under this Act, a consulting physician shall examine the patient and his or her relevant medical records and confirm, in writing, the attending physician's diagnosis that the patient is suffering from a terminal disease, and verify that the patient is capable, is acting voluntarily, and has made an informed decision.

3.03 Counseling Referral

If in the opinion of the attending physician or the consulting physician a patient may be suffering from a psychiatric or psychological disorder, or depression causing impaired judgment, either physician shall refer the patient for counseling. No medication to end a patient's life in a humane and dignified manner shall be prescribed until the person performing the counseling determines that the person is not suffering from a psychiatric or psychological disorder, or depression causing impaired judgment.

Probing: Ideas and Issues

Do you agree it is possible to create a sufficient means of verification in diagnosing patients (physically, psychologically, emotionally, spiritually)? What would be your greatest concern(s) in creating guidelines for ascertaining correct diagnoses?

5. Do we offer sufficient treatment and care to those who are dying or who are in pain?

On the One Hand:

By increasing access to euthanasia, there is less motivation to research pain control medications or to pursue alternative ways of offering comfort and care to the dying (e.g., spiritual or psychological support).

A. It is a clearly documented fact that those asking for assisted suicide almost always change their minds once we have their pain under control. We undermedicate terribly in American medicine (Dr. Kathleen Foley, a pain specialist at Memorial Sloan-Kettering Cancer Center in New York, as quoted in "Of Life and Death: A Jewish Response To Doctor Assisted Suicide" by Asher Lipner, *Viewpoint*: National Council of Young Israel, Winter, 1996, a paper posted on the web site of the Institute of Jewish Medical Ethics, www.ijme.org, 2001).

On the Other Hand:

Dying people often express a clear wish to continue or to discontinue treatment. We can persist in researching and offering "alternatives," but ultimately the choice of how one's life ends should be up to the patient.

a. As a punishment for teaching Torah, Rabbi Hananiah is to be burnt at the stake by the Romans. His disciples encourage him to open his mouth so that he will die more quickly and endure less suffering. They say to him,

> "Rabbi . . . open your mouth that the fire may enter [and you will die]." [Rabbi Hananiah] said to them, "It is better that God who gave my soul should take it and let no one harm himself." The executioner asked him, "Rabbi, if I intensify the fire and remove the mats from your body, will you bring me into the World To Come?" He said, "Yes." "Swear to me" [said the executioner]. He swore to him. [The executioner] immediately removed the mats and increased the flames. [Hananiah's] soul speedily departed. Then [the executioner] leaped up and fell into the fire. A heavenly voice [*bat kol*] went out and proclaimed, "Rabbi Hananiah and the executioner are prepared for the Life-to-Come." Rabbi [Judah Ha-Nasi] wept and said, "Some may attain their world in but one moment while others may take many years" (*Avodah Zarah* 18a).

Probing: Ideas and Issues

What is Dr. Kathleen Foley's concern in Text #5A? How should her concern be integrated into ethical decision making regarding euthanasia?

Refer to the story of Hananiah's execution in Text #5a. Why do you think the heavenly voice (*bat kol*) said that both Rabbi Hananiah and his executioner are prepared for the Life-to-Come? Do you agree? Why or why not?

6. **Will easing restrictions on euthanasia lead to abuses?**

On the One Hand:

Those without a strong advocate — the poor, young, elderly, mentally disabled — could be exploited.

A. You shall not mistreat any widow or orphan. If you do mistreat them, I will heed their outcry as soon as they cry out to Me, and My anger shall blaze forth and I will put you to the sword, and your own wives shall become widows and your children orphans (Exodus 22:21-23).

B. When strangers reside with you in your land, you shall not mistreat them. Strangers who reside with you shall be to you as your own citizens; you shall love them as yourself, for you were strangers in the land or Egypt; I the Eternal am your God (Leviticus 19:33-34).

C. I bring heaven and earth to witness that the Divine Spirit rests upon a non-Jew as well as upon a Jew, upon a woman as well as upon man, upon a maidservant as well as a manservant (*Yalkut Shimoni*, on Judges, section 42).

On the Other Hand:

Legal scholars could come up with safeguards so that all are protected equally under the law.

See Text Study #4a, excerpts from the Oregon Death with Dignity Act, plus the following summary of its provisions:

a. • The request must be voluntary.

• No doctor would be forced to comply.

• The patient must be an adult who is terminally ill and mentally competent.

• The request must be an enduring one; a 15-day waiting period is required.

• An examination by a mental health professional may be required.

• The request must be made orally and in writing and witnessed.

• All alternatives would be explained to the patient.

• The patient would receive a prescription for a lethal dose of medication that would be self-administered.

- The patient may change his or her mind at any time.

(Source: The Hemlock Society USA: www.hemlock.org)

Probing: Ideas and Issues

Do you agree that those without an advocate could be exploited in end of life decisions? Explain. Is it reasonable to believe that a legal document can prevent exploitation of the poor, young, elderly, and mentally disabled? Can such a document be effective in providing protection against economic or family pressures?

7. **Isn't choosing euthanasia or assisted suicide an expression of a person's free will?**

On the One Hand:

Those suffering with illnesses could, either blatantly or subtly, be coerced to die. Even mentioning euthanasia to dying patients compromises the notion that they would be choosing to die of their own free will.

A. Any act performed in relation to death should not be carried out until the soul has departed (*Tur, Yoreh Deah, 339*).

B. Not only are physical acts on the patient . . . forbidden, but one should also not provide a coffin or prepare a grave or make other funeral or related arrangements lest the patient hear of this and his death be hastened. Even psychological stress is prohibited (Fred Rosner, *Modern Medicine and Jewish Ethics*. Hoboken, New Jersey: KTAV Publishing House, Inc., New York: Yeshiva University Press, 1991, p. 207).

C. A doctor who suggests assisted suicide as an option to a patient, or relatives who

respond too readily to a patient's mention of euthanasia, send a powerful message that they believe the patient should not continue to live. In such cases we are not dealing with autonomy or the patient's right to die but with the will of the doctor and the relatives and their right to influence the ending of a life that has become a burden, or that they think is not worth living (*Seduced by Death* by Herbert Hendin, M.D., p. 185).

On the Other Hand:

It is appropriate to be honest with people who are dying about all of their options.

a. Those who deal deceitfully shall not live in My house; those who speak untruth shall not stand before My eyes (Psalms 101:7).

b. Teach your tongue to say, "I don't know," lest you be caught in a lie (*Brachot* 4a).

c. If I lie, may I incur the eternal wrath of God and God's angel Raphael, and may nothing in the medical art succeed for me according to my desires (Amatus Lusitanus, a Jewish physician, included in a section on honesty toward the patient, in *Lying: Moral Choice in Public and Private Life* by Sisela Bok, New York: Pantheon Books, a Division of Random House, 1978, p. 76).

For more texts on truth and trustworthiness, see:

"Emet: Truthfulness" in *Teaching Jewish Virtues: Sacred Sources and Arts Activities* by Susan Freeman, pp. 69-84.

"Trustworthiness — Emunah" in *The Jewish Moral Virtues* by Eugene B. Borowitz and Frances Weinman Schwartz, pp. 27-39.

Probing: Ideas and Issues

Do you think it is ever appropriate to mention euthanasia to a person who has a terminal and painful disease? Are there certain people who should be permitted to discuss "all the options"? If so, who would those individuals be?

8. **How do we compare "hastening a person's death" to "removing an impediment"?**

On the One Hand:

"Hastening a person's death" is equivalent to murder.

A. One who is in a dying condition is regarded as a living person in all respects. It is not permitted to bind the person's jaws, to stop up the organs of the lower extremities, or to place metallic or cooling vessels upon the person's navel in order to prevent swelling. The person is not to be rubbed or washed, nor is sand or salt to be put upon the person until the person expires. Anyone who touches the person is guilty of shedding blood. To what may this person be compared? To a flickering flame, which is extinguished as soon as one touches it. Whoever closes the eyes of the dying while the soul is about to depart is shedding blood. One should wait a while; perhaps the person is only experiencing a fainting spell (Maimonides, *Mishneh Torah, Hilchot Avel* 4:5).

On the Other Hand:

"Removing an impediment" to death is permitted.

a. If there is anything which causes a hindrance to the departure of the soul, such as the presence near the patient's house of a knocking noise, such as wood chopping, or if there is salt on the patient's tongue, and these hinder the soul's departure, it is permissible to remove them from there because there is no act involved in this at all but only the removal of the impediment (*Rema* on *Shulchan Aruch, Yoreh Deah* 339:1).

b. In truth, one cannot truly call the "removal of the impediment" a passive *action*: one must go to the woodchopper to tell him to stop and one must reach into the patient's mouth to remove the salt. There is certainly an "act involved"! . . . If at this moment, the sounds and the salt are keeping the patient alive, then stopping the one and removing the other, either "allow the patient to die" or "kill the patient" depending on sensibility. Like the prayers affected by the maid's dropped pot (see Text #3a above), that process . . . which has maintained the patient's life has been interrupted and the patient dies. How would this be essentially different from disconnecting a moribund patient's oxygen line? . . . Nowadays the patient is connected by tubing to the oxygen pipes which are in the walls of the hospital room: to disconnect the tubing one has to do something and that is *active* euthanasia . . . the acting or not acting is a function of technology not morality . . . I think that the issue of euthanasia must be rethought. For as a liberal Jew, texts of the past have votes but not vetoes; however, the texts adduced as we have seen, do not vote for what people have said they vote for . . . Euthanasia, we have said, applies to one who is in the process of dying and who is suffering; we must be sure of the first and unable to control the second. If that person be lucid and not wish the battle for life to continue, then his/her wishes should be followed as to when and how the end should come, whether that end comes by not doing something or by doing something . . . (Dr. Leonard Kravitz, "Euthanasia" in *Death and Euthanasia in Jewish Law*, 1995).

Probing: Ideas and Issues

Clarify the distinction between hastening a death and removing an impediment. In Text #8b above Dr. Kravitz says that in fact there is little difference between the two concepts. What exactly is his reasoning? Is his objection to differentiating between "hastening a death" and "removing an impediment" valid?

After studying the passages in the "Text Study" section, name what you believe are the greatest hazards in liberalizing legislation having to do with euthanasia and assisted suicide.

RELATED MIDDOT AND MITZVOT

Practicing the following virtues and commandments will help infuse our end of life decisions with Jewish values:

Anavah (Humility): In making decisions about medical treatment, all involved must maintain great humility. While we should try to make wise choices, we should appreciate the complexity of the situation, listen to each other, and avoid the arrogance of asserting the absolute rightness of our preference.

Eino Samayach BeHora'ah (Not Delighting in Rendering Decisions): Acknowledge and appreciate the gravity of making end of life decisions.

Emet ve'Emunah (Truth and Trustworthiness): The physician/patient relationship must be built on trustworthiness. Patients need to believe that their physician will truly listen to them and advocate for their needs. The same holds for family and friends — patients should be able to trust that their loved ones have their best interests in mind always. Furthermore, patients should be able to trust that the laws of society will protect them from potential abuses.

Ohev et HaMakom (Loving God): Taking care of others reflects our love for God.

Ohev veKavod et HaBriyot (Loving and Respecting Creation): Taking care of others reflects our love and respect for other human beings.

Rachamim (Compassion): The suffering patient should be treated compassionately.

Rofeh Cholim (Healing the Sick): We have a duty to do whatever we can to bring healing to those who are suffering from illness.

Talmud Torah (Study Jewish Sources): Learn what Jewish tradition says about the value of life, compassion, treatment of the dying, and the definition and determination of death. Also look for any examples of euthanasia, suicide, or assisted suicide in Jewish texts. Read contemporary *Responsa* on the subject, plus research how the secular courts in Israel are handling matters of this nature.

ACTIVITIES

A First Look: Key Issues and Ideas

1. How is death determined? Work with students to list all relevant factors in the texts above on how death might be defined from a Jewish point of view.

2. Have students refer to the eight questions and the two "On the One Hand/On the Other Hand" points of view for each shown in the chart in the "Text Study" section above. Have each person individually rank the 16 points from most important to least. In a group have them compare and explain their rankings. Ask: What do your results reflect about your attitude toward euthanasia and assisted suicide? What was most challenging about completing the exercise?

3. Review the provisions of the Oregon Death with Dignity Act (Text #6a above — the full

text of the Act can be found at www.finalexit. org). Then, have students draw up their own acts on death with dignity, perhaps in pairs. When they complete their drafts, have them compare their provisions with those of the Oregon Death with Dignity Act.

4. Discuss the meaning of "the slippery slope" as it applies to euthanasia and assisted suicide. For a case study, research policies and attitudes toward euthanasia in the Netherlands. The journey down the "the slippery slope" might begin with the acceptance of disconnecting a patient in a permanent vegetative state from a respirator. But with a continual liberalization of what is permissible in end of life "assistance," the following seriously controversial scenario eventually might be encountered. This scenario is a real-life case:

> "In the Dutch city of Assen in the spring of 1993, a court of three judges acquitted a psychiatrist who had assisted in the suicide of his patient, a physically healthy fifty-year-old woman who had lost her two sons and had recently divorced her husband. The court ruled that the psychiatrist, Dr. Boudewijn Chabot, was justified in his actions because his patient was competent to make the decision to die freely, her suffering was irremediable, and the doctor met the Dutch criterion for *force majeure*, meaning he was compelled by an overpowering force to put the welfare of the patient above the law, which formally prohibits assisted suicide and euthanasia" (See the chapter "Seduced by Death," pp. 63-110 in *Seduced by Death* by Herbert Hendin, M.D.).

In other words, a physically healthy 50-year-old woman was put to death at her request because she was suffering from the grief of personal loss. The woman's will to live seemed to have evaporated. The physician (a psychiatrist) who assisted in the woman's death was acquitted

of wrongdoing in the Dutch courts. Overall, it has been said that the Dutch courts have "moved from euthanasia for terminally ill patients to euthanasia for those who are chronically ill, from euthanasia for physical illness to euthanasia for psychological distress, and from voluntary euthanasia to non-voluntary and involuntary euthanasia" (Hendin, *Seduced by Death*, p. 135).

How would a Jewish court respond to Dr. Boudewijn Chabot's actions? Suppose a Jewish court, in making its judgment, wished to add a comment about the "slippery slope." What would it say?

5. Invite a doctor to class to explain the current status of pain medication, access to quality end of life care (and what the options are), artificial life support, and how death is defined in the hospital setting. What are the biggest challenges facing end of life care today? What needs to be done to improve care? The web site www.compassionindying.org is a helpful resource for learning about current efforts in addressing end of life care.

6. Invite a lawyer to discuss current legal options concerning end of life decisions. Ask him/her to explain living wills, the appointment of durable powers of attorney, and advance directives. A lawyer who works for a hospital will be especially informed about legal issues facing doctors and patients making end of life decisions. Ask what kind of legal advice is available to the chronically ill at hospitals and to residents of nursing homes. You also may wish to invite members of a hospital's Ethics Committee to address your group.

7. If there is an Israeli lawyer or a legal scholar in your vicinity, ask him/her to visit your group and to offer any insights into how biomedical related rulings are made in Israel. What is the influence of both Jewish and democratic principles; how are the two

realms of principles balanced? Is the guest able to offer insights as to how Israel's approach compares with that of other countries?

8. Compare Jewish perspectives on euthanasia and assisted suicide with the points of view of other religions. (As a start, you can refer to *Modern Medicine and Jewish Ethics* by Fred Rosner, pp. 202-204.)

9. Check out from your library (or from interlibrary loan) a book called *The Right to Die Debate: A Documentary History (Primary Documents in American History and Contemporary Issues)*, edited by Marjorie B. Zucker. Included in this collection are 138 documents — from Shakespeare's "Hamlet," act 3, scene 1 soliloquy ("To die — to sleep — to sleep! perchance to dream") to Supreme Court decisions on assisted suicide and euthanasia. Choose a selection of these documents. Then, refer to the "On the One Hand/On the Other Hand" points in the "Text Study" section above. Which points are demonstrated in each of the chosen documents? As a last step, judge whether or not to include a particular document in a collection reflecting attitudes toward euthanasia and assisted suicide consistent with Jewish beliefs.

Applying Middot and Mitzvot

Refer to the list of "Related *Middot* and *Mitzvot*" on p. 63 above. Ask participants to answer and explain their responses to the following questions:

1. Both *Rachamim* (compassion) and *Emet* (truthfulness) are important values in working with individuals suffering from illnesses. Would you consider one more important than the other? Why or why not?

2. How has engaging in *Talmud Torah* (studying Torah) shaped your beliefs concerning euthanasia and assisted suicide?

3. How might embodying *Anavah* (humility) impact the attitudes of individuals involved in an end of life decision: the doctor, the nursing staff, the patient, family members, close friends, the Rabbi?

4. For more information and activities on:

   Anavah (Humility): see *Teaching Jewish Virtues* by Susan Freeman, pp. 8-25.

   Bikur Cholim (Visiting the Sick): see *Teaching Mitzvot* by Barbara Binder Kadden and Bruce Kadden, pp. 157-161.

   Emet (Truthfulness): see *Teaching Jewish Virtues* by Susan Freeman, pp. 69-84.

   Ohev et HaMakom or *Ahavat HaShem* (Loving God): see *Teaching Mitzvot* by Barbara Binder Kadden and Bruce Kadden, pp. 215-221.

   Ohev veKavod et HaBriyot (Loving and Honoring Creation): see *Teaching Jewish Virtues* by Susan Freeman, pp. 179-194.

   Rachamim (Compassion): see *Teaching Jewish Virtues* by Susan Freeman, pp. 55-68.

   Rofeh Cholim (Healing the Sick): see *Teaching Jewish Virtues* by Susan Freeman, pp. 299-317.

   Talmud Torah (Studying Torah): see *Teaching Mitzvot* by Barbara Binder Kadden and Bruce Kadden, pp. 119-124.

5. For more information and activities related to "The End of Life: Death, Burial, and Mourning," see *Teaching Jewish Life Cycle* by Barbara Binder Kadden and Bruce Kadden, pp. 101-120.

Stories: Understanding through Listening

1. Read the imaginary situations presented in the "Scenarios: How Things Have Changed" section above. Discuss the following questions: How did each fisherman react to the emergency he witnessed? Did both fishermen act appropriately? Explain. If the modern fisherman didn't have a cell phone, would he have been negligent? If the modern fisher-

man had a cell phone but didn't use it, could he be accused of murder? How is the definition of death determined in each of the scenarios? Describe how our "stories" today differ from stories in ages past? What do you consider most challenging about end of life situations people face nowadays?

To go a step further, have group participants choose one of these four people: Shlomo, the fisherman in the year 1150 C.E., Sheldon, or the modern fisherman. Have each person rewrite the scenario from a first person perspective. That is, each writer describes what happened from his/her particular character's point of view.

2. Refer to the story of Hananiah in Text Study #5a above. Deepen your understanding of Hananiah and the executioner by studying the fuller account of Hananiah's story in the Talmud, *Avodah Zarah* 17b-18a. Then, imagine meeting Hananiah in the World To Come and write about or discuss the results of asking him the following questions: Do you (Hananiah) have any regrets about what you did before your execution? Elaborate on the responses you gave to your executioner's questions — what were you thinking? Do you believe the executioner truly merited assignment to the World To Come? What advice would you have for us in the modern age concerning the struggles we have with end of life decisions?

3. View the film *Whose Life Is It Anyway?* (1981, rated R, 188 minutes). It showcases the ethics of euthanasia, exploring a person's right to choose to live or die. The story is told of a sculptor who becomes a paraplegic after a car accident. The man, devastated by such loss of control over his life, pleads with hospital authorities to help him die. They refuse, however, and the man takes them to court.

4. Visit the National Public Radio web site: www.npr.org/programs/death. Have students choose one or more stories related to end of life issues to learn about, then report back to the group.

5. Read the young adult book *Stuck in Neutral* by Terry Trueman (New York: Harpercollins Juvenile Books, 2000). It is the story of a 14-year-old boy named Shawn who lives with cerebral palsy, a disease that leaves him with no muscle control. He can't speak, interact, or control his movements or bodily functions. Still, despite his frustrations, he is happy to be alive. That is why he panics when he begins to suspect that his father is thinking of killing him. Shawn knows that his father is trying to be kind; he imagines that his son's life is an endless torment. But his dad has no idea of the rich life that Shawn lives inside his head. And Shawn, helpless and mute, has no way of telling him.

6. Interview doctors and clergy about what they have witnessed and what they struggle with in terms of end of life issues. Generate a set of appropriate interview questions beforehand.

7. In a group in which there is a genuine level of trust, share personal stories related to difficulties in making end of life decisions.

Action: Getting Out, Getting Involved

1. Find out about hospice in your area. If there is a hospice-type facility, arrange a visit. (A Jewish hospice would be of particular interest.) Alternatively, invite a hospice worker to visit your group. Learn about the work hospices do and the philosophy they profess. Inquire how you might be helpful and supportive of their efforts.

2. List ways you can help or support a family that is facing the near death of a loved one. Possibilities might include preparing and delivering meals, volunteering to babysit children, taking care of the family's yard or garden, etc. When the need arises, make plans to follow through on one or more of the ideas on the list.

3. Create care packages that the Rabbi in your congregation or members of the *Bikur Cholim* (Visiting the Sick) Committee can take to individuals or families who are suffering from serious illness. Possible items to include: tea bags, a mug, good wishes in artwork and words, copies of prayers and Psalms, slippers, a cassette or CD of Jewish songs.

4. Find out about current discussions in your state regarding legislation for the terminally ill. Write to your legislators expressing your thoughts on the matter. Back up what you say with both facts from the best research and explanations of relevant ethical values.

Wrestling: Engagement with the Issues

1. Study the passage below in which King Saul, about to lose a battle, asks his arms bearer to kill him.

> The battle raged around Saul, and some of the archers hit him, and he was severely wounded by the archers. Saul said to his arms bearer, "Draw your sword and run me through, so that the uncircumcised may not run me through and make sport of me." But his arms bearer, in his great awe, refused; whereupon Saul grasped the sword and fell upon it. When his arms bearer saw that Saul was dead, he, too, fell on his sword and died with him. Thus Saul and his three sons and his arms bearer, as well as all his men, died together on that day (I Samuel 31:3-6).

Jewish discussions about the permissibility of assisted suicide often refer to the above passage. Choose two people to reenact the beginning of the encounter — to where it says, "But his arms bearer, in his great awe, refused . . . " Then ask the two actors to improvise the imagined conversation between Saul and his arms bearer. That is, what did the arms bearer say to Saul when "the arms bearer, in his great awe, refused" to

kill him. How did Saul respond? Encourage the actors to elaborate, to keep the conversation going for at least a couple of minutes.

As a last step, open the actors' stage to audience participation. The two actors (Saul and the arms bearer) should remain in character. Audience members ask the actors whatever questions they have about the actors/characters' motivations, inner feelings, beliefs, concerns, secrets, etc.

2. Learn about wills of inheritance, living wills, and ethical wills. It will be helpful to invite experts in to explain the various kinds of wills, show examples, and provide materials. Then, have students write their own.

Here are some things to keep in mind according to The National Center for Jewish Healing:

- Discuss your living will with your health care proxy and your doctor. They need to know your wishes, and you need to know their concerns and if they can comply.

- Individual state laws may require certain types of interventions to be specified on your health care proxy form (e.g., "do not resuscitate," artificial nutrition and hydration, etc.). You may want to discuss any questions with your doctor.

- You can get health care proxy forms from the Department of Health or from your local hospital.

- Make several copies of each document and distribute to your doctor, hospital, etc. Keep the originals safe and make sure they can be found when needed.

- Each major denomination of American Jewish life has prepared some form of living will and/or guide to preparing for the end of life. Ask your Rabbi or call your movement office to find out how to obtain copies.

(*The Outstretched Arm*, NY: The National Center for Jewish Healing, Winter 2001, p. 4)

More resources: *Ethical Wills: Handing Down Our Jewish Heritage* by Barbara Binder Kadden and Bruce Kadden; *So That Your Values Live On: Ethical Wills and How to Prepare Them*, edited by Jack Riemer and Nathaniel Stampfer.

3. Create a mock court to debate the following case which actually came before the Tel Aviv District court in 1990. The two sides are Eyal vs. Wilensky:

> Eyal has submitted a request for a declaratory judgment from the court that he not be connected to a respiratory machine should his condition deteriorate. Eyal is a 50-year-old man suffering from a terminal neurone disease, Amyotropic Lateral Sclerosis (A.L.S.). The doctor reports that the patient is approaching the final stages of the disease, characterized by an inability to swallow, speak, cough, or activate the breathing muscles — in the doctor's words, "a living hell." According to the doctor, without respiratory support, the man surely would die from oxygen starvation.

> The question for the court: In view of the circumstances and the patient's wishes, are the doctors legally authorized not to connect the patient to the respirator (in effect, to withhold treatment)?

> The two sides of the debate should prepare scrupulously — presenting arguments culled from both Jewish and scientific/social scientific sources. You might also want to assign "witnesses" who will need to do their own research and preparation. (Witnesses might include doctors, psychiatrists, the patient himself, family members, etc.)

> (What really happened? Judge Goren

ruled in Eyal's favor, with two qualifications. First, a decision regarding the respirator should be made only at the onset of the death process, not in advance of it. Second, the decision must be made with the confirmation of a senior doctor.)

4. Act out the situations described in the "Scenarios" section above (p. 54), or create your own to act out. If you create your own, try to include the following characters: the patient, the doctor or other health care providers, family members, and/or friends. The goal is to reflect the complexity involved in dealing with end of life definitions and decisions. The scenarios should highlight the particular realms of complexity we face in modern times.

5. In pairs, take turns listening to each other talk about fears, feelings, attitudes, and questions concerning end of life issues. The tenor of your listening is all-important. Listeners must be open hearted, nonjudgmental, and supportive. In addition, they are not to interrupt the speaker, nor offer any comment or reaction. The speaker should speak for three to five minutes (possibly longer for more mature participants). After one person has had a turn speaking, switch roles, so that the speaker now becomes the listener. You can do this as a journal exercise, too — the "listener" being the pages of the journal. After everyone has had an opportunity to speak (either to another person or to write in his/her journal), come back together as a group and allow participants to share their reactions to this experience.

6. Create a collage that visually captures the complexity of euthanasia and assisted suicide. Here are some words, phrases, and images to help trigger your own ideas:

> "You shall not murder", compassion, comfort, care, fear, search for meaning, pain, suffering, assisting, a court gavel, the slippery slope, "Love your fellow person as yourself" (Text #2b, p. 57),

"Behold, all souls are Mine" (Text #1B, p. 55), a heart dying (Text #1a, p. 55), becoming "stone-like" (Text #1a, p. 55), a goblet of wine — laced with poison? (Text #2a, p. 57), a shattered vase (see Text #3a, p. 57), breathing life into another person (see Text #4A, p. 58), a woodchopper (Text #8a, p. 62), salt (Text #8a, p. 62).

Empathy

1. Write a prayer to be recited by a person facing difficult decisions near the end of life. Or, write a prayer that could be said by one who visits, offers care, or gives comfort to such a person. Alternatively, "illuminate" a prayer — one that you or someone else has composed. That is, hand or machine copy a poem or prayer that resonates with you, place it in the middle of a larger piece of paper, then decorate the border around it. If you like, give the illuminated prayer to someone who will appreciate the gift. Here are a couple of possibilities of prayers to copy:

   For someone with a serious illness:

   Into Your hands I commend my spirit, both when I sleep and when I wake.
   Body and soul are Yours, O God, and in Your presence I cast off fear and am at rest.

   B'ya-do af-keed ru-chee, b'ayt ee-shan v'a-ee-ra, v'eem ru-chee g'vee-ya-tee. Adonai lee, v'lo ee-ra (from "*Adon Olam*").

   For those who visit, care, and comfort:

   May you be comforted by your ability to care and to give comfort.
   May you derive strength from your own deeply held faith to be emotionally present to suffering and grief.

   May your prayers give voice to the awesome state of our mortality in the face of the infinite.
   And may you find grace to help others see that rage against loss carries within it the feisty spark of its own divine energy.
   That our outcry is as important as our tears.

   (By Dr. Ken Gorfinkle, adapted from "When a Child Dies: Helping the Rabbi Help," presented as a keynote address to The National Center for Jewish Healing, November 30, 1999)

2. As part of a worship service, pray for someone who is ill — the traditional "*Mi Shebayrach,*" your own prayer, Debbie Friedman's version of the prayer, or the following version created by Marcia Falk:

   As those who came before us were blessed in the presence of the communities that sustained them, so we offer our blessings for one among us needing support.
   _____ (name)
   may your spirit be calmed and your pain be eased, may you receive comfort from those who care for you and may you drink from the waters of the ever-giving well.

   (Marcia Falk, *The Book of Blessings*, p. 276)

3. Have your group create a book of contemporary psalms for those coping with end of life issues, each person contributing one. To give yourself a more specific focus, think about this: Write a psalm appropriate for an 83-year-old woman to recite who has made a decision to discontinue her regular dialysis treatments (a kidney simulating process that is very difficult to tolerate). By discontinuing dialysis, the woman knows that she will die within a week or two. To get a sense of how

traditional Psalms were written, study a few from the Bible. Also, see *Flames To Heaven: New Psalms for Healing & Praise* by Debbie Perlman.

4. Look at the series "Lifelights," edited by Rabbi Nancy Flam and published by Jewish Lights Publishing. It includes several pamphlets on topics related to facing serious illness and providing care, including "When Someone You Love Is Dying," "Making Sacred Choices at the End of Life," "Jewish Hospice: To Live, To Hope, To Heal," "Caring for Yourself When You Are Caring for Someone Who Is Ill," and "When Someone You Love Needs Long Term Care." Those in your community who are struggling with such issues likely will find the pamphlets to be a source of support and comfort.

GLOSSARY

Euthanasia:

Literally, "a good death"; an act of inducing death painlessly, sometimes called "mercy killing."

Voluntary Euthanasia:

The patient asks to die or agrees with the physician's recommendation that he/she die.

Nonvoluntary Euthanasia:

A surrogate agrees, on the patient's behalf, with the physician's recommendation that the patient die.

Involuntary Euthanasia:

Someone other than the person involved performs an intentional act to terminate life without the consent of the person involved.

Passive Euthanasia:

Involves the withholding and withdrawing of life support, and is not technically euthanasia since the patient dies of the underlying disease.

Physician Assisted Suicide:

Intentional assistance given by a physician to enable a person to terminate his/her own life upon that person's request. Prescribing a lethal dose of medicine for the patient would be a typical method.

Double Effect:

Pain relief (or palliative) treatment given to a patient to reduce suffering may have the "double effect" of hastening a patient's death. The intent is to reduce suffering, not to end life. However, the patient's death may be a side effect of the treatment, and one that could be predicted. Administering increasing amounts of morphine is an example — this drug helps to relieve pain, but slows down the functioning of the body in a way that could bring death more quickly.[5]

Gosays:

A moribund patient whose death is imminent.

[5]These English definitions are adapted from "Euthanasia, Physician Assisted Suicide and the Dying Patient: Medical Status" by Philippa Newfield, M.D., a paper given at the Institute for Jewish Medical Ethics, 1997, 1.

BIBLIOGRAPHY

Books and Articles

Address, Richard F. *Making Sacred Choices at the End of Life*. Woodstock, VT: Jewish Lights Publishing, 2000.

Borowitz, Eugene B., and Frances Weinman Schwartz. *The Jewish Moral Virtues*. Philadelphia, PA: The Jewish Publication Society, 1999.

Dorff, Elliot. "End Stage Medical Care: A Halachik Approach." *Conservative Judaism* 43, no. 3 (Spring 1991).

Falk, Marcia. *The Book of Blessings*. San Francisco, CA: HarperSanFrancisco, 1996.

Flam, Nancy, ed. *Lifelights: Help for Wholeness and Healing*. Woodstock, VT: Jewish Lights Publishing, 2000.

Foley, Kathleen, and Herbert Hendin, eds. *The Case against Assisted Suicide: For the Right to End-of-Life Care*. Baltimore, MD: Johns Hopkins University Press, 2002. See also, Sherwin B. Nuland's review of this book: "The Principle of Hope," in *The New Republic*, May 27, 2002, pp. 25-30.

Freeman, Susan. *Teaching Jewish Virtues: Sacred Sources and Arts Activities*. Denver, CO: A.R.E. Publishing, Inc., 1999.

Friedman, Dayle A., ed. *Jewish Pastoral Care: A Practical Handbook from Traditional and Contemporary Sources*. Woodstock, VT: Jewish Lights Publishing, 2000.

Gordon, Dr. Harvey L. *Questions and Answers about Jewish Tradition and the Issues of Assisted Death*. New York: UAHC Press, 1997.

Hendin, Herbert. *Seduced by Death: Doctors, Patients, and Assisted Suicide*. New York: W.W. Norton & Company, Inc., 1998.

Herring, Basil F. *Jewish Ethics and Halakhah for Our Time: Sources and Commentary*. Hoboken, NJ: KTAV Publishing House, Inc. and New York: Yeshiva University Press, Volume I, 1984, Volume II, 1989.

Kadden, Barbara Binder, and Bruce Kadden. *Ethical Wills: Handing Down Our Jewish Heritage*. Denver, CO: A.R.E. Publishing, Inc., 1990.

———. *Teaching Jewish Life Cycle: Traditions and Activities*. Denver, CO: A.R.E. Publishing, Inc., 1997.

———. *Teaching Mitzvot: Concepts, Values, and Activities*. Rev. ed. Denver, CO: A.R.E. Publishing, Inc., 2003.

Kol Haneshamah: Shabbat Vehagim. Wyncote, PA: The Reconstructionist Press, 1994.

Kubler-Ross, Elisabeth. *Living with Death and Dying*. New York: Macmillan, 1981.

Lamm, Maurice. *The Power of Hope*. New York: Scribners, 1995.

Orenstein, Debra, ed. *Lifecycles: Jewish Women on Life Passages and Personal Milestones,* vol. 1. Woodstock, VT: Jewish Lights Publishing, 1994.

Perlman, Debbie. *Flames To Heaven: New Psalms for Healing & Praise*. Wilmette, IL: RadPublishers, 1998.

Riemer, Jack, and Nathaniel Stampfer, eds. *So That Your Values Live On: Ethical Wills and How to Prepare Them*. Woodstock, VT: Jewish Lights Publishing, 1993.

Rosner M.D., Fred. *Modern Medicine and Jewish Ethics*. Hoboken, NJ: KTAV Publishing House, Inc. and New York: Yeshiva University Press, 1991.

Sinclair, Daniel B. *Tradition and the Biological Revolution: Application of Jewish Law To the Treatment of the Critically Ill*. Edinburgh, Scotland: Edinburgh University Press, 1989.

Snyder, Carrie. *Death and Dying: Who Decides?* Farmington Hills, MI: Gale Group, Information Plus Reference Series, 2001.

Tendler, Moshe, and Fred Rosner. "Quality and Sanctity of Life in the Talmud and Mishnah". In *Tradition*, vol. 28, no. 1 (Fall 1993).

Stern, Chaim, ed. *On the Doorposts of Your House.* New York: CCAR Press, 1994.

Straus, Livia Selmanowitz. *A Flickering Candle: Death and End of Life Issues.* New York: The United Synagogue of Conservative Judaism Commission on Jewish Education, 1994.

A Time to Prepare: A Practical Guide for Individuals and Families in Determining One's Wishes for Extraordinary Medical Treatment and Financial Arrangements. New York: UAHC Press, 1994.

Trueman, Terry. *Stuck in Neutral.* New York: Harpercollins Juvenile Books, 2000.

Wahrman, Miriam Z. *Brave New Judaism: When Science and Scripture Collide.* Waltham, MA: Brandeis University, 2002.

Zucker, Marjorie B. ed. *The Right to Die Debate: A Documentary History.* Westport, CT and London: Greenwood Press, 1999.

Web Sites

Euthanasia.com: www.euthanasia.com

Information for research on euthanasia, physician assisted suicide, living wills, mercy killing. Committed to the fundamental belief that the intentional killing of another person is wrong.

Exit's Fast Access: www.aez61.dial.pipex.com/index.html

This site contains hundreds of pages of material explaining the arguments for and against euthanasia. It is promoted by Exit (formerly the Scottish Voluntary Euthanasia Society), which campaigns for a change in British law to promote individual patient choice, and strategies for improved palliative care and other resources at the end of life.

International Anti-Euthanasia Task Force: www.internationaltaskforce.org

An organization opposing euthanasia and assisted suicide.

Euthanasia Research and Guidance Organization: www.finalexit.org

The Hemlock Society of America: www.hemlock.org

Two organizations most sympathetic toward euthanasia and assisted suicide.

Religious Tolerance: www.religioustolerance.org/euthanas.htm

An organization that seeks to provide balanced information about euthanasia and assisted suicide.

Films

Specific sections of the following commercial films may be valuable for illustrating certain aspects of the topic of euthanasia, but it may not be appropriate to have students view the entire film. Prescreening is strongly recommended.

Whose Life Is It Anyway? (1981, 118 minutes, rated R)

An artist, paralyzed from his neck down, goes to trial to be allowed to die.

Peaceful Exit (1995, 50 minutes, no rating)

Left brain damaged after an operation, two-year-old Ian Stewart is in pain day and night and not expected to reach his teens. His parents, who have sacrificed their careers to care for Ian, feel his quality of life is negligible. This film records both their tragic situation and the moral dilemma they face: is euthanasia the answer?

CHAPTER 4

HARMFUL BEHAVIORS:
SMOKING, ALCOHOL ABUSE, AND OVER/UNDEREATING

Note: Much information is provided here, including details of current research and relevant statistics. You may not need it all. Consider the chapter a resource. Skim through the sub-headings to find and focus on what is most useful to you. You may notice the chapter format is a little different from the others, more suitable for this topic.

OVERVIEW

Judaism teaches us that we should do what we can to avoid harm. We are to take care of ourselves to the best of our ability. Our oldest Jewish sources warned against being careless or intentionally doing things that could hurt ourselves or others. In recent years, we have become more aware of the dangers of widespread behaviors such as smoking, drinking alcohol, and over/undereating. We begin with an overview of what Judaism teaches about taking care of the body. Then, we will focus on what makes smoking, drinking, and over/undereating potentially harmful, why people engage in these behaviors, and how to evaluate their risks.

Once we learn some general facts and theories about smoking, drinking, and over/undereating, we will have a clearer idea about the kind of Jewish guidance and wisdom that can be helpful to us. From our tradition we will seek practical advice: For example, is the specified behavior allowed or not? We also will raise spiritual questions: For example, what unfulfilled yearnings, brokenness of spirit, or painful feelings of emptiness might lead us to engage in practices that eventually hurt us? We will conclude by looking at ways of coping with harmful behaviors.

On Taking Care of Your Body and Avoiding Dangerous Practices

"Take heed, and guard your soul diligently . . . Take good care of your lives" (Deuteronomy 4:9, 15). Torah establishes the high regard we should have for our lives — cherishing our existence, avoiding danger and harm. We might even say the essence of Judaism — both in its origins and as it developed — is about sanctifying life: "Sanctify yourselves and be holy" (Leviticus 11:44).

Taking care of ourselves — mind, body, and soul — shows respect to God, in whose image we were created (Genesis 9:6). We affirm the sentiment expressed by the Psalmist who praises God for the wonder of our lives: "I praise You, for I am awesomely, wondrously made. Your work is wonderful; I know it very well (Psalms 139:14).

Over the ages, Jewish sages have discussed cleanliness, safety, adequate medical care, proper eating, and other health related issues. Especially pertinent to our topic is avoiding danger. Maimonides describes the prohibition against purposely exposing oneself to mortal danger. He rejects the notion that people should be able to do what they want with their bodies. He says that anyone who does dangerous things and says, "I am endangering myself and what does it matter to others," or "I don't care" is to be flogged (*Mishneh Torah, Hilchot Rotzayach* 11:5; also see *Pesachim* 113a, *Y. Terumot* 8:3). In detailing dangerous practices to avoid, Maimonides includes the obligation of land and home/building owners to keep up with repairs so that no one becomes injured or killed as a result of a collapsing roof or a fall into an empty well. He also warns of drinking water in which a leech, snake, or other poisonous reptile might be found. He cautions against putting coins in one's mouth (which might carry diseases or poisons), being careless with knives, walking near a leaning wall or over a shaky bridge, and entering a ruin or passing through any other dangerous place.

Later codifiers of Jewish law, such as Joseph Karo and Moses Isserles, underscore Maimonides' concerns. In fact, Joseph Karo devotes a whole chapter in the *Shulchan Aruch* to the commandment to "remove any object or obstacle which constitutes a danger to life" (*Choshen Mishpat* 427). Both Maimonides and Karo discuss the prohibition against deliberately wounding oneself (*Mishneh Torah, Hilchot Chovel Umazik* 5:1; *Shulchan Aruch, Choshen Mishpat* 420:31 and *Orach Chayim* 571).

By all accounts, Jewish law prohibits suicide. Generally, we think of suicide as an act someone commits that has immediate, lethal consequences (e.g., using a gun to kill oneself). But suicide can happen incrementally, as well, with slow acting "poisons." Both cigarette smoke and alcohol can have cumulative poisonous effects. Similarly, a suicide can happen because of an accumulation of damage to the body. An ongoing eating disorder can severely and even fatally damage one's internal organs.

Even though not everyone exposed to a particular danger will die because of that exposure, we are not to count on such a scenario. Though some may escape the most dire fallout from risky behavior, we are not to take chances. "When injury is likely, one should not rely on a miracle" (*Kiddushin* 39b).

So far, our discussion has implied that people make choices — sometimes risky ones. With our current understanding of the subject, we recognize the complexity of addictions (whether alcohol, nicotine, or drugs) and eating disorders. Sometimes we lose control of our behavior. We no longer feel we are making choices about what we're doing; rather, our bad choices seem to have taken us over. We begin to feel victimized by problems that have gotten too big for us to handle on our own. Therefore, we must invoke another Jewish teaching and place it above all other body care guidelines. That is, "If you're in pain, go to a physician" (*Baba Kamma* 46b). Depending on the circumstances, the "physician" may be a medical doctor, mental health professional, nutritionist, clergy person, or teacher.

When an occasional weekend cigarette with friends becomes a three-pack-a-day dependence . . . When a glass of wine at dinner becomes regular episodes of drunken stupor . . . Or, when a girl or boy is not "dieting," but rather starving him/herself, we are not simply talking about bad habits anymore. Rather, we are talking about complex, hazardous behaviors for which professional guidance and treatment is needed. In some cases, professionals will refer to a particular substance addiction or eating disorder as a serious "illness" for which attentive treatment is as necessary as it would be for any other serious illness.

What Makes a Behavior "Harmful"

Defining Use, Abuse, and Addiction: Smoking and Drinking

What is so mystifying about harmful habits is that no one can say for sure when moderate *use* of a substance becomes *abuse*, and when abuse becomes *addiction* or *dependency*. Patterns of abuse and addiction seem to vary from person to person and from substance to substance. Some occasional, social smokers ("chippers") will become "pack-a-day" users, and some "pack-a-day" users will become "chain-smokers." Some occasional drinkers will become heavy drinkers, and some heavy drinkers will become alcoholics.

Abuse is indicated by compulsive use, meaning a person feels obsessed by and driven to use a particular substance. Social relationships and work responsibilities begin to suffer. The more extreme patterns of abuse are called *addiction* or *dependency*. That is, a cigarette or alcohol user can become addicted to those substances. Addicts generally have developed physical tolerance to a substance, needing increasingly higher doses to experience the same effect. They also have withdrawal symptoms when the drug is stopped.

Addicts may become so entrenched in a negative habit that they become powerless to emerge from their problems without help. Doctors, therapists, other professionals, and loved ones may need to intervene. Anti-depressants, nicotine patches (for smokers), and other drugs also may be used to treat addictions.

Tragically, dependencies that are ignored can prove fatal either in the long run (e.g., smoking that leads to lung cancer) or in the short run (e.g., sudden death from an alcohol or alcohol/pill overdose). No one understands completely how the progression to addiction happens.

The American Psychiatric Association has published detailed definitions of both abuse and dependence. (See the Glossary, pp. 99-100.)

Defining Harmful Eating Behaviors

Though we might associate "use, abuse, and addiction" with smoking, drinking, or drugs, there are some parallels between such habits and compulsive eating and compulsive dieting. Just as we don't fully understand how "use" becomes "addiction," it is likewise difficult to pin down how eating habits go awry. At times, it may be perfectly appropriate, even beneficial, to make modifications to one's diet, either for gradual weight loss or weight gain. However, for certain individuals who become so intensely concerned with their bodies, a deep unhappiness with their body image can develop. They become estranged from the notion of the Psalmist — "I am awesomely, wondrously made; Your work is wonderful . . . " (Psalms 139:14). Consequences may include becoming obsessive about food and engaging in compulsive, harmful eating habits. Some occasional overeaters will become serious bingers — eating huge quantities of food over a short period of time. Some dieters will try laxatives or vomiting as a (misguided) means of con-

trolling their weight. Some bodybuilders will take steroids (a dangerous drug) in order to build muscle. It is important to note that there are eating behaviors so far outside the spectrum of reasonable eating habits that they require thoughtful intervention and may be more appropriately treated as mental disorders. (See the Glossary for the American Psychiatric Association's definitions for Anorexia Nervosa and Bulimia Nervosa.)

The Effects of Smoking: What Research Says

While not everyone who tries smoking will become a regular user, the nicotine in cigarettes is highly addictive and the long-term effects alarming. Specifically, smokers are more likely to suffer from heart attacks, strokes, and other serious cardiovascular disorders. Smoking greatly increases the possibility of developing lung cancer, is associated with other cancers (of the urinary tract, larynx, oral cavity, esophagus, kidney, pancreas, and cervix), and can cause other health problems, as well.

Smokers not only damage their own health. Pregnant women who smoke expose their unborn children to danger, e.g., low birth weight. Passive smoking — exposure to others' smoke — is a serious health risk, particularly for lung cancer and respiratory ailments.

Despite the dangers, smoking is widespread. Though the smoking rate has decreased among American adults since the mid-1990s, it has been on the rise among youth. In a 1999 study, 34.8 percent of students reported smoking at least some in the month prior to the survey, and 16.8 percent smoked on a regular or daily basis.[1] The World Bank estimates that in affluent countries, 14,000 to 15,000 children and young people take up smoking each day, In middle-income and low-income countries, the number is between 68,000 and 84,000.[2]

In its extensive study, the World Bank reports that the only two causes of death that are huge

---

[1]"Youth Risk Behavior Surveillance — United States, 1999," *Morbidity and Mortality Weekly Report*, vol. 49, no. ss-5, June 9, 2000.

[2]As reported in "Death in the Ashes" by Bob Herbert in his column "In America" for *The New York Times*, July 26, 2001, p. A23.

and growing worldwide are AIDS and tobacco-related illnesses. The Centers for Disease Control and Prevention expects tobacco to become the biggest killer in most developing countries within the next 20 years, causing more deaths than AIDS, malaria, tuberculosis, automobile crashes, homicides, and suicides combined. By the year 2030, tobacco is projected to be the single biggest cause of death worldwide, accounting for about 10 million deaths per year.[3]

The Effects of Alcohol Consumption: What Research Says

Excessive alcohol consumption over a period of time leads not only to physical addiction, but increases the risk of heart attack, stroke, brain damage, liver disease, and several cancers. Pregnant women who drink very heavily during pregnancy (six or more drinks a day) may give birth to babies with fetal alcohol syndrome, a pattern of irreversible abnormalities that include mental retardation, prenatal and postnatal growth deficiencies, and joint defects. Consuming as little as two drinks per day during pregnancy increases the risk of giving birth to low weight newborns.[4]

Because of its effect on the brain and central nervous system, alcohol is considered a drug. It is teenagers' drug of choice. The Bureau of Justice Statistics reports that in 1999, 73.8 percent of high school seniors had used alcohol in the previous 12 months and 51 percent in the last 30 days. Marijuana had the next highest use with 37.8 percent using it in the prior 12 months and 23.1 percent in the prior 30 days.[5]

Driving while under the influence is very risky and often leads to tragic accidents. Alcohol consumption impairs concentration and reaction time. The brain has difficulty processing information such as speed, distance, curves in the road, and even the difference between the gas and brake pedals. Motor vehicle crashes are the leading cause of death for Americans under the age of 21. Despite improved educational efforts regarding drinking and driving, a 1999 study found that in the month prior to a survey given, 13.3 percent of students reported they had driven a vehicle after drinking alcohol. Another 33.1 percent admitted they had ridden with a driver who had been drinking alcohol.[6]

Frequent drinking has serious emotional and interpersonal repercussions. Alcohol can bring to the surface feelings of anger and hostility that a person normally would keep under control. Nearly half of all murders in America occur while either the attacker or victim — or both — are under the influence of alcohol. Half of college students accused of violent crimes had either been drinking or taking drugs at the time of their crime. Often the victims were either drunk or on drugs, too. Alcohol is a major factor in many cases of child and spouse abuse and also can play a significant role in suicides.[7] A person who drinks heavily is less inhibited, becoming more susceptible to fighting, engaging in offensive behavior, and physically or verbally abusing others.

There are, of course, many dangers in abusing drugs besides alcohol — too many to cover in one chapter. We won't go into detail about other drugs, except to mention a particularly loathsome one whose misuse has increased since the mid-1990s, especially among young people. Rohypnol, called the "date rape" drug, is a powerful, low cost sleeping aid and tranquilizer. It is tasteless, odorless, and colorless, and can cause a person to pass out and be unable to recall events. Unsuspecting "dates," having been slipped this drug without their knowledge, frequently become victims of rape.

---

[3]Ibid.
[4]*The New Our Bodies Ourselves*, p. 56.
[5]"Drug Use in the General Population," *Drug and Crime Facts*, Bureau of Justice Statistics, December 1999.

[6]"Youth Risk Behavior Surveillance — United States, 1999," *Morbidity and Mortality Weekly Report*, vol. 49, no. ss-5, June 9, 2002.
[7]*Life Issues: Alcoholism*, p.31.

The Effects of Harmful Eating Habits: What Research Says

(Note: See the Glossary, pp. 99-100, for definitions of anorexia and bulimia.)

The Jewish Family and Children's Services relays some distressing facts about current eating patterns:

- On any given day, 48 million Americans are dieting.

- Individuals who diet are eight times more likely to develop eating disorders.

- There are at least 8,000,000 eating disorder victims in this country.

- 90% of eating disorder victims are female. Male cases are increasing.

- 1 in 200 girls aged 12 to 18 is anorexic.

- More than 75% of women say they "feel fat."

- The average fashion model weighs 25 pounds less than the average woman.[8]

The American Anorexia and Bulimia Association estimates that every year one million women develop eating disorders, and 150,000 die from anorexia. Anorexia has the highest death rate for any psychiatric disorder — some 5 to 15 percent die. Researchers point out that the cumulative effects of anorexia give it a death rate as high as 20 percent.[9]

Eating disorders are a serious and possibly fatal problem. But there are widespread instances of poor eating habits that professionals would not generally categorize as "mental disorders." Yet these, too, take their toll. Particularly worrisome is that a third of American adults are classified as obese (about 20 percent over their optimal weight)[10], as are roughly 12 percent of children ages 6 to 17. The number of obese children is about double what it was in 1974. The fact that overweight children often become overweight adults is a significant concern.[11]

Obesity kills an estimated 300,000 Americans a year.[12] Overweight adults are at an increased risk for a number of chronic medical conditions, such as coronary heart disease, hypertension, diabetes, gallbladder disease, respiratory disease, some cancers, and arthritis. Though regular physical activity is a key component of weight control (and healthy life style, in general), a large number of American adults trying to lose weight do not participate in any such activity.[13]

On the other hand, our culture overemphasizes thinness. While about 12 percent of children are overweight, nearly a third *think* they are overweight.[14] Such attitudes can lead to useless, unhealthful dieting. On and off dieting, fad diets, crash diets, and "failed" diets are hard on the body and often cause mental and emotional anguish.

The "Cost"

Certainly, we pay a high price with our health when we engage in harmful behaviors. Addictions usually take a toll on loved ones, as well. There are financial costs, too. Purchasing cigarettes, alcohol, and "binging" food is expensive and may strain the financial resources of individuals and/or their families. Treatment costs can also be expensive, e.g., for psychological therapy, medical care, or residency in a treatment center. But not all "therapies" are appropriate. Millions of dollars are spent on suspect treat-

[8]Jewish Family and Children's Services' "Begin from Within" web site, www.jfcs.org/bfwdidyouknow.html, 2000.

[9]*Bulimia/Anorexia: The Binge/Purge Cycle and Self-Starvation*, p. 219

[10]Robert J. Kuczmarski et al., "Increasing Prevalence of Overweight Among U.S. Adults," *Journal of the American Medical Association* 272 (3[20 July 1994]): 205-211.

[11]Center for Disease Control, The Third National Health and Nutrition Examination Survey (NHANES III: 1988-1994).

[12]JoAnn E. Manson et al., "Body Weight and Mortality Among Women," New England Journal of Medicine 333 (11[11 September 1995]): 677-85.

[13]According to a group of adults responding to a survey, approximately a third did not participate in any leisure time activity as part of their weight loss program. Only about a fifth of these adults exercised the recommended 30 minutes or more, five or more times a week. These findings are reported in "Prevalence of Leisure-Time Activity Among Overweight Adults — United States, 1998," *Morbidity and Mortality Weekly Report*, vol. 49, no. 15, April 21, 2000.

[14]"Youth Risk Behavior Surveillance — United States, 1999," *Morbidity and Mortality Weekly Report*, vol. 49, no. ss-5, June 9, 2000.

ments (e.g., unsubstantiated herbal remedies or fad diet books). In their desperation for a cure to their problems, some people are duped into futilely spending huge amounts of money.

Why Do People Do Harmful Things To Their Bodies?

General Factors to Consider

Finding an answer as to why people use, abuse, or become dependent on nicotine or alcohol is not an exact science. Some researchers believe that reasons for use have to do with social influences and peer pressure. Substance dependence (or addiction) is said to be more the result of psychological and physiological needs and pressures. Compulsive eating predominantly is attributed to emotional factors.[15] And where do so-called psychological pressures and emotional factors come from? Perhaps they originate from an inner emptiness akin to spiritual suffering.

Smoking and Drinking

Drugs — which include nicotine and alcohol — have physical effects. Mood altering substances affect brain processes, stimulating feelings of pleasure and/or release from pain.[16] These effects don't last long, however, and the "side effects" can be quite damaging (as outlined above). While pain may be temporarily masked, any enduring relief from problems is left wanting.

From studies of abuse patterns within families, it seems a genetic component is at work, though no one responsible gene has been identified. Still, parents who smoke influence their children's habits. Similarly, alcoholism occurs at much higher rates among the relatives of alcoholics than in the general population. Though to some extent substance abuse might be learned behavior, research suggests that risks for developing addictions (like the risks for developing heart disease or diabetes) tend to run in families.

Many young people begin to use harmful substances for social reasons. Typically, girls and boys start smoking because they want to experiment with something they see as fun, to act grown up, to be one of the crowd, or to rebel.[17] These reasons also may be why some young people begin to drink alcohol.

We like to belong to special groups. We may be drawn to a group in which most everyone drinks, smokes, and/or uses drugs liberally. It is easy to become influenced by group members who encourage or pressure us to use substances. In some communities, it can actually be hard to find an appealing social group or activity that excludes substance use. The acceptability of smoking or drinking in certain communities and cultures reinforces the legitimacy of these behaviors.

Once substance *use* becomes *dependence*, psychological and emotional factors are usually involved. It is said that one gets "high" from drugs, and "medium" from nicotine.[18] Smokers may rely on nicotine to help them maintain a more even tone, using the drug to moderate mood shifts brought on by stressful situations. Generally, addicts find that a little nicotine stimulates and a lot sedates. They may experience nicotine as helping them to feel alert and mentally efficient.[19]

People who abuse alcohol often say they like the way it makes them feel. Because of difficulties coping with problems, they drink to deaden pain and alleviate stress. They may consume alcohol to loosen up in social situations. The effects of alcohol make them feel more comfortable, less tense. Still, abusing alcohol ultimately does not solve troubles or enhance social skills. In the long run, problems usually get worse.

In sum, the self-destructive things we human beings do to ourselves may not seem self-destructive at first. Possible reasons for substance dependence are extensive. They may include individual circumstances, temperament, psycho-

[15]*Alcohol and Tobacco*, p. 5, 1997 ed.
[16]Ibid.
[17]*Youth Risk Behavior Surveillance — United States, 1997*; Centers for Disease Control and Prevention, Atlanta, Georgia, 1997.
[18]Krogh, p.149.
[19]Ibid., p. 44.

logical wounds, the meaning given to addiction, environment, social class, defeatism, bad self-image, negative outlook,[20] or weight control (for smokers). We may engage in harmful behaviors in response to pressures we feel, e.g., boredom, depression, anxiety, and/or domestic problems.[21] Feeling at a loss spiritually may contribute to our vulnerability to such pressures in the first place. The elusiveness of control in addiction gives it a complexity that makes it so dangerous.

Overeating and Undereating

In this section we will look at the social, cultural, psychological, and emotional factors that seem to contribute to harmful eating behaviors. There can be physiological reasons for being over-weight (e.g., thyroid dysfunction) or under-weight (e.g., an intestinal disease). Such problems need to be addressed by health care professionals and will not be our focus here.

So much of our socializing happens around food. Learning good habits and listening to our bodies can be difficult when we are besieged by tantalizing advertisements for food products, oversized portions, readily available "junk" (low nutrition) and instant foods, plus social opportunities that highlight food consumption. Bodies are different — usually a person with a large frame or tall height will be able to consume more than a smaller person. Even though both may be exposed to the same food temptations and participate in the same food-featured gatherings, what will be normal consumption for one person will be overeating for the other.

Contemporary culture is thought to have an influence on the development of eating problems. Body image disparagement and dissatisfaction can begin at a very early age. Glamour messages around us (in TV, movies, magazines, fashion advertisements) encourage girls to compare their bodies to thin "ideals." Boys especially are vulnerable to the bombardment of images of unnaturally muscle-bound "hunks." Popular pre-teen and teen fashion styles don't account for

varieties in body types, making it impossible for some young dressers to "fit in." Pressures to con-form can be stressful. For some, such stress leads to a sense of loathing for their bodies.

Not all children and adults who are exposed to these cultural messages develop eating prob-lems. Generally, a number of factors contribute to the onset of eating disorders, including cul-tural values, peer and parental influence, physi-ology/genetics, and individual circumstances and personality characteristics. Psychologists and others strive to understand a person's *internal* motivations for engaging in problematic eating behaviors. Addressing internal motivations is key in treating and trying to reverse damaging eating patterns.

One interesting idea has been proposed by the therapist Peggy Claude-Pierre. She says that entrenched negativity is a major contributing factor to eating disorders. This mental state — the culmination of a continual pattern of nega-tive assumptions about oneself — includes the loss of a sense of self and can precede other harmful behaviors, as well. This is not to say that external circumstances are insignificant. Whether or not a negative mental condition becomes dangerous depends substantially on the environment and on what is going on in a per-son's life.[22]

Certain personality types with a poorly defined sense of self seem particularly susceptible to serious eating disorders. The following risk factors for depression in adolescence also may fuel eating disorders: low self-esteem; the feeling of needing to please everyone; unassertiveness; lack of self-confidence; low expectations for being able to control important events; negative reinforcement of skills, talents, and activities; inadequate coping strategies; negativity; and learned helplessness.[23] Factors more directly related to eating disorders include feeling unde-serving of food, self-denial, negative body image, and being out of touch with body signals of full-ness and hunger. Though eating disorders may be more common among adolescents, they can

---

[20]Ibid., p. 133.
[21]Ibid., p. 129.

[22]Claude-Pierre, p. 48.
[23]Boskind-White, p. 228-229.

afflict individuals from early childhood to old age.

Can there be spiritual reasons for overeating and undereating? With these behaviors, perhaps we fill ourselves up with negativity (or extraneous, unhealthful food) rather than with what would nourish us most. We do so when we have lost hold of something more positive with which to fill ourselves. Displeasure with our bodies can alienate us from an essential aspect of the Jewish understanding of God. That is, we say that God is the One Who created and formed us, and to Whom we are to express gratitude for the miracle of our being (Psalms 139:14).

The section "When We're 'In Over Our Heads'" below addresses treatment possibilities and coping mechanisms. With supportive guidance, harmful eating behaviors can be overcome. They do not have to be disabling for life.

Is There an Acceptable Level of "Risk" for Smoking?

General Perspectives

Is there an amount that a person can smoke and yet remain reasonably protected from harmful consequences? While some researchers talk about reduced use as a treatment approach (which has some support in data), the overwhelming view is that only abstinence works. But what if you were just to smoke a couple of cigarettes on weekends with friends? Would that really be that damaging to your health? Maybe not. Still, from what we have learned so far, the progression from initial use to addiction is elusive. When a person begins to smoke, he/she may *intend* to limit the habit. However, there is no sure means for preventing casual use of nicotine from becoming serious dependence.

Jewish Perspectives

When tobacco first came into use in the Jewish community, there was a sense that it was beneficial for the body. As Rabbi Jacob Emden (1697-1776) wrote:

Tobacco is a healthful substance for the body . . . Its natural actions are important in helping to digest food, cleanse the mouth . . . and help the movement of essential functions and blood circulation, which are the root of health . . . It is indeed beneficial to every healthy man, not only because of the pleasure and enjoyment it affords, but because it preserves one's health and medical fitness (Jacob Emden, *Mor u-Ketziah*, O.H. 511).

Some 200 years later, tobacco's harmful effects came more into focus. The highly esteemed *halachist* of recent days, Rabbi Moshe Feinstein addressed the issue of smoking in his Responsa writings. He faced a difficult dilemma — how to reconcile the growing evidence of the dangers of smoking with the fact that the habit was widespread, having become a popular practice. He was well aware that the Talmud teaches, "We must not impose a restrictive decree upon the community unless the majority of the community will be able to endure it" (*Baba Kamma* 79b). He concluded that "since the multitude are accustomed to it, 'the Eternal will protect the foolish'" (*Shabbat* 129b, quoting Psalms 116:6). He also noted that "some of the great Torah Scholars of past generations and the present day were and are smokers" (Moshe Feinstein, *Iggerot Moshe*, H.M. 2, no. 18). In short, while Rabbi Feinstein would not encourage smoking, he would not prohibit it outright.

Subsequently, various Rabbis and scholars have come to less permissive conclusions. The Sephardi Chief Rabbi of Tel Aviv, Rabbi Chayim David Halevy, is one. A child asked him whether he must obey his father who sent him out to buy cigarettes. This was the Rabbi's response:

In view of the fact that physicians have universally warned against the great danger of smoking to human health, and since, in my opinion, it is forbidden by the Torah, which commands, "You shall carefully preserve your lives" (Deuteronomy 15:4), . . . you are not permitted to buy him cigarettes. Furthermore, whenever you see him with a cigarette in his mouth, . . . say to him, "Father, it is written in the Torah, 'You shall carefully preserve your lives,' and smoking is very harmful" — in the hope that he will understand, overcome his urge, and give up the habit (Chayim David Halevy, *Responsa Aseh Lecha Rav,* vol. 6, no. 59).

The charge to take care of our bodies and avoid danger was discussed in detail at the beginning of this chapter. As the dangers of tobacco use have become ever more apparent, Jewish leaders increasingly are taking harsher stances on smoking. Rabbi Moshe Zemer, in his book *Evolving Halachah,* summarizes the current consensus of *halachic* opinion:

1. Smoking near anyone who may be disturbed or harmed by smoke is prohibited.

2. It is forbidden to harm oneself by smoking. Accordingly, smokers who cannot break the habit "cold turkey" must make every effort to cut back gradually or receive professional help until they are weaned of their addiction.

3. It is forbidden for children and adolescents to begin or to become accustomed to smoking. Adults may not help or encourage them to acquire the habit.

4. Encouraging smokers in their habit, by offering them a cigarette or light, is prohibited.

5. Elected officials and spiritual leaders should sponsor serious educational campaigns to convince the public of the extreme danger of smoking.[24]

The permissiblity of working for a tobacco company is another area worthy of being addressed by *halachic* authorities.

---

[24]*Evolving Halachah: A Progressive Approach to Traditional Jewish Law,* p. 349-350.

Is There an Acceptable Level of "Risk" for Alcohol Consumption?

General Perspectives

The use of alcohol or drinking in moderation (by those of a legal age) tends to be acceptable in American culture. Drinking more than moderate amounts, to a harmful degree is abuse. Abuse of any drug, alcohol included, is unsafe, presenting dangerous risks to oneself and to others.

No simple formula exists for calculating risk free drinking. One or two drinks is usually a safe amount for a normal sized adult to drink. Still, one person may become "drunk" from one drink, whereas another will have a much higher level of tolerance. How much time elapses between drinks and whether or not a person drinks on an empty stomach also affects how quickly a person becomes impaired. A test which does help judge intoxication measures the ratio of alcohol to blood in drinkers — the BAC (blood alcohol content) test. In America a BAC of between .08 and .10 percent is considered legally impaired. (In Sweden it is .05 percent.) A level of .4 percent alcohol is enough to cause coma or even death. For a typical 150 pound man, three drinks will give him a BAC of .087. For a typical 125 pound woman, two drinks will give her a BAC of .08. Thus, three drinks legally pushes the limit for men, and two drinks for women. (A "drink" consists of three to five ounces of wine, 12 ounces of beer, or one ounce of hard liquor.)

If a person does drink, there are ways of reducing the risks:

- Eat something before or while drinking and sip drinks rather than gulp them down. These practices will slow down the rate at which alcohol enters the bloodstream.

- Don't drink and drive. Even small amounts of alcohol interfere with judgment, coordination, vision, and reaction time.

- Avoid using alcohol within a few hours of using any other drug, including over-the-counter medications. The mix can cause dangerous physical harm and even death.

- Don't drink when the body is in a vulnerable state, i.e., sick or tired. Don't drink during pregnancy (which can harm the fetus).

- Don't use alcohol as a problem solver. Drinking to escape troubles keeps one from dealing with underlying difficulties and tends to make one increasingly dependent upon alcohol and vulnerable to addiction.[25]

Jewish Perspectives[26]

References to alcohol consumption in Jewish sources suggest a continuum of attitudes — from acceptable to problematic. Consuming wine for *Kiddush* on Shabbat and holidays and as part of life cycle events is acceptable and even an integral part of our rituals. Greater quantities of wine may be consumed during special occasions. Four cups are drunk during the Passover *Seder*. The Purim festivities include drinking until one cannot tell the difference between "cursed be Haman" and "blessed be Mordecai" (*Megillah* 7b). The Talmud tells us that ten cups of wine are drunk in a house of mourning (*Semachot* 14:14). Clearly, consuming even more than "moderate" amounts of alcohol is tolerated at times.

However, Judaism does recognize a problematic side of drinking. Hebrew terms used for the continuum of drinking are: *shatui, shikur,* and *shikur k'Lot*. Roughly translated, they mean: tipsy or under the influence, drunk, and smashed (literally, "as drunk as Lot"). These different states are determined by quantities consumed and

degree of impairment. Someone who is "*shatui*" has drunk a quarter-*log* (2.9 ounces or about three drinks for a man), more than that is called "*shikur*" (*Yerushalmi Terumot* 1:4). A person's ability to talk coherently and walk normally are diminished at the level of "*shikur*" (*Eruvin* 64a-b).

Jewish sources recognize heaviness of limbs, drowsiness, difficulty in focusing, and impaired judgment as potential effects of alcohol consumption. Drinking beyond moderate amounts has consequences. A drunk person is constrained from fully participating in communal life. Princes, judges, priests, teachers, and ritual slaughterers must remain sober in order to carry out their duties properly.[27] Any individual who has been drinking faces restrictions in joining in communal prayer (*Yerushalmi Terumot* 1:4).

A person under the influence of alcohol is more prone to involvement in criminal activity. Jewish sources, like secular law, deem a person responsible for harm or damage caused during an episode of drunkenness (*Mishneh Torah, Hilchot Chovel U'mazeek* 1:11). However, in the Talmud Rabbi Chanina expressed an opinion that differed from that of the majority concerning a person's accountability for their actions while drinking. He said that when people become "smashed" or "*shikur k'Lot*" ("as drunk as Lot"), they can no longer be held responsible for what they have done (*Eruvin* 65a). Perhaps it is the community's responsibility to do whatever it can to prevent situations in which citizens abuse alcohol and cause serious harm. In our day, we see efforts along these lines. For example, there are laws against underage drinking (with "carding" at bars and liquor stores) and against driving while intoxicated. Judges often require individuals who have committed crimes while under the influence of alcohol to participate in a rehabilitation program.

We return now to the question that began this section: From a Jewish perspective, is there

---

[25]*The New Our Bodies Ourselves*, p.56

[26]Most of the material for this section is drawn from "Intervening in the Life of an Alcoholic" (1989) by Judith Brazen and Susan Freeman, in *Reform Jewish Ethics and the Halakhah*, edited by Eugene B. Borowitz. NJ: Behrman House,

Inc., 1994, pp. 79-95.

[27]*Sanhedrin* 42a with *Tosafot, Sh'elot U'teshuvot* of *Bayit Chadash* #41, Leviticus 10:9, *Mishneh Torah — Hilchot Biat Hamikdash* 1:3, *Shulchan Aruch — Yoreh De'ah* 1:8.

an acceptable level of risk for drinking? The answer is yes. Using alcohol in moderation and on special occasions is permissible. Abuse, however, is problematic and is to be avoided.

But there's a more complex issue. Traditional Jewish sources tend not to speak in terms of *addiction* to alcohol. In our day, we understand the dangers of alcoholism, what many experts consider to be a "disease." Some people are susceptible to a harmful and even life endangering dependence on alcohol. Most experts believe that once a person has been addicted to alcohol, it will be nearly impossible for him/her to return to "moderate use." From a Jewish point of view, we must conclude that complete abstention is necessary for such individuals. It is a matter of life and death.

Are the Risks of Dieting or Overeating Ever Worth Taking?

General Perspectives

If we were to condense the best advice on eating into one rule (with few exceptions), this would be it: *Only* eat when you're hungry, and when you are hungry, *always* eat. To do otherwise is to risk obesity or eating disorders.

Does this mean that it is never appropriate to make modifications in our eating behavior? No. Since being overweight poses serious health risks, weight problems need to be addressed appropriately. Modification in diet and lifestyle are not only acceptable, but advisable in such instances.

For the most seriously overweight people, consultation with a professional is an important first step. These are some of the basic guidelines that have been proven helpful: Those who have decided to lose weight need a personal weight loss plan to fit their lives. Successful plans usually include regular exercise or activity and a new healthier eating style. Being patient, being consistent with these lifestyle changes, and setting small, realistic goals are all important factors.[28]

Many weight loss strategies usually fail and can present health risks. They include using appetite suppressants, fasting, going on very restrictive diets, and relying on diet formulas. Other problematic factors are never permitting oneself any of the special foods one enjoys, not exercising, and repeatedly going to weight control groups and programs.[29] Purging, with laxatives or by forcing oneself to vomit, besides being injurious to the body, is not an effective method of weight loss.

We can make many reasonable and even healthful modifications in our eating habits. But once "modifications" become more extreme — with binging, purging, or starving oneself (i.e., bulimia or anorexia) — we are dealing with a different category of behavior. These "abuses" are serious disorders. The physical consequences of these behaviors (e.g., malnourishment, organ damage, vitamin/mineral deficiencies) and mental health issues involved (such as depression, low self-esteem, and/or entrenched negativity), require professional help.

Jewish Perspectives

There are times during the year for feasts and fasts, as part of holiday observances or life cycle events. But these occasions are exceptions to everyday eating practices. Eating in moderation is the Jewish ideal.

Maimonides reminds us to avoid whatever is injurious to our bodies, overeating included. We should not be gluttons, but eat food conducive to health, and of such food, not eat to excess. We should not be eager to fill our stomachs, like "those who gorge themselves with food and drink until the body swells." Maimonides warns that "overeating is like a deadly poison to any constitution and is the principal cause of all diseases." (See also Text Study, "On Eating," p. 90.)

Maimonides further teaches that eating is justified only by a feeling of hunger, when the

---

[28]Susan Kayman, William Bruvold, and Judith S. Stern, "Maintenance and Relapse after Weight Loss in Women: Behavioral Aspects," American Journal of Clinical Nutrition 52 (5[November 1990]): 800-807.

[29]Ibid., p. 44.

stomach is clear and the mouth possesses sufficient saliva. These are signals that we really are hungry. Likewise, we should drink only when we are truly thirsty. According to Maimonides, this means that if we feel hungry or thirsty, we should wait a little while, as occasionally we are led to feel so by a deceptive hunger and deceptive thirst (Maimonides, *Mishneh Torah, Hilchot De'ot* 4:15).

Maimonides also encourages physical exercise and activity. These help us to avoid disease and to increase our vigor. According to Maimonides, a sedentary life — one lacking in exercise — will cause us to be more subject to aches and pain, and will reduce our strength. Note that Maimonides' recommendations for moderate eating and engagement in exercise are quite consistent with currently accepted recommendations.

Certainly, Judaism would urge us to do whatever we can to avoid the risks of such eating disorders as self-starvation (anorexia) or binging and purging (bulimia). From our prior discussion of these matters, we know that if we are engaging in such destructive behaviors, it usually means we have lost control of what we are doing. Some would say that we have become dependent or addicted to damaging patterns of eating. If we are afflicted with an eating disorder, it is not acceptable to continue to expose ourselves (or watch as loved ones expose themselves) to potentially life threatening risks. Getting help is an urgent matter.

When We're "In Over Our Heads"

Do I Have a Problem?

Sometimes it's obvious to us when we're "in over our heads." But this is not always the case. Judging just how serious our habits are can be confusing. Our habits may have become such a part of our daily lives that we don't even notice the toll they have taken both on us and on those around us.

Questions to Ask about Substance Use

One way to judge the seriousness of our habits is to examine our behavior closely. Following are some questions to ask about substance abuse (nicotine, alcohol, or other drugs):

- Has someone close to you expressed concern about your substance use?

- Do you use a substance as a way of avoiding or coping with problems?

- Are you sometimes unable to meet home or work responsibilities because of substance use?

- Has use of a substance caused any problems in your relationships with family, friends, or co-workers?

- Do you rely on a substance to get you going in the morning?

- Do you find you have to take increasing amounts of a substance to achieve the same effects?

- Have you had distressing physical or psychological reactions when you have tried to stop the habit?

- Have you ever required medical attention as a result of your substance use?

- Have you often failed to keep promises you have made to yourself or others about controlling or cutting out your substance use?

- Do you ever feel guilty about your use of a substance or try to conceal it from others?[30]

- Are you in pain (physical, emotional, or spiritual)?

---

[30]These questions are adapted from *The New Our Bodies Ourselves*, p. 59.

Questions to Ask about Eating Disorders

The following are questions to ask yourself in regard to eating disorders:

- Has someone close to you expressed concern about your eating habits?

- Do you engage in harmful eating behaviors as a way of avoiding or coping with problems?

- Does your eating behavior have a negative impact on your home, school, or work responsibilities?

- Has your eating behavior caused any problems in relationships with family, friends, or co-workers?

- Has the intensity of your eating problems increased over time?

- Have you had distressing physical or psychological reactions when you have tried to stop engaging in a harmful eating habit?

- Have you ever required medical attention as a result of your eating behavior?

- Have you often failed to keep the promises you have made to yourself or others about controlling problematic eating patterns?

- Do you ever feel guilty about what you're doing or try to conceal it from others?[31]

- Are you in pain (physical, emotional, or spiritual)?

Getting Help

Answering yes to any of the questions in either category above signals the need for help. Harmful use of substances and problematic eating behavior significantly interferes with life. These habits can damage physical health, hurt relationships, and hamper school or other work. Answering yes also is a signal to pay attention to and take care of one's spiritual well-being.

Reiterating the injunction discussed in the opening section of this chapter is useful: "Take heed, take exceeding care of yourself . . . take good care of your lives" (Deuteronomy 4:9, 15). But we also must remember the charge that concluded that section: That is, "If you're in pain, go to a physician" (*Baba Kamma* 46b).

When we're "in over our heads," we cannot deal with our problems alone. For some, addressing any physical damage to the body may be the first step. This will be the case for those of us who are forced to face the severity of our problems because of health troubles.

With guidance and support, we can overcome incapacitating despair and negativity. Therapists can provide individual counseling. Many people find support groups very helpful. These include "Anonymous" groups (i.e., Alcoholics Anonymous, Narcotics Anonymous, Overeaters Anonymous), JACS (Jewish Alcoholics, Chemically Dependent Persons), and groups organized by local synagogues and such organizations as the Jewish Family Service.

Caring for the Spirit

Spiritual issues may be tied in to our experience of pain and our efforts to recover. Understanding our spiritual pain is something we may wish to explore with a Rabbi, close friend, and/or through meditation, study, and prayer:

- We may have strong feelings of spiritual emptiness.

- We may feel disconnected from ourselves and from the rest of the world.

- We may feel abandoned by or angry at God.

- We may have lost our will to participate in the religious life of our community.

---

[31]Questions from *The New Our Bodies Ourselves* about drug and alcohol use adapted here for eating disorders, p. 59.

- We may have experienced a loss of faith and a wish to abandon religious practices.

While it is unrealistic and unwise to think that we can completely eliminate pain from our lives, we can learn ways to reconnect to the things we care about and to the people we love. Judaism considers *teshuvah* (repentance and return) an essential value. We can "return" by taking care of our bodies, reentering the community, and working to improve strained relationships. We can return to God, as God is merciful and accepts us even when we are vulnerable and broken-hearted.

Summary of the Overview

1. Judaism teaches us to take care of our bodies and avoid dangerous practices.

2. Smoking, excessive alcohol consumption, and certain eating/dieting practices can be hazardous to our health and well-being. Sometimes we take risks without wholly understanding our motivations or fully realizing the potential for harmful consequences. There can be physical, psychological, social, and/or spiritual reasons for beginning or for continuing with a specific habit. Genetic patterning and/or cultural values also may influence us toward a self-destructive behavior.

3. It can be difficult to judge what is an acceptable level of risk for using potentially harmful substances (i.e., cigarettes or alcohol) or for engaging in potentially harmful practices (i.e., dieting, fasting, or bingeing). The potential for serious harm varies from individual to individual, from substance to substance, and from behavior to behavior.

4. If we find we are "in over our heads" in substance use or other self-destructive practices, we will need care and support from others — from doctors, therapists, clergy, teachers, family members, friends, and/or support groups. Besides professional assistance, renewed attention to our spiritual lives can help us to manage our pain and to overcome a dependence on the things that hurt us.

SCENARIOS: HOW THINGS HAVE CHANGED

Below are two imaginary scenarios dealing with our topic of harmful behaviors and taking care of one's self. They are intended to raise questions and spark discussion. Read each scenario to or with your students, and engage them in small or large group discussions. Use the "Focus the Discussion" section below to help identify the important issues and facilitate these discussions. Note that additional questions relating to the scenarios are found in the "Stories: Understanding through Listening" section below (pp. 94-95).

Following the discussions, have students continue on to the "Text Study" section to see what Jewish and other sources have to say on the subject. Finally, you may wish to have students discuss the questions a second time, to see if their views have changed.

Scenario 1: Russia in the Late 1800s

A Rabbi is concerned for the residents of his village. Lately, bands of marauders have come through, destroying property. Neighboring villages are reporting worse violence, including rapes and murders. The Rabbi decides he must address his community and insist they do whatever possible to avoid the dangers in their midst. In planning his comments, he realizes that the *parashah* (Torah reading) for the week is "*Va'etchanan.*" In the reading God urges the Israelites to "take heed, take exceeding care of yourself . . . take good care of your lives" (Deuteronomy 4:9, 15).

The Rabbi weaves together a *drash* (sermon), invoking the words from the *parashah*. He also refers to teachings from the Talmud and Maimonides about avoiding danger. Though the circumstances of his community are different, he plans to get his point across by applying the earlier teachings to the threats of his own times. He warns of being out alone or going to desolate areas. However, he knows that the marauders have no compunction about entering a village in broad daylight and mounting great devastation. Therefore, he also urges the community to be proactive, to create hidden safe havens wherever they can, such as in a basement, entered through a concealed opening.

Scenario 2: America in the Early Twenty-first Century

In their Confirmation class, a group of young people has gotten into a heart-to-heart conversation about problems they see concerning kids their age. They note how a lot of kids they know are unhappy or depressed; some seem angry all the time. Some kids do things which are really dangerous — drinking and driving, drugs, eating huge amounts and then making themselves throw up. Two kids from their high school were killed last month because they had been drinking and driving. It's scary and upsetting. Even so, some of the students admit they're curious about smoking, drinking, and drugs. A few have experimented with various substances. But they worry about going too far.

As the "heart-to-heart" unfolds, students talk about all the mixed messages they hear from parents, friends, teachers, media, and popular culture. They complain about how so many values get distorted. Advertisements try to make smoking and drinking seem glamorous. Only the most beautiful bodies are shown in ads, or in movies and magazines. And "beautiful" is almost always way too thin for women, plus the men's bodies are equally unrealistic. The whole media scene makes kids feel ugly and inadequate. The really sensitive kids have an especially hard time dealing with so many expectations of how they should look and how they should act. Everyone feels stressed out enough as it is! And the conversation continues.

As part of their Confirmation coursework, some of the students have recently been studying Jewish views of health and care for one's body. They were particularly intrigued by a verse from *parashat Va'etchanan,* an admonition to "take heed, take exceeding care of yourself . . . take good care of your lives" (Deuteronomy 4:9, 15). The students decide to make taking care of yourself the theme of their Confirmation presentation.

From their studies, observations of peers, and their own experiences, the students have become concerned about the dangers of abuse and addiction. In their presentation they urge people to get help if they become dependent on a harmful behavior. They conclude by expressing a commitment to working with the administration of the local high school to create a peer support group for students coping with addictions. In addition, they ask the synagogue Board to welcome "Anonymous" groups (i.e., Alcoholics Anonymous, Narcotics Anonymous, Overeaters Anonymous, JACS — Jewish Alcoholics and Chemically Dependent persons) to meet in the building and to sponsor a crisis hot line. The hot line would be for anyone in their community who is overwhelmed by a harmful behavior or for "standers by" who are concerned for loved ones.

Focus the Discussion

Avoiding danger is as important today as it ever was. Mostly, we associate danger "back then" with a threat to physical safety due to something in the environment (e.g., a snake, a leech, or an unsteady bridge) or because of an enemy. Certainly, vigilance continues to be necessary in regard to environmental and political issues that may threaten physical safety. But in addition, new dangers challenge us with their complexity. Tobacco had not been widely known in Jewish communities until the last 100 years or so. We have some sense of what the consequences used to be for alcohol abuse, but the issue does not seem to have been of major concern to earlier Jewish communities. We have little information about the incidence or treatment of abuse of other substances or eating disorders.

In recent decades though, we know the

impact of social pressures and cultural expectations on dangerous behaviors. We have discovered that "experimenting" may begin harmlessly enough (a few cigarettes, an occasional eating or drinking binge). But all too easily, such behaviors can get out of control. More evident now than ever is the problem of addiction. Today, when a behavior becomes so extreme that it is no longer part of a normal continuum, we may treat it more as an illness involving psychological, physical, and spiritual components.

TEXT STUDY

Note: In contrast to the other chapters, the "On the One Hand/On the Other Hand" structure does not provide the most useful way of examining harmful behaviors. Rather, we will study texts in a straightforward way, focusing on passages that reflect the various themes applicable to this topic.

1. **On Taking Care of Your Body and Avoiding Dangerous Practices**

   A. "Take heed, and guard your soul diligently . . . Take good care of your lives" (Deuteronomy 4:9, 15).

   B. Rabbi Akiba said, "A person is not permitted to harm him/herself" (*Baba Kamma* 90a).

   C. The Sages forbade many things that involve mortal danger. Anyone who does these things and says, "I am endangering myself and what does it matter to others," or, "I don't care," is to be flogged [by the Rabbinical court] (Maimonides, *Mishneh Torah, Hilchot Rotzayach* 11:5).

   D. One should aim to maintain physical health and vigor, in order that the soul may be upright, in a condition to know God. For it is impossible for one to understand sciences and meditate upon

them, when one is hungry or sick, or when any of one's limbs is aching (Maimonides, *Mishneh Torah, Hilchot De'ot* 3:3).

Probing: Ideas and Issues

Why is it important to take care of yourself from a practical point of view? From a spiritual point of view?

In Text #C, what does Maimonides believe the response should be to those who choose to endanger themselves? What is behind his thinking? Do you agree with him? What should our response be today to someone who says, "It's my business what I do with my body" or "I don't care?"

What does it say in Text #D above about "sickness" and our relationship with God? Some might argue that during sickness people often draw closer to God. How do you think abusive or addictive behaviors would affect a person's relationship with God?

2. **On Smoking**

Note: See other applicable texts in the Overview, beginning on p. 73.

   A. One should certainly take care not to start smoking, and to take proper care in desisting. But should one conclude that it is forbidden as an activity dangerous to one's health? The answer is that because the multitude are accustomed to smoking, and the *Gemara* [part of the Talmud] in such a case invokes the principle that "the Eternal will protect the foolish" (*Shabbat* 129b and *Niddah* 31a, [reflecting Psalms 116:6]), and in particular since some of the greatest Torah scholars of present and past generations do or did smoke [there is no prohibition] (Moshe Feinstein, *Iggerot Moshe, Yoreh Deah* 2:49).

   B. One must avoid anything that may be injurious to one's well-being and do everything that maintains and strengthens good health . . . Since smoking has been proven, beyond any shadow of a doubt, to be injurious to health and dangerous to life, one should do one's utmost to avoid it. According to some authorities, smoking is (in light of present medical knowledge) an offense prohibited by the Torah. If, as a consequence of smoking, we become ill and are thereby prevented from studying Torah or performing *mitzvot*, we are not considered as those who are exempt because of extraneous circumstances which prevent them from doing so. On the contrary, we are judged as those who willfully desist from Torah study or from performing *mitzvot*.

One may not smoke in public places since cigarette smoke has been proven to be injurious also to those in the vicinity of the smoker who inhale it (Compilation of Rabbinic views by Abraham S. Abraham, adapted, *The Comprehensive Guide To Medical Halachah*. Jerusalem: Feldheim Publishers, 1996, p. 25).

Probing: Ideas and Issues

What are the main points in Rabbi Feinstein's position? What are the main points in Rabbi Abraham's position? Within the last few decades, the number of Jewish smokers has declined. Plus, the seriousness of smoking related health problems has become better established. In what way do these factors challenge Rabbi Feinstein's opinion? Do you believe smoking — since we know it harms the body — is equivalent to a violation of other *mitzvot*?

3. On Alcohol Consumption

A. When the wine goes in, intelligence takes its leave. Wherever there is wine, there is no intelligence. When the wine enters, the secret (*sod*) comes out; the numerical total of wine (*yayin*) is 70 and the total of *sod* (secret) is 70 (*Numbers Rabbah* 10:8).

B. A drunkard (*shikur*) who has become as drunk as Lot (*shikur k'Lot*) — his judgment is like that of an idiot . . . (*Shulchan Aruch, Yoreh Deah* 1:8).

C. If a [drunk person] (*shikur*) committed a transgression involving the penalty of death, that person is to be executed; and if [a drunk person] committed one involving flogging, that person is to be flogged . . . Rabbi Chanina said: This applies only to one who did not reach the stage of Lot's drunkenness, but one who did reach such a stage is exempt from all responsibilities (*Eruvin* 65a).

D. The benefits of wine are many if it is taken in the proper amount, as it keeps the body in a healthy condition and cures many illnesses.

But the knowledge of its consumption is hidden from the masses. What they want is to get drunk, and drunkenness causes harm . . .

The small amount that is useful must be taken after the food leaves the stomach. Young children should not come close to it because it hurts them and causes harm to their body and soul . . . (Maimonides, *The Preservation of Youth*).

E. Do not take drugs because they demand periodic doses and your heart will crave them. You will also lose money. Even for medicinal purposes, do not take drugs if you can find a different medicine that will help (Rashbam, Rabbi Samuel ben Meir, lived 1085-1158, commentary on *Pesachim* 113a).

Probing: Ideas and Issues

Suppose these texts were all the information you had about Jewish views on alcohol consumption. How then would you summarize the "Jewish position"? In what ways do the texts reflect a permissive viewpoint; in what ways a restrictive one? What are the "gray areas"?

In Text #C above how does Rabbi Chanina's position differ from the majority opinion? What are the pros and cons of abiding by Rabbi Chanina's position? How do modern opinions compare with those expressed in this text? What standard of responsibility should we impose for those who drink — fully responsible for their actions, somewhat responsible, not responsible at all? Explain.

What would Maimonides (Rambam) and Rashbam (Texts #D and E) say are the greatest dangers of alcohol consumption? Do you agree with them? What does Maimonides mean (in Text #D) when he says that alcohol hurts children, that it causes harm to their body *and soul*? Have you witnessed situations in which drugs or alcohol seemed to have harmed someone's "soul"? Explain.

4. **On Eating**

   A. Have you found honey? Eat so much as is sufficient for you, lest you be filled with it and vomit it (Proverbs 25:16).

   B. If a man would take care of his body as he takes care of the animal he rides on, he would be spared many serious ailments. For you will not find a man who would give too much hay to his animal, but he measures it according to its capacity. However, he himself will eat too much without measure and consideration. Man is very attentive to his animal's movement and fatigue in order that it should continue in a state of health and not get sick, but he is not attentive to his own body . . .

      We should eat only when justified by a feeling of hunger, when the stomach is clear and the mouth possesses sufficient saliva. Then we are really hungry. We must not drink water unless we are truly justified by thirst. This means that if we feel hungry or thirsty we should wait a little, as occasionally we are led to feel so by a deceptive hunger and deceptive thirst (Maimonides, *Mishneh Torah, Hilchot De'ot* 4).

   C. It is our duty to avoid whatever is injurious to the body; therefore food should not be taken to repletion. We should not be gluttons, but eat food conducive to health; and of such food we should not eat to excess; we should not be eager to fill our stomachs, like those who gorge themselves with food and drink until the body swells. Overeating is like a deadly poison to any constitution and is the principal cause of all diseases. Most maladies that afflict humankind result from bad food, or are due to the patient filling the stomach with an excess of foods even though these be (in themselves) wholesome" (Compilation of Rabbinic views by Abraham S. Abraham, adapted, *The Comprehensive Guide To Medical Halachah*. Jerusalem: Feldheim Publishers, 1996, p. 26).

Probing: Ideas and Issues

Drawing from these three texts, define the Jewish ideal in eating habits. In Text #B, what is the relevance of Maimonides talking about animal owners being attentive to their animals? On a scale from 1 to 10, how would you rate "being attentive" as an important factor in good eating habits? Explain. In our day we recognize that sometimes people lose control over their eating habits. They may be diagnosed with an eating disorder. How might a scholar like Maimonides respond to such a circumstance?

5. **When We're "In Over Our Heads"**

   A. "If you're in pain, go to a physician" (*Baba Kamma* 46b).

   B. Those who have become slaves to habit are no longer their own masters, and cannot act differently, even if they want to. Their will is held in bondage by certain habits which have become second nature to them (Moses Hayyim Luzzatto, *The Path of the Upright*, p. 122).

C. Select a teacher for yourself; acquire for yourself a friend. When you assess people, tip the balance in their favor (*Pirke Avot* 1:6).

D. Seeking forgiveness from others (*teshuvah*), turning to God (*tefilah*), and reaching out to others in need (*tzedakah*) temper judgment's severe decree (High Holy Day *Machzor*).

E. Those whose anger is strong and their wrath intense are not far from the demented. And those who are given to anger, their life is no life (*Pesachim* 113b).

F. You support all who are falling, lift up all who are bowed down . . . You are near to all who call upon You, to all who call upon You in earnest (Psalm 145:14, 18).

G. Though I walk through a valley of deepest darkness, I fear no harm, for You are with me, Your rod and Your staff — they comfort me (Psalm 23:4).

Probing: Ideas and Issues

From these texts we can infer suggestions to help us when we are in over our heads, including:

- getting professional care
- seeking advice from "a teacher" (i.e., someone insightful and knowledgeable)
- finding support through friendship (including "support groups")
- not judging people, including yourself, overly harshly
- forgiving and seeking forgiveness (for things that happened as the result of an addiction)

- turning to and trusting in God
- helping others (especially those who have problems with which you can identify)
- dealing with anger (and other confusing feelings that might be feeding an addiction)
- summoning courage
- having faith

Which text (or message) do you think is most important for a person coping with a harmful behavior to pay attention to? Why? What other advice would you add to the list above? What suggestions would you give to your best friend if he/she became overwhelmed by something going on in his/her life? Would you be prepared to *take* the same advice that you would give others? Explain.

RELATED MIDDOT AND MITZVOT

Practicing these virtues and commandments helps to cope with harmful behaviors in a manner informed by Jewish values:

Anavah (Humility): Admitting feelings of powerlessness over an addiction is a humbling, but necessary first step in our efforts to make changes.

Chochmah (Wisdom) We will make wiser decisions when we heed the insights of our Sages and the advice gleaned from contemporary experience.

Emunah (Trust, Faith): When we put our trust in God, our faith in ourselves grows.

Kabbalat HaYisurin (Acceptance of Suffering): Everyone encounters pain at times. In acknowledging this, we can learn to cope with our pain in healthy, compassionate ways.

Ma'akeh (Preventing Accidents): Accidents are more prone to happen when one uses alcohol or other drugs. These substances can impair judgment, decrease alertness, diminish coordination, plus lead to less self-control and fewer inhibitions.

Ometz Layv (Courage): If we find ourselves dependent on a harmful behavior, we will need courage to take the necessary steps to reverse the course our lives have taken.

Shmiat HaOzen (Attentiveness, Being a Good Listener): To make the healthiest choices, we must pay careful attention to the signals our bodies give us and listen closely to our feelings and thoughts. Listening deeply to others will alert us to when others may need help.

Shmirat HaGuf (Taking Care of Your Body): This includes avoiding abuse of dangerous substances and being mindful of eating behavior.

Simchah (Joy and Happiness): Nurturing joy and happiness helps displace the negativity that feeds self-destructive behaviors. Feelings of optimism, vibrancy, and well-being are nourishing for body and soul.

Teshuvah (Returning, Repentance, Making Amends): Restoring care for our bodies, healing relationships with others, and turning to God are ways of "returning" from the confusion and pain of addiction.

ACTIVITIES

A First Look: Key Issues and Ideas

1. This exercise is a good way to open a unit about harmful behaviors (and will help guide teachers on how to gear study of the topic). Older children and teens likely have many questions on smoking, drinking (plus use of other drugs), and eating disorders. Ask group members to write down any questions they have. Assure them that this is a private exercise and that no one else will know who wrote which question.

Suggestions of ways to use the questions: (1) simply read them, which allows students to know that they are not alone in their curiosity and concerns; (2) use the questions as a guide when lesson planning, making an effort to address what really is on students' minds; (3) Organize the questions and assign them (or a selection of them) to small groups who will do research and create responses. The small groups then share their findings with everyone else.

A further consideration: You may want to do this exercise more than once during study of this topic. New questions will arise once students learn more and begin to wrestle with confusing issues.

2. What does it mean to take care of your body? Brainstorm with your group as many ideas as you can, listing them on the board. When you have exhausted that task, continue by brainstorming another list, on dangers to avoid.

Then, have students work individually, writing down five or so things (from the generated lists) they believe most need their peer group's attention (e.g., getting car rides from friends who have been drinking). Discuss responses — perhaps first in pairs, and then with the whole group together. Are there one or two harmful behaviors that emerge as being of particular concern?

3. To understand the ramifications of harmful behaviors, students need a grasp of the concepts of "use," "abuse," and "addiction" (or "dependence"). Go over definitions of these terms as they relate to substance use and eating behaviors. (Refer to the Overview above, also the Glossary, pp. 99-100.)

Next, divide into small groups and assign each a category: Tobacco, Alcohol, or Eating. Each group composes an imaginary scenario in which a person gradually goes from use to dependence (or moderate eating behavior to eating disorders, i.e., "dependence" on harmful eating patterns). When everyone is ready, reconvene and have the small groups share what they came up with.

4. We may think that because we understand so much about certain dangerous behaviors, we will know how to avoid falling victim to them. This is not true. There is much we don't understand. It is as necessary to appreciate the elusiveness of addiction as it is to master "the facts." Besides helping students become better informed, it is equally important to reduce student arrogance (if it exists) and impress on them that we are more vulnerable than we may realize.

Make two charts. On the first chart, brainstorm with students "What We Know" about harmful behaviors. You may want to divide the task into sections for smoking, drinking, and over/undereating. Thus, under smoking your list might include: causes lung damage, very addictive, popular in certain social groups, harms health of bystanders (i.e., secondary smoke), etc.

On the second chart, list "What We Don't (Fully) Understand." For smoking this might include: why people smoke, why some get addicted, what makes an individual vulnerable to social pressures, why some people can quit and others don't seem able to, who will develop lung cancer (or other serious health consequence), why some people turn to substances (rather than something healthier) to cope with life's stresses, how the media/ads influence people, etc.

5. Invite experts to class to discuss harmful behaviors and to field questions. Have students prepare beforehand by coming up with issues they would like the guests to address. Possible experts to invite include: psychologists, other mental health professionals, medical doctors, nutritionists, teachers, school counselors, and/or clergy who work with individuals with addictions; law enforcement officers (to talk about alcohol and drugs).

Applying Middot and Mitzvot

1. Refer to the list of "Related *Middot* and *Mitzvot*" above. Ask participants to answer and explain their responses to the following questions:

   - Which *middah* or *mitzvah* do you feel is most important to cultivate in order to avoid falling prey to harmful behaviors?

   - Are there *middot* or *mitzvot* you would add to this list?

   - Are there any you would leave off?

   - Which *middah* or *mitzvah* would *you* most like to work on, that you believe will most help *you* to avoid harmful behaviors?

   - How would you go about working on the chosen *middah* or *mitzvah*?

2. Focusing on *Shmiat HaOzen* (Listening, Paying Attention), list all the things a person should pay attention to in order to avoid harmful behaviors (related to substance abuse and/or problematic eating habits). Examples (on eating): body signals of hunger, body signals of fullness, times I'm tempted to overeat, quantities I eat/size of portions, social influences (munching at parties, holiday gatherings), nutritional value of food, feelings about my body, etc.

3. There's a credo used by some of the "Anonymous" groups (i.e., Alcoholics Anonymous, Narcotics Anonymous, Overeaters Anonymous):

   "God, grant me the serenity to accept the things I cannot change,
   The courage to change the things I can,
   And the wisdom to know the difference" (Reinhold Neibuhr).

   Several *middot* clearly parallel this powerful prayer. The first line corresponds to *Kabbalat HaYisurin* (Acceptance of Suffering) and *Anavah* (Humility); the second line to

Ometz Layv (Courage), *Teshuvah* (Repentance), and *Shmirat HaGuf* (Taking Care of Your Body); and the third to *Chochmah* (Wisdom).

"Anonymous" groups are geared to those who suffer from addictions, thus the prayer above speaks poignantly to their struggles. Now consider this perspective: Which *middot* or *mitzvot* should a person most focus on *from the beginning* — when making initial decisions about harmful behaviors? Write a three (or so) line credo/prayer that speaks to one or more of the following challenges:

- Making choices about risky behaviors
- Handling stress
- Coping with peer pressure
- Experiencing low self-esteem
- Dealing with expectations and disappointments
- Caring for yourself — body, mind, and spirit
- Nurturing faith
- Getting help

4. Create an exhibit of inspirational posters appropriate for a school on avoiding harmful behaviors. Alternatively, make the display for a center that treats substance abuse or eating disorders. Have individuals (or pairs) choose one *middah* or *mitzvah* to focus on. Using words and/or artwork in their poster design, they are to communicate a message that comforts, motivates, instructs, and/or inspires well-being.

5. For more information and activities on:

Anavah (Humility): see *Teaching Jewish Virtues* by Susan Freeman, pp. 8-25.

Chochmah (Wisdom): see *The Jewish Moral Virtues* by Eugene B. Borowitz and Frances Weinman Schwartz, pp. 11-23.

Emunah (Trust, Faith): see *The Jewish Moral*

Virtues by Eugene B. Borowitz and Frances Weinman Schwartz, pp. 27-40.

Ma'akeh (Preventing Accidents): see *Teaching Mitzvot* by Barbara Binder Kadden and Bruce Kadden, pp. 205-208.

Ometz Layv (Courage): see *Teaching Jewish Virtues* by Susan Freeman, pp. 195-210.

Shmiat HaOzen (Attentiveness, Being a Good Listener): see *Teaching Jewish Virtues* by Susan Freeman, pp. 255-268.

Shmirat HaGuf (Taking Care of Your Body): see *Teaching Jewish Virtues* by Susan Freeman, pp. 269-282.

Simchah (Joy and Happiness): see *Teaching Jewish Virtues* by Susan Freeman, pp. 283-298.

Teshuvah (Returning, Repentance, Making Amends): see *The Jewish Moral Virtues* by Eugene B. Borowitz and Frances Weinman Schwartz, pp. 263-276.

Stories: Understanding through Listening

1. Read over the imaginary situations in the "Scenarios: How Things Have Changed" section above. Discuss these questions:

- What concerns did the Rabbi face in the first scenario?
- What concerns did the students face in the second scenario?
- How are the dangers faced by the two communities similar? how different?
- How did the Rabbi/students respond to their concerns?
- Were their responses appropriate? adequate?
- "Marauders" leave victims in their wake. Nowadays, professionals may refer to those struggling with alcoholism (or other drug addiction) or anorexia as being victims. Why do you think the word "victim" might be used in cases of

substance addiction or anorexia? To what extent can a person prevent him/herself from becoming a victim?

2. Many people have written books in which they tell their "stories" of addiction. For a large collection of personal stories about recovering from alcoholism, see *Alcoholics Anonymous*, published by Alcoholics Anonymous World Services, Inc.

   Concerning eating disorders, current thinking is that it might not be a good idea to have young people read such books if they don't already have a problem. These stories may give ideas about engaging in harmful eating behaviors they otherwise would not have considered. Consult with an experienced therapist before recommending young adult books, such as: *My Sister's Bones* by Cathi Hanauer or *Stick Figure: A Diary of My Former Self* by Lori Gottlieb.

3. If you know someone in your community who is open to speaking with your group about his/her personal struggles with a tobacco, alcohol, or drug addiction, invite him/her in. Hearing another's personal story can be a profound experience.

   Note that inviting people in to share personal stories regarding eating disorders is not recommended as a prevention practice (see explanation in previous activity).

4. In a group which has a genuine level of trust, share personal stories regarding experiments and struggles with harmful behaviors. Before facilitating any such conversations, the leader should touch base with a psychologist for guidance. Or better, ask a psychologist to be present and assist in facilitating the conversation.

Action: Getting Out, Getting Involved

1. Over the course of a couple of weeks, have students be on the lookout for TV/radio public service announcements and for print ads that alert people to the dangers of harmful behaviors (such as smoking). Select a time for everyone to report their findings to the rest of the group and evaluate the effectiveness of each of the findings. (The leader should be sure to bring in a selection of his/her own, as well.) Then have students create their own radio/TV or newspaper/magazine ads publicizing a particularly risky or harmful behavior. If you have students create newspaper/magazine type ads, you may wish to display them on a wall, either in your own institution or in another appropriate venue.

   (A good resource for examples of anti-tobacco advertising: "Clearing the Smoke" by Ann Cooper in *Print: America's Graphic Design Magazine*, May/June 2001, p. 74, www.print-mag.com.)

2. Have the group research sources of help that are available in your area for people struggling with a substance addiction or eating disorder. Work together to compile information into a flyer that participants can hand out, display, and post in appropriate places. The flyer might include phone numbers of crisis hot lines, times and locations of "Anonymous" group meetings, helpful web sites, hospital and treatment centers, etc.

3. Work with students to organize a display that gathers together books and other resources for coping with harmful behaviors. Include brochures and other literature from various help organizations. The exhibited books should include reviews written by students (meaning they will have to select books, read them, and write up their thoughts as part of preparation for the display). Mount the book reviews so that they are displayed alongside the corresponding books.

4. Have members of the group (or the group as a whole) compose a letter to the editor or write an op-ed piece about what they feel most concerned about regarding smoking, drinking, poor eating habits, or other harmful behavior. The letter can be addressed to a school or college newspaper, town paper, or

synagogue newsletter. A variation: Direct the letter to one or more government officials.

5. Research and get involved in an action organization that works on a problem related to harmful behaviors, such as M.A.D.D. (Mothers Against Drunk Driving), S.A.D.D. (Students Against Drunk Driving), your local chapter of a Tobacco-Free Coalition, a lung cancer organization, etc.

6. Start a committee that includes students and possibly parents, teachers, and other community members to work on lively alternatives to Saturday night "partying" (i.e., drinking and drugs). The activities may include taking risks and engaging in challenges, but will avoid "harmful behaviors." For example, organize night gatherings at the health club (perhaps with wall climbing instruction/competition), night hikes/cross country ski adventures, mock casinos, etc.

Wrestling: Engagement with the Issues

1. Do role-playing improvisations or invent skits that develop some of the suggestions below.

   • A parent discovers a bottle of vodka under the bed of his/her teenage child.

   • While doing the laundry, a parent discovers cigarettes in the pocket of his/her child's jeans.

   • A student notices that a friend eats huge amounts at the cafeteria each day at lunch. Afterward, the friend hurries to the bathroom. The student strongly suspects the friend is regularly purging (vomiting) the food he/she has just consumed.

   • The older brother of a student you know buys alcohol for a group of underage teens. On a couple of occasions recently, you have seen these teens driving around town, obviously while under the influence of alcohol.

   • Your parents smoke and you can't stand it. You think it's dangerous and disgusting.

   • A friend has been gaining weight and seems very unhappy about it. He/she always tries to engage you in talk about diets and how ugly he/she feels, etc. You are really getting tired of this, yet you see what bad eating habits your friend has (eating overly large portions, eating lots of junk food, barely exercising, etc.).

   • A person loves and cares about someone else who drinks too much (or uses drugs).

   • People ignore the rule that prohibits smoking in the place where you work, including your boss.

   • At the playground, you come across two kids who you don't know, but who seem to be about nine years old, smoking.

   • Your school has planned a hot dog eating contest — i.e., whoever eats the most hot dogs within the given amount of time, wins a prize. You think the message this contest gives is really distorted — that deliberate gorging is a fun and humorous activity. But you also worry about being a spoil sport.

   • A doctor must explain to a patient that his/her lifestyle habits are life threatening.

   • Also see suggestions in "Empathy," activity #1 below.

   • Your own ideas!

   Allow time for participants to process this experience: how they felt about themselves while acting out their roles; how they felt about the other person/people; how their feelings changed during the role play (before, during, and after); what they learned.

2. A variation on the above activity: Have students choose a scenario to write about.

3. Have participants think about stressful situations and other times in which they feel

unhappy in one way or another. For example:

- Getting a poor grade or work evaluation

- Not being invited to something that most of your friends are

- Being excluded (in another way)

- Fighting with family members

- Being betrayed by a friend

- Having someone close to you get in serious trouble

- Losing something important

- Ending a romance

- Being disappointed about _____

- Having an accident

- Feeling jealous

- Feeling ugly

- Your own ideas

Next, give everyone an oversized piece of paper to use. Have them turn it on its side so that there is plenty of room to include three lists. In a column format, have them put these headings: 1. Stressful Situations; 2. Worst Responses; 3. Healthier Responses.

For each situation on their list, have participants first write down what might be their worst response to the situation (e.g., eat a bag of cookies, shout curses at anyone in the vicinity, smoke a cigarette, etc.). Next, have them put down what would be healthier responses (e.g., call and talk to a friend, go for a run, take a bath, go rent a funny movie, etc.).

3. Bring in a stack of popular magazines. Have participants go through them and cut out any and all images which in some way promote or condone harmful behaviors. As a group, decide which material is the most offensive. Discuss reasons why.

To extend this activity, write to the com-

panies or organizations responsible for the images and explain your thoughts to them (and why in the future you will not purchase their magazine or buy their product, etc.).

4. Create a collage which visually captures the complexity of harmful behaviors. Here are some words, phrases, and images to help trigger your own ideas:

"Take exceeding care of yourselves," avoid danger, cigarettes, alcohol, food that nourishes, food that harms, pain, confusion, media images, peer pressure, low self-esteem, abuse, addiction, dependence, risk, control/out of control, anger, listening, paying attention, ignoring negative "voices," surrender, making changes, seeking help, reaching out to others, turning to God.

Empathy

1. Have group members develop the details and role-play one of the following scenarios:

- A friend is hospitalized for anorexia — his/her weight has dipped to a dangerously low level. You go to visit.

- A friend is hospitalized as the result of a drunk driving accident. You go to visit.

- A friend is hospitalized, having had his/her stomach pumped because of a drug overdose. You go to visit.

- A friend has been jailed for a crime committed during an episode of drunkenness. You go to visit.

After engaging in the role-plays, allow plenty of time for processing what happened: i.e., how participants felt about themselves while acting out their roles; how they felt about the other person/people; how their feelings changed during the role play (before, during, and after); what they learned.

2. Everyone faces times in their lives when, for one reason or another, they don't feel good about themselves. Poor self-esteem, personal

problems, feelings of spiritual emptiness all may contribute to these low times. Write a prayer for yourself — something you can turn to and reflect on during difficult moments.

A variation: Write a prayer appropriate for a person to recite who has "hit bottom" in terms of an addiction. Imagine the prayer providing comfort and/or motivation for someone who has entered a treatment facility (even perhaps against his/her will).

You may want to weave in words from traditional Jewish sources, such as from Psalm 23 or 145. Also, these two prayers may help trigger your own writing ideas:

At a time of anxiety:

Eternal God, You abide though all things change. I am anxious and fearful, and I turn my heart to You, looking to You and leaning on Your strength.

It is written [Psalm 84:5], Blessed is the one whose strength is in You. Bless me now with faith and courage. Help me to feel that You are with me, steadying and sustaining me with the assurance that I am loved. Be with me and bring me hope, that in the days to come, my aspirations may be fulfilled for my good and the good of those I love and who depend on me. Banish my fears with the sense that you are always present, to uphold and sustain me, as it is written [Isaiah 41:10]: Have no fear, for I am with you; be not dismayed, for I am your God. I will strengthen you, I will help you, I will uphold you with the power of My righteousness. Amen.

When our burdens seem too heavy:

I come to You, O God, for Your gracious help. You dwell within my heart, You feel my distress, You know my pain, and how burdened I am. Give me strength to bear my burdens with courage, wisdom, and grace. Help me to be true to my better self, to discern my real work in life, and to do it with all my might. When I struggle within my own heart, stay by my side. Then I shall be able to say with Your prophet [Isaiah 40:31]: But those who hold fast to the Eternal shall renew their strength; they shall mount up with wings as eagles; they shall run and not be weary; they shall walk, and not faint.

May my work, and the ties that bind me to family and friends, make life rich in meaning for me, so that each day I live may be yet another step leading me nearer to You. Amen (*On the Doorposts of Your House*, p. 146-147).

GLOSSARY

The definitions below are adapted from the 1994 Fourth Edition of the American Psychiatric Association's *Diagnostic and Statistical Manual of Mental Disorders.*

Anorexia Nervosa:

A. Refusal to maintain body weight at or above a minimally normal weight for age and height (e.g., weight loss leading to maintenance of body weight less than 85 percent of that expected, or failure to make expected weight gain during a period of growth, leading to body weight less than 85 percent of that expected.).

B. Intense fear of gaining weight or becoming fat, even though underweight.

C. Disturbance in the way in which one's body weight or shape is experienced, undue influence of body weight or shape on self-evaluation, or denial of the seriousness of the current low body weight.

D. In postmenarcheal females, amenorrhea; i.e., the absence of at least three consecutive menstrual cycles.

Bulimia Nervosa:

A. Recurrent episodes of binge eating. An episode of binge eating is characterized by both of the following:

(1) eating, in a discrete period of time (e.g., within any two-hour period), an amount of food that is definitely larger than most people would eat during a similar period of time and under similar circumstances

(2) a sense of lack of control over eating during the episode (e.g., a feeling that one cannot stop eating or control what or how much one is eating)

B. Recurrent inappropriate compensatory behavior in order to prevent weight gain, such as self-induced vomiting; misuse of laxatives, diuretics, enemas, or other medications; fasting; or excessive exercise.

C. The binge eating and inappropriate compensatory behaviors both occur, on average, at least twice a week for three months.

D. Self-evaluation is unduly influenced by body shape and weight.

E. The disturbance does not occur exclusively during episodes of Anorexia Nervosa.

Substance Abuse:

An abnormal pattern of recurring use that leads to significant impairment or distress marked by one or more of the following in a 12-month period:

• Failure to fulfill major obligations at home, school, or work (for example, repeated absences, poor performance, or neglect).

• Use in hazardous or potentially hazardous situations, such as driving a car or operating a machine while impaired.

• Legal problems, such as arrest for disorderly conduct while under the influence of the substance.

• Continued use in spite of social or interpersonal problems caused by the use of the substance, such as fights or family arguments.

Substance Dependence (Addiction):

Present when three or more of the following occur in a 12-month period:

• Increasing need for more of the substance to achieve the desired effect (tolerance), or a reduction in effect when using the same amount as previously.

- Withdrawal symptoms if the use of the substance is stopped or reduced.

- Progressive neglect of other pleasures and duties.

- A strong desire to take the substance or a persistent but unsuccessful desire to control or reduce the use of the substance.

- Continued use in spite of physical or mental health problems caused by the substance.

- Use of the substance in larger amounts or over longer periods of time than originally intended or difficulties in controlling the amount of the substance used or when to stop taking it.

- A lot of time spent in obtaining the substance, using it, or recovering from its effects.

BIBLIOGRAPHY

Jewish Sources

Abraham, Abraham S. *The Comprehensive Guide To Medical Halachah*. Jerusalem: Feldheim Publishers, 1996.

Berg, Steven L., comp. *Jewish Alcoholism and Drug Addiction: An Annotated Bibliography*. Westport, CT: Greenwood Press, 1993.

Borowitz, Eugene B., and Frances Weinman Schwartz. *The Jewish Moral Virtues*. Philadelphia, PA: The Jewish Publication Society, 1999.

Brazen, Judith, and Susan Freeman. "Intervening in the Life of an Alcoholic" (1989). In *Reform Jewish Ethics and the Halakhah*, edited by Eugene B. Borowitz. Springfield, NJ: Behrman House, Inc., 1994, pp. 79-95.

Dorff, Elliot N. "Preventing Illness." In *Matters of Life and Death: A Jewish Approach to Modern Medical Ethics*. Philadelphia, PA: The Jewish Publication Society, 1998, pp. 245-254.

Freeman, Susan. *Teaching Jewish Virtues: Sacred Sources and Arts Activities*. Denver, CO: A.R.E. Publishing, Inc., 1999.

Goldwasser, Dovid. *Starving to Live: An Inspirational Guide To Eating Disorders*. New York: Judaica Press, 2000.

Herring, Basil F. "Smoking and Drugs." In *Jewish Ethics and Halakhah for Our Time: Sources and Commentary*, Volume I. Hoboken, NJ: KTAV Publishing House, Inc. and New York: Yeshiva University Press, 1984, pp. 221-243.

Kadden, Barbara Binder and Bruce Kadden. *Teaching Mitzvot: Concepts, Values, and Activities*. Rev. ed. Denver, CO: A.R.E. Publishing, Inc., 2003.

Luzzatto, Moses Hayyim. *The Path of the Upright*. Translated by Mordecai M. Kaplan. Philadelphia, PA: Jewish Publication Society, 1936.

Olitzky, Kerry M., and Stuart A. Copans. *Twelve Jewish Steps to Recovery: A Personal Guide To Turning from Alcholoism and Other Addictions*.

Woodstock, VT: Jewish Lights Publishing, 1991.

Rosner, Fred. "Cigarette and Marijuana Smoking." In *Modern Medicine and Jewish Ethics*. Hoboken, NJ: KTAV Publishing House, Inc. and New York: Yeshiva University Press, 1991, pp. 391-403.

Ross, Allen, and Stuart Copans. "A Jewish Way of Eating." In *Where We Stand: Jewish Consciousness on Campus*. Edited by Allan L. Smith. New York: UAHC Press, 1997.

Sherwin, Byron L., and Seymour J. Cohen. *Creating an Ethical Jewish Life*. Woodstock, VT: Jewish Lights Publishing, 2001.

Stern, Chaim, ed. *On the Doorposts of Your House: Prayers and Ceremonies for the Jewish Home*. New York: Central Conference of American Rabbis, 1994.

Zemer, Moshe. *Evolving Halachah: A Progressive Approach To Traditional Jewish Law*. Woodstock, VT: Jewish Lights Publishing, 1999, p. 345-350.

On Smoking

Books and Articles:

Note: Also see relevant books under "Jewish Sources" above.

Boston Women's Health Collective. *The New Our Bodies Ourselves*. New York: Simon & Schuster, 1992.

Quiram, Jacquelyn, et al, eds. *Alcohol and Tobacco: America's Drugs of Choice*. Wylie, TX: Information Plus, 1999.

Krogh, David. *Smoking: The Artificial Passion*. NY: W.H. Freeman and Company, 1991.

Web Sites:

Antismoking Master Support Site: www.mind-connection.com/interests/antismoking.htm

    "A page for those who want to put an end to the

destruction smoking wreaks on our loved ones and on ourselves."

Films:

The Insider (1999, rated R, 158 minutes)

True story of tobacco executive-turned-whistleblower Jeffrey Wigand and his relationship with "60 Minutes" producer Lowell Bergman.

Secrets Through the Smoke (2001, 55 minutes)

Documentary featuring former tobacco scientist Jeffrey Wigand (protagonist in *The Insider*) talking to teens about smoking. It also has skits, people talking about their smoking problems, and several non-smoking advertisements that have been on television.

The Teen Files: "Smoking: Truth or Dare" (1998, 52 minutes)

Obtain purchase information from www.aimsmultimedia.com.

On Alcohol

Books and Articles:

Note: Also see relevant books under "Jewish Sources" above.

Alcoholics Anonymous: The Story of How Many Thousands of Men and Women Have Recovered from Alcoholism. New York: Alcoholics Anonymous World Services, Inc. 1976.

Berg, Steven L., comp. *Jewish Alcoholism and Drug Addiction: An Annotated Bibliography.* Westport, CT: Greenwood Press, 1993.

Boston Women's Health Collective. *The New Our Bodies Ourselves.* New York: Simon & Schuster, 1992.

Quiram, Jacquelyn, et al, eds. *Alcohol and Tobacco: America's Drugs of Choice.* Wylie, TX: Information Plus, 1999.

Vaillant, George E. *The Natural History of*

Alcoholism, Revisited. Cambridge, MA: Harvard University Press, 1995.

Varley, Chris. *Life Issues: Alcoholism.* New York: Marshall Cavendish, 1994.

Web Sites

Dream Inc. (Developing Resources for Education in America, Inc.): www.dreaminc.org

A source for materials and information to aid in the fight against drug and alcohol abuse.

Jewish Alcoholics, Chemically Dependent Persons and Significant Others: www.jacsweb.org

This site gives information about retreats and programs, and also has a helpful bibliography of support materials, including ones with Jewish spiritual guidance.

Mothers Against Drunk Driving (M.A.D.D.): www.madd.org

MADD's mission is to stop drunk driving, support the victims of this violent crime, and prevent underage drinking.

The National Clearinghouse for Alcohol and Drug Information: www.health.org

An information resource run by the Substance Abuse & Mental Health Services Administration, an agency of the U.S. Department of Health and Human Services.

National Council on Alcoholism and Drug Dependence: www.ncadd.org

The NCADD fights the stigma and the disease of alcoholism and other drug addictions.

Students Against Destructive Decisions (also known as Students Against Driving Drunk and S.A.D.D.): www.saddonline.com

S.A.D.D. is a peer leadership organization dedicated to preventing destructive decisions, particularly underage drinking, other drug use, impaired driving, teen violence, and teen depression and suicide.

Films:

Bright Lights, Big City (1988, 110 minutes, rated R)

>A young man from Kansas moves to New York to work on a magazine and gets caught up in a world of drinking and drugs.

Days of Wine and Roses (1962, 117 minutes, unrated)

>An absorbing, frightening study of the insidiousness of alcohol addiction.

My Name Is Bill W. (1989, 100 minutes, unrated)

>Based on the true story of a successful stock broker who must come to grips with his alcoholism. He forms a support group that would evolve into Alcoholics Anonymous.

Shattered Spirits (1986, 93 minutes, rated PG-13)

>A dedicated middle-class family man has his life shattered by his uncontrolled drinking.

The Teen Files: "The Truth about Drinking" (1998, 30 minutes)

>Obtain purchase information from www.aimsmultimedia.com

On Eating Issues

Books and Articles:

Note: Also see relevant books under "Jewish Sources" above.

Boskind-White, Marlene, and William C. White. *Bulimia/Anorexia: The Binge/Purge Cycle and Self-Starvation.* New York: W.W. Norton & Company, 2000. (Includes excellent bibliography)

Boston Women's Health Collective. *The New Our Bodies Ourselves.* New York: Simon & Schuster, 1992.

Christian, Sandy Stewart. *Working with Groups to Explore Food and Body Connections.* Duluth, MN: Whole Person Associates, 1996.

Claude-Pierre, Peggy. *The Secret Language of Eating Disorders.* New York: Random House, 1997.

Cooke, Kaz. *Real Gorgeous: The Truth about Body and Beauty.* New York: W.W. Norton and Co., 1996.

Friedman, Sandra Susan. *When Girls Feel Fat: Helping Girls through Adolescence.* New York: Firefly Books, 2000. (Includes excellent bibliography)

Fumento, Michael. *The Fat of the Land: The Obesity Epidemic and How Overweight Americans Can Help Themselves.* New York: Penguin Putnam Inc., 1997.

Hall, Lindsey, and Leigh Cohn. *Anorexia Nervosa: A Guide To Recovery.* Carlsbad, CA: Gurze Books, 1998.

————. *Bulimia: A Guide To Recovery.* Rev. ed. Carlsbad, CA: Gurze Books, 1999.

————. *Self-Esteem: Tools for Recovery.* Rev. ed. Carlsbad, CA: Gurze Books, 1990.

Hutchinson, Marcia Germaine, ed. *Transforming Body Image: Learning to Love the Body You Have.* Freedom, CA: Crossing Press, 1985.

Roth, Geneen. *Why Weight: A Guide to Ending Compulsive Eating.* New York: Plume, 1989.

Schwartz, Rosie. *The Enlightened Eater: A Guide To Well-Being through Eating.* Toronto, Canada: Macmillan, 1998.

Web Sites:

Anorexia Nervosa and Related Disorders: www.anred.com

>*Explains the science of the disease and describes various eating disorders, their causes, and sources for treatment.*

Begin from Within: www.jrcs.org/bfw.heml

>*Workshops and therapy groups in Northern California.*

Gurze Books: www.gurze.com

>*Eating disorders resources and links to other sites.*

InnerSolutions: www.innersolutions.net

Loving, non-diet approach to healing, food, weight, and body-image issues.

Mirror-Mirror: www.mirror-mirror.org

Information to help individuals along the way to recovery.

National Association of Anorexia Nervosa and Associated Disorders: www.altrue.net/site/anadweb/

Provides counsel to eating disorder sufferers and their families, and referrals to specialists.

National Eating Disorders Association: www.nationaleatingdisorders.org

A prevention and advocacy organization providing information, sponsoring school programs, and offering a referral page for local eating disorder specialists.

Something Fishy: www.something-fishy.com

Huge web site with resources for eating disorders.

Films:

The Teen Files: "The Truth about Body Image" (2001, 21 minutes)

Obtain purchase information from www.aimsmultimedia.com

Full (2001)

A Canadian short film exploring a young man's eating disorders. Difficult to find.

The Karen Carpenter Story: A CBS TV Movie (1988, 97 minutes)

Story of the meteoric rise and sudden fall of Karen Carpenter, who became a famous singer while battling anorexia and bulimia.

Nova: Dying to Be Thin (2000)

A powerful PBS documentary on eating disorders. Each of the eight short episodes are available for viewing online at www.pbs.org/wgbh/nova/thin/program.html

CHAPTER 5

ETHICS OF BUSINESS

OVERVIEW

In business interactions, we face constant temptations to taint honesty and integrity. "If I cheat just a little bit, no one will know, no one will really suffer much . . . " "I could encourage this millionaire seeking my advice to invest in such-and-such company. What does it matter if I don't mention how her investment will benefit me personally . . . " "I don't have to tell this customer that the gold in the ring he plans to purchase from me is mixed with another metal. It looks genuine enough . . . " Even if no such thoughts have passed through *our own minds*, we can imagine how they might.

The various players in business transactions each bring to the table different needs and goals. For instance, the merchant wants to sell at the *highest* price possible; the buyer wants to purchase at the *lowest* price possible. Because of competing needs and goals, everyone involved in business transactions needs protections: employers and employees, merchants and customers, business owners and their neighbors, developers and community members.

While people should be able to run their businesses in ways they believe are most effective, there need to be safeguards against exploitation. Moral principles must guide business practices. The goal of business ethics is to ensure that no one is cheated, misled, taken advantage of, or otherwise treated unfairly.

Jewish Perspectives

The Talmud says that the first thing a person is asked in the world to come is, "Have you been honest in business?" (*Shabbat* 31b). Clearly, Judaism regards honorable business practice with high esteem. The Ten Commandments teach us not to steal and not to covet. The biblical "holiness code" enumerates ways to live in a sanctified manner. It includes warnings against dealing deceitfully or falsely with one another (Leviticus 19:11, 36 and 25:17) and oppressing others (Leviticus 19:13). One manifestation of these warnings is the command to be scrupulous in maintaining honest weights and measures (Leviticus 19:25). These principles underlie many of the intricate rules and regulations for monitoring business practices.

In our day, when making business decisions, we might ask ourselves these two questions: "What am I *legally* allowed to do?" and, "What is the *right* thing to do?" From a Jewish perspective, these two questions are not separated. What is *legal* and what is *right* go hand in hand. If what we're about to do is not moral — that is, if our intentions are not respectful, honorable, and dignified — then, what we're about to do is not legal, not allowed.

How do we balance the competing needs and goals of the various players in business transactions? This question is key to creating and imposing fair guidelines. A pious person will strive hard to keep in mind the highest values for righteous living: For example, treating others with dignity, loving one's neighbor as oneself, being just and merciful, and living humbly. While such values are laudable, more specifics are necessary. Jewish sources instruct us — extensive commentary included — not to rob, steal, exploit, deceive, misrepresent, coerce, conceal the truth, or in any other way intentionally put others at an unfair disadvantage.

We can place Jewish business concerns into subcategories. The remainder of the "Jewish Perspectives" section will address each of these:

G'nayvah (thievery), *G'zaylah* (robbery), *Ona'ah* (exploitation), *Ona'at Devarim* (verbal exploitation), *G'nayvat Da'at* ("stealing another's mind" or deception), *Lifnay Evare* (Not putting a stumbling block in the path of the blind), neighbors and others in the community, employer-employee relations, and *Dina d'Malchuta Dina* ("The law of the land is the law").

G'nayvah (Thievery): Stealing from others in secret, without their knowledge. Blatant examples of thievery include shoplifting, hot-wiring a car, pickpocketing, or using another's credit card number to acquire goods. Kidnapping falls into this category, as well. In addition, Judaism goes further, condemning more subtle ways of stealing. The Bible puts forth the law requiring that scales be set accurately (Leviticus 19:25, 36). A merchant who uses an imprecise weight — such as one that says "one pound," but is really a bit less than a pound — steals from the customer. Merchants are not to *own* inaccurate weights and measures, even if they have no intention of using them in business (Deuteronomy 25:13). Presumably the temptation to cheat the customer will be too much. Or, perhaps the deficient weights and measures might get into the wrong hands. In any case, customers should get exactly what they are paying for.

Nowadays, in Western countries, fewer individuals attend stalls in marketplaces and regularly use weights and measures. In a parallel venue, only a segment of the population works in the modern supermarket business where there is a need to maintain accurate scales, likely electronic ones. Still, we must attend to the issue of *G'nayvah* as its concerns go beyond weighing peaches or cucumbers. Tax evasion is one example. Another is padding one's expense account, such as ordering room service "extras" (like a sweatshirt with the hotel logo) when lodging in a hotel on the company's dollar. A third example is private use of employers' materials or facilities, such as using the company photocopier to make flyers advertising the used car you want to sell. Both shortchanging clients and cutting corners count as stealing from others in secret.[1]

G'zaylah (Robbery): Taking from others through force, coercion, or deceit. Using physical force to take something is a concrete example of *G'zaylah.* Exploiting a worker and denying the discovery of a lost article are *G'zaylah,* too. Abusing one's position, misusing power, or misapplying strength are all kinds of robbery.

Seven *mitzvot,* two positive and five negative, form the basis for prohibitions related to *G'zaylah.* These are to return the robbed article (Leviticus 19:23), to return a lost article (Leviticus 22:1), not to rob (Leviticus 19:13), not to oppress (Leviticus 19:13), not to covet (Exodus 20:14), not to desire (Deuteronomy 5:18), not to ignore the lost article (Leviticus 22:3).[2]

Ona'ah (Exploitation, overreaching): The origin of these laws is from the Bible: "When you sell property to your fellow, or buy any from your fellow . . . you shall not wrong (*lo tonu*) one another, but shall hold God in awe, for I am the Eternal Your God" (Leviticus 25:14, 17).[3]

In practical terms, we are not to wrong others by withholding important information. In particular, merchants may not sell items for more than their real worth. Overcharging by 1/6th is the marker above which *Ona'ah* is said to occur. Conversely, a buyer is not to purchase items for less than their real worth.

Ona'at Devarim (Verbal exploitation): Responsible business practice includes the avoidance of needless mental anguish to others. The Mishnah gives the example of a customer who asks the price of an object although he/she has no intention of buying the item. Here, the vendor is "exploited" because his/her hopes have been falsely raised in expectation of a sale (*Baba Metzia* 4:12).

---

[1]Meir Tamari mentions these categories of *G'nayvah* in his book *In the Marketplace,* 46.

[2]Tamari, 48-49.

[3]*"Tonu"* is a verbal form of the noun *"ona'ah."* Add the word *"lo"* to make the phrase negative — that is, *"lo tonu"* means "do *not* exploit."

G'nayvat Da'at (Stealing another's mind; misrepresenting or concealing the truth that puts another person at a disadvantage): We are forbidden to give any impression that we are acting to benefit others when such benefits are either absent or unintended. The generally accepted basis for this category of law is the biblical verse: "You shall not steal; you shall not deal deceitfully or falsely with one another" (Leviticus 19:11).

Over the centuries, Rabbis debated the nuances of prohibitions in this category. Maimonides says "*G'nayvat Da'at* includes flattery, any inconsistencies between what we say and what we're really thinking, and all manner of verbal deception. A person should always cherish truthful speech, an upright spirit, and a pure heart freed of all pretense and cunning" (*Mishneh Torah, Hilchot De'ot* 2:6, see Text Study #3d below).

How does *G'nayvat Da'at* apply in practical terms? What follows are traditional sources describing *G'nayvat Da'at*. We also look at how the underlying ideas might apply to contemporary circumstances.

There's the case of knowingly giving the wrong impression, but making no attempt to clear things up. An example from the Talmud (*Chullin* 94a): Samuel rebuked Shemaya for misleading a ferryman. What Shemaya did is pay the ferryman with a non-kosher chicken that the ferryman may have presumed to be kosher. Another opinion says Shemaya paid the ferryman with diluted wine (though doing so followed common practice, the ferryman may have thought the wine was undiluted). In today's market we can imagine a high-end store that sells designer shoes. The shop owner shows the customer a pair of black shoes made of synthetic materials. The shop owner suspects that the customer reasonably assumes the shoes are made of leather (rather than a synthetic substitute). Even so, the shop owner does not try to clarify the true quality of the item being sold.

What about luring customers into a shop using special treats and gifts? Rabbi Judah in the Mishnah says shopkeepers should not distribute parched corn or nuts (considered a "treat" in those days) to children. Such a practice would accustom the children to going to that particular shopkeeper. The Sages, however, allow the practice (*Baba Metzia* 60a; see Text Study #3A below). Luring potential buyers with treats and gifts is also a common business practice today. A parallel to the corn and nut ploy is offering prizes in cereal boxes. Manufacturers may stuff a small, cheap toy into the bottom of a sweet cereal box to manipulate children into begging their parents to purchase the product. Or, a bank franchise may offer a small gift, such as an electric coffee maker, to lure adult customers to open an account.

While the Sages did permit "bonus enticements," Rabbi Judah, and likely others, expressed discomfort about this practice. In the cereal box ploy, the buyer indeed receives the promised prize. But in gray areas of bonus enticements, perhaps the Sages would have adopted a more restrictive position. A more questionable lure is the promise of "a *chance* to win a prize." Children and others may be enticed into buying a product in the hopes that they will win a grand reward. Doubtfully, children (and some adults) fully understand the statistical improbability that they will ever win. The product pushers falsely raise hopes. We can reasonably suspect the sellers have (intentionally) misled.

Another example of *G'nayvat Da'at* is hiding the true quality of the merchandise. Put another way, you put the good stuff on top, hoping no one will notice the inferior quality of what is beneath or mixed in. An example is mixing fruits and vegetables so as to disguise the true condition of some of them. Other ploys involve repackaging meat that has exceeded its sell-by date and putting a layer of beans that have had the refuse sifted from them on the top of the barrel, thus hiding the mixed-quality beans that lay beneath (*Baba Metzia* 60a; see Text Study #2B below). An unethical caterer might mix inferior liquor into the bottle of an expensive brand, giving the mistaken impression that each drink poured is of a superior quality, and subsequently charge an inflated price.

A related subject is distorting the quality of merchandise by falsely "puffing up" its appearance or quality. In ancient days, the practice of feeding a certain type of bran broth to cows was forbidden. Doing so would cause the animal to become bloated, giving the appearance of "stiffness" (*Baba Metzia* 60b). Presumably, the animal would seem more sturdy and hearty than it actually was. A parallel from our day might be selling used cars. An unethical salesperson could paint and clean an old car, making it look appealing on the outside, but hide from the untrained eye the deteriorated inner mechanisms of the car. The Sages make a distinction between distorting an item's quality and simply sprucing the item up. Thus, a merchant can paint a new basket to make it look more appealing to buyers, but cannot paint a worn basket so as to make it *seem* new. Sprucing up new items is acceptable, but enhancing old items in order to pass them off as new is forbidden (*Baba Metzia* 60b; see Text Study #2A below).

But the prohibitions against deception do not end here. In the Talmud Rabbi Meir gives more encompassing examples of *G'nayvat Da'at* (*Chullin* 94a). One example is repeatedly inviting a guest knowing that the guest will not accept. Another is offering a gift knowing it will not be accepted. A third is opening a large container of food for a guest giving the mistaken impression that whatever is left will be uneaten and result in significant financial loss. Undoubtedly, the category of *G'nayvat Da'at* safeguards against a broad range of dishonest practices — in which true intentions are in any way falsified or distorted.

Lifnay Evare (Not putting a stumbling block in the path of the blind) (Leviticus 25:36). Applied to business, one party is "blind" to the full consequences of a transaction or to another's deceitful motivations. Selling weapons to known criminals is an example. Selling stolen goods to an unsuspecting buyer is another. The unsuspecting buyer unwittingly participates in an immoral enterprise. Today, some might argue that we should denounce as "putting a stumbling block in the path of the blind" anyone selling guns, cigarettes, or pornography.

Additionally, prohibitions in the category of *Lifnay Evare* include giving misleading advice or not disclosing a conflict of interest. As Rashi writes, "One must not tell another to sell a donkey and buy a field when one wishes to buy a donkey and sell a field."[4] In our day, financial consultants advise clients to invest money in particular companies. However, if a consultant does not disclose the fact that he/she has a major interest in a recommended company, he/she transgresses by way of *Lifnay Evare*.

Neighbors and Others in the Community: Thus far, we have focused our exploration of business ethics primarily on the relationship between merchants and customers. The broader community also needs protections. Protecting neighbors from pollution, from the noises and smells of businesses, has been a concern since the Mishnah (*Baba Batra* 2:3). On the other hand, just as neighbors need safeguards against invasive business practices, so, too, do businesses need protections. Business people are entitled to make a living, though restrictions may exist if they want to do so in a residential area.

The case of artisans reflects the effort to balance the needs and goals of businesses and their neighbors. The Mishnah says artisans can make their wares at home, but they are to go out to the marketplace to sell. Therefore, artisans can expect their neighbors to endure a certain amount of commotion due to their crafting goods for sale. Yet, the neighbors don't have to put up with the noise of customers entering and leaving their courtyard day and night. Still, not all businesses are treated the same — schools for example. When schools are in residential areas, the neighbors are to tolerate the extra noise, dirt, and general commotion in the name of Torah study.

---

[4] As quoted by Meir Tamari, 100.

Should the market allow everyone to enter freely? How should communities uphold fair competition? These concerns affect all members of a community. In some towns, local merchants used to have to shoulder the expense of a license to run a business. They also had to contribute to local taxes. Fair competition regulations were necessary. Otherwise, merchants that came in from the outside, who didn't carry certain local financial burdens, would have an unfair advantage.

In our own day, communities often must contend with developers. If someone wants to open a shopping mall or "big box" store, what restrictions need apply? What "costs" can developers expect the neighborhood to tolerate? Considerations of traffic, use of water and other utilities, increased pollution, and competition with other businesses are just a few of the pertinent factors to negotiate. Often local businesses do not have the means to compete with nationally financed businesses. The mega-businesses may be in a financial position to weather temporary losses until the local competition disappears. Thus, local businesses may find themselves in an unequal position to compete. Just how "free" can the "free market" be before becoming the unfair market?

Employer-Employee Relations: Though this chapter touches on only a few pertinent topics in this vast realm of business ethics, this category merits extensive attention. One emphasis in traditional Jewish sources is employers' obligations to employees in paying wages in a timely fashion (Deuteronomy 24:14-15, *Baba Metzia* 112a; see Text Study #5a and b below). The Mishnah discusses the practice of following local customs. For example, an employer cannot force a hired laborer to work late at night or early in the morning if that is not the local custom. If it is customary to give them dessert, the employer must do so (*Baba Metzia* 7:1; see Text Study #5c below).

On the flip side, the worker has responsibilities, too. Just as employers are instructed not to withhold or delay wages, so are workers not to deprive employers of the benefit of their work. Employees must not idle away time, a little here and a little there, thus wasting the whole day deceitfully. Indeed, workers must be very punctual concerning time (Maimonides, see Text Study #5A below). Workers also are not to engage in practices in their off-hours that will affect the quality of their work during their employed hours. For example, workers must not work at night at their own work and then hire themselves out during the day (presumably resulting in a compromised state of alertness); nor are workers to plow with their ox in the evenings and then hire the animal out in the mornings (*Tosefta, Baba Metzia* 8:2; see Text Study #5B below). Crime of the worker, incompetency, and improper behavior outside the workplace[5] may justify dismissal of an employee by an employer.

Abiding by local custom is an important aspect of Jewish views on employer-employee relations. Society has developed relevant, detailed, legally binding protocols. Employment lawyers continually hash out the meaning of "local custom." Union workers join together to express what they believe "local custom" should be. Countries' governing bodies include labor departments and ministries, committees, and task forces that attend to employment issues. Many large businesses have in-house counsel on their payrolls advising them on issues related to their employees.

Dina d'Malchuta Dina (The law of the land is the law) is a Jewish way of phrasing the idea of local custom. As described above, customs of the local community do play an important role in guiding business practices. But we must heed caution. It is unacceptable to insist that shoddy business practices are simply local custom, for example, by saying "everyone cuts corners." Justifying dishonesty in business is a slippery slope. Nourished by greed and envy, the descent can happen all too easily.

[5]These categories are discussed in detail in "Employee Rights in a Situation of Dismissal" by Gayle Pomerantz and

David Stern in *Reform Jewish Ethics and the Halakhah*, 278ff.

Like many ethical issues, the fundamental challenge of business ethics comes down to the question of freedom and restraint. It seems people should be free to realize their dreams, goals, and aspirations, including in business enterprises. After all, Judaism embraces freedom — the release from slavery, *yetziat Mitzrayim,* "deliverance from Egypt."

Yet, unrestrained freedom is not the goal. We were freed in order to receive Torah, to bind ourselves in a *brit,* a Covenant with God. Central to our Covenant is the teaching that all people are created in the image of God (*b'tzelem Elohim*), that all deserve dignified treatment. Reaching for goals doesn't tolerate trampling on others along the way. While we may strive to maximize earnings and profits, we cannot exploit or oppress others while doing so. Perhaps in an ideal world, everyone would check themselves, making sure not to take advantage of others. But such an ideal does not exist. Society must impose rules and guidelines to protect everyone's interests. It must regulate business practices so that fairness rules.[6]

General Perspectives

Jewish and general discussions of business ethics have many similarities. These include such concerns as balancing the needs of all those involved in business transactions, negotiating issues of freedom versus restraint (the free market versus the regulated market), preserving free competition, protecting the environment, and respecting local custom.

An area of difference between Jewish ethical business practice and general ethical approaches is this: In Judaism, legality and morality always stand together. In general business practice, this is not necessarily the case. As we discussed in "Jewish Perspectives," two key areas in which Judaism tends to be more restrictive are in *Ona'at Devarim,* verbal exploitation, and in *G'nayvat Da'at,* "stealing another's mind" or

deception. American business regulations do not go to the extent Judaism does to protect citizens from emotional manipulation and mental deception.

Even so, theoretically, secular democracies intend to ensure just and moral societies. The world of business has evolved over the centuries, with a dramatic acceleration of changes in the last decades. New technologies of transportation, communication, and information lead to new ethical challenges. Many of these challenges are in the realms of fair competition, expected product quality, worker protections, and environmental policy. Publicly owned companies (involving stock options and shareholders) have complicated our understanding of the employer-employee relationship. We face unrelenting pressures to keep up with the business essentials of "newer, faster, better, cheaper." Consequently, we continually need to upgrade our moral coping strategies, as well.

As we become more enmeshed in the "global economy," business ethics will need to be broadened. Before the modern era, much of the ethical discourse concerned itself with individuals acting upon other individuals — a buyer and a seller, an employer and an employee, an artisan and his courtyard neighbors, etc. Those types of one-on-one interactions still exist in our day. However, more so than ever, we must make sense of whole trends acting on other trends, economies acting on other economies. We face diffusion of responsibility, multinational corporations, monopolies, public stock offerings, and high stakes litigation. A single decision can affect the lives of thousands. A corporation can lay off thousands of workers at once. An oil or nuclear energy company can pollute the environment in proportions incomparable to what an individual might do in isolation. A vast chain of stores refusing to stock an item can affect sales to such an extent that the manufacturer may have to go out of business.

When "waves" of individuals are acting on

---

[6]See Gayle Pomerantz and David Stern's, "Employee Rights in a Situation of Dismissal" in *Reform Jewish Ethics and the Halakhah,* 297-299, for a thoughtful discussion about applying the principles of *b'tzelem Elohim, yetziat Mitzrayim,* and *brit* to business ethics.

"waves" of other individuals, the stakes are high; more is at risk. Communal responsibility for controlling and directing the trends in an ethical manner is a necessity. The marketplace requires proactive efforts for preserving honesty and fairness. Imagine a whole generation presenting itself at the gates of the World To Come. Imagine a whole generation being asked, "Were you honest in business? Did you oppress? Did you fear God?" (Leviticus 25:17). Can we justify our actions, beyond any doubt, from now to eternity? Will the gates of the next world be open when we arrive?

Summary of the Overview

The paragraphs below summarize key considerations regarding Business Ethics as discussed in the Overview.

1. We are not to cheat, mislead, take advantage of one another, or otherwise treat others unfairly.

2. Some unethical business practices are most comparable to stealing, as they lead to outright losses to another individual. Other practices deceive in more subtle ways, such as through withholding important information, concealing the truth, false flattery, misrepresentation, and so on. Judaism condemns both types of practices.

3. Judaism lays down basic ground rules for ethical business practice. Yet, the parameters of acceptable versus unacceptable business interactions always take local custom into account.

4. An emphasis on the immorality of mental deception is one of the distinguishing factors in Judaism's approach to business ethics.

5. A "global economy" increasingly characterizes our world today. This reality raises new ethical challenges for business.

SCENARIOS: HOW THINGS HAVE CHANGED

Below are two imaginary scenarios that illustrate aspects of our topic of the Ethics of Business, intended to raise questions and spark discussion. Read each scenario to or with your students, and engage them in small or large group discussions. Use the "Focus the Discussion" section below to help identify the important issues and facilitate these discussions. Note that additional questions relating to these scenarios are found in the "Stories: Understanding through Listening" section below (pp. 122-123).

Following the discussions, have students continue on to the "Text Study" section to see what our Jewish and other sources have to say on the subject. Finally, you may wish to have students discuss the questions a second time, to see if their views have changed.

Scenario 1: "Back Then"

Yosi is an apprentice hired by Reb Moshe, the sandal maker. Yosi is to show up every day at 8 a.m. He works until 10:30 a.m. when Reb Moshe, his employer, gives Yosi a 15-minute break. Reb Moshe provides Yosi with a light snack of pita bread and sweetened mint tea. Yosi usually sits in the courtyard during these breaks and enjoys the company of other apprentices. The other apprentices, in accord with local custom, also take a break each day at 10:30. At 1 p.m., Yosi returns to his family where he eats a full meal, takes a rest, and helps with chores. At 4 p.m., Yosi returns to Reb Moshe's shop where he works until 7 p.m. Before Yosi leaves, Reb Moshe hands him a few coins, Yosi's wages for the day.

Scenario 2: "Nowadays"

Josephine is a web site designer for footwear companies. As a single mother, she can't start her work day until her two children leave for school at 8 a.m. After rushing through household chores, Josephine sits down at her computer to work at 8:30 a.m. At 10:30, she takes a five minute break to brew a cup of coffee that she brings back to her desk to sip while continuing her work. Because competition has become so fierce in her field, Josephine feels she cannot lose a minute of valuable work time. Thus, she continues to work without stopping until 3:15 p.m. when her children come home. She fixes a snack for the children and pops a frozen meal for herself into the microwave oven (since she didn't have lunch). The family spends time together until 4 p.m. when the teenager from next door arrives. The teenager will stay until 6:30 p.m. Josephine returns to her computer work.

At 6:30, Josephine fixes the family a pasta dinner. After cleaning up and putting her children to bed, she returns a few phone calls while exercising on the stationary bike. In one of her phone calls, Josephine complains to a friend. She used to be able to count on a little extra income from doing web design for people in the community. But because those clients came to her home, some of her neighbors objected. The neighborhood is not zoned for private businesses.

Josephine returns to her computer at 9 p.m. She continues working until 11 p.m., then washes up and collapses into bed. Though she knows she has put in a hard day's work, she tosses and turns for a long time. She is unsure of whether the work she has done will bring in enough money to support her family.

Focus the Discussion

Times have changed! While there still are craftspeople and apprentices, there are more and more "Josephines." People like her face a different kind of marketplace with new employment "rules." This marketplace fosters fierce, far-ranging competition. Individuals are often businesses unto themselves, their talents and skills being insecure commodities. They may be self-employed and required to market themselves. To keep up, they may feel they cannot afford to place limits on the number of hours or on the

conditions under which they work. Their wages may fluctuate, leading to uncertainty and anxiety regarding their financial security. Benefits such as health insurance, pension contributions, and paid "personal days" may be nonexistent. Extended family members — people to help with the kids, with whom to pool resources, and share the burden of chores — may live far away. In sum, the complexities and "advances" of the modern world have led to a whole host of new ethical questions and concerns that businesses must address.

TEXT STUDY

Judaism holds honorable business practice in high esteem. Torah, Talmud, Mishnah, and scholars through the ages have all addressed the proper conduct of business in great detail. While these Jewish textual sources can provide us with guidelines, these guidelines sometimes highlight the tension between seemingly opposite considerations. The chart on the next page poses the questions and offers two opposing points of view. Text sources supporting each of these points of view follow below.

1. **How do the objectives of sellers and buyers differ?**

   On the One Hand:

   Sellers aim to maximize profits.

   Judaism considers both overcharging and underpaying to be *Ona'ah*, a type of fraud. The Rabbinic tradition understands the verse from Leviticus to refer to monetary exploitation.

   A. When you come to sell, you shall not wrong (*lo tonu*) one another (Leviticus 25:14).

   B. It is forbidden to defraud one's fellow person, whether in buying or in selling. Whoever of them [the parties to the

Ethical Business Practices: Questions to Consider

The Question	On the One Hand	On the Other Hand
1. How do the objectives of sellers and buyers differ? (see p. 114)	Sellers aim to maximize profits	Buyers want to purchase for the lowest price possible
2. What are fair strategies for sellers to use in promoting their merchandise? (see p. 116)	Sellers are entitled to make merchandise attractive and desirable to potential customers.	Buyers must not be deceived. Sprucing up items is acceptable; disguising the inferior quality of items is not.
3. How should sellers interact with potential customers? (see p. 116)	Impressing, enticing, and luring customers are all effective strategies for increasing business.	It is unethical to misrepresent, allow mistaken impressions to stand, or sell under false pretenses.
4. Are certain business unethical by their vary nature? (see p. 117)	If they'll buy it, you can sell it.	Selling harmful items or stolen items is prohibited. So is stockpiling basic commodities, then selling at inflated prices.
5. What should employers and employees expect of each other? (see p. 118)	Employers want to get as much work as they can from employees. They rightly expect employees to be competent, diligent, and scrupulous.	Employers must not oppress or treat their employees unfairly. They are in an advantageous position in relation to their employees.
6. What might developers/ business people and local citizens demand of each other? (see p. 119)	Developers and other business people should be able to run their enterprises in ways they feel are most effective.	The impact on neighbors, community members, and the environment must be taken into account.

transaction] does so, whether buyer or seller, transgresses a negative commandment [see verse from Leviticus above] (*Shulchan Aruch, Choshen Mishpat, Hilchot Mekach u'Memkar*, 227:1).

On the Other Hand:

Buyers want to purchase for the lowest price possible.

To avoid inflated or deflated prices, the buyer and seller must know the exact quality and quantity of the product(s) they're dealing with. Any type of stealing is forbidden, and accurate weights and measures are essen-

tial. (An *ephah* and *hin* are ancient measurements.)

a. You shall not steal (Exodus 20:13).

b. Just balances, just weights, a just *ephah*, and a just *hin* shall you have. I am the Eternal your God, who brought you out of the land of Egypt (Leviticus 19:36).

Probing: Ideas and Issues

Judaism condemns both overcharging and underpaying. What might be the damaging repercussions of such practices? The concept of

Ona'ah comes from *"lo tonu"* or "do not oppress." What is the connection? Have you had any personal experiences related to *Ona'ah*? How did you handle the situation(s)?

2. **What are fair strategies for sellers to use in promoting their merchandise?**

   On the One Hand:

   Sellers are entitled to make merchandise attractive and desirable to potential customers.

   A. Samuel permitted fringes to be put on a cloak. Rabbi Judah permitted a gloss to be put on fine cloth. Rabbah permitted hemp cloths to be beaten [to appear of finer texture]. Rava permitted arrows to be painted. Rabbi Pappa permitted baskets to be painted . . . (*Baba Metzia* 4:12).

   B. It is permitted to sift pounded beans [to remove the refuse, make them look better, and presumably raise their price] . . . [For the continuation of this text see #2b below.] (Maimonides, *Mishneh Torah, Hilchot Mechirah* 18, based on *Baba Metzia* 4:12).

   On the Other Hand:

   Buyers must not be deceived. Sprucing up items is acceptable; disguising the inferior quality of items is not.

   a. Painting new utensils is permitted, whereas old ones [to make them appear new] is forbidden (*Baba Metzia* 4:12).

   b. It is permitted to sift pounded beans — but not when the sifting is only at the top of the bin, because [sifting only at the top of the bin] serves to deceive the eye into thinking that the whole container is similarly sifted (Maimonides, *Mishneh Torah, Hilchot Mechirah* 18, based on *Baba Metzia* 4:12).

Probing: Ideas and Issues

Do these texts provide sufficient guidance as to the allowances and limits of enhancing items for sale? Is there anything you would add?

3. **How should sellers interact with potential customers?**

   On the One Hand:

   Impressing, enticing, and luring customers are effective strategies for increasing business.

   A. A shopkeeper may distribute parched corn or nuts to children and maidservants to accustom them to frequent his store. And he may reduce the price to increase his customer share. His competitors cannot prevent this for it does not constitute deception (Maimonides, *Mishneh Torah, Hilchot Mechirah* 18 and *Baba Metzia* 4:12).

   On the Other Hand:

   It is unethical to misrepresent, allow mistaken impressions to stand, or sell under false pretenses.

   a. You are not to steal, you are not to lie, you are not to deal falsely with each other (Leviticus 19:11).

   b. There are seven categories of fraud: the first among them is to misrepresent oneself to others [*gonev da'at ha-briyot*], one who insincerely invites another to his home, one who plies another with gifts that he knows the other will not accept, one who impresses his guest by opening a barrel of wine that is already sold to a vendor [thus the guest will believe that his host has on his account risked a financial loss, given that an open barrel of wine might spoil until such a time as a vendor comes along to purchase it], one who has improper measures, one who lies regarding his weights, and one who adulterates his merchandise . . . " (*Mechilta, Mishpatim*, chapter 13, *Tosefta, Baba Kamma* 7:3).

c. When one knows that there is some defect in one's merchandise, one must so inform the purchaser (Maimonides, *Mishneh Torah, Hilchot Mechirah* 18).

d. It is forbidden to accustom oneself to smooth speech and flatteries. One must not say one thing and mean another. The inward and outward self should correspond; only what we have in mind should we utter with the mouth. We must deceive no one, not even an idolater . . . Even a single word of flattery or deception is forbidden. A person should always cherish truthful speech, an upright spirit, and a pure heart freed of all pretense and cunning (Maimonides, *Mishneh Torah, Hilchot De'ot* 2:6).

Probing: Ideas and Issues

Do these texts provide sufficient guidance as to the allowances and limits of impressing, enticing, and luring customers? Is there anything you would add? Anything you disagree with? Have you ever had an experience in which you felt the merchant misrepresented his/her merchandise? How did you handle the matter? Is there a better way you could have handled it?

4. Are certain businesses unethical by their very nature?

On the One Hand:

If they'll buy it, you can sell it.

Jewish sources do not suggest this model of business.

On the Other Hand:

Selling harmful items or stolen items is prohibited. So is stockpiling basic commodities, then selling at inflated prices.

a. Everything that is forbidden to sell to non-Jews is similarly forbidden to sell to Jewish robbers, because by doing so, one strengthens the hands of the evildoers and leads them astray [if they would not be able to buy the weapons perhaps they would not rob. Similarly, without weapons, aggression becomes more difficult.] So, too, anyone who misleads others who are blind [who are not aware or knowledgeable], causing them to sin, and those who give others advice, which they themselves know is to the others' detriment [not only in money matters but even in referring to ways of travel, etc.], or those who strengthen the hands of evildoers who are actually so blinded by lust and desire that they are unwilling to see the true path — all these types transgress a negative commandment, as it is written, "You shall not place a stumbling block in the path of the blind" (Leviticus 19:14). (Maimonides, *Mishneh Torah, Hilchot Rotzayach u'Shmirat Hanefesh*, 12:14, bracketed commentary by Meir Tamari, p. 102)

b. It is forbidden to buy stolen goods from a thief. This is a grievous sin, since it strengthens the hands of those who transgress and causes them to steal again, because if they would not find a buyer, they would not steal (*Shulchan Aruch, Hilchot G'nayvah*, 356:1).

c. While Jewish sources limit profits from the sale of basic commodities, there are less restrictions in marketing luxury-type items.

> The *bayt din* (court) is obligated to fix prices and to appoint overseers to implement them. This applies only to basic goods, like wine, oil, and vegetables. But special goods like spices and similar articles do not have fixed prices, so everyone may earn what they wish (Maimonides, *Mishneh Torah, Hilchot Mechirah*, 14:1, 2).

Probing: Ideas and Issues

Selling weapons to robbers or buying stolen goods from thieves are examples of *Lifnay Evare*, placing a stumbling block before the blind. What other examples can you think of that fit this category of unacceptable commerce? Pornography? Cigarettes? Anything else? Also in the category of *Lifnay Evare* is giving ill-suited advice and advice based on a conflict of interest. What are specific examples of giving ill-suited business advice? On another matter — about making profits on basic commodities — should the government control or set prices on basic goods?

5. **What should employers and employees expect of each other?**

On the One Hand:

Employers want to get as much work as they can from employees. They rightly expect employees to be competent, diligent, and scrupulous.

A. Just as the employer is enjoined not to deprive poor workers of their wages or withhold wages from them when they are due, so are workers enjoined not to deprive employers of the benefit of their work by idling away time, a little here and a little there, thus wasting the whole day deceitfully. Indeed, workers must be very punctual concerning time (Maimonides, *Mishneh Torah, Hilchot Sechirut* 13:7).

B. Workers must not work at night at their own work and then hire themselves out during the day. [Nor are workers] to plow with their ox in the evenings and then hire the animal out in the mornings. Nor should workers go hungry and afflict themselves in order to feed their children — for by doing so, they steal labor from their employer (*Tosefta, Baba Metzia* 8:2).

C. Any [worker] who causes an irretrievable loss is liable to be dismissed immediately (*Baba Batra* 21b).

On the Other Hand:

Employers must not oppress or treat their employees unfairly. They are in an advantageous position in relation to their employees.

a. You shall not abuse needy and destitute laborers, whether they be your fellow citizens or sojourners in one of the communities of your land. You must pay them their wages on the same day, before the sun sets, for they are needy and urgently depend on it; else they will cry to the Eternal against you and you will incur guilt (Deuteronomy 24:14-15).

b. Whoever withholds an employee's wages, it is as though they have taken the person's life away (*Baba Metzia* 112a).

c. If an employer hires laborers and asks them to work in the early morning or late evening, at a place where it is not the local custom to work early or late at night, the employer cannot force the laborers to do so. Where it is customary to provide food for workers, the employer must do so. If it is customary to give them dessert, the employer must do so — it all depends on local custom (*Baba Metzia* 7:1).

Probing: Ideas and Issues

What do these texts define as the key responsibilities of the employer and employee? Would you say that these responsibilities are the most important? What other responsibilities do you think employers and employees owe each other?

6. **What might developers/business people and local citizens demand of each other?**

On the One Hand:

Developers and other business people should be able to run their enterprises in ways they feel are most effective.

A. This text comes from the secular world of business:

There is one and only one social responsibility of business: to use its resources and engage in activities designed to increase its profits so long as it stays within the rules of the game, which is to say, engage in open and free competition without deception or fraud (Milton Friedman, "The Social Responsibility of Business," in *The Essence of Friedman,* edited by Kurt R.Leube [Stanford, CA: Hoover Institution Press, 1987], p. 42).

On the Other Hand:

The impact on neighbors, community members, and the environment must be taken into account.

a. [If a person wished to open] a store in a courtyard, [the neighbors] can protest against the person, saying, "I cannot sleep because of the noise of those entering and leaving. An artisan may make utensils [at home] and go about and sell them in the marketplace. The others cannot protest . . . " (*Baba Batra* 2:3).

b. Carcasses, cemeteries, and tanneries must be kept at fifty cubits distance from a town [because of the bad odor]. A tannery must be established on the east side of town [because the east wind is gentle and will not carry the stench to town] (*Baba Batra* 2:9).

Probing: Ideas and Issues

What is the essence of what Milton Friedman says? Do you agree with him? The Mishnah gives some examples of what people in its day could justifiably protest concerning neighboring businesses. What kinds of things might you or others protest about today?

RELATED MIDDOT AND MITZVOT

Practicing these virtues and commandments supports ethical business practices.

Bal Tashchit (Not Destroying): Preserving the Earth. Businesses need to be responsible about their impact on the environment.

Emet (Truth): Speaking and acting truthfully is a key underlying value of business ethics.

Histapkut (Contentedness): If you're continually dissatisfied with your material lifestyle, you may be more likely to engage in questionable business practices, to cheat to get ahead.

K'vod et HaBriyot (Respecting Others): Treating others with dignity means not taking advantage of them in any manner.

Lo Tachmod (Not Coveting): Envy feeds greed and possibly underhanded competitiveness. Controlling envy is an important component of maintaining moral business standards.

Malachah (Work/Industriousness): Being dependent on others when you are able to work or living in poverty can be demoralizing. Engaging in business can provide a suitable way to live a secure and honorable life.

Nedivut (Generosity): Generous people are less likely to want to take advantage of others. Generous employers will take to heart their employees' welfare and the community's well-being and act accordingly.

Yirah (Awe and Reverence): We are not to oppress, but are to have *yirah* or "fear God" (Leviticus 25:17). If we deceive others in our day-to-day business interactions, it's not as if no one knows. God knows and God sees. Doing wrong will catch up with us one way or another.

ACTIVITIES

A First Look: Key Issues and Ideas

1. To increase familiarity with key vocabulary, create a matching game. On one set of index cards, write the glossary words from the Appendix of this chapter. On the other set, write the definitions. Have individuals or teams try to match up the cards correctly. You may choose to do this exercise for reinforcement purposes after introducing students to the material. Or, do it as an opening to the unit — requiring students to do research to discover the correct answers.

   Besides the words in the Glossary, here are other ideas you can include:

   • An example of *G'nayvah*: Shoplifting

   • An example of *G'zaylah*: Not returning a lost object

   • An example of *Ona'ah*: Overcharging by more than 1/6th of an item's worth

   • An example of *Ona'at Devarim*: Asking about the price of an item when you have no intention of purchasing it

   • An example of *G'nayvat Da'at*: Mixing fruits and vegetables in a shop display in order to disguise the true condition of some of them

   • An example of *Lifnay Evare*: Selling weapons to a known thief

   • One key responsibility of employers: Pay wages on time

   • One key responsibility of employees: Don't waste time

   • First question asked in the World To Come: Were you honest in business?

2. The major challenge of business ethics is balancing the needs and goals of all who are affected by a transaction or policy. List five possible needs or goals for each of the following people:

   • Merchants/Sellers

   • Customers/Buyers

   • Employers

   • Employees

   • Developers

   • Community Members

   Discuss what you think are the main points of contention between the various "stakeholders" in business. What are the most effective ways of balancing everyone's needs and goals?

3. What were some pressing business concerns in ancient days? What are they now? Divide the group in half. One section represents ancient issues, the other modern ones. Each group comes up with at least ten distinct concerns in their era. Then, stage a conversation across the ages. The leader facilitates a discussion about the pressures, changes, and challenges faced by each group. The goal is to help participants grasp the unique complexities businesses must cope with today and discover ways ancient wisdom might offer relevant guidance.

4. Refer to the 12 "On The One Hand/On The Other Hand" points listed in the table on p. 115 (six points from one side, plus six from the other). Individually, each person ranks all 12 points from what he/she thinks is the most important business principle to what is least important. Reconvene, and have group members compare and explain their rank-

ings. Ask: What do your results show about your attitude toward business ethics? What was most challenging about completing this exercise?

Applying Middot and Mitzvot

1. Business schools increasingly require students to study business ethics. Decide the topics and/or *middot* your group believes a business school should cover in a course on ethics. Then, assign each individual or small groups a topic, such as fair competition, truth in advertising, avoiding conflicts of interest, etc. They are to flesh out more details on how to teach their topic. Here are some pointers to help the "course-preparers":

   - What are five main points business students should know concerning (whatever the topic is)?

   - Give a clear example or scenario that teaches each of the five points.

   - What discussion question or short activity will help students understand each point?

   - After everyone has prepared their topic, share ideas, or better yet, teach each other.

2. We could argue that *Emet* (Truth) is the key principle underlying ethical business practices. Hold a discussion, giving participants the opportunity to elaborate on each of the following:

   - When a merchant is untruthful . . .

   - When a customer is untruthful . . .

   - When an employer is untruthful . . .

   - When an employee is untruthful . . .

   - When businesses in the neighborhood are untruthful . . .

   - When neighbors of businesses are untruthful . . .

   - When developers are untruthful . . .

   - When community members (in discussion with developers) are untruthful . . .

   After completing this exercise, ask if participants agree that being truthful is the most important virtue for business practice. Why or why not?

3. There are companies that make posters and other paraphernalia for businesses that use photographs, words, and messages of inspiration for workers. Perhaps a poster illustrated with a hawk would say "Success" and include a short quotation about success by a famous author.

   Have your group create a series of Jewishly-inspired posters for businesses. Each poster should include an uplifting word, message, and illustration related to good business practice. See www.successories.com for examples.

4. For more information and activities on:

   Bal Tashchit (Not Destroying, Preserving the Earth: see *Teaching Mitzvot* by Barbara Binder Kadden and Bruce Kadden, pp. 199-203. Also: *Let the Earth Teach You Torah* by Ellen Bernstein and Dan Fink, Wyncote, PA: Shomrei Adamah, 1992.

   Emet (Truth): see *Teaching Jewish Virtues* by Susan Freeman, pp. 69-84.

   Histapkut (Contentedness): see *Teaching Jewish Virtues* by Susan Freeman, pp. 211-227, and *The Jewish Moral Virtues* by Eugene B. Borowitz and Frances Weinman Schwartz, pp. 161-172.

   K'vod et Ha-Briyot (Respecting Others): see *Teaching Jewish Virtues* by Susan Freeman, pp. 179-194.

   Lo Tachmod (Not Coveting): see *Teaching Jewish Virtues* by Susan Freeman, pp. 211-227.

   Malachah (Work/Industriousness): see *Teaching Jewish Virtues* by Susan Freeman, pp. 136-148.

Nedivut (Generosity): see *Teaching Jewish Virtues* by Susan Freeman, pp. 165-178, and *The Jewish Moral Virtues* by Eugene B. Borowitz and Frances Weinman Schwartz, pp. 93-104.

Yirah (Awe and Reverence): see *Teaching Jewish Virtues* by Susan Freeman, pp. 332-346.

Stories: Understanding through Listening

1. Read over the imaginary scenarios in the "Scenarios: How Things Have Changed" section above. These scenarios highlight issues related to conditions of employment. After reviewing the scenarios, have a couple of students describe in their own words the basic conditions of Yosi's and Josephine's employment. Then, discuss these questions:

   • What are the differences between the employment situations of Yosi and Josephine?

   • What would you expect to be most challenging to Yosi in his work? and to Josephine?

   • How would Yosi have managed the challenges he faced?

   • How might Josephine manage the challenges she faces?

   • How might the community infrastructure support (or detract) from Yosi's ability to succeed in his work?

   • How does the community infrastructure support (or detract) from Josephine's ability to succeed in her work?

   • How could the community infrastructure be more supportive for people like Josephine?

   • Describe the ideal work scenario for yourself. Make it realistic!

2. We derive many of our principles related to business ethics from stories or specific cases. Ask individuals or pairs to create stories that

will include several scenes. In short, the flow of each story will be: Character sins (in a number of ways); character changes; character seeks to rectify the damage.

Here are the specifics. The authors imagine and describe a corrupt character who transgresses in each of the following categories: *G'nayvah, G'zaylah, Ona'ah, Ona'at Devarim, G'nayvat Da'at,* and *Lifnay Evare* (see the Glossary, p. 126, for definitions). For each category of transgression, the authors must come up with an example of what their character does. After they complete this part of the story, the authors continue by imagining that their corrupt character suddenly (or gradually) reforms him/herself. The authors describe what causes their character to change. They then go back through this character's transgressions, showing how the character attempts to rectify the damage he/she did in each of the categories of *G'nayvah,* etc. In some cases, perhaps the character could undo the damage; in other cases, perhaps not. When the stories are complete, share them in a group.

3. A variation on the above activity: Use art rather than writing to complete the exercise. Fold large sheets of paper into thirds. Have participants choose a transgression and illustrate three story scenes, one on each third.

   • Scene (Picture) 1: Person does wrong (in terms of *G'nayvah, G'zaylah, Ona'ah, Ona'at Devarim, G'nayvat Da'at,* or *Lifnay Evare*).

   • Scene 2: Person changes behavior for some reason.

   • Scene 3: Person tries to rectify wrong done in Scene 1.

4. Another variation (on the above two activities): Do the exercise through the creation of skits.

5. To understand more fully the issues of employer-employee relations in your community, plan a series of interviews. In a

group, brainstorm a list of places you might want to conduct interviews regarding conditions of employment. The list might include: the hospital, the ice cream shop downtown, a certain school, the bottle factory, the national chain department store, the computer repair shop, a lawn service, a fast food restaurant, an elegant hotel, etc. Have participants choose one or more businesses in which to conduct their interviews. They may prefer to do this individually or in pairs.

Proper preparation will be necessary to carry out this exercise successfully. First, participants must attain permission to interview. The most efficient way to do this is to have the leader contact the business, explain the purpose of the activity, and secure permission to interview an employer and one or more employees. Then give the students the name of the contact person and have them take it from there.

A simpler option: Have students interview parents and/or neighbors about their jobs.

The other important preparation is creating appropriate interview questions. You will need one list for employers and another for employees. Here are a few sample questions for employers: What do you like most about being an employer at your current job? What is most challenging? What are the biggest problems you face related to your employees? What happens if you suspect an employee is wasting time? Etc.

6. Have everyone do research and then present a biographical report on a "whistle-blower." "Whistle-blowers" are ethical resisters who expose corruption in government or industry, often at risk to themselves. For example, they could lose their jobs or become victims of vengeance. Their stories provide an impressive standard for moral action. This exercise allows participants to learn more about these admirable individuals.

An excellent resource is *The Whistle-blowers: Exposing Corruption in Government & Industry* by Myron Peretz Glazer and Penina Migdal Glazer, and "People of the Year," cover story in *Time Magazine*, the last week in December, 2002. There also are several films that tell the stories of whistle-blowers and others who speak out against business violations. They include *Silkwood* (1983, 131 min., rated R), about dangerous conditions at a nuclear plant; *Erin Brockovich* (2000, 131 min., rated R), about a corporation's responsibility for polluting a community's water supply; *A Civil Action* (1998, 115 min., rated PG-13), about a lawyer who puts big corporations on trial for their polluting practices; *Norma Rae* (1979, 114 min., rated PG), about establishing unions; and *The Insider* (1999, 157 min., rated R), which tells the true story of Jeffrey Wigand who, after being fired from his top level company job, turns whistle-blower, claiming his employers lied about the dangers of cigarettes. These films can be rented at video stores.

7. Invite a labor attorney to visit your group. Find out what are the most common issues encountered related to employer-employee relations. What are the most controversial issues? What legislation currently under consideration might affect places of employment? What does the attorney know about labor issues in this country compared with the issues faced by other countries around the world? Etc.

Action: Getting Out, Getting Involved

1. Write a letter to a business in which you feel *G'nayvat Da'at* or misrepresentation is an issue. The misrepresentation may have to do with deceptive advertising, product quality that is inferior to what a customer would rightfully expect, etc.

2. Some of the frenzy to build the "newest, fastest, cheapest . . . " is fed by consumers' demands. To what extent do *you* demand and desire the latest in material possessions? And to what extent do you embrace *histapkut*, contentment with what you have?

After examining your own attitudes and possible excesses, make a commitment to curb some aspect(s) of consumerism in your life. Set an amount of time to follow through with your commitment, perhaps a week or two. Then, report back to the group about the experience. Possible "curbing" strategies: drive less and walk more; use fresh foods rather than prepackaged ones; check out books, music, and videos from the library rather than purchasing them; repair items and mend torn clothes rather than buying new things; give away some of the overload of things you own to others who are in need.[7]

3. Find out how to get involved with an organization that deals with labor and/or environmental issues. Issues of concern might include: abuses of foreign workers, trafficking in slave labor, exploitation of child labor, or industrial pollution. You may want to write to government or United Nations officials about concerns you have and what actions might be taken to address particular issues. A good place to begin educating yourself about current issues is by checking out the web site of the International Labor Organization, www.ilo.org. A few environmental organizations to contact are:

Environmental Defense Fund
257 Park Avenue S.
New York, NY 10010
(212) 505-2100
www.edf.org

Greenpeace
1436 U Street, NW
Washington, DC 20009
(202) 462-1177
www.greenpeace.org

Clean Water Action
317 Pennsylvania Ave., SE
Washington, DC 20003

(202) 547-1196
www.cleanwater.gov

Environmental Protection Agency (EPA)
401 M Street, SW
Washington, DC 20460
Public Affairs: (202) 382-4361
www.epa.gov

Wrestling: Engagement with the Issues

1. Have several small groups act out the situations from the "Scenarios: How Things Have Changed" section above. Each group should extend the scenario to include a "what happens next" scene or two.

2. Create your own scenarios to act out which highlight difficult business issues. Coach the actors to incorporate ideas and values from Jewish sources. Here are a few ideas:

   • A customer who feels she's been overcharged

   • A customer who didn't receive the product he paid for

   • A business owner manipulating a potential client with flattery and insincere invitations

   • Workers confronting an employer about unsuitable working conditions

   • Community members approaching a business about its noise pollution in their neighborhood

3. Refer to the "Text Study" section above. Assign different groups to create scenarios that illustrate all or a selection of each grouping of texts.

4. Stage a debate. One side is developers; the other is community members. In addition, assign a group to be "Jewish Sages." The developers want to build a new strip mall. Several nationally owned "big box" fran-

---

[7]Chapter 10 in this book, "Consumerism: How Much Is Too Much?" deals in depth with this activity's focus.

chises will go into this mall. These include a huge general store ("All Things"), a drug store ("Druggy's"), a book store ("Endless Books"), and an office supply store ("MuchStuff"). Downtown is less than a mile away from the proposed mall's location. Main Street has been the center of the small town for the last 200 years. Some local businesses on Main Street have been around for several generations, including "Downtown Dry Goods," "Joey's Drugs," "Books for Our Town," and "Pencils," a family owned office supply store. Concerns about the developers' plans include protecting fair competition and likely increases in traffic, noise, and pollution. The developers argue that they should be allowed to build their business, that we live in a free market economy.

Give the two sides time to formulate arguments. The "Jewish Sages" spend their time doing some research, too, but for now they refrain from forming a set opinion.

Next, appoint a presiding judge (i.e., the leader of the group) to facilitate a "public debate." The Jewish Sages listen carefully during the debate. When the two sides exhaust their arguments, the presiding judge will send the case for arbitration by the Jewish Sages. The Jewish Sages will need to draw on their initial research, plus consider the arguments before them so that they can offer a fair judgment. They will address whether to allow the developers to build in the manner they would like.

5. Collect a stack of assorted magazines. Have your group go through them and look at the advertisements. Assess which ones offer a fair portrayal of what is being marketed and which are suspect according to Jewish criteria. Set aside ten to 20 questionable ads. Then, assign half the group to be business owners and advertisers. Assign the other half to be members of a consumer protection organization. Everyone together forms a business ethics panel. This panel must clear each advertisement before it is allowed to be pub-

lished. Which ads will the panel allow to go through and which will they reject, and why?

6. Play a "Find What's Wrong with This Business" game. Divide into small groups. Each group should come up with a business skit. The actors should focus on developing the interactions between people. They should pay attention to props, imaginary or real, as well. For the set, they should think carefully about how to present merchandise and how to advertise their services and/or products. The skit should incorporate at least five business transgressions (i.e., things you're *not* supposed to do in business). For example, a skit might include misrepresentation of the quality of merchandise, ill-suited advice, and three other transgressions. When the whole group reconvenes, actors perform the skits. Can the audience figure out what was "wrong" in each of the skits?

Empathy

1. Every year, the Colorado Ethics in Business Awards committee gives the Daniel L. Ritchie Award, recognizing a business person who has exemplified high moral character and ethical practices in their professional business career. Divide into small groups. Each group will act as this committee, deciding the criteria for this award and how often to give it. When the whole group reconvenes, have the "committees" share their ideas.

2. Have the group study the texts below that speak about the demoralizing plight of poverty and the value of work. The task for participants is this: Choose a text as a jumping off point for an unstructured journal exercise. Write about your reaction to the text, what you think the text means, your feelings about poverty and work, etc. Try to increase your sensitivity to poverty by imagining (or reporting on) how you might feel if you found yourself in such dire circumstances.

Poverty is one of three things that drive people out of their minds (*Eruvin* 41b).

Poverty in one's house is harder to bear than 50 plagues (*Baba Batra* 116a).

People should love work and not hate work. For just as the Torah was given as a covenant, so work was given as a covenant, as it is said: "Six days you shall labor and do all your work, but the seventh day is a Sabbath of the Eternal your God" (Exodus 20:9) (*Avot de'Rabbi Natan*, Chapter 11).

Hire yourself out to a work which is strange to you rather than become dependent on others (*Yerushalmi, Sanhedrin* XI, 7, 30b, line 68).

There is nothing harder than poverty. It is hardest of all the afflictions of the world . . . Our Sages say, "All other suffering in one pan, and poverty in the other, and the scales would balance." There is no lot which is harder than poverty, for those who are crushed by poverty are as if they were crushed by all the afflictions of the world, and as if all the curses enumerated in Deuteronomy had befallen them, as our Sages say, "All afflictions in one pan, and poverty in the other, and the scale of poverty would fall" (*Exodus Rabbah, Mishpatim* XXXI, 12, 14).

GLOSSARY

Dina d'Malchuta Dina:

"The law of the land is the law."

Ephah:

Ancient unit of measurement. (Merchants must ensure that weights and measurements are accurate.)

G'nayvah:

Thievery; taking in secret.

G'nayvat Da'at:

"Stealing another's mind"; deception.

G'zaylah:

Robbery; taking by force.

Hin:

Ancient unit of measurement. (Merchants must ensure that weights and measurements are accurate.)

Lifnay Evare:

"In front of a blind person" (Leviticus 25:36). One party provides the means to sin or gives unsuitable advice to someone who is "blind" to the full consequences or implications of a transaction. (The means to sin or unsuitable advice are kinds of "stumbling blocks.")

Ona'ah:

Exploitation; withholding important information.

Ona'at Devarim:

Verbal exploitation.

BIBLIOGRAPHY

Books and Articles

Blumberg, Paul. *The Predatory Society: Deception in the American Marketplace.* New York: Oxford University Press, 1989.

Glazer, Myron Peretz, and Penina Migdal Glazer. *The Whistleblowers: Exposing Corruption in Government and Industry.* New York: BasicBooks, a division of HarperCollins Publishers, 1989.

Herring, Basil F. "Truth in the Marketplace." In *Jewish Ethics and Halakhah for Our Time, Volume II.* Hoboken, NJ: KTAV Publishing House, Inc. and NY: Yeshiva University Press, 1989.

Levine, Aaron, and Moses Pava, eds. *Case Studies in Jewish Business Ethics.* Hoboken, NJ: KTAV Publishing House, Inc. and NY: Yeshiva University Press, 2000.

Pava, Moses L. *Business Ethics: A Jewish Perspective.* Hoboken, NJ: KTAV Publishing House, Inc., and New York: Yeshiva University Press, 1997.

Pomerantz, Gayle, and David Stern. "Employee Rights in a Situation of Dismissal." In *Reform Jewish Ethics and the Halakhah,* ed. by Eugene B. Borowitz. New Jersey: Behrman House, Inc., 1988.

Reich, Robert B. *The Future of Success.* New York: Alfred A. Knopf, 2001.

Repa, Barbara Kate. *Your Rights in the Workplace.* Berkeley, CA: Nolo Press, 1999.

Straus, Livia Selmanowitz. "Jewish Business Ethics: Teaching toward Moral Living." In *Jewish Education News* 20, No. 1, Spring 1999.

Tamari, Meir. *The Challenge of Wealth: A Jewish Perspective on Earning and Spending Money.* Northvale, NJ: Jason Aronson Inc., 1995.

———. *In the Marketplace: Jewish Business Ethics.* Southfield, MI: Targum/Feldheim, 1991.

———. *With All Your Possessions.* Northvale, NJ: Jason Aronson Inc., 1998.

Web Sites

Sites related to business ethics:

Business Ethics – Corporate Social Responsibility Report: www.business-ethics.com

A magazine promoting ethical business practices. Publishes an annual list of the 100 best Corporate Citizens.

Corporate Social Responsibility News: www.csrnews.com

An international news service dedicated to the publication and distribution of corporate social responsibility news.

Department of Labor (of the United States Government): www.dol.gov

The Department of Labor fosters and promotes the welfare of all workers through a wide range of programs and policies.

International Business Ethics Institute (IBEI): www.business-ethics.org

"Fostering Global business practices which promote equitable economic development, resource sustainability, and just forms of government."

International Labor Organization: www.ilo.org

A United Nations agency which seeks the promotion of social justice and internationally recognized human and labor rights.

Environmental organizations that have concerns that relate to business ethics:

Clean Water Action: www.cleanwater.gov

A government organization responsible for restoring and protecting America's watersheds.

Environmental Defense Fund: www.edf.org

A leading national nonprofit organization linking science, economics, and law to create innovative, equitable, and cost-effective solutions to our society's most urgent environmental problems.

Environmental Protection Agency: www.epa.gov

The U.S. governmental agency whose mission is to protect human health and safeguard the natural environment — air, water, and land — on which life depends.

Greenpeace: www.greenpeace.org

Greenpeace is an international non-profit organization that focuses on the most crucial worldwide threats to our planet's biodiversity and environment.

Films

Specific sections of the following films may be valuable for illustrating certain aspects of the Ethics of Business, but it may not be appropriate for students to view the entire film. Prescreening is strongly advised.

A Civil Action (1998, 115 minutes, rated PG-13)

The true story of a lawyer who brings a case against two large corporations for their polluting practices. Available from video stores.

Erin Brockovich (2000, 130 minutes, rated R)

The true story of a legal assistant who almost single-handedly brings down a California power company accused of polluting a community's water supply. Available from video stores.

The Insider (1999, 157 minutes, rated R)

The true story of Jeffrey Wigand, who after being fired from his top level job with a tobacco company, turns whistle-blower, claiming his employers lied about the dangers of cigarettes. Available from video stores.

Norma Rae (1979, 114 minutes, rated PG)

The story of a southern textile worker employed in a factory with intolerable working conditions. She struggles to unionize the workers in order to protect their rights. Available from video stores.

Silkwood (1983, 131 minutes, rates R)

The true story of Karen Silkwood, a worker in a nuclear power facility who might have been murdered to prevent her from exposing dangerous conditions at the power plant. Available from video stores.

Wall Street (1987, 125 minutes, rated R)

A young and impatient Wall Street stockbroker is willing to do anything to get to the top. Available from video stores.

CHAPTER 6

DEATH PENALTY

OVERVIEW

Can people do something so wrong, so horrifying, that they deserve to die? Those who support the death penalty would say yes. People who commit a violent, murderous act must forfeit their life. Society demands and victims' families deserve this response. In addition, within many religious traditions, including Judaism, one can find support for the death penalty.

Death penalty opponents believe a government should not punish criminals by executing them. Abolitionists (death penalty opponents) argue against the death penalty on several fronts, including the general immorality of killing, especially when there are alternative punishments. They claim the death penalty does not realize many of its intended objectives, such as deterring other would-be offenders or providing "closure" for grieving family members. Furthermore, grave injustices can occur.

Jewish abolitionists say death penalty supporters interpret our religious sources too narrowly. That is, necessary conditions for a death sentence effectively eliminate the possibility that such a penalty would ever take place.

It might seem the ethical choice is this: You are either for the death penalty, or you're against it. That is, you either believe it is permissible to punish others by executing them, or you believe that killing criminals is wrong. However, a compromise perspective may exist. This position would forbid the death penalty except in the rarest of instances, for the most heinous of crimes.

Jewish Perspectives

What Offenses Warrant the Death Penalty?

Biblical law mandates the death penalty for 36 offenses. These include murder, kidnapping, adultery, incest, certain instances of rape, idol worship, public incitement to apostasy (worshiping other gods), disrespecting parents, and desecrating Shabbat. Over the centuries, Judaism reflects mixed attitudes toward the death penalty. While at various times and places, certain communities were willing to carry it out, restrictions were severe. In fact, widespread Jewish opinion contends that in post-biblical days, communities rarely carried out death sentences (see Text Study #1a, #1g, #2a, and #5a below).

Why Punish and Why the Death Penalty?

Important objectives for punishment in the Bible were the realignment of God with creation, retribution, deterrence,[1] and restoring the moral order of society. Another objective, particularly regarding the death penalty, was "special prevention" (i.e., executing "mid-level" criminals, such as burglars, to prevent them from committing further and possibly worse crimes, such as murder). Over the centuries, Jewish attitudes toward these objectives continually evolved.

Realignment of God with Creation: God demands that human beings behave in certain defined ways. Criminal acts transgress God's will, God's blueprint for an ethical society. From the Bible's

---

[1] Elie Spitz, "The Jewish Tradition and Capital Punishment," in *Contemporary Jewish Ethics and Morality,"* 344. See Text Study #5b.

perspective, we must execute violators of God's laws (Numbers 25:4), those who profane God's name. Doing so helps make amends, helps "realign us" with God. Putting offenders to death will turn God's "fierce anger" (Deuteronomy 13:18) away from Israel (Numbers 25:4). Being "realigned with God" means we recommit as a society to living rightly. We get back into God's good graces.

Additionally, the Bible taught that besides offending God, a murderer "offended" the land itself. Executing a "blood spiller" made expiation for "contaminating the land": "The land will not be purged of the blood that has been shed upon it except through the blood of the one who shed it" (Numbers 35:33).

Today, we would be hard pressed to find Jews who would suggest that killing criminals "turns God's fierce anger away from Israel." With such language, the Bible marked certain crimes as abhorrent and offensive to God. Most modern Jews recognize that we can fulfill the objective of realigning God with creation through other punishments. Namely, effective courts of justice can mark certain crimes as abhorrent by imposing stiff prison sentences. In addition, courts may require fines and/or community service.

Retribution: "Eye for an eye" retribution is known as *lex talionis* (see Text Study #3A below). The basic logic is this: If I inflict on you the same injury that you inflicted on me, we're "even." In the post-biblical period, Rabbis allowed monetary compensation for injuries (e.g., a monetary fine rather than an actual eye for an eye).

With murder — as opposed to injury — things get more complicated. According to Jewish sources, it is more difficult to accept compensation when a murder is involved. As it says in Genesis, "Whoever sheds the blood of humankind, by humankind shall that one's blood be shed, for in God's image did God make humankind" (Genesis 9:6).

Of course, the Rabbis made it very difficult to carry out the death penalty. Some necessary conditions seem nearly impossible to fulfill. That is,

the offender had to receive a warning before committing the crime (*hatra'ah*), and two eyewitnesses had to observe the offender in the act (*edut mechuvenet*). Clearly, traditional Jewish sources struggled with the laws of capital punishment. But they did not actively question whether the death penalty is inherently unjust.

Many Jews today *do* consider the death penalty to be inherently unjust. They struggle with questions about the morality of the death penalty: Is it *ever* right for a society to put somebody to death, to kill someone for his/her crime? Many contemporary Jews are wary of the death penalty. Some recommend banning it in most, if not all cases. An alternative, severe punishment, such as life imprisonment, should serve the needs of retribution well enough. To serve justice, we don't actually need to kill someone.

Deterrence: In several instances, after pronouncing a death penalty for a particular offense, the Bible adds, "All will hear and be afraid" (Deuteronomy 17:13, 19:20, and 21:21). In other words, "If you do what this evil thug did, you, too, will die! See how horrible it is to be executed? Next time it could be *you* if you're not careful!" The objective of deterrence is to prevent others from committing offenses.

Nowadays, Jews who follow discussions of deterrence know of its inadequacies. Deterrence is a faulty justification for the death penalty. Modern democracies cannot defend capital punishment by saying it deters other would-be offenders. This claim simply has not been proven (see Text Study #4b, c, and d below).

Restoring the Moral Order of Society: Judaism holds that living according to God's will reinforces the moral order of the universe. Unlawful acts, such as murder, threaten the moral order. Too much crime can undermine and unravel civilization. Therefore, the Bible declares, "Put away evil from your midst" (Deuteronomy 17:7, 12; 19:19; 21:21; 22:24; 22:27). By "putting away evil," the Bible means executing offenders. When a community identifies certain conduct as being so abhorrent as to deserve judicial punishment, it makes an important statement: "We resent, disapprove of, and outlaw criminal conduct!"

Modern Jews might agree that punishing criminals can help restore the moral order of society, but question the necessity of killing a criminal to realize this objective. Other punishments can be as effective and ethically more justifiable.

Special Prevention: Special prevention means cutting off known criminals before they strike again, possibly in more lethal ways. A death sentence will decisively prevent an offender from committing further crimes. Maimonides explains: a "stubborn and rebellious son" (Deuteronomy 21:18-21), a kidnapper (Exodus 21:16), and a stealer caught in a break-in (Exodus 22:1) can be put to death because of the concern that in the future they will become shedders of blood (*Guide of the Perplexed*, 3:41, see Text Study #4C below).

Mainstream Jewish thinkers today do not support killing individuals for crimes they may or may not commit in the future. They would suggest society look for alternate ways to restrain criminals from striking again, and alternate ways to protect the public.

By What Authority — A Sentence of Death?

In the days of the Temple, a court of 23 judges could pass a death sentence, but only by fully complying with due process. Due process included *hatra'ah*, warning the culprit before the crime, and *edut mechuvenet*, impeccably qualified witnesses able to withstand severe cross-examination[2] (see Text Study #1b-f below).

Alternatively, the king could pass a death sentence. This might happen if the courts were unable or unwilling to impose capital punishment, even when overwhelming evidence pointed to the suspect's guilt. Why give the king

such power? Tradition justified this privilege as a necessary alternative to the courts, to ensure "the well-being of society, as dictated by the needs of the hour."[3]

Thus, in principle, if the conditions are right, Jewish law seems to allow the death penalty. Even so, Jewish communities have practiced it only with extreme caution. A well-known passage regarding the death penalty comes from the Mishnah (*Makkot* 1:10, see Text Study #1a below). The passage begins by saying a Sanhedrin that passes a death sentence once in seven years is a violent court. Rabbi Eleazar ben Azariah says once in 70 years. Rabbi Tarfon and Rabbi Akiva say, "If we had been members of the Sanhedrin, no one ever would have been executed." The Talmud suggests Rabbi Tarfon and Rabbi Akiva would scrutinize and challenge the evidence to such a degree that a conviction would become nearly impossible (*Makkot* 7a).

Still, no one opinion about death penalty "wins out" over the others in the Mishnah passage. In fact, Rabbi Shimon ben Gamaliel presents the stiffest challenge to Rabbi Tarfon and Rabbi Akiva's position. He states, "[By avoiding all capital punishment] they would have caused a proliferation of murderers in Israel" (see Text Study #4A below).

Contemporary scholars offer their own interpretations of the commentary by Rabbi Tarfon and Rabbi Akiva. Some suggest Rabbi Tarfon and Rabbi Akiva were concerned about the possibility of a mistaken verdict — executing an innocent person. Other scholars believe these Rabbis rejected the death penalty *in principle*. Seeing the death penalty as inconsistent with the "entire body of Jewish tradition," which opposed "any and all executions."[4]

In any case, *hatra'ah* (warning criminals) and *edut mechuvenet* (eyewitnesses) are difficult enough conditions for a death sentence. But another hurdle is the absence of a Sanhedrin or a king — a reality today, as throughout most of

---

[2]Basil F. Herring, *Jewish Ethics and Halakhah for Our Time*, 155. For details of court procedure in capital cases, see Maimonides, *Mishneh Torah, Hilchot Sanhedrin* 11-15.

[3]Herring, 155, drawing on Maimonides, *Mishneh Torah, Hilchot Melachim* 3:10.

[4]Herring, 157.

Jewish history. Without these authorities, who can pronounce a sentence of death? One opinion would allow contemporary courts to carry out a death sentence. Courts would justify such an emergency measure as protecting the well-being of society and the Torah. Another opinion would claim that without the Sanhedrin and the unbroken chain of ordained judges, a death sentence is no longer a legitimate response to murder.[5]

In the same vein, without a king, what happens to "executive privilege"? A king could override the courts and order the death penalty. Can someone nowadays take over this royal privilege? Specifically, can judicial authorities (put in place by contemporary communities) order a death sentence the way a king could? Some scholars would forbid this. Others suggest today's judicial authorities may exercise the equivalent of royal powers.

Thus, suppose a Jewish community today were to decide the fate of a violent criminal. We would have several *halachically* defensible alternatives for punishment. The scholar Basil F. Herring summarizes these:[6]

> On the one hand, we could sentence the criminal to death, defending the "emergency ruling" as being "necessary for the well-being of society." We would require a court with religiously impeccable credentials to make such a decision. Or, a representative body standing at the head of a given Jewish society could impose the death penalty.
>
> On the other hand, we might conclude that, without a Sanhedrin, capital punishment is not possible. That is, in the absence of a "properly empowered judicial body," we cannot allow even "an emergency decree."

Jewish sources also discuss a third possibility. Courts could impose some kind of substitute corporal punishment or imprisonment. But no consensus emerges regarding the advisability of this option. Some authorities favor it, and others oppose it.

In short, these are three possibilities, given the modern societies in which Jews live:

- Permitting only the highest, most scrupulous courts to pronounce death sentences

- Banning the death penalty under all circumstances

- Imposing alternative sentences

(The second and third possibility are not mutually exclusive. That is, we could ban the death penalty, but still impose an alternative sentence.)

The Death Penalty in America and Israel

Now, what does the above analysis mean for us today? From a Jewish perspective, are our communities' death penalty policies legitimate?

America, in the early twenty-first century, had hundreds of individuals on death row (more details on this in the next section). Political activists, legal analysts, and others voice serious concerns about the fairness of American courts, with proven instances of mistakes and discrimination. Those dedicated to Judaism's values and laws cannot support frequent and liberal use of the death penalty. In rare instances, a Jewish opinion may legitimately defend a particular death sentence imposed by the American courts. But overall, mainstream Jewish leaders and scholars criticize the death penalty in America as being terribly flawed and misguided.

In the first 50 years of its existence, the modern state of Israel carried out one death sentence. The offender was the Nazi master of genocide, Adolf Eichmann. Some religious authorities might stand firm in the position that today no Jewish authority can pronounce a death penalty sentence. Still, by imposing capital punishment once in 50 years, for a certified mass killer, the Israeli courts acted in a Jewishly defensible way. In 1954, Israel passed the Penal Law Revision (Abolition of the Death penalty for Murder). The country retained the death penalty, however, for

---

[5]Herring, 169.

[6]Herring, 170.

crimes of genocide and for treason committed in times of warfare.

General Perspectives

What Offenses Warrant the Death Penalty?

America has gone through both abolitionist (anti-death penalty) and retentionist (pro-death penalty) periods in its history. A retentionist position dominates. As of the early part of the twenty-first century, federal courts and most, but not all, American states allowed death sentences. Most democracies around the world have abolished the death penalty, including Canada, Australia, and the nations of the European Union.

Murder is potentially a capital crime in American states that allow the death penalty. Though it varies from state to state, these are the types of homicide considered capital crimes: murder carried out during the commission of a felony (e.g., while robbing a store); murder of a peace officer, corrections employee, or firefighter engaged in the performance of official duties; murder by an inmate serving a life sentence; and murder for hire (contract murder).[7] Accounting for aggravating circumstances is a key part of judging the severity of a murder. Examples of aggravating circumstances include: murder involving torture, murder related to rape or child molestation, and murder during a kidnapping.

As stated, many American states and most democratic countries do not accept the death penalty. Furthermore, even within the states that allow it, the issue is controversial. American abolitionists actively work to ban executions, a practice they deem "cruel and unusual." Thus, when we ask, "What offenses warrant the death penalty?" we must include this response: Many believe that *no offense* warrants the death penalty. Some countries are abolitionist for ordinary crimes only (such as murder, kidnapping,

rape). They allow the death penalty, but only for very limited crimes. Israel is an example of a country that is abolitionist for ordinary crimes. In a given generation in Israel, a death sentence should rarely, if ever take place.

Why Punish and Why the Death Penalty?

As we learned above, some democratic societies retain the death penalty. The objectives likely include: retribution, "closure," deterrence, restoring the moral order of society, and special prevention.

Retribution: People in favor of the death penalty do not see execution as "murder," but as punishment. Offenders receive what they deserve. Revenge is not the stated objective of the American justice system, though retribution may be.

Robert Jay Lifton and Greg Mitchell, the authors of *Who Owns Death* explain: Whereas *revenge* is a "visceral, personal desire to hurt the wrongdoer," *retribution* is a "deep felt desire to uphold society's values." Retribution comes from the Latin word *retribuere*, meaning "to pay back." A punishment that "pays back" means it is deserved and is appropriate to the crime. The authors continue, "Revenge combines retribution with the infliction of an extreme punishment. It requires that the murderer truly suffer his evil act, which could extend to a painful and violent death (hanging or electrocution). The lethal injection confuses everything, because it seems to snuff a life out so gently that nothing much has happened."[8]

Death penalty defenders support capital punishment as a "deserved and appropriate" response to certain crimes. It is *retribution* for a reprehensible act.

Death penalty opponents, on the other hand, might say that capital punishment is such an extreme response to crime, that it is as much about *revenge* as retribution. "Gentler" methods

---

[7] Mei Ling Rein, *Capital Punishment*, 44.

[8] *Who Owns Death*, 200-201.

of execution, such as lethal injection, distort the enormity of the fact that carrying out an execution is killing a human being. Execution is *murdering*; it is murdering the murderer. Interestingly, Hebrew uses the same root, *r-tz-ch* for execution and murder. An execution is law enforcers who "kill" and a murder is a criminal who "kills."[9]

Closure: Related to the idea of retribution is the concept of "closure." In essence, this is the logic of closure: When a murderer is put to death, family members and living victims will breathe a sigh of relief. The certainty that the criminal is dead will lift a huge burden of waiting and wondering what will happen to the offender. The execution will alleviate the anxiety that persists simply by knowing the brutal perpetrator still walks the earth.

The problem is the closure objective often falls short. Traditional Jewish sources do not focus attention on the closure justification for the death penalty. One reason may be that closure is not a reliable death punishment objective. While victims may feel some satisfaction when the criminal dies, an execution doesn't make grief and pain simply disappear. Marie Deans, founder of Murder Victims' Families for Reconciliation writes:

> After a murder, victims' families face two things: a death and a crime. At these times, families need help to cope with their grief and loss, and support to heal their hearts and rebuild their lives. From experience, we know that revenge is not the answer. The answer lies in reducing violence, not causing more death. The answer lies in supporting those who grieve for their lost loved ones, not creating more grieving families. It is time we break the cycle of violence. To those who say society must take a life for a life, we say: "not in our name" (www.mvfr.org, January 26, 2002).

Deterrence: In theory, deterrence is a reasonable objective for the death penalty. In essence, this is the logic: We'll execute this one really bad guy and make sure everyone hears about it. The horror of being put to death will be such a frightening prospect that would-be killers will think twice about getting involved in crime. Better yet, they will realize that a life of crime is not worth it and will turn to more productive ways of living.

Like the elusive objective of closure, the problem with deterrence is there is no reliable evidence of its effectiveness. We would hope that if we put a few murderers to death, other volatile individuals would see the wrongness of their ways and throw away their guns. But this is not the case.

States with the death penalty have higher crime rates than those without. Democratic countries that have abolished the death penalty have lower crime rates than does the United States, which has retained it. No significant changes in crime and murder rates appear when states either abolish capital punishment or institute it.[10] Over 80 percent of criminologists do not believe deterrence is a justification for the death penalty.[11] Significantly, police chiefs asked to rank the factors that, in their judgment, reduce the rate of violent crime, put the death penalty last. Curbing drug use, putting more officers on the street, longer sentences, and gun control were viewed as more effective.[12] (See also Text Study #4a–d below.)

Restoring the Moral Order of Society: Advocates of the death penalty might claim it helps us define and commit to what our society holds to be right, moral, and lawful. With capital punishment we are making the important statement that we distance ourselves from evil, embrace civilized values, and affirm an uncompromising dedication to justice and order.

---

[9]See "Capital Punishment — The Classic Jewish Definition" by Gerald J. Blidstein for a detailed discussion on the meaning of *r-tz-ch*.

[10]*Who Owns Death*, 200-201.

[11]Ibid.

[12]Richard Dieter, Death Penalty Information Center, *On the Front Line*, 1995, 2.

Abolitionists see the situation differently. As the anti-death penalty activist Hugo Adam Bedau puts it, "An execution is a violent public spectacle of official homicide . . . [Endorsing] killing to solve social problems [is] the worst possible example to set for the citizenry. Governments worldwide have often attempted to justify their lethal fury by extolling the purported benefits that such killing would bring to the rest of society. The benefits of capital punishment are illusory, but the bloodshed and the resulting destruction of community are real."[13] (See also Text Study #3a–e below.)

Special Prevention: One reason juries may impose a death sentence is concern that once the killer is released from prison, he/she may strike again. The death penalty conclusively prevents a proven criminal from ever again becoming a menace to society. American juries have been influenced by the fact that over the years, many violent criminals are released from prison. Convicted murderers under a "life sentence" might serve 20 or more years, but eventually get out.

But prison sentencing regulations have changed in America. Most states now have a provision in which a convicted murderer can be sentenced to "life without parole," meaning the convict will never be released from prison. The option of sentencing the most violent criminals to life without parole has shifted attitudes away from the death penalty. Many who might support the death penalty would opt instead for life without parole when this alternate sentence is available.

Who Gets the Death Penalty and by What Authority?

There are those who will continue to support capital punishment after analyzing pro and con arguments, such as those above. However, they still must confront some of the most disturbing arguments against it. Statistics show the death penalty is ridden with inconsistencies, prejudices, and mistakes.

Here are a few specifics: The American judicial system imposes the death penalty disproportionately upon those whose victims are white, upon offenders who are people of color, and upon people who are poor and uneducated.[14] Some question the policies of jury selection. That is, prosecutors in capital cases can reject potential jurors based on their opposition to the death penalty. This kind of selective process does not seem consistent with a suspect's right to be judged by a representative "jury of his/her peers." A particularly controversial matter is that over the years, American courts have allowed minors and mentally retarded people to be executed. Some see the fact that not all states have the same rules as problematic. While a criminal might receive a prison sentence, possibly even life without parole in one state, he/she might be executed for the same crime in another state.

Most troubling of all is that mistakes happen. When they do, no one can correct or undo the consequences. The death penalty is final and irreversible. On June 12, 2000, Professor James Liebman of Columbia University Law School released a comprehensive study of the death penalty in America. Over a 23-year period, he found a national error rate of 68 percent. That means two out of three convictions were problematic. Incompetent representation and prosecutorial misconduct were the most common errors.[15]

Between 1973 and 2001, 95 people were released from death row because evidence of their innocence turned up. The Religious Action Center of Reform Judaism (RAC) reports that many of these cases were not discovered through the normal appeals process. Rather, new scientific techniques, investigations by journalists, and the dedicated work of expert attorneys were

---

[13]Hugo Adam Beadau, "The Case Against the Death Penalty," www.aclu.org.

[14]Ibid.

[15]This information is discussed in a position paper pub-

lished by the Religious Action Center of Reform Judaism ("Issues: Death Penalty," www.rac.org, June 11, 2001, 2) and publicized in a statement made by the American Civil Liberties Union, www.aclu.org.

responsible. The typical death row inmate does not have access to such services. As of 2001, DNA testing had reversed the convictions of eight inmates. However, testing is not available to most. The RAC explains, "States and their judicial systems have been reluctant to authorize it for old cases because testing is expensive, there is a backlog of death row cases already, and they do not want to overturn old convictions."[16]

On January 11, 2003, Governor George Ryan commuted all Illinois death sentences to prison terms for life. By sparing the lives of 163 men and four women, Governor Ryan's order represented the largest emptying of death row in history. "Our capital system is haunted by the demon of error: error in determining guilt, and error in determining who among the guilty deserves to die," claimed Governor Ryan. He condemned a system in which half of the nearly 300 capital cases in Illinois had been reversed for a new trial or resentencing. He denounced substandard legal representation for defendants, racial discrimination, higher rates of death sentences in rural areas, and dozens of convictions based on jail informants. Of 13 men recently proved innocent, 12 had been executed. The efforts of journalism students, new DNA technology, and other independent investigations led to the freeing of 17 men from death row. For the state nearly to have put that many people mistakenly to death is "outrageous and unconscionable," exclaimed Governor Ryan, and is "nothing short of a catastrophic failure" (see also Text Study #8d below).

Staking Out Positions

Capital punishment is a controversial practice in the United States. Among western industrialized nations, the United States is the only country that retains it. Within the United States, voices on both sides of the issue express passionate views regarding its legitimacy. Though the death penalty remains legal, an abolitionist movement is strengthening. Anti-death penalty forces present formidable challenges to those who would put scores of people to death each year, and defend the practice as *not* being cruel or unusual.

Summary of the Overview

- A defensible position exists within Judaism that accepts the death penalty *in principle*.

- However, most Jewish communities, for most of Jewish history, did not apply the death penalty. Thus, *in practice*, capital punishment rarely took place.

- Today, the likelihood of fulfilling many commonly cited death penalty objectives is highly questionable.

- For modern nations, two death penalty positions are consistent with Jewish thinking: One is that it should be wholly abolished. The other is that it should happen only on the rarest of occasions, by impeccably thorough courts, and for the most heinous of crimes (such as genocide).

SCENARIOS: HOW THINGS HAVE CHANGED

For centuries, the death penalty question has been fraught with controversy. Do we really fulfill our intended objectives with the death penalty? Can we justify responding to violent crime by executing the offenders? These are difficult philosophical questions, and those on both sides of the debate hold strong opinions and deep convictions.

Below are two imaginary scenarios, one set in ancient days and the other in contemporary

---

[16]Religious Action Center of Reform Judaism, "Issues: Death Penalty," www.rac.org, June 11, 2001, 3.

times, intended to raise questions and spark discussion. Read each scenario to or with your students, and engage them in small or large group discussions. Use the "Focus the Discussion" section below to help you identify the important issues and facilitate these discussions. Note that additional questions relating to these scenarios are found in the "Stories: Understanding through Listening" section below (p. 151).

Following the discussions, have students continue on to the "Text Study" section to see what Jewish and other sources have to say about our topic. Finally, you may wish to have students discuss the scenarios a second time to see if their views have changed.

Scenario I: Adapted from the Talmud, Sanhedrin 37b, around 500 C.E.

A shepherd sat under a tree, on the side of a hill, tending his flock. Suddenly two men ran past — Ya'akov was chasing another man. The chase led the two men into some ruins. The shepherd got up and quickly followed them. By the time the shepherd got to the entrance of the ruins, Ya'akov was coming out. In his hand he held a bloody sword. Just inside the ruins, on the ground, was the other man, wounded and writhing, taking his last breaths of life.

The shepherd exclaimed to Ya'akov, "How wicked you are! Who slew this man? It is either me or you. Obviously, you're the murderer! Yet you know the courts won't be able to convict you since two witnesses didn't actually see you kill him" (Deuteronomy 17:6).

The shepherd continued, "But God knows what you did, Ya'akov. The courts might not be able to get you, but God will set things right. A killer eventually gets what he deserves."

The shepherd began to turn away from the murderer to go get help when a snake appeared. It bit the murderer so that he died.

Scenario II: Nowadays

Ms. Jackson was on trial for murder. A witness stood for questioning. She was asked to explain what she had seen regarding an incident that left a woman dead.

The witness explained: "I was sitting in my car outside QuickStop, a gas station with a convenience store. My friend and I had stopped to pick up a few things. Before we left, my friend decided to run across the street to buy a doughnut. So, I was alone in my car. As I looked out, I saw the gas station attendant with the defendant, Ms. Jackson. It looked as if the attendant was helping Ms. Jackson with one of the gasoline pumps. Suddenly, Ms. Jackson seemed to be pushing the attendant back toward the store. I looked closer; Ms. Jackson had a knife in her hand. I quickly dialed 911 on my cell phone, then got out of my car. As I took a few steps toward the store, Ms. Jackson was running out with a bloodied knife in her hand. The attendant lay just inside the doorway. She had a huge wound across her chest and was dying."

The trial continued with prosecutors presenting a few other important pieces of testimony against Ms. Jackson. These included the absence of an alibi for her whereabouts at the time of the murder, and documentation of a recent knife purchase she made. Still, the QuickStop witness's testimony was the central evidence against Ms. Jackson. The jury returned a guilty verdict. A sentencing jury would decide the punishment. Because the murder took place in a state that allows the death penalty, jury members could consider it if sufficient aggravating circumstances were found.

Focus the Discussion

As we have learned, both similarities and differences exist between traditional Jewish attitudes toward capital punishment and general modern perspectives. Regarding these scenarios, in the first, the suspect could not be convicted because the requirement for eyewitnesses was absent. That is, two witnesses did not see the suspect in the act. (Also, besides seeing Ya'akov in the act, they, or someone else, would have had to warn him not to carry out the crime.) The second scenario showed different requirements and standards for incriminating evidence.

However, one other difference is worth pointing out. A traditional Jewish attitude toward justice includes a role for God. That is, human courts must strive to maintain the most scrupulous standards possible. But in doing so, some highly suspicious individuals may escape conviction. We must do our human best to attain justice, but realize that occasions may arise that call for us to trust in a "Higher Source of Justice." The Talmud (*Sanhedrin* 37b) suggests that God, who knows each person's thoughts, is the final arbiter of justice. People do get what they deserve, one way or another.

TEXT STUDY

As we have seen, the ethics of the death penalty raise many difficult questions. Jewish and other textual sources provide helpful responses, but these responses often highlight tensions between opposing considerations. The chart on the next page poses the questions and offers two opposing points of view. Text sources supporting each of these points of view follow below.

1. **Is the death penalty a legitimate punishment?**

On the One Hand:

It is appropriate to consider capital punishment for the perpetrator of certain crimes.

A. The Bible is the earliest Jewish source to mention the death penalty, with biblical law mandating the death penalty for 36 offenses. Rabbinic and later sources add provisions and restrictions.

> He that strikes a man, so that he dies, is to be put to death, yes, death . . . When a man schemes against his neighbor, to kill him with cunning,

you shall take him away from My altar, to die (Exodus 21:12, 14).

B. Authorities could defend the death penalty because of the "needs of the time" (*Sanhedrin* 46a):

> A court may execute one not subject to the death penalty. This would not be in violation of the Torah but to protect it. Thus, if the court recognizes that the people willfully ignore the law, the court may issue special decrees to strengthen the law as it sees fit. This is by way of a temporary decree, not as a permanent statute for all generations . . . Such was the case of the man who rode a horse on the Sabbath . . . and was stoned, and such was the case when [*Sanhedrin* 45b] Shimon ben Shetach hanged 80 women on one day, even though there was no proper cross-examination, warning, or unequivocal evidence. He acted by way of a temporary measure as he saw fit (Maimonides, *Mishneh Torah, Hilchot Sanhedrin* 24:4).

C. If there are murderers who are not subject to the death penalty, then an Israelite king may execute them by his royal prerogative and by reason of societal need, if he so wishes. Likewise if a court wishes to execute such a person as a temporary measure, it may do so if such are the needs of the hour (Maimonides, *Mishneh Torah, Hilchot Rotzayach* 2:4).

On the Other Hand:

The death penalty is so severe, so final that to carry it out should be very difficult, if not impossible.

a. A Sanhedrin that passes the death penalty once in seven years is called a violent court. Rabbi Eleazar ben Azariah says this is true of a court that passes

TEACHING HOT TOPICS

Evaluating the Death Penalty: Questions to Consider

The Question	On the One Hand	On the Other Hand
1. Is the death penalty a legitimate punishment? (see p. 138)	It is appropriate to consider capital punishment for the perpetrator of certain crimes.	The death penalty is so severe, so final that to carry it out should be very difficult, if not impossible.
2. Can we enforce the death penalty meaningfully and effectively? (see p. 141)	There are procedures and methods for executing criminals.	Whatever the method, the fact is that executions turn the state into a killer.
3. Is retribution a legitimate objective for the death penalty? (see p. 141)	The death penalty is retributive justice — giving criminals what they deserve (i.e., *lex talionis* or "an eye for an eye . . . ")	The death penalty only aggravates cycles of crime as it feeds a culture of violence.
4. Is the death penalty a deterrent for those who would consider committing violent crimes? (see p. 142)	The possibility of receiving the death penalty will deter those who would commit violent crimes.	There is no evidence that the death penalty deters criminals from unlawful acts.
5. Does the death penalty help communities identify and recommit to moral values? (see p. 144)	The death penalty restores the moral order of society, realigns the community with God, and lifts a vile contamination from the land.	Alternative punishments can achieve the same goals.
6. Does the process preceding and surrounding an execution contribute to *teshuvah* (restitution and repentance)? (see p. 145)	Being put to death serves as expiation (compensation) for a murderer.	The death penalty prevents rehabilitation and thwarts *teshuvah* (restitution and repentance).
7. How are the victims' loved ones affected by the execution of the offending criminal? (see p. 146)	Once the perpetrator is executed, the victim's family finally can experience a well deserved sense of "closure" to their tragedy.	Putting the criminal to death won't bring back a loved one.
8. Do democracies that continue to enforce the death penalty have reliable standards? (see p. 147)	The American judicial system requires reasonable standards for imposing the death penalty.	Mistakes, unreliable witnesses, incompetent lawyers and judges, biased juries, and racial and economic discrimination make the death penalty a gross distortion of justice.

such a sentence even once in 70 years. Rabbi Tarfon and Rabbi Akiva say, "Had we been members of the Sanhedrin, no one would ever have been executed" (*Makkot* 1:10).

b. If anyone kills a person, the murderer may be murdered only on the evidence of witnesses; the testimony of a single witness against a person shall not suffice for a sentence of death (Numbers 35:30).

c. A death sentence passed by a court of 23 judges required full compliance with due process. Necessary conditions included *hatra'ah*, i.e., warning the culprit before the crime, and *edut mechuvenet*, i.e., impeccably qualified witnesses able to withstand severe cross-examination[17] (see Text Study #8b below for a related passage):

> Once the witnesses say, "We gave him due warning and we know him," the court gives [the witnesses] a solemn charge [regarding the gravity of their position] (Maimonides, Mishneh Torah, Hilchot Sanhedrin 12:3).

d. They used to examine [the witnesses] with seven inquiries: In what Sabbatical year [of the Jubilee did the crime occur]? in what year [of the seven year cycle]? in what month? on what date of the month? on what day [of the week]? in what place [was the suspect observed committing the crime]? Rabbi Yosi says: [They need only ask] on what day, in what hour, and in what place. [Also witnesses were asked]: Do you know him? Did you warn him? Is he an idolater? Whom does he worship? What is the manner of his worship?

> The more [a judge] examines, the more praiseworthy he is. It once happened that ben Zakkai probed the evidence regarding the stalks of fig trees

(*Sanhedrin* 5:1-2).

e. It is a Scriptural decree that the court shall not put a man to death or flog him on his own admission (of guilt) (Maimonides, *Mishneh Torah, Hilchot Sanhedrin* 18:6).

f. "You shall do no unrighteousness in judgment" (Leviticus 19:15). This refers to the judge who perverts judgment, acquits the guilty, and condemns the innocent. It also refers to the judge who delays judgment, who discusses at undue length things that are obvious in order to annoy one of the parties to the suit. He, too, is included among the unrighteous (Maimonides, *Mishneh Torah, Hilchot Sanhedrin* 20:6).

g. It is clear that with such a procedure [restrictions and provisions imposed by the Rabbis], conviction in capital cases was next to impossible, and that this was the intention of the framers of the rules is equally plain (George Foot Moore, *Judaism*, Harvard University Press, 1927, Vol. II, p. 186).

Probing: Ideas and Issues

Once the death penalty is "on the books" (as it is in the Bible), authorities must decide how and when to apply it. What considerations do the texts above address? Many Jewish texts discuss the conditions necessary for imposing the death penalty. However, if we were to consult only the texts above, what would we find the Jewish attitude toward death penalty to be — in favor, not in favor, somewhere in between? Explain.

Read the continuation of Text Study #1a above as presented in #4A below. Who do you agree with the most — the unnamed Rabbinic opinion (i.e., the first sentence), Rabbi Eleazar ben Azariah, Rabbi Tarfon and Rabbi Akiva, or Rabbi Shimon ben Gamaliel? Explain.

---

[17]Basil F. Herring, *Jewish Ethics and Halakhah for Our Time*, 155.

2. **Can we enforce the death penalty meaningfully and effectively?**

On the One Hand:

There are procedures and methods for executing criminals.

A. And you shall come unto the priests, the Levites, and unto the judge that shall be in those days; and you shall inquire and they shall declare unto you the sentence of judgment (Deuteronomy 17:9).

B. Bat Tali, the daughter of a priest, had illicit sexual relations. Rabbi Chama bar Tuvia wrapped her in branches and burned her to death. Said Rabbi Joseph, "Rabbi Chama thereby erred doubly. He contradicted Rabbi Matna [in using that particular mode of execution], and he contradicted the *Beraita* that says . . . that capital punishment occurs only when there is a priest [and Sanhedrin functioning in the Temple] (*Sanhedrin* 52b).

C. See also Text Study #1b–e above.

On the Other Hand:

Whatever the method, the fact is that executions turn the state into a killer.

a. In all the lands of my acquaintance, the death penalty is not practiced, except here in Spain. When I arrived here, I was most surprised that this was done without a Sanhedrin. I was told that it was by way of a royal dispensation utilized by the Jewish court to save lives that would be lost were they to be left to Gentile courts. And while I permitted them to maintain this practice, I never agreed with their taking of life in such a fashion (Rosh, Responsum 17:8).

b. In the late 1990s, SueZann Bosler declared that if the state killed the man who killed her father:

We become murderers, too. We become just like him. I don't want to be like him. I don't want his blood on my hands (*Who Owns Death*, p. 212).

(For a related passage from a Jewish source, see Text Study #8b below.)

c. See also Text Study #3e below.

Probing: Ideas and Issues

How would the authors of each of the texts above respond to the statement that the death penalty turns the state into a killer? What do you believe?

3. **Is retribution a legitimate objective for the death penalty?**

On the One Hand:

The death penalty is retributive justice — giving criminals what they deserve (i.e., *lex talionis* or "an eye for an eye . . . ")

A. But if harm should occur, then you are to give life in place of life — eye for eye, tooth for tooth, hand for hand, foot for foot, burnt-scar for burnt-scar, wound for wound, bruise for bruise (Exodus 14:23-25).

B. Certain crimes constitute such outrageous violation of human and moral values that they demand retribution. It was to control the natural human impulse to seek revenge and, more broadly, to give expression to deeply held views that some conduct deserves punishment, that criminal laws, administered by the state, were established. The rule of law does not eliminate feelings of outrage but does provide controlled channels for expressing such feelings . . . The death penalty's retributive function thus vindicates the fundamental moral principle that a criminal should receive his or her just desserts.

Through the provision of just punishment, capital punishment affirms the sanctity of human life and thereby protects it (Statement of Paul G. Cassell, Associate Professor of Law, University of Utah, Salt Lake City, before the Senate Judiciary Committee, April 1, 1993).

On the Other Hand:

The death penalty only aggravates cycles of crime as it feeds a culture of violence.

a. Forty years prior to the destruction of the Second Temple, the Sanhedrin moved from the Temple and met in the marketplace, so as not to judge capital cases. What was the reason? Because they recognized the proliferation of capital crimes which they were unable to judge properly, thus they relocated so as not to pass the death sentence (*Avodah Zarah* 8b).

b. The Bible is clear: *midah keneged midah* — measure should be met with like measure. Yet a lifetime sentence without probation, which is appropriate for murder in the first degree, provides a severe enough punishment that can be equated with the death penalty. After all, money can never replace an eye either, yet for the sake of justice our Rabbis were willing and able to make moral equivalencies (Elie Spitz, "The Jewish Tradition and Capital Punishment," in *Contemporary Jewish Ethics and Morality*," p. 344, 346-347).

c. Some would argue that the death penalty will teach society at large the seriousness of crime. Yet we say that teaching people to respond to violence with violence will, again, only breed more violence (A Joint Statement, *To End the Death Penalty*, by the National Jewish/Catholic Consultation [co-sponsored by the National Council of Synagogues and the Bishops' Committee for Ecumenical and Interreligious Affairs of the National Conference of Catholic Bishops],

December 3, 1999).

d. Executions are bad for our minds because of their effect on our violent and vengeful impulses . . . Capital vengeance, the principle of "a death for a death," sustains and legitimates those violent impulses. It encourages us to remain "stuck" in them rather than transforming them into constructive advocacies and actions (*Who Owns Death*, p. 236).

e. With each new death penalty statute enacted and each execution carried out, our executive, judicial, and legislative branches, at both the state and federal level, add to a culture of violence and killing. With each person executed, we're teaching our children that the way to settle scores is through violence, even to the point of taking a human life (Statement of Senator Russell Feingold, on introducing the Federal Death Penalty Abolition Act of 1999 [S. 1917] before the Senate, November 10, 1999).

Probing: Ideas and Issues

What are the possible advantages (if any) of punishments that are meant to be equal in gravity to the crime? What are the disadvantages? To what extent should retribution ("getting back at the bad guy") be a consideration in coming up with an appropriate punishment for a criminal?

4. **Is the death penalty a deterrent for those who would consider committing violent crimes?**

On the One Hand:

The possibility of receiving the death penalty will deter those who would commit violent crimes.

A. See passage #1a above. That passage continues with these words:

Rabbi Shimon ben Gamaliel says, "[By avoiding all capital punishment, as do Rabbi Tarfon and Rabbi Akiva] they would have caused a proliferation of murderers in Israel" (*Makkot* 1:10).

B. If those who testified are false witnesses, if they have testified falsely against their fellow, you shall do to them as they schemed to do to their fellow. Thus you will sweep out evil from your midst; others will hear and be afraid, and such evil things will not again be done in your midst. Nor must you show pity: life for life, eye for eye, tooth for tooth, hand for hand, foot for foot (Deuteronomy 19:18-21).

C. Whether or not capital punishment will deter others, it definitely will prevent the offender him/herself from committing further crimes. (This idea is known as "special prevention.")

> As for a "stubborn and rebellious son" (Deuteronomy 21:18-21), he must be put to death because of what he will become, for necessarily he will murder later on. "He that kidnaps" (Exodus 21:16) likewise must be punished in this manner, for he exposed him to death. Also "he that comes breaking in" (Exodus 22:1), for he too is prepared to kill, as [the Sages], may their memory be blessed, have explained. These three, I mean a stubborn and rebellious son, a kidnapper, and a thief, will become shedders of blood (Maimonides, *Guide of the Perplexed*, 3:41).

D. If the death penalty can deter one murder of an innocent life or if it can make a statement to the community about what will and will not be tolerated, then it is justified (Statement of James C. Anders, Solicitor, Fifth Judicial Circuit of South Carolina, before the Senate Judiciary Committee, September 19, 1989).

On the Other Hand:

There is no evidence that the death penalty deters criminals from unlawful acts.

a. In a climate of increasing crime, the Sanhedrin moved its meeting site away from where it could proclaim death sentences. The court wasn't prepared to put so many people to death. Perhaps they understood that executing criminals does not necessarily deter other would-be offenders. Such punishments may only add to an environment of violence (see Text Study #3a above).

b. Some would argue that the death penalty is needed as a deterrent to crime. Yet the studies that lie behind our statements over the years have yet to reveal any objective evidence to justify this conclusion. Criminals tend to believe they will escape any consequences for their behavior, or simply do not think of consequences at all, so an escalation of consequences is usually irrelevant to their state of mind at the time of the crime (A Joint Statement, *To End the Death Penalty*, by the National Jewish/Catholic Consultation [co-sponsored by the National Council of Synagogues and the Bishops' Committee for Ecumenical and interreligious Affairs of the National Conference of Catholic Bishops], December 3, 1999).

c. Following the logic of death penalty supporters who believe it is a deterrent, you would think that our European allies, who don't use the death penalty, would have a higher murder rate than the United States. Yet, they don't, and it's not even close. In fact, the murder rate in the United States is six times higher than the murder rate in Britain, seven times higher than in France, five times higher than in Australia, and five times higher than in Sweden. [In America] during the period 1995-1998, Texas [the highest percentage death penalty user] had a murder rate that [was] nearly double the murder rate in Wisconsin [free of the death penalty for nearly 150 years] (Statement of Senator Russell Feingold, on introducing the Federal Death Penalty Abolition Act of 1999 [S. 1917] before the Senate, November 10, 1999).

d. I have inquired for most of my adult life about studies that might show that the death penalty is a deterrent. And I have not seen any research that would substantiate that point (Attorney General Janet Reno, at a Justice Department news briefing, 2000).

Probing: Ideas and Issues

Which texts are more convincing: those that would claim the death penalty deters others from criminal acts, or those what would disagree with that conclusion? Is proven deterrence an important justification for death penalty? Is proven deterrence a *necessary* justification? Explain.

5. **Does the death penalty help communities identify and recommit to moral values?**

On the One Hand:

The death penalty restores the moral order of society, realigns the community with God, and lifts a vile contamination from the land.

A. You are not to corrupt the land that you are in, for the blood — it will corrupt the land, and the land will not be purged of the blood that has been shed upon it except through the blood of the one who shed it (Numbers 35:33).

B. Punishment (which includes the death penalty) expresses the emotions of the society wronged, the anger and outrage felt, and it solidifies and reinforces the

goals, values, and norms of acceptable behavior in the society . . . (Statement of James C. Anders, Solicitor, Fifth Judicial Circuit of South Carolina, before the Senate Judiciary Committee, September 19, 1989).

On the Other Hand:

Alternative punishments can achieve the same goals.

a. There is an established procedure, one which we follow in practice, whereby a person who is guilty of a crime for which the punishment is death is instead excommunicated and whipped, and never given an opportunity for pardon. The reason is that today we no longer carry out the death penalty (Maimonides, Commentary on the Mishnah, *Chullin* 1).

b. There are three overarching objectives for punishment to be found in the Bible: the realignment of God with creation, retribution, and deterrence . . . We live in a time with a punitive option which our tradition lacked, namely, prisons. This new factor plus [several] practical considerations constitute a moral challenge to the death penalty in our current U.S. penal system . . . Prisons today do meet the three goals of execution in the Bible (Elie Spitz, "The Jewish Tradition and Capital Punishment" in *Contemporary Jewish Ethics and Morality*," p. 344, 346-347).

c. See also Text Study #3b above.

Probing: Ideas and Issues

Do you agree with the statement that the death penalty restores the moral order of society, realigns the community with God, and lifts a vile contamination from the land? Explain. How important do you think these three objectives of punishment are? Can alternative punishments achieve these objectives? How so or how not?

6. **Does the process preceding and surrounding an execution contribute to *teshuvah* (restitution and repentance)?**

On the One Hand:

Being put to death serves as expiation (compensation) for a murderer.

A. When he was about ten cubits from the place of stoning, they would say to him: "Make confession": for it was the custom of those condemned to death to make confession, and all who confess have a share in the World To Come . . . And if the condemned does not know how to make confession, they say to him, "Repeat these words: 'May my death be an atonement for all my sins.'" Rabbi Yehudah says, "If he knew he had been sentenced through false evidence, he says, 'Let my death be an atonement for all my sins except this sin.'" [The Sages] said to [Rabbi Yehudah], "If that were what he would say, then every convicted criminal would say likewise to exonerate himself" (*Sanhedrin* 6:2).

B. Notwithstanding the high regard for humanity, the cherished value of every unique individual, and the great love that we have for every individual made in the image of God, even those condemned to death . . . nonetheless an evil person cannot be permitted to remain alive, for by his death he gains atonement, even as he is removed from life (Rabinowitz-Teomim, *Mishpetei Nefashot*, p. 48-49 as quoted by Basil Herring, *Jewish Ethics and Halakhah for Our Time*, p. 157).

On the Other Hand:

The death penalty prevents rehabilitation and thwarts teshuvah (restitution and repentance).

a. Judaism expects a person to make ongoing efforts to repent. Traditionally, a Jew recites the *"Amidah"* prayer three times each weekday. The prayer includes these passages:

> Our Parent, bring us back to Your Torah. Our Ruler, draw us near to Your service. Lead us back to You, truly repentant. Praised are You, Eternal who welcomes repentance.

> Forgive us, our Parent, for we have sinned; pardon us, our Ruler, for we have transgressed, for You forgive and pardon. Praised are You, Eternal who is gracious and forgiving.

> Behold our affliction and deliver us. Redeem us soon because of Your mercy, for You are the mighty Redeemer. Praised are You, Eternal, Redeemer of the people Israel.

b. Justice didn't do a thing to heal me. Forgiveness did . . . I've seen mankind's idea of ultimate justice. I have more faith in God's . . . I want people to know that our hope for healing is not in the legal system (Debbie Morris, a woman raped and nearly murdered when she was 16, quoted in *Who Owns Death*, p. 207).

Probing: Ideas and Issues

According to these texts, does remaining alive provide worthwhile opportunities for a violent criminal to repent? What do you believe is the most valuable way a murderer might receive expiation for his/her crime?

7. How are the victims' loved ones affected by the execution of the offending criminal?

On the One Hand:

Once the perpetrator is executed, the victim's family finally can experience a well deserved sense of "closure" to their tragedy.

A. We victims need a closure to our grief. I did not rejoice when Wallace Norrell was executed July 13, 1990, for murdering [my daughter] Quenette, but I certainly felt relief . . . (Statement of Miriam Shehane, State President, Victims of Crimes and Leniency, Montgomery, Alabama, before the Senate Judiciary Committee, April 1, 1993).

B. A mother in Ohio who had waited 15 years for the killer of her two daughters to die claims:

> [I would have] no problem injecting him (with lethal poison) myself. I could lie down and have a good night's sleep, knowing that justice had been done (*Who Owns Death*, p. 199).

On the Other Hand:

Putting the criminal to death won't bring back a loved one.

a. See the passage written by Marie Deans, founder of Murder Victims' Families for Reconciliation above, in "Why Punish and Why the Death Penalty" in the "General Perspectives" section above, p. 134.

b. Betty Slusher refused to attend the execution of the killers of her husband in South Carolina in 1998:

> I thought when this day came that I wouldn't be sad, that I would be happy, but I am sad. Let's face it, we're taking two men's lives (*Who Owns Death*, p. 202).

c. The words of a mother of a young girl murdered in Pennsylvania:

> The gaping wound will never heal. And it is because of this intense pain that I have come to know that I would not, and could not, inflict it on another mother . . . Justice would only be served if, in taking his life, Aimee could come back to life, and that is impossible (*Who Owns Death*, p. 204).

d. The strongest argument [for the death penalty] is the deep pain and grief of the families of victims and their quite natural desire to see punishment meted out to those who have plunged them into such agony. Yet it is the clear teaching of our traditions that this pain and suffering cannot be healed simply through the retribution of capital punishment or by vengeance. It is a difficult and long process of healing, which comes about through personal growth and God's grace. We agree that much more must be done by the religious community and by society at large to solace and care for the grieving families of the victims of violent crime (A Joint Statement, *To End the Death Penalty*, by the National Jewish/Catholic Consultation [co-sponsored by the National Council of Synagogues and the Bishops' Committee for Ecumenical and interreligious Affairs of the National Conference of Catholic Bishops], December 3, 1999).

Probing: Ideas and Issues

What do you think "closure" means as it relates to the death penalty? Why do you suppose families of victims might feel they would experience closure if the offender were executed? What might be arguments against justifying death penalty because it provides closure to the victim's loved ones?

8. **Do democracies that continue to enforce the death penalty have reliable standards?**

On the One Hand:

The American judicial system requires reasonable standards for imposing the death penalty.

A. The Fifth Amendment provides that "no persons shall be held to answer for a capital crime, unless on a presentment of indictment of a Grand Jury . . . nor be deprived of life . . . without due process of law." This clearly permits the death penalty to be imposed and establishes beyond doubt that the death penalty is not one of the "cruel and unusual punishments" prohibited by the Eighth Amendment" (From Justice Antonin Scalia's concurring opinion in the Supreme Court decision "Callins V. James" [510 U.S. 1141, 1994], denying review of the death penalty case [in response to Justice Blakmun's dissent).

B. The system imposes a vast array of due process protections to assure that no innocent person is convicted of a crime (Statement of Paul G. Cassell, Associate Professor of Law, University of Utah, Salt Lake City, before the Senate Judiciary Committee, April 1, 1993).

C. Lest we forget, in addition to the extensive appeals of the courts, every state with a capital punishment statute has a procedure for executive clemency . . . (Statement of Miriam Shehane, State President, Victims of Crimes and Leniency, Montgomery, Alabama, before the Senate Judiciary Committee, April 1, 1993).

On the Other Hand:

Mistakes, unreliable witnesses, incompetent lawyers and judges, biased juries, and racial and economic discrimination make the death penalty a gross distortion of justice.

a. You shall have one standard for stranger and citizen alike: for I the Eternal am your God (Leviticus 24:22).

b. In capital cases, authorities were to impress upon witnesses the gravity of their position. If witnesses' testimony were to cause an injustice:

> The blood of the accused and his unborn offspring stain the perjurer forever. Thus, in the case of Cain, Scripture says, "The voice of the bloods of your brother call to Me." Observe that the text reads in the plural — not "blood" but "bloods." For Abel's blood and that of his unborn seed were alike involved. It is for this reason that God created only one human in the beginning, a token to humanity that if one destroys one life, it is as though one had destroyed all humankind; whereas if one preserves one life, it is as though one had preserved all humankind (*Sanhedrin* 4:5).

c. Some would argue that our system of justice, trial by jury, can ensure that capital punishment will be meted out equitably to various groups in society and that the innocent will never be convicted . . . Statistics, however weighted, indicate that errors are made in judgment and convictions. Recent scientific advances, such as DNA testing, may reveal that persons on death row, despite seemingly "overwhelming" circumstantial evidence, may in fact be innocent of the charges against them. Likewise, suspiciously high percentages of those on death row are poor or people of color. Our legal system is a very good one, but it is a human institution. Even a small percentage of irreversible errors is increasingly seen as intolerable. God alone is the author of life (A Joint Statement, *To End the Death Penalty*, by the National Jewish/Catholic

Consultation [co-sponsored by the National Council of Synagogues and the Bishops' Committee for Ecumenical and Interreligious Affairs of the National Conference of Catholic Bishops], December 3, 1999).

d. On January 11, 2003, Governor George Ryan of Illinois commuted 167 death sentences to prison terms for life. See page 136 for some statements by Governor Ryan. The following are additional excerpts of his remarks explaining this action:

> You are five times more likely to get a death sentence for first-degree murder in the rural areas of this state . . .
>
> Half . . . of the nearly 300 capital cases in Illinois had been reversed for a new trial or resentencing. How many . . . professionals can get by with 50 percent accuracy?
>
> Thirty-three of the death row inmates were represented at trial by an attorney who had later been disbarred or at some point suspended from the practice of law. Of the more than 160 death row inmates, 35 were African-American defendants who had been convicted or condemned to die not by a jury of their peers, but by all-white juries (Excerpts from Governor's "Speech on Commutations," *The New York Times*, Sunday, January 12, 2003, "National" section, p. 22).

Probing: Ideas and Issues

Why should we trust the American legal process? What are the problems with trusting the American legal process with death penalty cases? If we believe that "God alone is the author or life" (Text Study #8c), does that mean the courts should never impose the death penalty?

RELATED MIDDOT AND MITZVOT

We should keep in mind these virtues and commandments as we evaluate the ethics of the death penalty.

Anavah (Humility): Taking anyone's life, even a criminal's, is a momentous action. We must be extremely humble as we weigh justification of the death penalty.

Ayd Shahkeyr (Not Bearing False Witness): Any level of falsity in accusing a suspect could contribute to him/her wrongly being put to death. We must do everything possible to prevent such a tragic scenario.

Charatah (Regret): Expressions of regret on the part of the offender sometimes help shift the angry emotions of the victim's family and society so that they are more willing to consider alternatives to the death penalty.

Emet (Truth): No sentence should be pronounced upon the suspect without certainty of the truth of the accusations.

Lo Tikom (Not Taking Revenge): Revenge is not an acceptable objective of punishment.

Lo Tirtzach (Not Murdering): Even if we say that executing a criminal is an exception to this commandment, we must recognize the gravity of purposefully killing any human being.

Mishpat Echad (One Standard of Justice for All — Leviticus 24:22): Any justice system that discriminates against the poor or against a particular race of people is corrupt and has no right ever to enact a death penalty sentence.

Salchanut (Forgiveness): To forgive a violent criminal may be too much to ask of those harmed by his/her actions. Even so, striving for forgiveness helps many victims (and victims' families) to begin healing. Aspiring toward forgiveness is a difficult but worthy struggle.

Teshuvah (Repentance): Some say a criminal's death will atone for his/her wrongs. We must weigh such a belief against the atonement that could happen if a person worked to make amends on this side of life.

ACTIVITIES

A First Look: Key Issues and Ideas

1. A set induction: Survey students about their feelings and attitudes regarding capital punishment. On the board write the word "Death." Have participants "free associate" words and ideas that come to them when they think of the word. Continue with some or all of these words: Punishment, Execution, Life Imprisonment, Murderer, "Eye for an Eye," Vengeance, Lethal Injection. Conclude with "Death Penalty."

   After completing the above, ask: How would you characterize our group's overall attitude toward the death penalty? Which word(s) aroused the most variety in types of associations, and which aroused the least? Why do you suppose this is?

2. Another set induction: Survey students about what they know and what they've heard about the death penalty. What current events are happening that relate to death penalty issues and concerns? What are the most problematic controversies? (An example of a controversy might be: poor and uneducated inmates on death row often have received substandard legal support.)

3. Give students an Overview of the Death Penalty. The Overview should include both Jewish and General Perspectives on the bulleted subtopics below. Alternatively, assign individuals or small groups a subtopic to research, then present their findings to the rest of the group.

   - What Offenses Warrant the Death Penalty?
   - Why Punish and Why the Death Penalty?
     - Realignment of God with Creation
     - Retribution
     - Deterrence
     - Restoring the Moral Order of Society
     - Special Prevention
     - Closure
   - Who Gets the Death Penalty and by What Authority?
   - The Death Penalty in America and Israel

4. Have group members imagine they serve on an advisory committee to the president/prime minister of the country. Their charge is to give a recommendation to the president/prime minister regarding the death penalty. Refer to the 16 points listed in the "On the One Hand/On the Other Hand" table in the "Text Study" section above. Committee members assign a number value to each of the 16 considerations. A "10" means *most* important to take into account; a "1" means *least* important. For example, they might rank #8 (the possibility of mistakes and injustices in applying the death penalty) as a "10" and #6 (being put to death serves as expiation for a murderer) as a "1." You may want participants to work in pairs, then come back together as a group to discuss conclusions.

5. After some initial study of the topic, ask students to consider this statement:

   "Judaism accepts the death penalty *in principle*, but not *in practice*." Guide a discussion of this statement with these questions:

   - How is the statement accurate?
   - How is the statement not accurate?

- Is accepting something in principle, but not in practice ethically sound? Why or why not?

- Is accepting the death penalty in principle, but not in practice a useful ethical guideline? Why or why not?

- "Judaism's attitude toward the death penalty is . . . " As mentioned, one way to complete this sentence is: "Judaism's attitude toward the death penalty is that it accepts it in principle, but not in practice. How would *you* complete the sentence?

Applying Middot and Mitzvot

1. Go around the room and ask each participant to complete this sentence: When there *is not* one standard of justice for all (*mishpat echad*) . . .

    Repeat, but have participants complete this sentence: When there *is* one standard of justice for all . . .

2. Have the group (or small groups) write a memo to jury members seated on a court that will judge a violent criminal. This memo should guide and inspire jurists to maintain the highest moral attitudes and intentions. In composing their memo, participants should use six or more words from the "Related *Middot* and *Mitzvot*" section above, pp. 148-149.

3. Explain these terms: Forgiveness (*salchanut*), repentance (*teshuvah*), and regret (*charatah*). Emphasize how important these Jewish values are. Explore how these values might be consistent with views expressed in Text Study #6b, #7b, and #7c.

    Continue by saying: "Even though Judaism embraces forgiveness, and even though we believe people should have the opportunity to regret their actions and repent, our tradition warns us not to 'cave in' to mercy." Share the following passage. It expresses the sentiment that we must respond unyieldingly to murder:

"Do not pity him": This is an admonition not to spare the killer out of mercy. One should not say that a person has already been killed, of what use is the killing of another? Rather than neglect the execution, therefore, the murderer should be executed. Abba Chanon says in the name of Rabbi Eliezer, "Wherever the Torah specifies an [apparently] unjust punishment, it is written 'do not pity'" (*Midrash Tannaim*, Deuteronomy 19:13).

Discuss this question:

How do we account for the seeming discrepancy between encouraging forgiveness, repentance, and regret on the one hand, and saying "do not pity" on the other?

To take this activity one step further, read the following statement put out by Murder Victims' Families for Reconciliation:

Reconciliation means accepting that you cannot undo the murder, but you can decide how you want to live afterwards (www.mvfr.org).

Discuss this question:

Is this statement consistent with a valid Jewish response to murder?

4. For more information and activities on:

Anavah (Humility): see *Teaching Jewish Virtues* by Susan Freeman, pp. 195-210.

Ayd Shahker (Not Bearing False Witness): see *Teaching Mitzvot* by Barbara Binder Kadden and Bruce Kadden, pp. 107-111.

Din V'Rachamim (Balancing Justice and Mercy): see *Teaching Jewish Virtues* by Susan Freeman, pp. 55-68.

Emet (Truth): see *Teaching Jewish Virtues* by Susan Freeman, pp. 69-84.

Lo Tikom (Not Taking Revenge): see *Teaching Mitzvot* by Barbara Binder Kadden and Bruce Kadden, pp. 187-192.

Lo Tirtzach (Not Murdering): see *Teaching Mitzvot* by Barbara Binder Kadden and Bruce Kadden, pp. 169-173.

Teshuvah (Repentance): see *The Jewish Moral Virtues* by Eugene B. Borowitz and Frances Weidman Schwartz, pp. 263-276, and *It's a Mitzvah!* by Bradley Shavit Artson, pp. 186-195.

Stories: Understanding through Listening

1. Invite one or more criminal lawyers to address your group, ideally a defense lawyer and a prosecutor. A prison chaplain also would make an interesting guest. Have guests discuss their experiences and feelings regarding penalizing violent criminals. Ask them to describe their attitudes toward the death penalty. For Jewish guests, ask how their religious commitments and beliefs influence their feelings about the death penalty. If you have invited guests from other backgrounds, compare how their religious beliefs influence them.

2. Read over the scenarios in the "Scenarios: How Things Have Changed" section above. Discuss these questions:

   • What did Ya'akov's crime *seem* to be (in the first scenario)?

   • Could a Jewish court convict him? Explain.

   • How is Ya'akov's case similar to Ms. Jackson's (in the second scenario)?

   • How might standards of conviction differ in modern secular courts from standards in traditional Jewish courts?

   • What can/should modern courts learn from Jewish standards of justice?

   • Today, criminologists use forensic techniques, such as DNA testing, to identify a suspect with a crime. Such techniques were not available to our ancestors. Traditionally, Judaism taught that neces-

sary conditions for convicting suspects included *hatra'ah* (forewarning the culprit before the crime), and *edut mechuvenet*, (impeccably qualified witnesses able to withstand severe cross-examination). Should these two Jewish standards be relaxed in light of forensic testing or other strategies for convicting criminals?

3. Have group members read *Dead Man Walking* by Sister Helen Prejean (New York: Vintage Books, 1993). As they read, ask students to note ideas consistent with Jewish attitudes and values regarding death penalty, criminals, victims, truth, forgiveness, healing, spiritual counsel, etc. Does the book contain ideas not consistent with Judaism? It may be helpful to assign one or two chapters at a time.

   Alternatively, watch and discuss the movie version of *Dead Man Walking* (1995, 122 min., rated R), available from video stores.

Action: Getting Out, Getting Involved

1. Many organizations have missions involving issues related to crime, death penalty, and/or victims' families. Assign individuals or small groups to research and report back on various organizations. In their reports they should:

   • Summarize what the organization does.

   • Discuss whether it would be appropriate for a committed Jew to become involved in the organization, explaining why or why not.

   • Suggest ways to get involved (assuming the presenters believe in the organization's mission). Mention things to do *now* to help support the organization's work (for example, publicize the needs of a specific murder victim's family, or write letters to officials working for governments that retain the death penalty explaining why it should be abolished).

Also, mention *potential* ways to support the organization (for example, become a lawyer who assists poor and uneducated inmates).

- For suggestions of organizations to research, see those included in the Bibliography below, under "Web Sites."

2. Contact a prison chaplain. Perhaps your Rabbi can help you get in touch with such an individual. Find out from this person if there are inmates who would benefit from receiving cards, holiday messages, and/or letters from your group. Ask the chaplain for guidance regarding appropriate and helpful ways to engage with prisoners.

3. Ask: How well does our judicial system fulfill the principle "One standard of justice for all" (*Mishpat Echad*, Leviticus 24:22)? Have students research and evaluate their government's successes and failures regarding this important value. Sources for information include books, articles, and web sites mentioned in the Bibliography below. Additional insights are sure to be gained by interviewing lawyers, law enforcement officers, prison chaplains, (former) prisoners, etc.

Wrestling: Engagement with the Issues

1. Establish three groups. Give participants the option of joining the one which most closely reflects their beliefs:

- Pro-death penalty (e.g., for violent criminals)

- Anti-death penalty (under any circumstances)

- Death penalty only for genocidal murderers or for those who commit treason during wartime

Each group imagines it is a campaign committee for a political candidate. The group must prepare their candidate to inform the public about the candidate's beliefs on the death penalty. It must compose a position statement on the death penalty. When the statements are complete, each group selects one person to pose as the candidate.

Reassemble everyone together. Have one group's candidate read his/her statement. The members of the other political group(s) act as members of the press. These reporters question and challenge the candidate's position. The candidate may consult with his/her supporters before responding to the press. When the first group's candidate has been sufficiently questioned, continue with the other candidates.

2. Debate the ethics of executing a specific inmate currently on death row. Newspapers, magazines, television, and other media often highlight and discuss particularly controversial capital cases. Include this question as part of the debate: Would executing the death row inmate be acceptable from a Jewish point of view?

3. Jewish opinions on the death penalty frequently cite this famous Mishnah (also quoted above in Text Study #1a and #4A):

> A Sanhedrin that passes the death penalty once in seven years is called a violent court. Rabbi Eleazar ben Azariah says that this is true of a court that passes such a sentence even once in 70 years. Rabbi Tarfon and Rabbi Akiva say, "Had we been members of the Sanhedrin, no one would ever have been executed." Rabbi Shimon ben Gamaliel says, "[By avoiding all capital punishment, as do Rabbi Tarfon and Rabbi Akiva,] they would have caused a proliferation of murderers in Israel" (*Makkot* 1:10).

Hold a mock talk show panel discussion. Assign some students to pose as the guests, one student (or the leader) to pose as the show host, and everyone else to be audience members. The guests are: Rav Stam (who represents the anonymous position that opens the Mishnah passage), Rabbi Eleazar ben

Azariah, Rabbi Tarfon, Rabbi Akiva, and Rabbi Shimon ben Gamaliel. The "host" begins by thanking the "guests" for traveling through many centuries to participate in the talk show panel.

The topic is the death penalty in America, in the twenty-first century. The host facilitates the discussion, seeking comments and views from all the guests. A sample first question might be, "Rabbi Stam, what are your impressions of death penalty practices in America today?" The host also may solicit questions from audience members.

4. Students create a collage which visually captures the complexity of the death penalty. Here are some words, phrases, and images to help trigger participants' own ideas: killing, murdering, executing, hanging, electric chair, lethal injection, prison, punishment, "an eye for an eye," cycles of violence, the state as killer, courts, juries, realignment with God, moral order, retribution, revenge, restitution, reconciliation, rehabilitation, forgiveness, pity, "do not pity," mistaken judgments, distortions of justice, etc.

5. Instead of making a collage, students use various images in the previous activity to create a painting or poem related to the death penalty.

6. Choreograph a dance which explores one or more of these themes: retribution, revenge, restitution, reconciliation, rehabilitation, forgiveness, realignment with God, and/or establishing/reestablishing moral order.

7. In pairs, take turns listening to each other talk about fears, feelings, attitudes, and questions about the death penalty. The tenor of your listening is all-important. Listeners must be open hearted, nonjudgmental, supportive. In addition, they are not to interrupt the speaker, nor offer any comment or reaction. The speaker should speak for 3-5 minutes (possibly longer for more mature participants). After one person has had a turn speaking, switch roles, so that the speaker now becomes the listener. You can do this as a journal exercise too — the "listener" being the pages of the journal. After everyone has had the opportunity to "speak" (either to another person or to write in his/her journal), come back together as a group and allow participants to share their reactions to this experience.

Empathy

1. Pose the question: Should we have empathy for murderers? After some initial discussion, share the following information about Mario Marquez, who murdered his wife and niece "during an outburst of jealous anger toward his wife":

   > Mr. Marquez had an I.Q. of 65 and was savagely abused as a child. At times his father would beat him with a horsewhip until he passed out. His parents abandoned him to the streets when he was 12.
   >
   > Mr. Marquez was too limited mentally to talk with his lawyer about his case. They talked about animals and the things Mr. Marquez liked to draw.
   >
   > He was executed in 1995 (by the state of Texas) (*New York Times*, "Deciding Who Will Live" by Bob Herbert, Op-Ed, p. A27, March 18, 2002).

   Discuss the specific case of Mario Marquez. Should we have empathy for him? What would the implications of empathy be? Should empathy be a factor in sentencing a murderer?

2. Choose one of the following categories of individuals. Write a prayer that might be recited by:

   - Someone involved in deciding a murder case; for example, a judge, a jury member, a lawyer, or a witness;

   - A family member of a murder victim;

   - A family member of an inmate on death row;

   - An inmate on death row.

GLOSSARY

Edut mechuvenet:
Impeccably qualified witnesses able to withstand severe cross-examination.

Hatra'ah:
Warning the culprit before the crime.

Lex Talionis:
Translates as "The Law of the Talon/Claw." "An eye for an eye" type of punishment.

Sanhedrin:
A court, made up of Sages.

BIBLIOGRAPHY

Books and Articles - Jewish Sources

Artson, Bradley Shavit. *It's a Mitzvah!* West Orange, NJ: Behrman House, Inc., 1995.

Bleich, J. David. "Capital Punishment in the Noachide Code." In *Jewish Law in Our Time*, edited by Ruth Link-Salinger. New York: Bloch, 1982.

Blidstein, Gerald J. "Capital Punishment — The Classic Jewish Discussion." In *Contemporary Jewish Ethics*, edited by Menachem Marc Kellner. New York: Sanhedrin Press, 1978.

Borowitz, Eugene B., and Frances Weidman Schwartz. *The Jewish Moral Virtues*. Philadelphia, PA: The Jewish Publication Society, 1999.

Cytron, Barry D., and Earl Schwartz. *When Life Is in the Balance*. New York: United Synagogue, 1986.

"Capital Punishment." *Encyclopedia Judaica*. Jerusalem, Israel: Keter Publishing House Jerusalem Ltd., 1974.

Freeman, Susan. *Teaching Jewish Virtues: Sacred Sources and Arts Activities*. Denver, CO: A.R.E. Publishing, Inc., 1999.

Herring, Basil F. *Jewish Ethics and Halakhah for Our Time*, Vol 1. New York: KTAV Publishing House, Inc., and Yeshiva University Press, 1984.

Kadden, Barbara Binder and Bruce Kadden. *Teaching Mitzvot: Concepts, Values, and Activities*. Rev. ed. Denver, CO: A.R.E. Publishing, Inc., 2003.

Kazis, Israel J. "Judaism and the Death Penalty." In *Contemporary Jewish Ethics*, edited by Menachem Marc Kellner. New York: Sanhedrin Press, 1978.

Lipskar, Rabbi Sholom D. "A Torah Perspective on Incarceration as a Modality of Punishment and Rehabilitation." www.jlaw.com/Articles/PrisonerRights.html, 1996, copyright by Ira Kasden, 1997-2002.

Miller, Judea B. "Capital Punishment." In *Where We Stand: Jewish Consciousness on Campus*, edited by Allan L. Smith. New York: UAHC Press, 1997.

"Punishment." *Encyclopedia Judaica*. Jerusalem, Israel: Keter Publishing House Jerusalem Ltd., 1974.

Spitz, Elie. "The Jewish Tradition and Capital Punishment." In *Contemporary Jewish Ethics and Morality*, edited by Elliot N. Dorff and Louis E. Newman. New York and Oxford: Oxford University Press, 1995.

Books and Articles - General Sources

Ferro, Jeffrey. *Prisons and Jails: A Deterrent To Crime?* Farmington Hills, MI: Gale Group, 2002.

Henslin, James M. "Crime and Criminal Justice." In *Social Problems*, Englewood Cliffs, NJ: Prentice Hall, 1990.

Herman, Peter G., ed. *The American Prison System*. The Reference Shelf, Volume 73, Number 5. Bronx, NY: The H.W. Wilson Company, 2001.

Lifton, Robert Jay, and Greg Mitchell. *Who Owns Death?: Capital Punishment, the American Conscience, and the End of Executions*. New York: HarperCollins Publishers, 2000.

Prejean, Helen. *Dead Man Walking*. New York: Vintage Books, 1993.

Rein, Mei Ling. *Capital Punishment: Cruel and Unusual?* Farmington Hills, MI: Gale Group, 2000.

Web Sites

American Civil Liberties Union: www.aclu.org.
　　A longtime activist organization pursuing individual rights.

Citizens United for Alternatives to the Death Penalty: www.cuapd.org.
　　Campaigns for public education and the promotion of tactical grassroots activism.

Death Penalty Focus: www.deathpenalty.org.

Dedicated to the abolition of capital punishment.

Death Penalty Information Center: www.death-penaltyinfo.org

A non-profit organization that provides comprehensive information on the death penalty.

Equal Justice USA: www.quixote.org/ej/

A faith-based organization coordinating a campaign for a moratorium on death penalty.

Jewish Law — Articles: www.jlaw.org

Examines halachah, Jewish issues, and secular law.

Justice Denied: www.justicedenied.org

A magazine for the wrongly convicted.

The Justice Project; www.thejusticeproject.org

Educates about the flaws of capital punishment in the American justice system.

Moratorium 2000: www.moratorium.org

A global petition drive for a moratorium on the death penalty.

Murder Victims Families for Reconciliation: www.mvfr.org

Works to abolish the death penalty while supporting programs that address the needs of victims.

National Center for Victims of Crimes: www.ncvc.org

Information and support for crime victims.

National Coalition to Abolish the Death Penalty: www.ncadp.org

Coalition of individuals and organizations dedicated to the abolition of the death penalty.

Pro Death Penalty: www.prodeathpenalty.com

Information and arguments in favor of the death penalty.

Religious Action Center of Reform Judaism: www.rac.org

Builds a case against the death penalty, drawing on analysis of the American legal system and Jewish values.

The Religious Organizing Against the Death Penalty Project: www.deathpenaltyreligious.org.

Provides people of faith with tools and resources for becoming effective advocates for abolition. Site coordinated by the American Friends Service Committee.

Films

The following films deal with the death penalty in a frank and sometimes graphic way. While specific sections may be valuable for illustrating certain aspects of the topic, but it may not be appropriate for students to view the entire film. Pre-screening is strongly advised.

Dead Man Walking (1995, 122 minutes, rated R)

The true story of a caring nun who struggles with the moral and spiritual issues of comforting a death row inmate awaiting execution. Based on the book by Sister Helen Prejean (New York: Vintage Books, 1993). Available from video stores.

The Executioner's Song (1982, 136 minutes, unrated)

The true story of Gary Mark Gilmore, the first man to be executed in the United States after the death penalty was reinstated in 1976. The film spans the last nine months of his life. Available from video stores.

The Green Mile (1999, 188 minutes, rated R)

The story of the lives of Death Row prison guards in the 1930s, leading up to the execution of a wrongly accused man. Available from video stores.

The Life of David Gale (2003, 130 minutes, rated R)

An advocate for the abolishment of capital punishment is falsely convicted of rape and murder, and finds himself on death row. Available for purchase online at www.amazon.com. Video store release date not yet announced.

CHAPTER 7

SCHOOL VIOLENCE

OVERVIEW

Unfortunately, school violence is an increasingly problematic issue in our society. There are many schools in which students and teachers fear for their safety. In addition, some schools that "feel" safe unwittingly harbor students on the verge of causing great harm. The general mission of schools is to educate children. We understand that schools cannot fulfill every personal need of every child. But everyone can agree on this: that our children will *not be hurt* at school. Learning cannot happen at an optimal level, if at all, when violence at schools is a threat.

In this chapter we will look at several general questions regarding school violence: What is responsible for the increase in violence? How should we deal with it? Who should take charge of implementing strategies for change — school administrators, teachers, parents, students, politicians, religious leaders, psychiatrists, social workers, social psychologists, media executives, philosophers, philanthropists, charitable outreach divisions of community businesses, police, security guards?

As a point of clarification, this English definition for the word violence will be used: "exertion of any physical force so as to injure or abuse."[1] All kinds of incendiary words and actions can hurt another person. Though we will look at many problematic behaviors throughout this chapter, we reserve the word "violence" for the specific problem of physical assault.

Jewish Perspectives

Traditional Jewish texts do not speak directly to the phenomenon of school violence as we witness it today. However, Jewish insights provide us with useful guidelines for approaching this complex problem. They include various *halachic* concepts, ethical principles, and *middot* (Jewish virtues).

The Ben Sorer U'Moreh: "The Stubborn and Rebellious Child"

We begin our inquiry by focusing on teenagers (or preteenagers) who are at the hub of violent episodes at schools. What does Jewish tradition teach about youth who deviate from the standards of civility that we expect in our communities? The Torah speaks about *ben sorer u'moreh*, a "stubborn and rebellious son" (Deuteronomy 21:18ff). This son listens neither to the voice of his father, nor the voice of his mother. Though his parents discipline him, he still does not listen to them. Therefore, according to the text, the parents are to seize their wayward son and bring him to the elders of the town. The parents are to say to the elders, "Our son, this one, is a stubborn one and a rebel who does not hearken to our voice — he's a glutton and a drunkard!" Then, all the men of the town are to pelt the rebellious son with stones, so that he dies. Hearing that evil has been burned from their midst, all Israel can expect to become "filled with awe."

Public humiliation?! Stoning?! Such parental "discipline" may sound rather extreme to modern ears. Still, we can glean several critical

---

[1] *Webster's Third New International Dictionary* (Springfield, MA: Merriam-Webster, Inc., 1986), 2554.

insights from the text. The first relates to how Jews interpret the passage over the centuries, i.e., that so many conditions were built into identifying these outrageously unruly sons that Jewish scholarship concludes capital punishment for such children never happened and never will happen (see *Sanhedrin* 8:1-5, plus later commentaries). In other words, no Jewish community ever actually stoned wayward children because it could not justify labeling any son so irredeemable. We never get to the point of calling children wholly evil. Therefore, we never get to the point of engaging in ritual stoning nor any kind of "burning of evil [children] from our midst."

Judaism so narrowly defines the "stubborn and rebellious son" as to preclude any child from being so labeled. Thus, we realize that the lesson of the *ben sorer u'moreh* is not what it at first seems. Traditional interpretations of the text hold that children are never "so far gone" that the community gives up on them. The case of the "stubborn and rebellious son" challenges us to go beyond simplistic laying of blame. The potential for good and for evil exists in every one of us. The Hebrew terms for these two inclinations are *yetzer ha-tov* and *yetzer ha-ra*. Any approach to the issues of problematic children should consider this Jewish teaching as it recognizes the vast and varied potential of every person.

Besides essentially defining the "stubborn and rebellious son" out of existence, the text offers another important guideline. It concerns the people dealing with the unruly child. The child himself and his parents do not bear the total brunt of coping with the problematic situation. That is, the elders of the town, all the men of the town, and to some degree all Israel have a role in responding to the child's unacceptable behavior. There is broad responsibility for handling volatile situations in the community.

We can apply lessons of the stubborn and rebellious son to challenges of school violence. What causes such wanton acts of violence? While we don't have a clear-cut answer, at least we can say that simply shaking our heads and blaming some kind of plague of "evil in our

midst" is not satisfactory. How do we deal with violence? Again, there's not one straightforward answer, but we do learn one important thing from the *ben sorer u'moreh* discussion. Tempted as we may become to deal harshly with a wayward child, the legal commentary ties our hands from meeting violence with violence (i.e., we are restrained from stoning troublemakers!).

The Rodef: "The Pursuer"

Another relevant area of Torah-based law concerns the *rodef*, or "pursuer." While scholarly discussions and interpretations of these laws are extensive and complex, the basic principles apply to school violence. The core principle derived from the *rodef* is this: we must do what we can to help a fellow person whose life is in jeopardy, who is being "pursued" by someone who appears to have evil intentions. Torah teaches, "Do not stand idly by the blood of your fellow" (Leviticus 19:16). Relating this idea to schools means protecting school community members from (being "pursued" by) potentially violent youths.

Conversely, "pursuers" themselves must be saved from their own transgressions. We must *help them to help themselves* not to become criminals (not to become out of control killers). We must try to prevent potentially violent individuals from carrying out criminal actions, even at the cost of their own lives (*Sanhedrin* 73a). This means doing whatever we can to steer pursuers away from causing serious harm. From the previous paragraph, we learn that we are to protect the pursued, the potential victim. Here we learn of our duty to "protect" the pursuer, that is, to save the pursuer from doing wrong.

In the case of school violence, just who is the *rodef* may be cause for debate. Let's say we see a girl we'll call "Armed," with a knife in her hand, running after a girl we'll call "Unarmed." We might say "Armed" is the *rodef*, the pursuer, and "Unarmed" is the pursued (the potential victim). But what if we find out that "Armed" has been the subject of bullying and taunts for months? What if we learn that because of the hostile circumstances at her school, "Armed" has attempted suicide several times? And what if we find out that "Unarmed" spearheaded unremitting, emotionally painful, and stressful acts of humiliation toward "Armed"?

This pursuer case is not so simple. We could argue that in fact it is "Armed" who is engaged in self-defense. Before this incident, she felt her life was in danger, and the teachings of Judaism permit a person to act in self-defense when life or limb is threatened. "Armed" may consider *herself* the one who is pursued by a *rodef*. "Armed" — who has been "pursued" relentlessly with harmful words and intimidating acts — may claim that she is justified in chasing and threatening "Unarmed." "Armed" may proclaim that she is protecting her own threatened life.

Whether we decide that the oft-humiliated "Armed" falls into the category of "the pursued" or not, she does have a justifiable complaint. Judaism recognizes humiliation as a legitimate grievance. Our tradition unequivocally condemns humiliating others. The perpetrator may incur a specific penalty (such as a fine) for the harm he/she causes. Moreover, a person who shames others may meet punishment "in the next world."

According to teachings about the *rodef*, just who is obligated to become involved in halting school violence? Maimonides says: "All Israel is commanded to save a person being pursued for his/her life, even if it means killing the pursuer, and the pursuer is a minor" (*Mishneh Torah, Hilchot Rotzayach*, 1:6). "All Israel" means community responsibility for protecting people who are at risk of being harmed. This idea underscores the more general Jewish ethical principle: *kol Yisrael aravin zeh ba-zeh* — all of Israel is responsible for one another. If all Israel (the whole community) is responsible for the violence, just what are they supposed to do about it? Though we do not have an exact formula about *what to do*, one thing is absolutely clear. The community is not to "stand idly by."

While we use the term "Israel," we know from another concept — *mipnay darkay shalom* (for the sake of peace) — our concerns must expand to include all people. But it is not only for peace that our obligation extends to the welfare of the larger community. It is also because of our belief in the dignity of all individuals. All people are created in the image of God (*ha-adam nivra b'tzelem Elohim*).

Who Is Responsible for a Crime? What We Learn from the Eglah Arufah

Our discussions of the stubborn and rebellious son, *ben sorer u'moreh* and the pursuer, the *rodef*, provide some guidelines for a Jewish approach to school violence. A third concept is the *eglah arufah*. This term refers to an elaborate ritual concerning a slain man found in a field between two cities, whose murderer is unknown. When such a body is found, the elders slaughter a calf (the *eglah arufah*) to purge the community of the crime. As part of the cleansing ritual, they say, "Our hands did not shed this blood, our eyes did not see!" (Deuteronomy 21:7). The elders are not suspects in the murder of the slain man. Yet, the Mishnah explains that they must nevertheless proclaim their innocence. They do so because there may be a question of indirect causation of death (*Sotah* 9:6). That is, it is possible that the crime happened because a hungry man was not able to find food or because an unescorted traveler entered a danger zone. The Sages view such circumstances as requiring a response by the community leadership. There must be a safe and healthy community infrastructure that provides vital needs such as food and security. The leadership must answer for circumstances that lead to such tragedy as murder.

What guidance for the prevention of violence can we derive from the *eglah arufah*? We can make sure vital needs are provided for in the community. Safety must be assured. In the modern era, safety guarantees likely would require an examination of access to guns, influence of media violence, school security procedures, parental/adult supervision of teens, and school cultures that condone bullying and exclusion. In the *eglah arufah* scenario, vital needs also include provision of food. In our own day, we might understand that category more broadly. That is, society has a responsibility to protect individuals from falling so deeply into poverty, despair, and degradation that they feel pressed to engage in criminal acts. Who is responsible for all these community safeguards? The leadership of the community. If something goes terribly wrong, the "elders" must examine their leadership and commit themselves to whatever changes are necessary to improve the fabric of the society.

Jewish Values and Virtues

Judaism has a great deal to say regarding values (*middot*) to live by. We could argue that many of these, if deliberately incorporated into the school culture, would promote an environment in which violence is less likely to occur. (See the section, "Related *Middot* and *Mitzvot*," p. 175.)

General Perspectives

The Problem

Yes, school violence is a problem. It is on the increase, and the stakes are higher with sophisticated weapons more widely available. A 1997 survey conducted by the National Center for Education Statistics reports the incidence of crime and violence that occurred in public schools during the 1996-1997 academic year:

- 57% of public elementary and secondary school principals reported that one or more incidents of violence (reported to the police or other law enforcement officials) had occurred in their school during the school year.

- Of the nonviolent crimes reported, about 190,000 were incidents of physical attacks or fights without a weapon, about 116,000 were incidents of theft or larceny, and 98,000 were incidents of vandalism.

- Of the violent crimes reported, about 4,000 were incidents of rape or other sex-ual battery, 7,000 were robberies, and 11,000 were physical attacks or fights in which weapons were used.

- 45% of elementary schools reported one or more violent incidents compared with 74% of middle and 77% of high schools (National Center for Education Statistics, *Violence and Discipline Problems in Public Schools*: 1996-1997, *Executive Summary,* February 1998, 2-4).

What or who is responsible for the increased incidence of school violence? All over, communities discuss this baffling question. Perhaps locating the cause of the problem will lead to a solution. Thoughtful individuals write books, publish newspaper editorials, and wage debates in teachers' lounges and on the floors of Congress. Geneticists conduct studies, as do endocrinologists (hormone doctors), and psychiatrists. Social scientists test theories. "Experts" back up their conclusions with statistics, scientific study results, and/or personal observations. We will list the violence-generating "suspects" experts most often cite.

Possible Biological/Psychological Factors

Genetics: Some people are born with a genetic make-up that "naturally" predisposes them to violent behavior.

Hormones: Young males (who are disproportionately involved in violent crimes) have high testosterone levels. Hormonal surges during adolescence exacerbate aggressive responses to provocative situations.

Immature Brains: The pre-frontal cortex of the teenage brain is biologically immature. This part of the brain is responsible for inhibiting impulses. A teen involved in a provocative situation (with deadly weapons in reach) will not necessarily exert the same self-control as that same person will later in life.[2]

---

[2]"A Brain Too Young for Good Judgment" by Daniel R. Weinberger, *The New York Times*, Op-Ed, March 10, 2001.

Psychiatric Conditions: These aren't necessarily a direct *cause* of violence. Still, a "side effect" of certain conditions can be comparatively more aggressive behaviors. The conditions include Mental Retardation, Attention Deficient/Hyperactivity Disorder (ADHD), Reactive Detachment Disorder, Serious Mental Illness (such as schizophrenia, mania, and recurring depressive episodes), Post-traumatic Stress Disorder (PTSD), Alcohol/Drug Abuse, and Suicidal Depression.[3]

Personality Disorders: Recurring patterns of active defiance, disobedience, and open hostility toward adult authority figures characterize Oppositional Defiant Disorder, and the more extreme Conduct Disorders.

Substance Abuse: Drugs and alcohol impair judgment and impede self-control. Addictions to illicit drugs may lead to criminal activity, and criminal activity often entails violence.

Possible Environmental Factors

Economic Environment: Poverty may lead a person to such a degraded and desperate condition that engaging in criminal activity becomes increasingly likely, perhaps just to survive. Affluence, too, can have problematic effects, including working parents who have little time for their children and families, and who may be strapped with credit card debt (a significant cause of divorce). Financial pressures and competition often lead to the pursuit of material goods. Such stresses may make certain individuals more vulnerable to substance abuse, domestic violence, marital breakups, suicides, vandalism, bullying, robberies, etc.

Inadequate Schooling: An inferior school environment (the building itself, lack of supplies, shortage of teachers and other staff, low standards and expectations) compromises education. Academic failure may relegate certain individuals

to the permanent underclass and possibly a life of crime. Students who have trouble academically may drop out of school, join gangs, and become involved in violent street life.[4]

Discrimination: Innocent people may be victimized because of their race, ethnicity, religion, sexual preference, medical or mental disability, age, or gender. On the flip side, being the target of senseless and prejudicial hatred may arouse the victim to violent response.

Domestic Violence: Acts of abuse against members of one's own family are found among all races, ethnic groups, social classes, age groups, and both genders. Abuse victims and witnesses often become filled with such rage that they become batterers and criminals themselves.

Availability of Weapons: With the increasing availability of guns, when conflicts between students escalate, the results can be deadly.

The Media: Violence saturates our media — TV, movies, music, and video games. While children respond to media violence in different ways, strong evidence shows that watching violence increases the frequency of aggressive behavior in children.[5]

Minimal Presence of Responsible Adults/Weak Leadership: Lack of adult supervision, adult listening ears, and adult mediation and counsel forces troubled students to turn elsewhere for guidance and relief. That "elsewhere" may be unhealthy and dangerous (i.e. violent web sites, gangs, other troubled teens, drugs/alcohol, suicide).

Suburban Anonymity: A sense of strong community connection is difficult to nurture in suburbia. It is difficult to create the social fabric of closely knit neighborhoods among residents who are isolated from each other in increasingly bigger houses on bigger lots.

---

[3]*Preventing Youth Violence*, 32-33.

[4]*Preventing Youth Violence*, 37.

[5]*Nobody Left to Hate*, 59.

Cultural Factors

Primacy of Self: A sense of personal entitlement and the belief that "I always come first" may compromise feelings of responsibility toward others.

Materialism: Success becomes identified with the accumulation and consumption of material goods. Amassing wealth and prestige supersedes dedication to communal and spiritual values.

Expectations of Instant Gratification: Easy access to sex, drugs, pornography, and crude music undermines motivation for self-restraint. Our culture does not encourage us to curb our desires. If anything, it entices us to indulge our desires, and to indulge them *now*.

Lack of Conflict Resolution Skills: Many conflicts could be kept from escalating if students and teachers had the skills to resolve problems peaceably.

Bullying, Taunting, Humiliating: Students who continually are subjected to this type of emotional stress may become filled with rage. They may turn feelings of powerlessness into plans for violent retaliation.

Exclusion and Cliques: School cultures often revolve around groups of individuals who cluster together for all sorts of reasons. When these groups become cliques that exclude in hurtful ways, those left out may redirect painful feelings of alienation into revenge.

Gangs: Empowerment, risk taking, peer pressure, and approval are all associated with membership in gangs. Gang activities can turn lethal when violence takes center stage. There are gangs that become involved in brutal initiation rites, murder, armed robbery, drive-by shootings, and vicious assaults that include torture and dismemberment of victims.[6]

Inadequate Moral Education: A dearth of character education promotes a "free-for-all" atmos-phere of behavioral expectations for students.

Incoherent School Core Values, Rules, and Consequences: When schools do not spend the time and effort to identify, agree upon, and commit to live by core values, rules, and consequences, serious repercussions may follow. A lack of clear expectations feeds an atmosphere of apathy or confusion. Without adequate means of disciplining with dignity, an atmosphere develops in which violent intentions can grow without notice.[7]

Conclusions about the Factors

Clearly, theories about the roots of school violence abound. Most likely, several factors are present each time a youth turns into a killer. Since the complexity and breadth of possible causes of violence are vast, finding a means of prevention is a daunting task. Promising strategies, however, have been identified.

About Interventions

The social psychologist Elliot Aronson divides the strategies for dealing with youth violence into two categories: "Pump-Handle Interventions" and "Root Cause Interventions." The term "pump-handle intervention" comes from the 1854 cholera epidemic in London. Dr. John Snow, a well-known physician, traced the epidemic to a contaminated well. His first course of action was not to try to find the cause of the contamination. He did not, at first, attempt to clean up the water, educate the people living in the area, or persuade them not to drink the water. Rather, he simply removed the pump handle from the wellhead, and thereby stanched the epidemic. Later, Dr. Snow looked for the "root cause" of the contamination. After discovering the source of contamination was raw sewage, he helped instigate changes to building codes, improving the health and welfare of millions of people.[8]

---

[6]*Preventing Youth Violence*, 40.

[7]*As Tough as Necessary*, 24ff.

[8]*Nobody Left to Hate*, 46.

This analogy applies well to school violence. In the next section are some possible "pump-handle" steps to take for helping stem school violence.

"Pump-handle" Interventions

Psychological Support: Make adequate psychological support available, including individual counseling; plus anger management, stress reduction, and social skills workshops.

Decrease Weapons: Reduce youth access to weapons. Require gun locks, licensing, and background checks. Enhance safety mechanisms on guns.

Outreach To Troubled Families: Provide support to families in crisis.

Confront the Problem of Substance Abuse: Educate about the dangers of drugs and alcohol; make treatment programs available.

School Security: Improve building security at schools.

Reduce Media Violence: Pressure media executives to tame violent content in their productions.

"Root Cause" Interventions

Much of the school violence debate focuses on "pump-handle" interventions. But proponents of "root cause" interventions contend that the "pump-handle" methods, even if adequately implemented, are only a start and will not resolve the problem of school violence. "Root cause" interventionists argue that unless we address underlying fundamental causes, the system will remain "contaminated." These fundamental causes tend to fall in the category of cultural factors (see above) and, according to many educators and leaders, are amenable to the following root cause interventions:

Character Education: Different organizations and communities have ideas regarding the content of this type of education. The Character Counts Coalition (almost 100 organizations representing more than 40 million Americans) proposes one model. Their "Six Pillars of Character" teach that a person of character: (1) is trustworthy, (2) treats people with respect (3) is responsible, (4) is fair, (5) is caring, and (6) is a good citizen.

Conflict Resolution Skills: Learn, practice, and implement them. While teachers take the lead, students must learn these skills, as well.

Core Values: Identify and live by core school values, rules, and consequences. (An example of a value: school is a place where we learn that my way is not the only way. An example of a rule: settle disagreements with words, not fists.[9])

Confront Bullying: Implement anti-bullying initiatives. Involve the whole school community, including parents.

Broaden Pedagogical Techniques: Include pedagogical methods that require cooperation and collaboration.

Practice What You Preach: Urge administrators and teachers to model the values they want their students to learn.

Affirmative Environment: Implement practices that make students see school as an affirming, competence building place. Some examples include warmth, clearly defined limits, democratic atmosphere, recognizing and resolving conflict, and handling group behavior in a dignified fashion.[10]

Who Is Responsible?

Obviously, for any of these interventions to work, people who would implement them need to be identified and trained. "Pump-handle" interventions require particular groups of specialists to take leadership roles. For example, psychologists need to address psychological factors.

---

[9]*As Tough as Necessary*, 31.

[10]Ibid., 41-77.

Law enforcement officials need to take charge of policing neighborhoods and schools. Counselors and social workers work with troubled families and substance abusers. Politicians and media executives are the major players in wrestling with violent media content. Politicians, political action committees, and other grass roots organizations take center stage in the gun control debate.

The challenge of the "root cause" interventions is that the whole community must get involved — students, teachers, administrators, parents, and town residents. To change school culture to one that is affirming and accepting requires a broad based effort. This call to the whole community is similar to the Jewish concept of *kol Yisrael aravin zeh ba-zeh* — all Israel is responsible for one another.

Still, who gets the "broad based" effort started? Let's go back to something we looked at earlier in our Jewish discussion and try to apply it here. The ideas behind the *eglah arufah* highlight the responsibility of the "elders of the community." Who is responsible for responding to a culture that seeds school violence? We might say that the initiators of reform should be the "elders of the community." The elders — the adult leaders — must step forward and navigate the call to change.

Summary of the Overview

The following summarizes key considerations regarding school violence as discussed in the Overview.

1. Some Jewish insights to guide our approach to school violence include:

    *   The community shares responsibility for and involvement in the problems of our youth.

    *   All people, youth included, have the potential to do good and to do wrong.

    *   Individuals may protect themselves from others who threaten their life.

*   We are not to stand idly by when someone else's life is threatened.

*   Since everyone is created in God's image, we must treat all people respectfully.

*   A society's adult leaders ("the elders") must accept responsibility for conditions that lead to crime or tragedy. The onus is upon them to safeguard the emotional and physical well-being of the members of the community.

2. A combination of forces seems responsible for the increase in school violence, reflecting psychological and biological factors, environmental factors, and cultural factors.

3. An effective strategy for stemming school violence will use interventions that address both immediate dangers (such as easy access to weapons) and underlying causes (such as an environment that tolerates bullying).

SCENARIOS: HOW THINGS HAVE CHANGED

Below are two imaginary scenarios regarding violent behavior among young people, intended to raise questions and spark discussion. Read each scenario to or with your students, and engage them in small or large group discussions. Use the "Focus the Discussion" section below to help identify the important issues and facilitate these discussions. Note that additional questions and activities relating to these scenarios are found in the "Stories: Understanding through Listening" section below (pp. 179-181).

Following the discussions, have students continue on to the "Text Study" section to see what Jewish and other sources have to say on the subject. Finally, you may wish to have students discuss the scenarios a second time, to see if their views have changed.

Scenario 1: In a Jewish Community

Aryeh ("Lion") is holding a knife and chasing another youth, named Shalom ("Peace"). Shalom, seeing he is danger, stops in his tracks, buries his head in his arms, and tries to protect himself. Ezra ("Help") is standing nearby and witnesses Aryeh threatening Shalom. Ezra picks up a rock and hurls it at Aryeh's shoulder. Aryeh drops the knife. Ezra quickly grabs the weapon, and both he and Shalom tackle Aryeh. By this time, others are gathering round. Some community elders are summoned. They break up the fight. Aryeh, cradling his injured arm, plus Shalom and Ezra are led off with the elders. The elders decide that Aryeh's actions, like that of a *rodef*, a "pursuer," were serious enough to deserve punishment.

Scenario 2: Uncovering Additional Motivations

In the "Jewish Perspectives" section above (pp. 157-160), we discuss in depth a scenario in which the weapon wielding "Armed" chases after "Unarmed." Refer to this scenario. Note that at first, "Armed" seems to be the criminal. But when we learn that "Armed" has been the subject of "Unarmed's" bullying, taunts, and other humiliations for months, we realize that the case is more complex.

Focus the Discussion

The first scenario is fairly straightforward. In the second, we probe possible motivations for seemingly irrational behavior and consider how the effects of humiliation might influence behavior.

Traditional Jewish texts do not address school violence per se. Nevertheless, they do address rebellious children, what to do when faced with the threat of a pursuer, procedures and justifications for self-defense, and the responsibilities of community leaders. They discuss repercussions of shaming others and causing emotional injury, as well as the topics of self-

mastery, self-restraint, and the pursuit of peace. Our tradition deals with physical threats, plus emotional and psychological harm people can cause one another, and how individuals should strive to live righteous lives.

In our world today, we share many concerns discussed for centuries in Jewish sources. Moreover, we face new challenges, as the environmental and cultural factors outlined above illustrate (see "General Perspectives" above, pp. 160-164). Adding to the complexity is our growing understanding of human biology and psychology. We can forge an approach to school violence, informed by both Jewish values and modern insights. But it will take courage, wisdom, and leadership to do so.

TEXT STUDY

School violence forces us to ask difficult questions. Jewish and general textual sources provide many answers, but these answers often highlight the tension between seemingly opposing considerations. The chart on the next three pages poses these important questions and offers two opposing points of view. Text sources supporting each of these points of view follow below.

1. **What role should a school play in the life of its students?**

    On the One Hand:

    Schools aren't rehabilitation centers. They should focus on well-behaved students who want an education. Problem-atic students should be expelled. Perhaps they should be put in their own schools.

    A. Wisdom is too lofty for a fool;
        He does not open his mouth in the gate.
        He who lays plans to do harm
        People call a schemer.

TEACHING HOT TOPICS

Forging Strategies to Deal with School Violence: Questions to Consider

The Question	On the One Hand	On the Other Hand
1. What role should a school play in the life of its students? (see p. 165)	Schools aren't rehabilitation centers. They should focus on well-behaved students who want an education. Problematic students should be expelled. Perhaps they should be put in their own schools.	Schools have an obligation to try to salvage the lives of students who have gone astray. Troublemaking students should be given chances to mend their ways. Expelling them means they simply will go elsewhere (e.g. to the mall) where they may cause trouble, and where there will be no supervision. The danger will just change locations. Problematic students need to be around well-behaved kids, rather than in a situation where they will only reinforce each other's bad behavior.
2. To what extent should schools tolerate student misbehavior? (see p. 168)	A "Zero Tolerance" policy is in order for certain behaviors (such as bringing weapons to school, using drugs). Mandatory expulsions or other serious consequences would automatically apply.	We need to listen and pay attention to the unique circumstances of each individual. Not everyone should be treated equally. Rigidity of school authorities only breeds student hostility toward them.
3. Will improved security make a difference in safety and quality of life for schools? (see p. 169)	Beef up security: Install metal detectors in schools, hire more security guards, and increase monitoring of students.	Monitoring students more rigorously will lead to abuse of privacy. Killers intent on harm can kill outside of school grounds. Moreover, all the extra security will increase anxiety.
4. What restrictions should be placed on media regarding violent content? (see p. 169)	Clamp down on violence in media.	Freedom of the press is guaranteed by the First Amendment to the United States Constitution.

(continued on next page)

5. What do we do about the proliferation of guns in our midst? (see p. 170)	Ban gun ownership for private citizens.	Eliminating the threat of guns is unrealistic. While there are ways to reduce gun violence (with licensing, safety devices, education, etc.), wide access to dangerous weapons will not go away any time soon.
6. How much effort should we make in trying to help troubled individuals? (see p. 171)	Some people are inherently evil. Some are naturally despicable.	Everyone has vast potential for a variety of behaviors. Labeling people or expecting bad things of them can lead to "self-fulfilling prophecies."
7. Do cliques contribute to causing school violence? (see p. 171)	Cliques are a part of school culture, and there's not that much you can do about them. Large high schools, with their numerous periods a day, are impersonal places. Cliques help to close the gap. Students should be able to choose their own friends. Gangs are a type of clique that give the security of a substitute kind of family to certain kids who really need that.	Effective means for addressing exclusion must be sought. Exclusion breeds loneliness, resentment, and alienation. Those who are left out may turn to harmful behaviors as coping mechanisms. They may use violence as a means to get back at those who have hurt them.
8. How concerned should we be about bullying? (see p. 172)	Let's not overreact to bullying. Some teasing helps everyone not to take themselves so seriously. Kids should learn to stick up for themselves.	Bullying can cause serious harm — the potential damage must not be underestimated. Schools must make it a priority to implement strategies aimed at eliminating bullying.
9. If we think there might be a problem, should we let someone know? (see p. 173)	"Reports" of suspicious behaviors can go astray. Rumors, denials, and/or lack of parental support can make follow-through difficult. Further, the "reporters" may be shunned or endangered for revealing information to authorities.	Timely interventions and rebukes can deter more serious crime.

(continued on next page)

| 10. Will character education (teaching values and social skills) make a measurable difference in improving school culture? (see p. 174) | How can schools be expected to shoulder the burden of so many learning agendas, such as character education, conflict resolution, empathy training, cooperative learning techniques, values clarification, etc.? Schools barely have the time to teach the basics of academics! Besides, values should be taught by parents and through students' religious education. Schools can't be expected to change a whole culture. | Character education and the teaching of social skills is as critical a part of a child's learning as anything else. When deprived of this kind of learning, the school environment — academic and social — will suffer. Learning core values intersects with the teaching of literature and history. There are (non-religious) values all segments of the school community can agree on. What happens now in schools *will* affect the culture of future generations. |

The schemes of folly are sin,
And a scoffer is an abomination to people (Proverbs 24:7-9).

B. An intelligent son heeds instruction,
But he who keeps company with gluttons disgraces his father (Proverbs 28:7).

On the Other Hand:

Schools have an obligation to try to salvage the lives of students who have gone astray. Troublemaking students should be given chances to mend their ways. Expelling them means they simply will go elsewhere (e.g. to the mall) where they may cause trouble, and where there will be no supervision. The danger will just change locations. Problematic students need to be around well-behaved kids, rather than in a situation where they will only reinforce each other's bad behavior.

a. Rabbi Hamnuma said: Jerusalem was destroyed only because the children did not attend school . . . and loitered in the streets (*Shabbat* 119b).

Probing: Ideas and Issues

Describe a possible sequence of 5 to 10 things that might contribute to a city's demise if chil-

dren were not attending school. (You might start with something like this: First kids would be bored and not know what to do with themselves. Next they would . . .)

2. **To what extent should schools tolerate student misbehavior?**

On the One Hand:

A "Zero Tolerance" policy is in order for certain behaviors (such as bringing weapons to school, using drugs). Mandatory expulsions or other serious consequences would automatically apply.

A. Rabbi Shimon ben Lakish says: "Those who are compassionate when hard-heartedness is called for will end up being hard-hearted when compassion is called for" (*Kohelet Rabbah 7*).

On the Other Hand:

We need to listen and pay attention to the unique circumstances of each individual. Not everyone should be treated equally. Rigidity of school authorities only breeds student hostility toward them.

a. I bring heaven and earth to witness that the Divine Spirit rests upon a non-Jew as well as upon a Jew, upon a woman as well as upon a man, upon a maidservant as well as a manservant. All depends on the deeds of the particular individual (*Yalkut Shimoni*, on Judges, section 42).

b. Happy is the generation whose great [leaders] listen to the small, for then it follows obviously that in such a generation, the small will listen to the great (*Rosh HaShanah* 25b).

Probing: Ideas and Issues

What dangers do you see in being overly compassionate? What dangers are there in not listening well enough to the particular circumstances of each individual? (A story is told of a young girl who arrived to school with seven knives in her backpack. Since the school had "zero-tolerance" for weapons, her mother was contacted and given the knives. The girl was given a long-term suspension, and the police were called. While waiting for the police, the girl broke down and told school officials that the night before her mother had attempted suicide. Fearing that her mother might take her life while she was at school, the girl took every knife she could find in the house with her that day to school.)

3. **Will improved security make a difference in safety and quality of life for schools?**

On the One Hand:

Beef up security: Install metal detectors in schools, hire more security guards, and increase monitoring of students.

A. Those who can prevent members of their household from committing a sin, but do not, are punished for the sins of their household.

   If they can prevent their fellow citizens from committing sins, but do not, they are punished for the sins of their fellow citizens.

   If they can prevent the whole world from committing sins, but do not, they are punished for the sins of the whole world (*Shabbat* 54b).

On the Other Hand:

Monitoring students more rigorously will lead to abuse of privacy. Killers intent on harm can kill outside of school grounds. Moreover, all the extra security will increase anxiety.

a. Balaam blessed the people of Israel when he saw the tribes dwelling together in tents, in such a way that everyone's privacy was respected:

   > He saw each tribe dwelling by itself, not intermingled one with another; he saw that the entrances of their tents were not exactly facing each other so that one could not peer into the other's tent (Rashi on Numbers 24:2, also *Baba Batra* 60a).

Probing: Ideas and Issues

What do you think is the greater value — ensuring safety or respecting privacy? Explain. Which value seems to be a higher priority at your school? Do you think the balance of safety and privacy in your school is appropriate?

4. **What restrictions should be placed on media regarding violent content?**

On the One Hand:

Clamp down on violence in media.

A. Hate evil and love good (Amos 5:15).

B. An enemy dissembles with his speech,
   Inwardly he harbors deceit.
   Though he be fair-spoken, do not trust him
   For seven abominations are in his mind.
   His hatred may be concealed by dissimu-

lation (false pretense),
But his evil will be exposed to public
view (Proverbs 26:24-26).

C. The research results are clear: In spite of
the protestations of media executives,
exposure to violence in films, on TV, and
in video games can and does have an
important impact on the behavior and
feelings of children and adolescents.

But . . . it is important that we don't
get carried away . . . Millions of kids
watch a lot of violent stuff on TV and
don't go around shooting their classmates. At the same time, it would be
naive to believe that TV violence is not a
contributing factor — especially if the
youngsters watching all that TV are frustrated, angry, or prone to violence
(*Nobody Left to Hate*, p. 62).

On the Other Hand:

Freedom of the press is guaranteed by the
First Amendment to the United States
Constitution.

a. Congress shall make no law respecting an
establishment of religion, or prohibiting
the free exercise thereof; or abridging the
freedom of speech, or of the press; or the
right of the people peaceably to assemble,
and to petition the government for a
redress of grievances (First Amendment to
the Bill of Rights of the United States
Constitution).

b. What Congress can do is exert pressure
on the entertainment industries to show
some restraint, police themselves, and
establish a useful rating system so that
parents can attempt to exercise sensible
vigilance over what their children watch.
If broadcasters and filmmakers would
succumb to this pressure, this would be a
small step in the right direction (*Nobody
Left to Hate*, p. 62).

Probing: Ideas and Issues

Freedom of the press, as we understand it today,
is not an emphasis of traditional Jewish texts.
Rather, the emphasis is more on the dangers of
lashon hara — "evil speech" — gossip, rumors,
and slander. Write a Jewish commentary to the
First Amendment — that is, what you believe
freedom of speech should and should not cover.

5. **What do we do about the proliferation of
guns in our midst?**

On the One Hand:

Ban gun ownership for private citizens.

A. You shall not stand idly by when your
fellow's blood is being shed (*Leviticus*
19:16).

B. It is forbidden to sell a heathen or a rob-
ber weapons of war, which might be used
in violating a *mitzvah*, although it is permitted to sell them defensive weapons,
such as shields (*Mishneh Torah, Hilchot
Rotzayach* 12:14).

On the Other Hand:

Eliminating the threat of guns is unrealistic.
While there are ways to reduce gun violence
(with licensing, safety devices, education,
etc.), wide access to dangerous weapons will
not go away any time soon.

a. [Eliminating guns would result in] a
sharp reduction in multiple killings in
our schools — and everywhere else, for
that matter. Needless to say, this would
be impossible. We would have to confis-
cate every gun in America. But in
America, we believe in individual liberties, so it should not surprise you that an
overwhelming majority of the population
opposes the confiscation of guns. A less
extreme and far more feasible [approach
. . .] would require the licensing of guns
and restricting juveniles' access to guns
(*Nobody Left to Hate*, p. 49).

Probing: Ideas and Issues

When biblical and Rabbinic texts were written, Jewish communities didn't face the staggering prevalence of such dangerous weapons as guns that we face today in America. What are Jews to do now if we want to strive "not to stand idly by," yet understand that the complete elimination of guns in America is just about impossible?

6. **How much effort should we make in trying to help troubled individuals?**

   On the One Hand:

   Some people are inherently evil. Some are naturally despicable.

   Jewish thought does not support this point of view.

   On the Other Hand:

   Everyone has vast potential for a variety of behaviors. Labeling people or expecting bad things of them can lead to "self-fulfilling prophecies."

   a. See, I set before you today life and good, and death and evil: in that I command you today to love the Eternal your God, to walk in God's ways and to keep God's commandments, laws, and regulations . . . Life and death I place before you, blessing and curse; now choose life, in order that you may stay alive, you and your seed, by loving the Eternal your God, by hearkening to God's voice, and by cleaving to God, for God is your life and the length of your days . . . (Deuteronomy 30:15-20).

   b. Ben Azzai said: Do not despise anyone. Do not underrate the importance of anything, for there is no one who does not have his/her hour, and there is no thing that does not have its place (*Pirke Avot* 4:3).

   c. Ben Zoma taught: Who is mighty? Those who conquer their evil impulse. As it is written: "Those who are slow to anger are better than the mighty, and those who rule over their spirit than those who conquer a city" [Proverbs 16:32] (*Pirke Avot* 4:1).

Probing: Ideas and Issues

What are the most challenging choices you face regarding treatment of others? (For example: "One challenge I have is choosing calm explanation of my feelings over the yelling of accusations. Another challenge is choosing patience over impatience." Etc.)

7. **Do cliques contribute to causing school violence?**

   On the One Hand:

   Cliques are a part of school culture, and there's not that much you can do about them. Large high schools, with their numerous periods a day, are impersonal places. Cliques help to close the gap. Students should be able to choose their own friends. Gangs are a type of clique that give the security of a substitute kind of family to certain kids who really need that.

   This idea is foreign to traditional Jewish ways of thinking.

   On the Other Hand:

   Effective means for addressing exclusion must be sought. Exclusion breeds loneliness, resentment, and alienation. Those who are left out may turn to harmful behaviors as coping mechanisms. They may use violence as a means to get back at those who have hurt them.

   a. Hillel taught: Do not withdraw from the community (*al tifros min ha-tzibur*) (*Pirke Avot* 2:5).

   b. Belong to the persecuted rather than to be the persecutors (*Baba Kamma* 93a).

c. Rabbi Eleazar said: Since the destruction of the Temple, the gates of prayers are locked [making it harder for prayers to reach heaven]. But even though the gates of prayers are locked, the gates of tears are not. Rabbi Hisda said: All gates are locked except the gates through which pass the cries of people who have been wronged (*Baba Metzia* 59a).

d. The Rabbis hold that disgrace is worse than physical pain . . . (*Sotah* 8b).

e. Some people make vows out of hatred of their neighbor, swearing, for example, that they will not let this or that person sit at the same table with them or come under the same roof. Such people should seek the mercy of God so that they may find some cure for the diseases of their soul (Philo of Alexandria).

Probing: Ideas and Issues

Imagine a dialogue between a panel of Rabbis and a school committee (made of students, parents, and teachers). What would the Rabbis advise concerning cliques? What might school committee members respond? "Reconstruct" how such a dialogue might continue . . .

8. How concerned should we be about bullying?

On the One Hand:

Let's not overreact to bullying. Some teasing helps everyone not to take themselves so seriously. Kids should learn to stick up for themselves.

A Jewish way of thinking would argue that responding to bullying is important.

On the Other Hand:

Bullying can cause serious harm — the potential damage must not be underestimated. Schools must make it a priority to implement strategies aimed at eliminating bullying.

a. A *tanna* (one who memorized oral teachings) recited before Rabbi Nahman ben Isaac: "A person who publicly shames a neighbor is like someone who has shed blood." To which Rabbi Nahman answered, "You have spoken well. I have seen that when someone is shamed, the color leaves the person's face and the person becomes pale."

Abbaye asked Rabbi Dimi "What do people in Palestine most carefully try to avoid?" He answered, "Putting others to shame" (*Baba Metzia* 58b).

b. Three categories of people are condemned to eternal hell: one who commits adultery with a married woman; one who publicly shames a neighbor; and one who calls a neighbor by a degrading nickname, even if the other is accustomed to that name . . . It would be better for one to throw oneself into a fiery furnace than publicly to put a neighbor to shame (*Baba Metzia* 58b-59a).

c. If a man pulls another man's ears, plucks his hair, spits in his face, or removes his garments, or if he uncovers the head of a woman in the marketplace [married women always kept their heads covered as a sign of modesty], he must pay the other person four hundred *zuz* . . . (*Baba Kamma* 8:6).

Probing: Ideas and Issues

Elaborate on what you think would be a generally accepted Jewish attitude toward bullying. Do you think the Rabbis get carried away in their condemnation of those who cause others shame? Explain.

9. If we think there might be a problem, should we let someone know?

On the One Hand:

"Reports" of suspicious behaviors can go astray. Rumors, denials, and/or lack of parental support can make follow-through difficult. Further, the "reporters" may be shunned or endangered for revealing information to authorities.

A. You shall not deal deceitfully or falsely with one another. You shall not swear falsely by My name . . . You are not to commit corruption in justice; do not favor the poor or show deference to the rich; judge your kinsman fairly. Do not go about as a talebearer among your people (Leviticus 19:11, 15-16).

B. You are to inquire, to examine, and to investigate well, and [determine] if the claim is certain and true, the fact is established, that this abomination was indeed done in your midst . . . (Deuteronomy 13:15, referring to idol worship).

C. We must exercise the most scrupulous care, so as not to give an ill-considered and hasty decision, and so harm the innocent (*The Commandments*, vol. 1, pp. 192-193).

On the Other Hand:

Timely interventions and rebukes can deter more serious crime.

a. You are not allowed to withhold information that could help someone (*Choshen Mishpat* 426:1).

b. Those who see sin in their home and do nothing in protest are indicted as if they committed the sin (*Shabbat* 54b).

c. If a person permitted certain sins to go on without strongly objecting, that person is considered a murderer (*Moed Katan* 5a).

d. Where harm is being caused to others, the story can be told if the following seven guidelines are followed:

   i. You saw the act yourself and it is not a rumor from others, unless substantiated later.

   ii. You must be careful not to decide quickly if the issue is one of stealing or damage.

   iii. You must reprimand the sinner first in soft language. Perhaps it will be effective and the sinner will return to the right way. If the sinner does not listen, then you can tell the public of this person's willful evil.

   iv. You must not make the sin out to be greater than it is.

   v. Your intention must be for the (favorable) end result and not, God forbid, to enjoy the harm you are causing to your fellow or to be motivated by hatred that you harbor for your fellow.

   vi. You can achieve this aim in a different way without telling *lashon hara* (i.e., talking behind someone's back), then it is totally forbidden to tell it.

   vii. The telling must not cause more damage to the person than appearing in court for breaking that law would cause.

(Chafetz Chayim: *Laws of Lashon Harah* 10:2)

Probing: Ideas and Issues

Using the texts above as a measure, overall, do you think Judaism would fall to the side of reporting or not reporting suspicious behavior? And just how "suspicious" would the behavior have to be to merit reporting on it? Some schools favor an anonymous tips hotline for students to call when something seems to be amiss.

Would such a hotline be acceptable from a Jewish point of view?

10. Will character education (teaching values and social skills) make a measurable difference in improving school culture?

On the One Hand:

How can schools be expected to shoulder the burden of so many learning agendas, such as character education, conflict resolution, empathy training, cooperative learning techniques, values clarification, etc.? Schools barely have the time to teach the basics of academics! Besides, values should be taught by parents and through students' religious education. Schools can't be expected to change a whole culture.

A. No one is poor except those who lack knowledge . . . Those who have knowledge have everything. Those who lack knowledge, what do they have? . . . (*Nedarim* 41a).

B. Rav said to Rav Samuel the son of Shilat: Before the age of six do not accept pupils; from that age you can accept them, and stuff them with Torah like an ox (*Baba Batra* 21a).

On the Other Hand:

Character education and the teaching of social skills is as critical a part of a child's learning as anything else. When deprived of this kind of learning, the school environment — academic and social — will suffer. Learning core values intersects with the teaching of literature and history. There are (non-religious) values all segments of the school community can agree on. What happens now in schools *will* affect the culture of future generations.

a. A heathen went to Hillel [and said to him, "Accept me as a proselyte on the condition that you teach me the whole Torah . . .]." Hillel . . . said to him,

"What is hateful to you do not do to your fellow — that is the whole Torah, all the rest is commentary — now, go and learn" (*Shabbat* 31a).

b. Let people first do good deeds, and then ask God for [knowledge of] Torah. Let people first act as righteous and upright people act, and then let them ask God for wisdom. Let people first grasp the way of humility, and then ask God for understanding (*Tanna de be Eliyahu*, p. 31).

c. Rabbi Elisha ben Abuyah said that a person who has learnt much Torah and has good deeds is like a horse that has reins. The person who has the first, but not the second, is like a horse without reins — it soon throws the rider over its head (*Avot de Rabbi Natan*, verse I, xxiv, 39a).

d. Rabbi Beroka of Khuzistan often visited the market at Be Lapat. There he would meet Elijah the prophet (who, according to tradition, sometimes descended from heaven to appear to the pious on earth).

"Does anybody in this market have a share in the world to come?" Rabbi Beroka asked one day . . . While they were talking, two men came by.

Elijah said, "Those two have a share in the world to come."

Rabbi Beroka went to them and said, "What do you do?"

They said, "We are jesters. When we see a person depressed, we try to cheer that person up. And when we see two people quarreling, we work hard to make peace between them" (*Ta'anit* 22a).

Probing: Ideas and Issues

In Jewish tradition learning and good deeds often are linked together. To what extent are these two values incorporated into your school? How about your synagogue school? Do you believe the balance is the right one? If so, describe why you think this is so. If not, how could the balance be improved?

RELATED MIDDOT AND MITZVOT

Practicing these virtues and commandments can help diffuse the pressures that lead to school violence.

Derech Eretz (Civility): Schools that make explicit efforts to create an environment of civility reap both academic and social benefits.

Din V'Rachamim (Justice and Mercy): We must strive to find a sensitive balance between justice and mercy when dealing with troublemaking students.

Erech Apayim (Slow to Anger): Potentially violent students should be taught skills to control and channel anger appropriately.

Hachnasat Orchim (Welcoming the Stranger): Inclusion and cooperation should be stressed in the classroom and on the playground, both informally and formally (i.e. through regular use of cooperative pedagogic techniques). Special outreach should be made to newcomers who are more easily left out.

K'vod HaBriyot (Respecting Others' Dignity): School rules and consequences for breaking them must reflect fairness and the value of treating others with dignity. Otherwise, feelings of resentment and alienation will be exacerbated, possibly leading to increased hostility.

Lo Levayesh (Not Embarrassing or Humiliating Others): An atmosphere in which embarrassing, humiliating, and bullying others is tolerated is one which "invites" acts of vengeance.

Rodef Shalom (Pursue Peace): An environment of peace is most conducive to learning.

Sayver Panim Yafot (A Pleasant Demeanor): When teachers model friendliness and warmth toward others, they set a tone that helps students see school as affirming and committed to their success.

Shmiat HaOzen (Being a Good Listener): Adults in the school community must really listen to their students in order to understand what is troubling them and how they might help them. Modeling good listening will encourage students to listen better to each other, too. Good listening is a huge part of effective problem solving.

Tochechah (Rebuking): Troublemaking behavior (bullying, carrying weapons, threatening violence, etc.) needs to be addressed immediately with rebukes that fit the offense and that are given in a dignified manner.

ACTIVITIES

A First Look: Key Issues and Ideas

1. You might want to do this exercise twice — before beginning this unit and afterward. Attitudes are likely to change! The "Overview" section of this chapter asks: what is the cause in the increase in violence, what can be done, and who is responsible? Divide the group into pairs. Ask: What are your top three responses to each of the three questions? When the pairs have completed this task, the whole group reassembles. Each pair should be prepared to defend its position. If the two can't agree, each must be prepared to go solo in defending his/her position. Here is an example of what a pair might come up with:

   What is the cause in the increase in violence?

   - Kids being excluded and taunted.
   - Too many guns, too easily available.
   - Parents and teachers not caring enough.

   What can be done?

   - Expel troublemakers who threaten either with weapons or with words.

- Hire more school counselors to check in with kids on a regular basis.
- Have schools use the same kind of security checks that airports use, like putting backpacks through X-ray machines and having kids walk through metal detectors.

Who is responsible?

- All the students in the school
- The teachers
- Parents

After you cover the relevant factors thoroughly, you can have participants do this exercise a second time. Doing so will force them to reexamine their preconceived ideas and confront the complexity of school violence from a broader perspective.

2. Refer to the Glossary, p. 186. Write the terms (or a selection of them) on the board or large sheet of paper. Ask students if they are already familiar with any of them. Give straightforward definitions for the ones students are not able to explain adequately. Keep this list of terms visible so that the group can refer to them as they study school violence.

3. To convey the complexity of school violence, study all the pertinent components. First, review the three questions: What is responsible for the increase in school violence? How should we deal with it? Who should take charge of implementing strategies for change?

   Then, assign subtopics to learn about. You will want to have copies of the appropriate sections from this chapter available. Students can work individually or in pairs. Ask them to concentrate on understanding the material as best they can. Then, have them write down every question they can think of related to the material. Here are the subtopics:

a. Explain the category of *ben sorer u'moreh* and its relevance to school violence. (See "Jewish Perspectives" above.)

b. Explain the category of the *rodef* and its relevance to school violence. (See "Jewish Perspectives" above.)

c. Explain the significance of the *eglah arufah* to the topic of school violence. (See "Jewish Perspectives" above.)

d. What are the biological/psychological, environmental, and cultural factors affecting violence? (See "General Perspectives" above.)

e. What steps can be taken to help stem school violence? (See "General Perspectives" above.)

f. What points must we consider when forging strategies to deal with school violence? (See the chart in the "Text Study" section above, pp. 165-174.)

g. Explain how "Related *Middot* and *Mitzvot*" apply to school violence (p. 175).

After about ten minutes, students present the material they studied to the rest of the group. They explain the gist of the material, what details they think are important, any difficulties in understanding what they studied, and questions they have.

4. Refer to the 20 points listed in the chart found in the "Text Study" section above (pp. 166-168) — 10 points from one side, plus 10 from the other. Individually, each person ranks all 20 points from what they believe to be most compelling to least. In a group compare and explain rankings. Ask: What do your ranking results show about your attitude toward school violence? What was most challenging about completing this exercise?

5. The leader explains each of the following cultural factors that may affect increases in school violence. (Find more information on each in the Overview, "General Perspectives.")

Primacy of Self

Materialism

Expectations of Instant Gratification

Lack of Conflict Resolution Skills

Bullying, Taunting, Humiliating

Exclusion and Cliques

Gangs

Inadequate Moral Education

Incoherent School Core Values, Rules, and Consequences

Ask: How many of these factors describe problems with which you yourself grapple? Which of the factors do you think most afflict your school community? How about the broader community in which you live — which factor do you think is of the greatest concern? Explain. How would your school environment change if you were able to resolve or successfully address that factor? What ideas do you have for doing so?

6. Arrange for a series of guest speakers or organize a panel discussion. Invite to class people who might be considered "the elders of the community," the leaders or adults to whom we look for guidance and to whom we ascribe responsibility for the community's safety and well-being. These are the people we might consult to help choose strategies to reduce school violence. Include individuals from a variety of backgrounds, with a range of areas of expertise. Possible guests could include: school administrators, teachers, parents, politicians, religious leaders, psychiatrists, pediatricians, social workers, social psychologists, media executives, philosophers, philanthropists, community business people, police, or security guards.

In advance, prepare for the guests a list of questions related to youth violence that you wish to address. Then, after the guests make their presentations (and leave), have the group discuss reactions to what the guests said. Whose ideas were most compelling, and why?

7. This activity will involve research and presentations. Access to computers for web research will help participants find information most efficiently. Have the group imagine they are members of a school board. They have decided they want to include some kind of character education in their school. They are looking for the kinds of strategies that reflect "root cause interventions" (to youth violence, as discussed in the "General Perspectives" section of the Overview, p. 163). Divide everyone into groups of two or three. Assign each group one of the following web sites to research:

www.charactercounts.org — see The Character Counts Coalition's "Six Pillars of Character."

www.goodcharacter.com

www.character.org — see their "11 Principles of Effective Character Education."

www.charactered.net — see their curriculum and lesson plans.

www.jigsaw.org — learn about a pedagogic technique that enhances cooperation and empathy.

www.nccre.org — The National Center for Conflict Resolution Education.

www.responsiveclassroom.org — see their archives of articles that discuss ways to pay attention to children's social, as well as academic education.

Each group should try to understand the rationale and methodologies suggested by their organization.

An advanced challenge: each group plans a short activity for the rest of the group based on their research. Once the presentations happen, the presenting groups try to "sell" their program to the "school board."

As board members listen, they note questions they have. When the presenters finish, the board members ask their questions. The questions should be thoughtful and (politely) challenging.

After the presentations, the whole group should select the program (or programs) they want to implement. The next step would be to figure out how their strategy would translate to a Jewish school. Jewish resources related to character education include:

> *Exploring Jewish Ethics and Values* by Ronald H. Isaacs (Hoboken, NJ: KTAV Publishing House, Inc.), 1999.

> *The Jewish Moral Virtues* by Eugene B. Borowitz and Frances Weinman Schwartz (Philadelphia, PA: The Jewish Publication Society), 1999.

> *Judaism and Spiritual Ethics* by Niles E. Goldstein and Steven S. Mason (New York: UAHC Press), 1996.

> *Striving for Virtue: A Contemporary Guide for Jewish Ethical Behavior* by Kerry M. Olitzky (Hoboken, NJ: KTAV Publishing House, Inc.), 1996.

> *Teaching Jewish Virtues: Sacred Sources and Arts Activities* by Susan Freeman (Denver, CO: A.R.E. Publishing, Inc.), 1999.

Applying Middot and Mitzvot

1. Ask: If you were designing a workshop for potentially violent kids, on which *middot* or Jewish virtues would you have them focus? On which *middot* would you focus for the general population of your school to help improve the social environment? Two traditional lists of *middot* can be found in *Pirke Avot* 6:6 and in *Orchei Tzadikim/The Ways of the Righteous*. You also might want to look at the virtues covered in *Teaching Jewish Virtues* by Susan Freeman (this book also cites those from *Pirke Avot* and *Orchei Tzadikim* in Appendix 8, pp. 355-356). Other good

resources are: *The Jewish Moral Virtues* by Borowitz and Schwartz, and *Exploring Jewish Ethics and Values* by Ronald H. Isaacs.

2. Instruct your group in this way: Commit to becoming better listeners. Do a *shmiat ha-ozen/*"a listening ear" journal exercise daily (or nightly) for a week. When you are at school, concentrate on opening your ears . . . and eyes and heart more deeply. What do you notice? Are there people who are left out, bullied, excluded? Are there people who are hurting, who feel humiliated, who are struggling? How does "paying attention" make you a better person? How might better listening skills improve the atmosphere at a school (or your school)?

   Tell participants to try to notice these specific details both about their own and their peers' listening skills and habits:

   - Does the listener look at the speaker? (Do I look at the speaker?)

   - Does the listener interrupt? (Do I interrupt?)

   - Does the listener talk to others while the speaker is talking? (Do I talk to others . . . ?)

   - Does the listener's body show attentiveness? (Does my body show attentiveness?)

   - Does the listener think about what the speaker is saying or is his/her mind wandering on other topics? (Do I listen to what the speaker is saying . . . ?)

   - Does the listener ask questions to make sure he/she really understands? (Do I ask questions?)

   - Can the listener repeat or recap the speaker's ideas? (Can I repeat the speaker's ideas?)

3. Have the group create a series of posters for your school (or an imaginary school). These posters will serve as tools for publicizing ways to enhance *sayver panim yafot*, "a pleas-

ant demeanor" and/or *derech eretz*, "civility" in your school. You can broaden the definition of *sayver panim yafot* to include a general sense of exuding warmth and friendliness. You may want to brainstorm ideas beforehand. Here are a few ideas to get you started:

- Holding the door open for the person behind you

- Greeting others every day with a "good morning" or "*boker tov*"

- Remembering after school to call and check in on a classmate who was absent

- Stopping to help someone who has dropped his/her belongings (i.e., rather than laughing at the person)

- Standing up *against* bullies and standing up *for* the bullied

- Your own ideas!

4. For more information and activities on:

Derech Eretz (Civility): see *The Jewish Moral Virtues* by Eugene B. Borowitz and Frances Weinman Schwartz, pp. 53-65.

Din V'Rachamim (Justice and Mercy): see *Teaching Jewish Virtues* by Susan Freeman, pp. 55-68.

Erech Apayim (Slow To Anger): see *Teaching Jewish Virtues* by Susan Freeman, pp. 85-101.

Hachnasat Orchim (Welcoming the Stranger) see *Teaching Jewish Virtues* by Susan Freeman, pp. 102-118, and *Teaching Mitzvot* by Barbara Binder Kadden and Bruce Kadden, p. 151-155.

K'vod HaBriyot (Respecting Others' Dignity): see *Teaching Jewish Virtues* by Susan Freeman, pp. 179-194.

Lo Levayesh (Not Embarrassing or Humiliating Others): see *Teaching Jewish Virtues* by Susan Freeman, pp. 119-135.

Rodef Shalom (Pursue Peace): see *The Jewish Moral Virtues* by Eugene B. Borowitz and

Frances Weinman Schwartz, pp. 237-248; also "The Pursuit of Peace" by Moshe Sokolow, New York: CAJE, 1993.

Sayver Panim Yafot (A Pleasant Demeanor): see *Teaching Jewish Virtues* by Susan Freeman, pp. 228-240.

Shmiat HaOzen (Being a Good Listener): see *Teaching Jewish Virtues* by Susan Freeman, pp. 255-268.

Tochechah (Rebuking): see *Teaching Jewish Virtues* by Susan Freeman, pp. 318-331.

Stories: Understanding through Listening

1. Read over the imaginary scenarios in the "Scenarios: How Things Have Changed" section above (p. 164-165). Have students recap the stories in their own words. Then, review the basic laws of the *rodef*. Discuss these questions:

- How would you judge who is at fault in each of the scenarios?

- What additional information would you seek in order to understand these conflicts?

- What should a "stander-by" do in each of the scenarios?

- Under what circumstances would you *not* consider Aryeh a *rodef*? (Scenario 1)

- Under what circumstances would you *not* consider "Armed" a *rodef*? (Scenario 2)

- What consequences/punishments would you mete out if you were mediating these conflicts?

2. Refer to the story of the jesters in Text Study #10d (p. 174). Ask: What do you think those jesters did to cheer up others and to help make peace between quarreling people?

   Have group members come up with ten things the jesters might have done to cheer up people and ten of the jesters' possible peacemaking strategies. After doing so, have the group name ten ways for cheering others up and ten ways for making peace in their own community (or school community). They can use some of the same ideas. To get more peacemaking strategies, research books and web sites related to conflict resolution. (A good web site to check out is The National Center for Conflict Resolution Education: nccre.org.)

3. Tell the group: Plan at least two interviews — one with a parent and another with a grandparent or other senior adult. Possible interview questions:

   • What were schools like when you were growing up?

   • How did students behave with each other?

   • How did students act toward the teachers?

   • What were the rules?

   • What happened if you broke the rules?

   • How were conflicts resolved?

   • Were there cliques?

   • What was done about bullies?

   • What were the underlying values of the school community?

   • How were parents involved in the school?

   • Other questions . . .

   After participants collect their information, have them chart how the culture of schools has and hasn't changed in three generations — their own generation, that of their parents, and that of their grandparents.

4. Participants may enjoy doing this exercise in pairs. Have them research an actual "story" in which a youth committed an act of violence. (Or the leader can bring in one or more stories). Instruct students: First write (or rewrite) the story as a news article (in a journalistic style). The "article" should briefly answer the questions: who, what, when, where, why, and how. Next, rewrite what happened, this time as a fictional short story. You will draw on some details of the actual news story. But with this new version, you are to take liberties in making changes so that the story turns out peaceably. When everyone finishes the exercise, participants present their stories to the whole group. After sharing their work, presenters can invite questions from their listeners.

5. This exercise will involve writing from various people's points of view. But first, the background:

   One of the most disturbing incidences of school violence in recent years took place at Columbine High School in Littleton, Colorado in April 1999. Two enraged students, armed with an arsenal of weapons, went on a rampage at their school, killing 12 of their classmates, a teacher, and themselves. In addition, 23 more students needed to be hospitalized, many of whom are now plagued with long-term disabilities. Before committing this massacre, the two perpetrators, Eric Harris and Dylan Klebold, made videotapes about their violent intentions. After the content of the videotapes was made public, here is what one student, a member of the Columbine football team, had to say:

   > "Columbine is a good clean place except for those rejects. Most kids didn't want them there. They were into witchcraft. They were into voodoo. Sure we teased them. But what do you expect with kids who come to school with weird hairdos and horns on their hats? It's not just jocks; the whole school's disgusted with them. They're a bunch of homos, grabbing each other's private parts. If you want to get rid of someone, usually you tease 'em. So the whole school would call them homos, and when they did something sick, we'd tell them, 'You're sick and that's wrong'" (*Nobody Left to Hate*, p. 71-72).

Have group members choose one of the following people to represent in their writing: another member of the football team, an injured student, a parent of Klebold or Harris, a parent of a victim, a teacher, a security officer, a student in the school who often is bullied and excluded, the principal, a school neighbor, etc. The writers imagine they have just spent time with the jock who has shared the above words with them. After hearing from the jock, the writers take leave of him and go to sit alone. They take out a piece of paper and express their feelings about the words they have just heard. The writers should strive hard to be true to their adopted "voice." When everyone is finished, have participants share their writing and/or how they felt about engaging in this exercise. Older students might view and discuss the film *Bowling for Columbine* (2002, 119 min., rated R).

6. In a group in which there is a genuine sense of trust, share your own "stories." These might include provocative incidents group members have witnessed, personal concerns about schools, situations that feel difficult to handle, etc. This exercise can work well in a parent-student program.

Action: Getting Out, Getting Involved

1. Organize sessions on anger management, stress management, peer counseling, peer mediation, and/or social skills. Specialists should lead these sessions. Start with a synagogue/religious school class or youth group. Then, consider bringing what you have learned are good programs to the wider community, such as a public high school, after school clubs, a teen community center, etc.

2. Plan a *Derech Eretz* Day at your religious or day school. What are some ways you can add warmth, kindness, manners, and respect to your environment? You may want to refer to ideas you came up with in activity #3 under "Applying Middot and Mitzvot" above

and/or in activity #2 under "Stories." If you do not attend a Jewish day school, how might you bring your ideas for improved *derech eretz* into your other school (or work) environment?

3. Imagine your group represents members of a parent-teacher-student committee. You are to develop protocol for welcoming newcomers to your school community. Create protocol for those things that students can carry out on their own to welcome newcomers — both during school and outside school hours.

4. Create a two sided bulletin board or hall display. On one side post examples of violence; on the other side include what could be considered deterrents to violence. This display can be as concrete or abstract as you like. For concrete material, use newspaper and magazine clippings. For a more abstract display, include original artwork expressing the two themes.

5. Encourage students to reach out to someone who is left out. In a group discuss what this might mean (for example, inviting someone to join your group at lunch). Also, discuss what you might do if you yourself feel left out (for example, get to know people you may have overlooked as potentially good companions). Ask students to follow through on some of the suggestions. In a week, check in and see how everyone did with this challenge.

6. Have your group become active in a gun control organization, such as the Center to Prevent Handgun Violence (www.cphv.org). Find out what current issues are being focused on. How can you become involved in furthering their efforts?

7. Have participants write letters to members of Congress asking them to pressure the entertainment industry to curb violent content and to institute a useful ratings system. You can also speak out against media violence through letters to the editor and/or writing

to companies that advertise during violent shows. A useful place to begin a protest is simply by *not* attending violent movies, watching violent TV shows, purchasing music with violent lyrics, or playing violent electronic games, etc.!

8. Organize CPR (cardiopulmonary resuscitation) classes at your school or synagogue. CPR training provides specific skills in intervening in life and death emergencies, perhaps saving lives. The training teaches a person how, in certain situations, "not to stand idly by . . . " (Leviticus 19:16). While CPR gives a person confidence with important life sustaining skills, it also teaches an underlying value. In supplementary (or complementary) sessions with the CPR classes, study the commandment of "not standing idly by." Discuss other ways to apply CPR-type skills/ values to other situations. That is, how can you "not stand idly by" when you witness bullying, teasing, discrimination, genocide? What skills and values would you need? For a useful resource, see the chapter *"Lo Ta'amod al Dam Rayecha"* in *Teaching Mitzvot* by Barbara Binder Kadden and Bruce Kadden, pp. 181-185.

Wrestling: Engagement with the Issues

1. Act out the scenarios from the "Scenarios: How Things Have Changed" section above. Or create your own scenarios to act out. If you create your own, include the following characters: the pursuer, the pursued, person/ people standing by, community leaders. The goal is to capture the complexity of volatile school situations.

2. Study the *"ben sorer u'moreh"* text and commentary. See the beginning of the "Jewish Perspectives" section in the Overview for a synopsis. Imagine a modern account of a stubborn and rebellious school student. Have your group flesh out some particulars and assign roles. Roles might include:

- Rebellious student
- Mother
- Father
- "Elders" (Teachers, principal, Rabbi, or others)
- various community members
- one or two interviewers

Suppose all the significant players in the story have been invited to participate in a TV interview or documentary. Present this event as a scripted play, an improvisation, or a filmed video "documentary."

3. Hold a debate on "What to Do about School Violence." One group represents "the hardliners;" the other is the "moderating forces" group. Refer to the material in the "Text Study" section above for some points of controversy.

4. Survey participants about how they respond to conflicts. Have them answer each question with Always, Sometimes, or Never (use "A" for Always, "S" for Sometimes, or "N" for Never).

When there is a conflict, I try to:

a. hit the other person

b. run away

c. get help from a peer

d. talk it out

e. understand the other point of view

f. make a joke of it

g. get help from an adult

i. make the other person apologize

j. apologize myself

k. find out what the problem is

l. listen to the other person

m. tell the other person to leave me alone

n. say swear words

o. get friends to gang up on the other person

(This exercise is adapted from one that appears in the Appendix of *Creative Conflict Resolution* by William J. Kreidler.)

As a next step, have the group go back through the list and discuss which responses to conflict would be considered acceptable Jewish responses. Ask them to elaborate on and defend their reasoning.

5. Tell your group that it represents a mini-school community. Assign subgroups to be the students, parents, teachers, and administrators. You are to have a meeting in which you determine your school's core values. Try to come up with about ten. It may be helpful to begin the wording of each value with: "School is a place where . . . " Two examples:

   • School is a place where everyone is treated with dignity and respect.

   • School is a place where everyone can feel safe.

   After determining some core values, define rules that would apply based on each of the values. Two examples:

   • (School is a place where everyone is treated with dignity and respect, so . . .) No name-calling.

   • (School is a place where everyone can feel safe, so . . .) No weapons allowed.

   Finally, think of what consequences would apply if someone broke a rule. But remember, the consequences can't go against any of the school's core values. That means a consequence for name calling couldn't be that the victim gets to call the name caller bad names in front of a lot of people. Such a humiliating consequence would go against the value of treating everyone with respect and dignity. Would your list of values look different if you were designating them for a Jewish school? (An excellent resource for this activity is the book *As Tough as Necessary* by

Curwin and Mendler.)

6. Create collages out of torn paper. Have available various colors and textures of paper and glue. Study the *"ben sorer u'moreh"* (see the "Jewish Perspectives" section in the Overview for a synopsis). Then have students create collages depicting a modern stubborn and rebellious child. The pieces of torn paper might represent the child him/herself, peers of the child, the parents, community leaders and other community members, cultural forces, the school, etc.

Other themes for torn paper collages:

   • A modern *rodef* (pursuer), i.e., in the model of the one mentioned in Scenario #2 in the "Scenarios: How Things Have Changed" section above (pp. 164-165)

   • The words from Leviticus 19:16: "You shall not stand idly by when your fellow's blood is being shed"

7. Choose one of the above collage suggestions, but use paint or watercolors, rather than torn paper, to express your ideas.

8. Create a collage or poem using words and images related to the topic of school violence. Here are some words to trigger ideas:

   rebellion, stubbornness, in pursuit (*rodef*), humiliation, bullying, exclusion, inclusion, peace, conflict, loneliness, being left out, anger, rage, self-control, guns, threats, violence, a listening ear, the community, the elders, intervening.

9. Read the text below:

   It is not those outside our community who can destroy the fabric of our lives, values, and ethics; nor can they mend it. We are the weavers. We are the threads. And it is our actions that determine the patterns and textures of the fabric ("We Are the Weavers" by Gila Gevirtz, *Jewish Education News*, Spring 1999, front cover).

Have your group create a weaving. Choose which kinds of threads (strips of material) you want to have represent the community. Then choose a second group of strips to weave through the "community" threads. On the second group of strips, use fabric markers (or paint) to write values, virtues, and/or rules that you believe your community needs to live by. You may want to repeat the word several times on the strip (in Hebrew and/or in English). Then, through group collaboration and cooperation, begin to weave the piece of art.

Empathy

1. Instruct students: Write a letter of apology to someone you teased or excluded. Don't censor yourself as you compose the words you want to say. That is, don't worry as you write about whether you really will send the letter. The letter might refer to a current circumstance in your life, or it may refer to something that happened years ago. There is a saying that it's never too late to apologize. Do you believe that? Should you actually send the letter? You be the judge.

2. Do a *Hachnasat Orchim* ("Hospitality") exercise in which participants physically experience a taste of inclusion and exclusion. Have all but one or two people create an inviting space with their bodies. They will become a group sculpture, making shapes with their bodies that are welcoming. In this part of the exercise, the majority of the participants "become" hospitality. Then have the one or two other people enter the inviting space, walk/move around it, through it, and exit. In this part of the exercise, selected participants experience or receive hospitality. Repeat a few times, giving others the opportunity to experience the welcoming energy of the "human hospitality sculpture."

Share reactions. Have those who entered the group sculpture describe what it was like. Conversely, what was it like "being" hospital-

ity, being the welcoming sculpture?

Now contrast the first experience with its opposite. Have a group make an unwelcoming group sculpture, an uninviting space. Then, have one or two people enter, walk/move around, and exit. Repeat a few times, taking turns with different people creating the sculpture and entering the space.

An advanced extension: Allow the "sculptures" to move with their upper bodies and arms only, keeping their feet planted in place, or with complete freedom to move (but not touch those entering).

Discuss. Do you have new insights about inclusion and exclusion, about being a welcoming versus unwelcoming community because of this experience? For those who entered the sculptures, what was the best moment? What didn't you like, and why? Can you apply anything you learned through this movement exercise to life situations? (This exercise is adapted from *Teaching Jewish Virtues: Sacred Sources and Arts Activities* by Susan Freeman, p. 114.)

3. Plan and hold a creative service for peace. Include songs, prayers, published poems and prose, plus participants' own creative writing. Include selections that express hopes and prayers for peace in oneself, in the community, and in the world.

4. Create a memorial to victims of school violence. This might be a sculpture or other piece of art, or it might be a book of poems written and bound by members of your group.

5. Emulate the students in the Rabbi Joseph H. Lookstein Ramaz Upper School. They expressed great empathy following the tragic school shootings at Columbine High School in Littleton, Colorado, in April, 1999.

   a. Take out an ad in the local paper of the community in which violence has occurred. The Ramaz students took out a quarter page ad featuring a picture of a dove with an olive branch, with the words from Psalms 122: "May there be peace within your walls, serenity within your palaces." The text of the ad read: "The faculty and students at the Rabbi Joseph H. Lookstein Ramaz Upper School in Manhattan offer their heartfelt condolences to the families and friends of those who were killed tragically at Columbine High School. As high school students, we feel connected to those who lost their lives in this massacre and pray that God will comfort their families."

b. Collect *tzedakah*, charity to help injured individuals pay for their medical expenses.

c. Launch a "green ribbon" campaign, wearing green ribbons as a symbol of "life, hope, and rebirth."

d. Have students create and sign a "scroll of honor" taking a stand against school violence and disrespect. The text of the pledge signed by Ramaz students reads:

> This contract states that you won't pass by when a person is in physical or emotional trouble. By signing this contract, you are showing Jonesboro, Arkansas, Littleton, Colorado (sites of tragic shootings), the rest of the United States, and the whole world

that you will not tolerate violence or disrespect in your schools and communities. You are taking a stand. There are no easy answers, no simple solutions. No food drive, Band-Aid, or memorial is big enough to bring back those who have died. Signing this contract and wearing these ribbons is something you can do. They symbolize your dedication to ending all acts of senseless violence and disrespect. The color green symbolizes hope — and nothing can take that away.

(Resource for this activity: "Do Not Separate Yourself from the Community," New York: CAJE, 1999, p. 9.)

6. Ask everyone to make a small poster to take home and hang in a place where it can be seen often (such as next to your bed). This poster will serve as a reminder for you to take care of yourself and be safe, to care about others and not stand idly by, and to accept these important realms of responsibility now, today. You might choose to highlight these words:

> If I am not for myself, who will be for me? If I am only for myself, what am I? And if not now, when? (*Pirke Avot* 1:14)

GLOSSARY

Hebrew Terms

Ben sorer u'moreh:

A stubborn and rebellious son.

Eglah arufah:

A slaughtered calf (literal meaning); the elders of a community make an offering of a calf when the murderer of an abandoned corpse cannot be found.

Ha-adam nivra b'tzelem Elohim:

All people are created in the image of God.

Lo ta'amod al dam rayecha:

Do not stand idly while the blood of your fellow person is shed. (Leviticus 19:16)

Kol Yisrael aravin zeh ba-zeh:

All of Israel is responsible for one another.

Middot:

Jewish virtues.

Mipnay darkay shalom:

For the sake of peace.

Mitzvot:

Jewish commandments, practices.

Rodef:

A pursuer (after another person).

General Terms:

Biological/Psychological Factors:

How our physical make-up may affect our actions.

Environmental Factors:

How circumstances in our immediate surroundings might influence our actions.

Cultural Factors:

How certain values, habits, and trends in our society might influence our behavior.

Pump-handle Interventions:

Measures that may help reduce violent acts, but won't necessarily get at the deeper causes. (For example, gun control, metal detectors in schools, reducing media violence.)

Root Cause Interventions:

Measures to reduce violent acts that attempt to get at the deeper causes. (For example, character education, conflict resolution training, anger management, identifying and living by a school's core values, etc.)

Character Education:

Teaching values and good character traits (directly or through literature, history, and social studies).

Conflict Resolution:

Skills for resolving conflict peaceably.

BIBLIOGRAPHY

Books and Articles

Aronson, Elliot. *The Jigsaw Classroom.* Beverly Hills, CA: Sage, 1978.

Aronson, Elliot. *Nobody Left to Hate.* New York: Worth Publishers, 2000.

Bonilla, Denise M., ed. *School Violence.* New York: The H.W. Wilson Company, 2000.

Capozzoli, Thomas K., and R. Steve McVey. *Kids Killing Kids: Managing Violence and Gangs in Schools.* Boca Raton, FL: CRC-St. Lucie Press, 2000.

Center to Prevent Handgun Violence. *Straight Talk about Risks: A Pre-K-12 Curriculum for Preventing Gun Violence.* Washington, DC: Center to Prevent Handgun Violence, 1992.

Curwin, Richard L., and Allen N. Mendler. *As Tough as Necessary: Countering Violence, Aggression, and Hostility in Our Schools.* Alexandria, VA: Association for Supervision and Curriculum Development, 1997.

Flannery, Raymond B., Jr. *Preventing Youth Violence: A Guide for Parents, Teachers, and Counselors.* New York: The Continuum Publishing Company, 1999.

Harris, Judith Rich. *The Nurture Assumption: Why Children Turn Out the Way They Do; Parents Matter Less than You Think and Peers Matter More.* New York: The Free Press, 1998.

Johnson, David W., and Roger T. Johnson. *Reducing School Violence through Conflict Resolution.* Alexandria, VA: Association for Supervision and Curriculum Development, 1995.

Kreidler, William J. *Creative Conflict Resolution: More that 200 Activities for Keeping Peace in the Classroom.* Glenview, IL: GoodYear Books, 1984.

Myers, David G. *The American Paradox: Spiritual Hunger in an Age of Plenty.* New Haven, CT: Yale University Press, 2000.

Web Sites

The Center for Effective Collaboration and Practice: cecp.air.org/school_violence.htm

> *Promotes a reoriented national preparedness for dealing with children who have or are at risk of developing serious emotional disturbances. See especially "Early Warning, Timely Response — A Guide To Safe Schools")*

The School Violence Watch Network: www.cyberenforcement.com/schoolviolencewatch.htm

> *Assists school administrators, teachers, and law enforcement officials in dealing with threats and rumors of violence, bullying, or drug abuse occurring within schools.*

School Safety Report Card: www.schoolsafetyreportcard.com

> *An opportunity for stakeholders in the educational system — parents, teachers, students, counselors, administrators, taxpayers, business people, law enforcement, government officials, media, and community residents — to provide input and complete a report card to grade their school district and school.*

These web sites are helpful in searches for the latest stories and issues:

Education Week: www.edweek.org
> *The online version of Education Week magazine. Search for articles about school violence.*

Yahoo: www.yahoo.com
> *Click "news," then search for "school violence."*

The following web sites deal with character education:

Character Counts!: www.charactercounts.org
> *A nonprofit, nonpartisan, nonsectarian coalition of schools, communities and nonprofit organizations working to advance character education by teaching the Six Pillars of Character: trustworthi-*

ness, respect, responsibility, fairness, caring, and citizenship.

Good Character.com: www.goodcharacter.com

Character Education resources, materials, and lesson plans.

The Character Education Partnership: www.character.org

" . . . a nonpartisan coalition of organizations and individuals dedicated to developing moral character and civic virtue in our nation's youth as one means of creating a more compassionate and responsible society."

The Character Education Network: www.charactered.net

A place for students, teachers, schools and communities to facilitate character education. The site provides ready-to-use curriculum, activities, and resources.

The Jigsaw Classroom: www.jigsaw.org

"The jigsaw classroom is a cooperative learning technique that reduces racial conflict among school children, promotes better learning, improves student motivation, and increases enjoyment of the learning experience."

National Center for Conflict Resolution - Conflict Resolution Education, Inc.: www.resolutioneducation.com

Promote the development of conflict resolution education programs in schools.

The Responsive Classroom: www.responsiveclassroom.org

A practical approach for creating safe, challenging, and joyful schools.

Films

The Teen Files is an Emmy Award winning series that helps teens identify, understand, and deal with many of the issues confronting teens today. *The Teen Files Flipped* is a newer series from MTV that offers teens a fresh perspective on complex issues by "flipping" them into the shoes of young people who are coming to grips with life-changing issues. Obtain purchase information from www.aimsmultimedia.com.

The Teen Files — The Truth about Violence (2000, 57 min.)

The Teen Files Flipped — Gun Awareness (2002, 21 min.)

The Teen Files Flipped — Bullies, Loners, and Violence (2001, 21 min.)

The Teen Files Flipped — Doing Hard Time (2002, 21 min.)

The Teen Files Flipped — Tolerance (2001, 21 min.)

The following commercial films deal with issues of school violence, bullying, cliques, and alternate methods of conflict resolution. While specific sections may be valuable for illustrating certain aspects of these topics, it may not be appropriate for students to view the entire film. Prescreening is strongly recommended.

Revenge of the Nerds (1984, 89 min., rated R)

My Bodyguard (1980, 96 min., rated PG)

Back to the Future (1985, 116 min., rated PG)

Carrie (1952, 118 min., not rated)

The Rage: Carrie 2 (1999, 97 min., rated R)

Bowling for Columbine (2002, 119 minutes, rated R)

CHAPTER 8

ETHICS OF WAR

OVERVIEW

"War is hell." We've all heard the expression. War is violent, destructive, brutal, and devastating. Yet, war has been a reality of human existence since humankind appeared on earth. And sadly, despite its horrors, war doesn't seem close to disappearing. Even so, we must ask ourselves if there are ways to mitigate some of war's evils.

People battle for different reasons. Some wars may qualify as worth fighting, others not. There are nations that will fight a war only to defend their very survival. Others are willing to fight to spread ideological beliefs. How do we determine a *just cause* for war? Who is obliged to fight? Does war have "rules"? That is, are there *just means* of fighting a war? How does war affect our relationship with God? How does war affect our humanity?

In this chapter we will examine difficult questions regarding the ethics of war. By definition, ethical inquiry suggests an absence of easy answers. But nowhere are the stakes as high as they are in war.

Jewish Perspectives

How Do We Determine a Just Cause for War?

Killing, murder, and the intentional harming of people and other creatures are antithetical to Jewish values. Furthermore, those who cause wanton damage and destruction to property and the environment are denounced. Such violent individuals deserve severe punishment. How is it possible for war ever to play a legitimate role in a Jewish worldview?

In war, values we take for granted, values we've studied and believed in, values we hold dear to our hearts are called into question. When we agree to war, we face wrenching contradictions: We said "never kill," and now we knowingly accept the fact that masses of people will likely die at our hands. We said "never harm," and now we are responsible for widespread injury. We said not to "cause destruction purposefully," and now we fight, leaving massive environmental and property damage in our wake. That is war — civilization turned upside down.

Still, Judaism teaches we can sanction armed conflict at times. Moreover, there are circumstances when fighting is mandatory. Jewish law distinguishes between two types of war: (1) *milchemet mitzvah*, an "obligatory war" and (2) *milchemet reshut*, an "authorized or optional war."[1]

Obligatory wars fulfill specific biblical commandments, including the conquest of Canaan (under Joshua) and attacks against the tribe of Amalek (Exodus 17:8-16). Maimonides includes as obligatory "a war to deliver Israel from an enemy who has attacked them" (see Text Study #1c below).

Optional wars are for increasing territory or "diminishing the heathens so that they shall not march against them" (*Sotah* 44b, see Text Study #1b below). Various *halachic* authorities explain the parameters of diminishing the heathens in different ways. Traditionally, optional wars must

---

[1] Some *halachic* sources further distinguish types of obligatory wars, naming a third category called *milchemet chovah,* or "a compulsory war."

be initiated by a king, approved by the Sanhedrin (an ancient legislative body), and sanctioned by the *urim ve'tumim* (a priestly device for obtaining oracles). Since these institutions no longer function, *halachic* authorities generally agree that launching a so-called "optional war" is not authorized in our day.

Besides the two war categories discussed above, the laws of the pursuer are applicable to our discussion. These laws apply the teaching: "If someone comes to slay you, forestall by slaying the person" (*Sanhedrin* 72a, see Text Study #1a below). We are allowed to defend ourselves. If a nation is under attack (or attack is imminent), engaging in a war of self defense is legitimate. Coming to the aid of a third party under attack can be justified as well under the laws of the pursuer. The "third party" under attack would not be a single individual then, but a whole nation.

There is a significant caveat in justifications for wars of self defense. Let's say someone is pursuing me with the intent to kill, and I could save myself by injuring the pursuer. If I kill the pursuer instead, *I* am guilty of a crime and am subject to punishment — execution! (*Sanhedrin* 74a, Text Study #1a below). Applying this concept to warfare introduces restrictions in terms of going after an enemy. That is, force must be used only to the extent necessary for obtaining the military objectives of self-preservation.

A difficult question is whether preemptive strikes are permissible. When survival is at stake, authorities may consider preemptive strikes necessary, and therefore warranted. However, they would prohibit killings that take place in a war not based on immediate self defense. Such killings could be seen as murder.

Who Is Obliged to Fight?

As long ago as the Bible, our tradition did not compel every man who is physically able to fight to actually do so. In Deuteronomy, when the priests addressed the people as they prepared for battle, they granted exemptions for military service. These exemptions included: one who has built a new house, but not lived in it; one who has planted a vineyard, but not reaped its fruits; one who has betrothed, but not consummated the marriage; and one who is afraid and "soft-hearted" ("*rach layv*") who might melt the hearts of his brothers, as well (Deuteronomy 20:5-9; see Text Study #3A below). "Soft-hearted" suggests someone who is sensitive, emotionally vulnerable, and perhaps cowardly.

In essence, there are two distinct categories of exemptions in the Bible. One is for those whose death would halt the completion of a life cycle event. The other is for those whose fear would have a negative influence on the morale of the troops. Later commentators, including Maimonides, say that life cycle exemptions do not apply in obligatory wars (*milchamot mitzvah*). Those who are afraid and "soft-hearted" would be exempted from fighting despite the type of war. However, even those released from combat duty could be called to support the war through other means, i.e., by supplying water and food, and repairing roads for the army (*Sotah* 44a).

Sages have puzzled over the meaning of what it is to be "afraid and soft-hearted" ("*ha-yaray v'rach ha-layvav*"). Is such a person lacking in courage? Is he terrified by the prospect of witnessing violent deaths? Is he burdened with sins, fearing punishment during war? (*Sotah* 44a) Whatever the case, the "afraid and soft-hearted" status was not considered a matter of conscience, something a person could *choose*. Specifically, opposing a war for political reasons or objecting to fighting would not exempt a person from military duty. Rather, the exemption addresses those who are psychologically unfit for the rigors of battle.

Judaism holds the path of peace in the highest esteem, yet does not support a position of unwavering pacifism. Jewish sources say war may be necessary at times. Clearly, peace is the ideal. Thus, the thrust of our tradition urges us to reject violence to whatever extent we possibly can and still survive.

Does War Have Rules?

The laws of the pursuer (mentioned above) teach that we cannot kill an enemy if we can stop him/her using non-lethal means, such as a strike to a limb. An important Jewish rule of war comes from the laws of the pursuer: Use of force must not exceed the minimum necessary to repel the enemy. In keeping with this principle, it is prohibited to apply force for revenge, to punish the enemy for their aggression, and for terrorizing or humiliating the enemy.

Military force is defensible only when used for deterrence. Of course, deterrence is not easy to define. Through the ages, military leaders and sages have argued over what is considered deterrence. For instance, just how threatening does the enemy have to be before a preemptive attack is justified? Though defining legitimate military strategy can get complex, again, the bottom line rule is: An army must not use more force than is absolutely necessary.

Along these lines, as part of its ethical code, the Israel Defense Forces upholds the principle of *tohar ha-neshek*, "purity of arms." This principle teaches use of weapons only to the extent necessary to subdue the enemy. Soldiers are to avoid unnecessary harm to life and property.

Another important rule is not to attack enemies before giving them ample opportunity to make peace through nonviolent means. This principle originates in the Bible (Deuteronomy 20:10-12; see Text Study #4a below). Over the centuries, Sages and leaders have upheld this requirement of war (e.g., Maimonides, see Text Study #4b below).

Judaism requires protection of the civilian population. Especially notable are the rules regarding a siege. Our tradition teaches: when the Jewish army surrounds a city to siege it, it is to surround the city only on three sides, leaving an opening for inhabitants to flee should they wish to do so (Maimonides, see Text Study #5a below). Cutting off food and water supplies is an objectionable siege tactic since the civilian population perishes along with enemy troops.

Civilians must be allowed to escape the fate "chosen" by enemy combatants. Civilians who remain, despite the opportunity to flee, surrender their noncombatant status. They may face the same war consequences as the enemy soldiers do. Some may become captives. Those who take captives are subject to regulations. These regulations protect the captives from what might otherwise be their fate.

The Talmud prohibits waging a war that will destroy a sixth or more of the population (*Shevuot* 35b). In our day, we face war situations that potentially could lead to "Mutually Assured Destruction" (MAD). The launching of nuclear weapons during war could escalate to the point of massive, widespread casualties — well beyond a sixth of the population. From a Jewish point of view, justifying the use of nuclear weapons is nearly impossible.

Besides rules to limit the use of force against the enemy and rules to protect civilians, there are rules to protect the environment. A prohibition against cutting down fruit trees outside a besieged city originates from the Bible (Deuteronomy 20:19, see Text Study #6a below). Maimonides adds more generally that wanton destruction is forbidden, such as smashing household goods, tearing clothes, demolishing buildings, or stopping up springs (Maimonides, see Text Study #6c below). Maintaining sanitary conditions within the camp is a noted value. A rule that exemplifies this is the requirement to dig a hole with a trowel and "turn and cover that which comes from you" (Deuteronomy 23:14).

How Does War Affect Our Relationship with God?

Judaism teaches that God abhors senseless bloodshed. God despises cruelty, violence, and wanton destruction. Thus, we become alienated from God's will when we participate in a clearly prohibited war. Our wrongful actions distance us from God and Jewish sacred teachings. Our lives become tainted with sin. The words God once spoke through the prophet Isaiah become applicable to us:

Cry with full throat, without restraint;
Raise your voice like a ram's horn;
Tell My people of their wickedness (Isaiah 58:1).

In the second section of this chapter (see p. 189), we considered wars that were authorized by God, *milchamot reshut* (e.g., certain biblical battles for territorial expansion). We concluded that the vehicle for declaring such wars no longer exists. We learned that throughout the ages, Judaism disapproved of many kinds of wars, that essentially wars in our time should be fought only for purposes of self defense. Outside the Jewish world, some modern army leaders do allow fighting to expand territory, to take vengeance on an enemy, or for ideological reasons. But from a Jewish viewpoint, it is audacious to justify these kinds of wars "in the name of God" or to claim that God is fighting "on our side." Such wars defy God's will. They likely lead to violence, destruction, and the shedding of innocent blood. Doubtfully, a meaningful and honest relationship with God can exist under these circumstances.

What about a war whose purpose is less controversial? For example, suppose we are battling hostile troops that have invaded our country. We honestly believe we have a right to defend ourselves, that our tradition accepts and teaches this to be so. While we might not say that such a battle *pleases* God, we feel we are not betraying God's will, we are not sinning. How then does war affect our relationship with God?

It seems that God wants us to be the best people we possibly can be in whatever situation we find ourselves. War forces us to face what might be the greatest challenge in terms of rising to our highest selves.

Judaism teaches, "In the image of God did God make humankind" (Genesis 9:6). Furthermore, we are to strive to emulate God's ways, to aspire to God's greatest attributes: "Walk in My ways and be blameless . . . " (Genesis 17:1). We ascribe to God such *middot* (virtues) as: mercy, justice, love, wisdom, compassion, slowness to anger, and generosity. Additionally, we say God is a source of comfort, hope, friendship, healing,

and support. Especially relevant is God's role as "Maker of Peace." As we pursue and seek to master *middot*, we become more "God-like."

For instance, the more we strive for peace, the more we come to know and understand the attribute of God that is peace. Our relationship with God becomes closer. In war, as in any other stage of life, to the extent that we can elevate our actions and our demeanor, we must aspire to do so. Thus, we will nurture a "true and enduring" relationship with God.

Judaism also teaches: "In a place where there are no worthy persons, strive to be a worthy person" (*Pirke Avot* 2:6). Again, this is a call to our higher selves. Applied to war, this teaching tells us that we cannot sink to the inhumanity that war tends to bring out in people. We must push ourselves to rise above the inclination to do evil (*yetzer hara*). We are to be compassionate when compassion seems to have disappeared, to be hopeful when hope seems shattered, to pursue peace fiercely when peace seems remote. These efforts are a way of tenaciously pursuing God's will. With these efforts, a relationship with God can endure.

General Perspectives

What Is a Just Cause for War?

There are many reasons for war. Nations, opposition forces within nations, religious groups, and ideological movements have ways of judging the legitimacy of war. This section first mentions general reasons for war. Next, we will examine whether there might be universal just causes for war, causes that rise above the orientations of individual fighting groups.

Here are some major reasons people have waged war throughout the ages. Often, more than one reason will apply in any given war.

- Self defense: A nation defends its territory and safety against an aggressor.

- Rescue of Hostages: A military operation seeks the safe return of citizens captured by an enemy.

- Military Security/Deterrence: Preemptive strikes are mounted to halt or impede an enemy's military capabilities (e.g., destruction of a weapons manufacturing plant).

- Extension of Territory: Political power, influence, and riches are expected with territorial gains.

- Economic Benefit: Access is sought to natural resources, treasures, trade routes, and markets.

- Ideology: A military force imposes a political system or forcibly converts others to a particular religious belief.

- Vengeance: The enemy is punished for an insult, injury, or other perceived injustice.

- Credibility of Threats: A nation stages a military operation in order to prove to the enemy (and to other nations, as well) just how strong it really is and that it will back up threats with action.

- Social Integration: Rival groups within a nation are united against a common enemy. Focus on a common enemy deflects attention away from a nation's own internal troubles, helping to ensure peace within that nation's own borders.

- "Feeding" the Military Machine: Certain political leaders, military officials, and corporate executives draw power, wealth, and prestige from continual warfare.[2]

Just because a reason is coherent, doesn't mean it is right or good. The reasons listed above are simply descriptive. They highlight *why* a group might go to war, not if it *should* go. Figuring out if there is just cause for war is the more difficult task.

Some might argue that (1) there is just cause for declaring war on nations that ignore human rights, and (2) that attacks on such "rogue nations" are legitimate. But can we agree on what rights and values should be standard for all people? The United Nations took on the challenge, and on December 10, 1948, the General Assembly adopted without dissent the "Universal Declaration of Human Rights." Here is a synopsis of the main ideas:

- Article 1: Right to freedom and equality in dignity and rights.

- Article 2: Freedom from discrimination.

- Article 3: Right to life, liberty and security of person.

- Article 4: Freedom from slavery and servitude.

- Article 5: Freedom from torture or degrading treatment.

- Article 6: Right to recognition as a person before the law.

- Article 7: Right to equal consideration before the law.

- Article 8: Right to remedy through a competent tribunal.

- Article 9: Freedom from arbitrary arrest, detention, or exile.

- Article 10: Right to a fair trial or public hearing.

- Article 11: Right to be considered innocent until proven guilty.

- Article 12: Freedom from interference with privacy, including home, family, and correspondence.

- Article 13: Right to freedom of movement and residence in one's own country, and to leave and return at will.

- Article 14: Right to asylum.

---

[2]These reasons are gleaned from the chapter "War, Terrorism, and the Balance of Power" in *Social Problems* by James M. Henslin, pp. 578-611.

- Article 15: Right to a nationality and freedom to change it.

- Article 16: Right to marriage and protection of family.

- Article 17: Right to own property.

- Article 18: Freedom of belief and religion.

- Article 19: Freedom of opinion and information.

- Article 20: Right to peaceful assembly and association.

- Article 21: Right to participate in government and in free elections and to equal access to public service.

- Article 22: Right to social security.

- Article 23: Right to work and fair pay for work.

- Article 24: Right to rest and leisure.

- Article 25: Right to adequate standard of living for health and well-being.

- Article 26: Right to education.

- Article 27: Right to participate in the cultural life of the community.

- Article 28: Right to social order assuring human rights.

- Article 29: Responsibility to community essential to free and full development of the individual.

- Article 30: Freedom from State or other interference in any of the above rights.

Today, a significant consortium of nations agrees that disregard for human rights is a serious offense. The one abuse most likely to be singled out as possibly justifying armed response is an attack on Article 3 — the right to life, liberty, and security of person. For the most part, however, nations are reluctant to condone going to war over human rights abuses. The essential point here is that the disregard for human rights creates dangerous living conditions.

An environment that denies basic freedoms can become so volatile that it can easily erupt into war. While people might debate whether or not human rights abuses justify war, such abuses may help explain why war happens.

In 1941, the president of the United States, Franklin D. Roosevelt, stated four major reasons for going to war, called the "Four Freedoms":[3]

"The freedoms we are fighting for, we who are free: the freedoms for which the men and women in the concentration camps and prisons and in the dark streets of the subjugated countries wait, are four in number.

The first is freedom of speech and expression — everywhere in the world.

The second is freedom of every person to worship God in his own way — everywhere in the world.

The third is freedom from want — which, translated into world terms, means economic understandings which will secure to every nation a healthy peacetime life for its inhabitants — everywhere in the world.

The fourth is freedom from fear — which, translated into world terms, means a worldwide reduction of armaments to such a point and in such a thorough fashion that no nation will be in a position to commit an act of physical aggression against any neighbor — anywhere in the world."

Every nation may not *fully* agree on what circumstances justify war. Still, the general humanistic perspective that emerges from the "Universal Declaration of Human Rights" and the "Four Freedoms" provides important guidelines for war. Suppose we compare the principles laid out in those two documents with the straightforward reasons for war listed at the beginning of this section (see pp. 192-193). A

---

[3]From "The Four Freedoms," a booklet published by the Office of War Information, Washington, DC, 1942, which includes prior remarks made by Roosevelt on January 6, 1941.

humanistic perspective would assert that some reasons for war are more worthy than others. It would reject altogether certain rationalizations for war, for example, wars waged for territorial expansion, wars waged to convert others forcibly to certain religious beliefs, wars waged out of vengeance, and so on. On the other hand, it is more likely to justify war for reasons concerning defense of "life, liberty, and security of person." No matter what, a humanistic perspective would demand that warring factions work as hard as possible to resolve conflicts peacefully.

Who Is Obliged to Fight?

Who can, may, or will serve in the armed forces differs from nation to nation, and from conflict to conflict. In Israel, with few exceptions, able bodied men and women must serve a term of full-time duty in the military, and then as part of the Reserves. At times, the United States has maintained an all-volunteer army. During war or other tense periods, the country has drafted civilians into the armed forces.

In our day, there are many interesting controversies over who must fight. We will mention two of these. One has to do with "conscientious objectors": specifically, should you be exempt from a draft if you are a conscientious objector to war? What if you are a "selective conscientious objector," that is, you have moral objections to a *particular* war? Suppose an army is willing to exempt conscientious objectors from the draft. What should the criteria be for granting that status?

Another controversy has to do with women's role in the military. In a society that values equality of the sexes, should women serve in the military in the same capacity as men? For instance, should an army that drafts men to fight, draft women equally?

Issues of military exemptions are complex. Our aim here is not to analyze in great detail questions about who must serve. Rather, it is simply to point out that there is, in fact, a good deal of debate on the topic.

Does War Have "Rules"?

We have discussed what might be just causes for war. A related question is, are there *just means* of fighting wars? That is, putting aside whether a war should be fought in the first place, are there rules that should be followed? It may seem odd to talk about ethical fighting — how can we speak about violent action and ethics in the same breath? But since for the time being, war is not disappearing, we must resist the most base cruelties of war. We must work to eliminate as many of the horrors as we can, even if humankind is not ready to eradicate war altogether.

Following the September 11, 2001 terrorist attacks on the World Trade Center in New York and the Pentagon in Washington, DC, the scholar Richard Falk wrote an article entitled "Ends and Means: Defining a Just War."[4] He looks at how we derive legitimacy with respect to use of force in international settings. He suggests that we do so through these mutually reinforcing legacies: "the traditions of the 'just war' doctrine, international law, and the ideas of restraint embedded in the great religions of the world." In essence, civilized people can agree on certain key ideas concerning just use of force:

- The principle of discrimination: force must be directed at a military target, with damage to civilians and civilian society being incidental.

- The principle of proportionality: force must not be greater than that needed to achieve an acceptable military result and must not be greater than the provoking cause.

- The principle of humanity: force must not be directed against enemy personnel if they are subject to capture, wounded, or under control (as with prisoners of war).

[4]Richard Falk, professor emeritus of international law at Princeton University. "Ends and Means: Defining a Just War," *The Nation*, October 29, 2001.

- The principle of necessity: force should be used only if nonviolent means to achieve military goals are unavailable.

He points out that "the justice of the cause and of the limited ends will be negated by the injustice of improper means and excessive ends." In other words, there are those who go too far in what they are trying to accomplish in a war and fight "dirty." Consequently, any good reasons they originally may have had for going to war don't count. Their "reasonable" intentions are canceled out by their evil or unjust actions.

The Geneva Convention is a key source for international humanitarian law. There are many rules discussed "Relative To the Protection of Civilian Persons in Time of War." An overarching provision is that "persons taking no active part in the hostilities . . . shall in all circumstances be treated humanely" (Article 3). Here is a sampling of topics covered in this extensive document.

- No murder, mutilation, cruel treatment, or torture.

- No taking of hostages.

- No outrages upon personal dignity, in particular humiliating and degrading treatment.

- No executions without previous judgment pronounced by a regularly constituted court.

- The wounded and sick shall be collected and cared for.

- Safety and neutralized zones may be created to protect vulnerable individuals.

- No attacks on civilian hospitals, medical vehicles and aircraft, or medical workers.

- Provide care for children under fifteen who are orphaned or are separated from their families as a result of the war.

- Women shall be protected against any

attack on their honor, in particular against rape, enforced prostitution, or any form of indecent assault.

- No pillaging.

- Those who want to leave the area of conflict are entitled to do so.

In addition, there are many rules concerning the conduct of occupying forces and the treatment of internees.

In the first section of "General Perspectives" above we looked at principles established in the Universal Declaration of Human Rights. Many of those principles not only help us evaluate just causes for war, but also just means or rules for war. To address the conditions that create war more broadly, we might add a few more "rules." Over twenty human rights organizations signed onto a statement of ten core principles in the wake of the September 11, 2001 terrorist attacks on New York and Washington.[5] These principles are applicable to events that go beyond that particular episode:

1. Condemn Attacks: Condemn indiscriminate attacks on innocent civilians.

2. Mourn the Victims: Mourn the loss of innocent lives.

3. Bring the Perpetrators To Justice and Prevent New Attacks.

4. Safeguard Liberty while Protecting Security.

5. Reject Scapegoating: Avoid blaming whole communities for the deeds of a few; plus investigate and prosecute hate crimes.

6. Promote and Respect Human Rights Worldwide.

7. Respect the Laws of War (see our discussion above).

8. Ensure Humanitarian Access and Protect Those Seeking Refuge: Governments and other parties must ensure safe access to

---

[5]From the web site of Human Rights Watch, www.hrw.org.

humanitarian aid and security for humanitarian workers in order to provide urgent assistance required by innocent civilians.

9. Promote Human Development: Freedom from fear must go hand in hand with freedom from want (see Roosevelt's words above in the first "General Perspectives" section, p. 194).

10. Promote and Defend Open Societies: These are societies that respect the rule of law, promote tolerance, and guarantee people's rights of free expression and peaceful dissent.

How Does War Affect Our Humanity?

In the last part of the "Jewish Perspectives" section above, we asked how war might affect our relationship with God. Here we will shift the question to the more general concern of how war affects who we are as human beings. We've already addressed issues on how war might affect others. There are "rules" against torture, hostage taking, humiliation, pillaging, and other degradations precisely because these things can happen too easily during wartime. We know that such brutal acts are horrifying for the victims. But the effects can reach further.

Treating others as objects rather than as people can have consequences beyond harm to the victims. Abusive actions and brutal killings often have a devastating effect *on the perpetrators*. They may become paranoid, emotionally distant, rigid, indiscriminately loyal to "the cause," unable to resist immoral attitudes and pressures, and lack a sense of personal responsibility.

We ended the "Jewish Perspectives" section with the teaching, "In a place where there are no worthy persons, strive to be a worthy person" (*Pirke Avot* 2:6). We said that God demands this of us. Here we can add that not only God, but all of humanity demands, and deserves, no less.

Summary of the Overview

The points below summarize key considerations regarding war as discussed in the Overview.

- We have a sacred duty to love and preserve life and to protect God's earth. We must avoid causing harm to creatures, the environment, and property.

- War has the potential to cause widespread death, suffering, and destruction, throwing into turmoil some of our most cherished values and deeply held commitments.

- Yet, when hostile forces threaten and endanger life, we must respond.

- Still, we must always seek to make peace with our enemies through nonviolent means. If that is impossible, we may use force, but limit it to demands concerning self defense.

SCENARIOS: HOW THINGS HAVE CHANGED

Below are two scenarios dealing with issues related to war, intended to raise questions and spark discussion. Read each scenario to or with your students, and engage them in small or large group discussions. Use the "Focus the Discussion" section below to help identify the important issues and facilitate these discussions. Then continue on to the "Text Study" section to see what Jewish and other sources have to say on the subject. Finally, you may wish to have students discuss the scenarios a second time, to see if their views have changed.

Scenario 1: In Biblical Days: Exodus 17:8-16

Before the Israelites received the Torah at Sinai, they dwelt in the wilderness. While they resided in Refidim, Amalek and his men attacked. Moses instructed Joshua to prepare men for a counter-attack, to make war on Amalek. Joshua did as Moses instructed him. The Israelites battled the Amalekites. Using swords, Joshua's forces overwhelmed Amalek and his people. The Israelites demonstrated perseverance, strong leadership, and faith in God's will. These elements helped them to defeat the Amalekites.

Scenario 2: During World War II: 1939-1945

Many Jews lived in Europe, though they were a small minority of the population. A powerful dictator named Adolph Hitler arose, leading a political movement called Nazism. Besides intending to take over Europe and other lands, Hitler was determined to annihilate the Jews. Most Jews didn't realize the extent of Hitler's intentions until it was too late. While some Jews staged resistance efforts and others tried to escape, they were in the main overwhelmed by Hitler's forces. Responding to Hitler's aggressive efforts to seize land, control territory, and impose his fanatical ideology, many nations became entangled in a war.

At the same time, for reasons that include Japan's attack on America's Pearl Harbor, many nations began to battle in the Pacific. Much of the world was at war.

After years of fighting and millions of deaths — both of soldiers and innocent civilians, including six million Jews — Hitler was defeated. In the Pacific the war ended when the United States dropped two nuclear bombs on Japan. The bombs "scorched" the earth, killing between 130,000 and 170,000 people, plus causing wide-spread injury.

Focus the Discussion

War has changed over the centuries. Warfare has grown from battles between tribes, to battles between nations, to battles between groups of nations. We refer to two twentieth century wars as "World Wars." But tribal war has not disap-peared. In modern times, there are all kinds of violent conflicts between peoples — some are more regional and confined, while others have involved much of the world.

As Jews, our governing autonomy — our power to rule ourselves — has shifted over the centuries. There are times and places in which we have made our own decisions regarding war.

We had the liberty to do so informed by our understanding of Jewish laws and values. In other times and places, we have been subject to the ruling authorities of the countries in which we lived. In still other situations, our voices have been among many other voices participating in the democratic processes that make decisions.

Whatever the governing forces that exist around the world, the stakes are high in war today. Technology has provided a steady stream of ever more deadly (and costly) weapons. While killing with the sword is bloody and violent, that weapon can be directed precisely toward the enemy. Guns are a step up in deadliness, killing more quickly and easily and at a greater distance than swords. Biological and chemical weapons have the potential to cause wide scale suffering and death. Then, there are bombs. In World War I, bombs killed approximately 3 out of every 100,000 people in England and Germany. By World War II, that number grew to 300 out of every 100,000. Most devastating are nuclear weapons which can kill millions with a single, powerful blast. Besides causing human casualties, chemical or nuclear warfare can cause massive destruction to the environment.

Clearly, we who live in the world community have a growing capacity to kill each other. Because of this dire situation, many nations rec-ognize the urgent need for a growing capacity to work for peace. To that end, international law, treaties, and charitable organizations have important contributions to make. We have dis-cussed these topics above (see pp. 195-197).

Is there a particular contribution we, as Jews can make toward world peace? Whether we are in a governing position or not, our Jewish war ethics have a great deal to offer the world com-munity. When we are responsible for governing ourselves, we must apply the highest standards of compassion and justice in making decisions concerning the use of force. When we are one voice among many, we must speak out and stand up for compassion and justice when talk turns to war.

In the face of such challenges, it is our tradi-tion to turn our hearts to God for guidance and sustenance. While we work for peace, we pray: "God who is Maker of Peace make peace among us, among our people, and among all the peoples of the world."

TEXT STUDY

As we have seen, the ethics of war present us with many difficult questions and no easy answers. Clearly, killing, murder, and the intentional harming of people and other creatures are antithetical to Jewish values. Yet Judaism teaches that we can sanction armed conflict at times, and does recognize circumstances when fighting is mandatory. Jewish texts have addressed these complex issues and provide us with some insight, but these guidelines often highlight the tension between seemingly opposing considerations. The chart on the next page poses the questions and offers two opposing points of view. Text sources supporting each of these points of view follow below.

1. **Is war ever justified?**

On the One Hand:

Killing is abhorrent. It violates the sixth commandment.

A. You shall not kill.

   (Alternate translation: "You shall not *murder,*" Exodus 20:13)

B. In the following Rabbinic text, an individual is ordered by the governor of his locale to put a certain man to death. If he refuses to obey the order, he himself will be put to death. Raba is consulted, ruling that the individual must not put the innocent third party to death to save himself:

   > Let him slay you rather than you commit murder. Who knows that

your blood is redder? Perhaps his blood is redder? [That is, who is to say that you deserve to live more than he does?] (*Sanhedrin* 74a)

C. Whoever saves a single life, scripture regards that person as though he/she has saved the entire world, and whoever destroys a single life, scripture regards that person as though he/she has destroyed the whole world (*Sanhedrin* 4:5).

On the Other Hand:

There are just causes worth fighting for, even if killing must be involved.

a. If someone comes to slay you, forestall by slaying that person (*Sanhedrin* 72a).

   > [However,] Rabbi Jonathan ben Saul has taught: If one was pursuing his fellow to slay him, and the pursued could have saved himself by maiming a limb of the pursuer, but instead killed his pursuer, the pursued is subject to execution on that account (*Sanhedrin* 74a).

b. After reading the following passage, recall that a so-called "discretionary war" (*milchemet reshut*) requires these three conditions: the initiative of a king, approval of the Sanhedrin (legislative body), and a sanctioning of the war by the *urim ve'tumim* (a priestly device used for obtaining oracles). Meeting these criteria is not possible in our day.

   > Said Rava: All [the Sages] agree that the wars of Joshua to conquer [the land of Canaan] were obligatory (i.e., *milchamot mitzvah*). All agree that the wars of the House of David for territorial expansion were discretionary (*milchamot reshut*). They differ with regard to [wars for the purpose of] diminishing the heathens so that they shall not march against them.

TEACHING HOT TOPICS

Considerations for Making Ethical Decisions Regarding War

The Question	On the One Hand	On the Other Hand
1. Is war ever justified? (see p. 199)	Killing is abhorrent. It violates the sixth commandment.	There are just causes worth fighting for, even, if need be, killing is involved.
2. For what, if any reason might we knowingly risk our lives? (see p. 201)	We are to avoid endangering ourselves, putting our lives at risk.	There are causes for which risking our lives may be justified.
3. Who is obligated to participate in war? (see p. 202)	Though a war may be permissible, participating in combat is not appropriate for everyone.	There are wartime circumstances for which serving in the armed forces becomes obligatory for every mentally stable, able-bodied person.
4. How can we continue to embrace the value of peace even as we prepare for or engage in war? (see p. 203)	War is a rejection of the paramount Jewish value of pursuing peace.	The enemy cannot be attacked before being given ample opportunity to make peace through nonviolent means.
5. In war, can we adequately protect innocent bystanders from harm? (see p. 204)	In war, innocent people are likely to get killed.	Efforts must be made to prevent unnecessary deaths and injuries, including giving those on the enemy side who wish to escape a conflict continual openings to do so.
6. What might be the long term effects of war, and can some of the damage be avoided? (see p. 205)	Long after a war is over, extraordinary suffering may persist for weeks, and even years as a result of environmental destruction and the lingering poisons of weapons.	While carrying out a war mission, environmental destruction and the suffering of civilians must be minimized to whatever extent possible.
7. Do we spend too much time on war? (see p. 206)	The cost of war is shameful when compared with what could be purchased alternatively.	Though the cost of military preparedness is high, if our "survival" depends on it, we have to be willing to spend what is necessary.
8. Is it possible to preserve our humanity during wartime? (see p. 207)	War breeds dehumanization. Combatants are vulnerable to becoming brutal, cruel, and immune to human suffering.	Grassroots organizations, individual countries, and international alliances must be vigilant in counteracting dehumanization.

(continued on next page)

9. How might beliefs about God shape attitudes toward war? (see p. 208)	God is the Creator of all things. Since war kills and destroys, it is a desecration to God.	People may look to God for support in their efforts to achieve certain war goals.

[Rabbi Judah] calls it commanded and [the Sages] call it discretionary (*Sotah* 44b).

c. According to Maimonides, there are a number of reasons for which a king is obliged to wage war [*milchemet mitzvah*], including:

> [A war] to deliver Israel from an enemy who has attacked them (Maimonides, *Mishneh Torah, Hilchot Melachim* 5:1).

d. Defensive response to an attack is mandatory in order to save lives. Yet, although a preemptive strike is warranted when there is reason to anticipate danger, such preemptive action is not mandatory in the absence of overt aggression (J. David Bleich, *Contemporary Halakhic Problems*, vol. III, p. 284).

Probing: Ideas and Issues

There are many issues presented here. Go through the texts, one by one, and in your own words, restate the main idea(s) communicated in each. According to these passages, for what reasons might killing/war be justified? What restrictions are mentioned? Why would approval of the Sanhedrin be a necessary criteria for launching a *milchemet reshut* (discretionary war)? Overall, what ideas do you definitely agree with in the texts? What ideas are you less sure about? Why? Which is more ethically justifiable — a *milchemet mitzvah* or a *milchemet reshut*? Explain.

2. **For what, if any reason might we knowingly risk our lives?**

On the One Hand:

We are to avoid endangering ourselves, putting our lives at risk.

A. The following "watch out!" statement concerns passing through another people's territory (where the descendants of Esau reside).

> . . . Take good care of yourselves. Take heed, and guard your soul diligently . . . Take good care of your lives (Deuteronomy 2:4; 4:9, 15).

B. Rabbi Akiba said, "A person is not permitted to harm him/herself" (Mishnah, *Baba Kamma* 90a).

C. Throughout the ages, Jewish sages have wrestled with the ethics of giving up one life to save others. A great deal of discussion develops from these two texts:[6]

> Caravans of men are walking down a road, and they are accosted by non-Jews who say to them: "Give us one from among you that we may kill him, otherwise we shall kill you all." Though all may be killed, they may not hand over a single soul of Israel. However, if the demand is for a specified individual like Sheba son of Bichri, they should surrender him rather than all be killed (Jerusalem Talmud, *Trumot* 7:20; *Genesis Rabbah* 94:9).

---

[6]For a thorough study on this topic, see *A Responsum of Surrender* by Elijah J. Schochet.

Resh Lakish stated: "[He may be surrendered] only if he is deserving of death as Sheba son of Bichri." Rabbi Yochanan said: "Even if he is not deserving of death as Sheba son of Bichri" (Palestinian Talmud, *Trumot* 47a).

On the Other Hand:

There are causes for which risking our lives may be justified.

See Texts #1a-c above. Also, Text #2C applies here, as well.

Probing: Ideas and Issues

To what extent is the desire not to risk one's life a valid stance to take for opposing war? For what reasons would *you* be willing to risk your own life?

3. Who is obligated to participate in war?

On the One Hand:

Though a war may be permissible, participating in combat is not appropriate for everyone.

A. Then the officials are to speak to the people, saying:

Who is the man that has built a new house and has not (yet) dedicated it? Let him go and return to his house, lest he die in the war and another man dedicate it!

And who is the man that has planted a vineyard and has not (yet) made common use of it? Let him go and return to his house, lest he dies in the war and another man make common use of it!

And who is the man that has betrothed a woman and has not (yet) taken her (in marriage)? Let him go and return to his house, lest he die in the war and another man take her!

And the officers are to continue to speak to the people, they are to say:

Who is the man, the one afraid and soft of heart? Let him go and return to his house, so that he does not melt the heart of his brothers, like his heart!

And it shall be, when the officials finish speaking to the people, the commanders of the armed forces are to count by head the fighting people (Deuteronomy 20:5-9; also see *Sotah* 8:4).

On the Other Hand:

There are wartime circumstances for which serving in the armed forces becomes obligatory for every mentally stable, able-bodied person.

a. It must be noted that in some circumstances a *milchemet reshut* [discretionary war], once undertaken, may be governed by the regulations applying to a *milchemet mitzvah* [obligatory war]. As noted [in text #3A above], Deuteronomy 20:5-7 provides for the deferment of military service for certain categories of men. These exclusions apply only to a *milchemet reshut*. Hence, a king may not legitimately undertake a *milchemet reshut* unless he is confident of victory without finding it necessary to conscript such persons. However, once a war is declared and the tide of battle threatens to overwhelm the Jewish forces committed to battle, the situation is entirely different. *Chazon Ish, Orach Chayim-Mo'ed* 114:3, quite logically asserts that once a battle has been undertaken and there is danger of losing the encounter, response to such danger constitutes a *milchemet mitzvah* and, accordingly, even those persons otherwise exempt from military service are obligated to participate if their services are necessary to achieve victory. The selfsame consideration would logically apply even in the case of a war whose inception was entirely illicit. The danger of defeat creates a situation requiring the "deliverance of Israel from an enemy" which constitutes a *milchemet mitzvah* (J. David Bleich, *Contemporary Halakhic Problems,* vol. III, pp. 290-291).

Probing: Ideas and Issues

According to Text #3A, who should be exempt from serving in military operations? Why do you suppose those particular exemptions are permitted? Do you think the exemptions are fair? Why or why not? Are there exemptions you would add or eliminate? According to Text #3a, what limits must be placed on exemptions? Why?

4. How can we continue to embrace the value of peace even as we prepare for or engage in war?

On the One Hand:

War is a rejection of the paramount Jewish value of pursuing peace.

A. Whoever desires life and is eager for years of goodness . . . (Psalms 34:13).

Avoid evil and do good.
Seek peace and pursue it (Psalms 34:15).

B. And they shall beat their swords into plowshares
And their spears into pruning hooks;
Nation shall not lift sword against nation,
They shall never again know war (Isaiah 2:4).

C. In that day, there shall be a highway from Egypt to Assyria. The Assyrians shall join with the Egyptians and Egyptians with Assyrians, and then the Egyptians together with the Assyrians shall serve [the Eternal].

In that day, Israel shall be a third partner with Egypt and Assyria as a blessing on earth; for the Eternal of Hosts will bless them, saying, "Blessed be My people Egypt, My handiwork Assyria, and My very own Israel" (Isaiah 19:23-25).

D. Three days before the Messiah arrives, Elijah will come and stand upon the mountains . . . Elijah's voice will be heard from world's end to world's end. And then he will say: "Peace has come to the world" (*Pesikta Rabbati*, Piska 35).

On the Other Hand:

The enemy cannot be attacked before being given ample opportunity to make peace through non-violent means.

a. When you draw near to a town, to wage war against it, you are to call out to it terms of peace.

And it shall be: if peace is what it answers you, and it opens (its gates) to you, then it shall be that all the people that are found in it shall belong to you as forced laborers, and they shall serve you. But if they do not make peace with you, and make war against you, you may besiege it . . . (Deuteronomy 20:10-12).

b. If the inhabitants [of a warring nation] make peace, accept the seven Noahide commandments, and submit to certain conditions of taxation and service, one may not kill a single person (Maimonides, *Code,* "Laws Concerning Kings and Wars," 6:1).

c. Joshua, before he entered the land of Israel sent three letters to its inhabitants. The first one said that those that wish to flee [the oncoming army] should flee. The second one said that those that wish to make peace should make peace. The third letter said that those that want to fight a war should prepare to fight a war (Maimonides, *Code,* "Laws Concerning Kings and Wars," 6:5).

Probing: Ideas and Issues

According to these texts, what are the necessary conditions for peace? What conditions for peace could a modern democratic nation reasonably demand of its enemy? What do you believe are the most worthwhile strategies for avoiding violent conflict between nations?

5. **In war, can we adequately protect innocent bystanders from harm?**

On the One Hand:

In war, innocent people are likely to get killed.

A. Following Abram's participation in the War of the Kings, the next chapter in Genesis begins with these words: "After these things, the word of the Eternal came unto Abram in a vision, saying 'Fear not, Abram . . .'" (Genesis 15:1). Commentators probe possible reasons for Abram's fear:[7]

> Abram was afraid, saying: "I have killed the sons of a righteous man, and now he will curse me and I shall die . . . " (*Midrash Tanchuma* on "*Lech Lecha*" 19, ed. Buber).

> Still another reason for Abraham's fear after killing the kings in battle was his sudden realization: "Perhaps I violated the Divine commandment that the Holy One Who Is Blessed commanded all people, 'You shall not shed human blood' (Genesis 9:6). Yet how many people have I killed in battle?" (*Ibid.*)

> "Abraham was filled with misgiving, thinking to himself: Maybe there was a righteous or God-fearing man among those troops which I slew . . . " (*Midrash Rabbah* on Genesis 44:4).

B. This passage from Josephus refers to the Roman siege of Jerusalem in 72 C.E.:

> The restraint of liberty to pass in and out of the city took from the Jews all hope of safety, and the famine now increasing consumed whole households and families; and the houses were full of dead women and infants; and the streets filled with the dead bodies of old men. And the young men, swollen like dead men's shadows, walked in the market place and fell down dead where it happened. And now the multitude of dead bodies was so great that they who were alive could not bury them; nor cared they for burying them, being now uncertain what should betide themselves. And many endeavoring to bury others fell down themselves dead upon them . . . And many being yet alive went unto their graves and there died. Yet for all this calamity was there no weeping nor lamentation, for famine overcame all affections. And they who were yet living, without tears beheld those who being dead were now at rest before them. There was no noise heard within the city . . . (Josephus, *The Wars of the Jews*, Book VI, ch. XIV, p. 721).

C. In this modern situation, the American army did not allow innocent people to escape. The repercussions were devastating.

> In August 1967, during Operation Benton, the "pacification" camps became so full that Army units were ordered not to "generate" any more refugees. The Army complied. But search and destroy operations continued. Only now the peasants were not warned before an air strike was called

---

[7]The three texts here are cited in "War in the Jewish Tradition" by Everett Gendler, in *Contemporary Jewish Ethics*, 205.

on their village. They were killed in their villages because there was no room for them in the swamped pacification camps (Orville and Jonathan Schell, letter to *The New York Times*, Nov. 26, 1969).

On the Other Hand:

Efforts must be made to prevent unnecessary deaths and injuries, including giving those on the enemy's side who wish to escape a conflict continual openings to do so. (For additional texts which question the morality of "sacrificing" innocent lives, see Texts #1B and #2C above.)

a. When siege is laid to a city for the purpose of capture, it may not be surrounded on all four sides but only on three sides in order to give an opportunity for escape to those who would flee to save their lives . . .

    It has been learned by tradition that this was the instruction given to Moses (Maimonides, *Code*, "Laws Concerning Kings and Wars," 6:7).

b. It is forbidden to sell to idolaters any weapons of war. Neither may one sharpen their weapons nor make available to them knives, chains, barbed chains, bears, lions, or anything which might cause widespread injury. One may sell to them shields or shutters which are purely defensive (Maimonides, *Code*, "Laws of Murder and Defense," 12:12).

    That which is prohibited for sale to idolaters is also prohibited for sale to Jews who are suspected of then selling such material to idolaters. Likewise, it is forbidden to sell such weapons to Jewish thieves (Maimonides, *Mishneh Torah*, "Law of Idolatry," 9:8).

Probing: Ideas and Issues

What precautions do these texts mention for avoiding the harming of innocent people? What are some of the tactics used today to protect innocent people? How effective are these tactics? Who counts as innocent?

6. **What might be the long term effects of war, and can some of the damage be avoided?**

On the One Hand:

Long after a war is over, extraordinary suffering may persist for weeks, and even years as a result of environmental destruction and the lingering poisons of weapons.

The following passages are all modern, twentieth century examples of war's effects.

A. In the First World War, an entirely different category of mutilated soldiers returned from the war with these horrific wounds that were inflicted by modern ammunition. There were soldiers who returned who had suffered psychological shock. Some had been buried for hours in their dugouts and had no longer control over their extremities. These were the soldiers who had suffered and who showed, and continued to show, what suffering in the trenches had meant. They had not turned themselves into heroes. They were not even capable of functioning in the society at the end of the war. But, they were a continuous reminder of what they had gone through in the gas attack, in the bombardment, in being buried for hours under the earth, and being at the brink of psychological collapse. And, many of the population did not like to have to face these war cripples. They did not wish to be reminded continuously of what it was really like (PBS, "The Great War and the Shaping of the 20th Century," interview with Bernd Huppauf, New York University).

B. The [presumably Soviet] biplane came out of a clear sky at 9:30 one morning. It made a single run over the Laotian village of Va Houng, unleashing a stream of yellow gas that fell like rain along a one kilometer strip and formed droplets on the ground. To the villagers, it smelled like burning peppers.

According to Gnia Pao Vang, a subdistrict chief in Vientiane Province, the gas killed 83 of the 473 residents of Va Houng, as well as all village animals, the chickens succumbing first.

The people died in pain, usually after two or three days of intense diarrhea and vomiting. Like other survivors, Mr. Gnia suffered for weeks from headaches and dizziness, impaired vision, a running nose, painful breathing and a swollen throat. For days he spit phlegm and blood (Barry Wain, "The Chemical Warfare in Southeast Asia." *Wall Street Journal*, September 21, 1981).

C. Long after peace returned to Mozambique, the number of war casualties continued to grow. Civilians, especially women and children, were the main victims of land mines that had been buried throughout the country. They were usually planted off main roads on bush paths, at water sites, or in people's fields. These have claimed over 10,000 lives and wounded many more. With these hidden dangers, it is very difficult for people to feel secure in peace (Report by Oxfam: "Mozambique — The Effects of War").

On the Other Hand:

While carrying out a war mission, environmental destruction and the suffering of civilians must be minimized to whatever extent possible.

a. When you besiege a town for many days, waging war against it, to seize it: you are not to bring ruin on its trees, by swinging away (with) an ax against them, for from them you eat, you are not to cut them down — for are the trees of the field human beings, (able) to come against you in siege? Only those trees of which you know that they are not trees for eating, them you may bring to ruin and cut down, that you may build siege works against the town that is making war against you (Deuteronomy 20:19-20).

b. It is forbidden to cut down fruit bearing trees outside a (besieged) city, nor may a water channel be deflected from them so that they wither, as it is said: "You are not to bring ruin on the trees . . . " (Deuteronomy 20:19) (Maimonides, *Code*, "Laws Concerning Kings and Wars," 6:8).

c. Not only one who cuts down (fruit producing) trees, but also one who smashes household goods, tears clothes, demolishes a building, stops up a spring, or destroys articles of food with destructive intent, transgresses the command: "You shall not destroy" (Maimonides, *Code*, "Laws Concerning Kings and Wars," 6:10).

Probing: Ideas and Issues

What destructive effects of war might outlast the conflict itself? Can some of these be eliminated? How? If destructive repercussions of war cannot be eliminated entirely, how might lasting damage be minimized?

7. **Do we spend too much on war?**

On the One Hand:

The cost of war is shameful when compared with what could be purchased alternatively. Contemporary concerns confront this issue more directly than do traditional Jewish sources.

A. Every gun that is made, every warship launched, every rocket fired signifies, in the final sense, a theft from those who hunger and are not fed, those who are cold and are not clothed. This world in arms is not spending money alone. It is spending the sweat of its laborers, the genius of its scientists, the hopes of its children (Dwight D. Eisenhower, quoted in *Peace Prayers*, p. 23).

B. Think of what a world we could build if the power unleashed in war were applied to constructive tasks! One-tenth of the energy that the various belligerents spent in the war, a fraction of the money they exploded in hand grenades and poison gas, would suffice to raise the standard of living in every country and avert the economic catastrophe of worldwide unemployment. We must be prepared to make the same heroic sacrifices [for peace that we make] for the cause of war. There is no task that is more important or closer to my heart (Albert Einstein, quoted in *Peace Prayers*, p. 35).

On the Other Hand:

Though the cost of military preparedness is high, if our survival depends on it, we have to be willing to spend what is necessary.

a. Like other nations, the United States finds itself boxed in. While military expenditures are costly in terms of benefits foregone, failing to make them may well open us to attack. In light of [the majority of humankind's] bellicose history . . . , such an assumption, unfortunately, appears well-founded. Only in the event of a miracle by which all nations become pacifists and all danger of attack ceases will lack of military preparedness make sense. And there is no indication of any such miracle in the offing (James M. Henslin, *Social Problems*, p. 589).

Probing: Ideas and Issues

What are some of the "costs" of war besides the loss of human lives? What might be the long-term effects of spending such high sums on military preparedness? Is there an alternative to this kind of spending and use of resources?

8. **Is it possible to preserve our humanity during wratime?**

On the One Hand:

War breeds dehumanization. Combatants are vulnerable to becoming brutal, cruel, and immune to human suffering.

The following texts warn against dehumanizing the enemy. Clearly, the assumption is that such a tendency is a hazard during times of conflict.

A. Do not rejoice when your enemy falls, And do not let your heart be glad when [your enemy] stumbles. If your enemy is hungry, give bread to eat, and if [your enemy] is thirsty, give water to drink. Happy are those who always have a sense of fear, but those who harden their hearts (or consciences) will fall into evil (Proverbs 24:17, 25:21, 28:14).

B. In that hour when the Israelites crossed the Red Sea, the ministering angels wanted to sing a song of praise before God. But God said to them: "My handiwork [the Egyptians] is drowning in the sea, yet you want to sing a song before me!?" (*Sanhedrin* 39b).

On the Other Hand:

Grassroots organizations, individual countries, and international alliances must be vigilant in counteracting dehumanization.

a. A medieval Jewish source movingly tells us that one hundred shofar sounds at our New Year services correspond to the one hundred groans by the mother of Sisera (Judges 5:28) when she saw [that] her son [was] killed in his battle against the Israelites.

Sisera was a brutal tyrant, wreaking terror on our people. His death was our salvation. Yet, he had a mother, and to this day we hear her cries and recall her grief over the death of her child.

Even terrorists have mothers, and we must not be indifferent to their anguish. This is but one of the remarkable features of Judaism in an effort to ensure that even war does not harden us to the point of not caring for the loss and suffering of our enemies (Sir Immanuel Jacobovitz, "The Morality of Warfare," in *L'EYLAH*, vol. 2, no. 4, 1983).

b. No one shall be subjected to torture or to cruel, inhuman or degrading treatment or punishment (From "The Universal Declaration of Human Rights," Article 5, adopted by the United Nations, December 10, 1948).

Probing: Ideas and Issues

What does "dehumanization" mean? What happens when the enemy is dehumanized? Do you believe there are effective ways to minimize dehumanization? In modern Israel, one aspect of military policy is *tohar haneshek* — "purity of arms." This principle states that Israeli soldiers are to use their firearms only to defend themselves, never to oppress or loot an enemy. Is this policy realistic? enforceable?

9. How might beliefs about God shape attitudes toward war?

On the One Hand:

God is the Creator of all things. Since war kills and destroys, it is a desecration to God.

A. After the flood, God addresses Noah regarding murder:

Whoever now sheds human blood, for that human shall his/her blood be shed, for in God's image did God make humankind (Genesis 9:6).

B. If one sheds blood, it is as if that person had diminished God's image (*Mechilta* to Exodus 20:13).

C. David said to Solomon, "My son, as for me, it was in my heart to build a house unto the name of the Eternal my God [the First Temple]. But the work of the Eternal came to me, saying, 'You have shed blood abundantly and have made great wars; you shall not build a house unto My name, because you have shed much blood upon the earth in my sight'" (I Chronicles 22:7-8).

On the Other Hand:

People may look to God for support in their efforts to achieve certain war goals.

a. For the Eternal your God is the one who goes with you, to wage war for you against your enemies, to deliver you! (Deuteronomy 20:4).

b. David replied to the Philistine, "You come against me with sword and spear and javelin; but I come against you in the name of the Eternal of Hosts, the God of the ranks of Israel, whom you have defied . . . And this whole assembly shall know that the Eternal can give victory without sword or spear. For the battle is the Eternal's, and God will deliver you into our hands" (I Samuel 17:45, 47).

Probing: Ideas and Issues

How might religious beliefs shape the course of a conflict between nations? What dangers might there be in "bringing God" into war? When, if ever, is it appropriate to suggest that God plays a particular role in a war? Explain. Does God "take sides"?

RELATED MIDDOT AND MITZVOT

These virtues and commandments can help infuse war decisions with Jewish values:

Anavah (Humility): Any decisions about use of force should come from a place of humility. The mastery of *anavah* is probably the best "guarantee" against the abuse of power.

Bal Tashchit (Protecting the Environment/Not Destroying): War efforts must avoid causing any more harm to the environment than is absolutely necessary.

Din (Law and Justice): Jewish law establishes grounds for fighting wars — only for a just cause and in a just manner. International law can help promote justice in war on a world level.

Lo Tignov (Not Stealing): Looting and pillaging are equivalent to stealing, and are forbidden.

Lo Tikom (Not Taking Revenge): Using force to punish or take vengeance on the enemy is forbidden.

Lo Tirtzach (Not Murdering): Killing enemies in war, for reasons unrelated to self defense, is murder.

Nedarim (Keeping Promises): Treaties are promises among nations and other autonomous groups. When treaties are honored, there is a better chance that peace will prevail.

Ometz Layv (Courage of Heart): Beyond physical might and bravery, this *middah* encompasses the will to act morally and responsibly.

Rachamim (Compassion): We must have compassion, even on our enemies.

Rodef Shalom (Pursuing Peace): Solving conflict through nonviolent means is the ideal. We must be relentless in our pursuit of peaceful alternatives to war.

ACTIVITIES

A First Look: Key Issues and Ideas

1. A set induction: Survey students about their feelings and attitudes on war-related issues. On the board write the word "Kill." Have participants "free associate" words and ideas that come to them when they think of that word. Continue with some or all of these words: Defend, Peace, Vengeance, Hatred, Siege, Fight, Treaty, Surrender, Weapon, Refugee, etc. Conclude with the word "War."

   After completing the above, ask: How would you characterize this group's overall attitude toward war? Which word(s) aroused the most variety in types of associations, and which aroused the least? Why do you suppose this is?

2. Another set induction: Ask participants to recall the first time they knew about, experienced, or understood what war is. (An example: "Flipping through my parents' *Newsweek* magazine when I was about seven years old and seeing photos of dead and injured people in Vietnam, then reading and asking about this situation, feeling shocked by the horror and tragedy of this conflict . . . I didn't understand . . . ") Give time for people to share their personal reflections.

3. The Overview, pp. 189-197, states that the chapter will look at these questions:

   - How do we determine a *just cause* for war?

   - Who is obliged to fight?

   - Does war have "rules"? That is, are there just means of fighting a war?

   - How does war affect our relationship with God?

   - How does war affect our humanity?

   Orient students to war ethics by summarizing major ideas that respond to these questions. Include both Jewish and general perspectives.

4. Give details from the Overview which explain *milchemet mitzvah* (an obligatory or commanded war) and *milchemet reshut* (an authorized or optional war). Ask participants to think of examples of these kinds of wars from history and from current events.

5. After initial study of the topic, ask participants to come up with three or four essential points of a Jewish war ethic. They can do this task individually, in pairs, or in small groups. When everyone is finished, ask some (or all) participants to share their ideas. Then, have students compare their ideas with those listed at the end of the Overview. Note similarities and differences between the ideas. Would anyone change their summary points now that they've heard what others have had to say?

6. Students rate each of the 18 "On the One Hand/On the Other Hand" points found in the chart in the "Text Study" section above (pp. 200-201). Individually, everyone assigns a level of importance to each of the 18 points, with "10" meaning very important and "1" meaning not important at all. Reconvene and have group members compare and explain their ratings. Ask: What do your results reflect about your attitude toward war? What was most challenging about completing this exercise?

Applying Middot and Mitzvot

1. Refer to the "Related *Middot* and *Mitzvot*" section above (p. 209). Have students rank these items from most to least important in terms of developing a proper attitude toward war. Students should discuss and explain their rankings.

2. Imagine the United Nations asks different religious groups to contribute to a world exhibit on preventing war. Your group will represent the Jewish viewpoint. With your students, design an exhibit — such as a series of posters — highlighting some of the *middot* and *mitzvot* in the "Related *Middot* and *Mitzvot*" section above (p. 209), plus others if desired. Since displaying these posters at the real U.N. may not be possible, find another appropriate venue in which to share this work.

3. Ask: If you yourself were in a war situation, which *middah/mitzvah* would you try to keep foremost in your mind and heart? Why?

4. Go through each of the *middot* and *mitzvot* one at a time. Discuss the consequences during wartime of *not* paying attention to what each one demands.

5. Some say peace in the world begins with peace within one's more intimate sphere — peace within self, family, and community. Study Jewish texts on peace, including those related to *Sh'lom Bayit* ("Peace in the Home/Peace in the Family"). For one resource, see *Teaching Jewish Virtues* by Susan Freeman, pp. 241-254.

   Then, have everyone write "contracts" for themselves describing specific efforts they will make to promote and maintain peace within the areas of life most under their control. (For example: "I will commit once a week not to argue with my mother about cleaning my room," or "I will silently count to ten before criticizing members of my family. That way I give myself a chance to evaluate whether what I'm going to say is really necessary or just mean-spirited.")

   Follow up on the contracts, checking in to see how everyone is doing with them.

6. For more information and activities on:

   Anavah (Humility): see *Teaching Jewish Virtues* by Susan Freeman, pp. 8-25.

   Bal Tashchit (Protecting the Environment/Not Destroying: see *Teaching Mitzvot* by Barbara Binder Kadden and Bruce Kadden, pp. 199-203, and *It's a Mitzvah!* by Bradley Shavit Artson, p. 50.

Din (Law and Justice): see *Teaching Jewish Virtues* by Susan Freeman, pp. 55-68.

Lo Tignov (Not Stealing): see *Teaching Mitzvot* by Barbara Binder Kadden and Bruce Kadden, pp. 175-179.

Lo Tikom (Not Taking Revenge): see *Teaching Mitzvot* by Barbara Binder Kadden and Bruce Kadden, pp. 187-192.

Lo Tirtzach (Not Murdering): see *Teaching Mitzvot* by Barbara Binder Kadden and Bruce Kadden, pp. 169-173.

Nedarim (Keeping One's Word): see *Teaching Mitzvot* by Barbara Binder Kadden and Bruce Kadden, pp. 101-105.

Ometz Layv (Courage of Heart): see *Teaching Jewish Virtues* by Susan Freeman, pp. 195-210.

Rachamim (Compassion): see *Teaching Jewish Virtues* by Susan Freeman, pp. 55-68.

Rodef Shalom (Pursuing Peace): see *It's a Mitzvah!* by Bradley Shavit Artson, p. 118.

Stories: Understanding through Listening

1. Invite to class one or more of the following individuals to share their stories: a war veteran, someone currently in the military, a politician, a war survivor (from the Holocaust and/or other war), a refugee. Have each discuss both their experiences and feelings during the war itself, plus their current attitudes about war. For Jewish guests, ask how their religious commitments and Jewish beliefs influenced their feelings about and actions during the war. If you have invited guests from other backgrounds, compare how their religious beliefs influenced them.

2. Read a selection of war letters to get a sense of how people felt and what they saw on the front lines of war. A good resource is *War Letters*, edited by Andrew Carroll (New York: Scribner, 2001). Have participants write their own war letter, choosing a situation in which a Jew may have found him/herself.

Examples: a warrior in biblical times (see Scenario 1 above, p. 197), someone fighting to defend Masada from the Romans, a rebel fighter with Bar Kochba, a planner of the Warsaw Ghetto uprising, an Israeli soldier during one of the recent wars, a soldier fighting in one of America's wars (Revolution, Civil War, Korean War, Vietnam War, Gulf War, War in Afghanistan, etc.). A good background resource for Jewish/Israel material is the *Encyclopaedia Judaica*. An American history textbook or secular encyclopedia can provide other background.

3. Create a skit based on the passage in Text Study #2C above. This is the story of caravans of men who are accosted and told to give up one of their group or risk being killed themselves.

4. Over the course of a week or two, have participants bring in newspaper and magazine articles or photos related to war and conflict. Create a display that captures the current world situation. Have students prepare labels for each item. Labels should include a Jewish teaching. For example:

   - The individuals in this photo are violating the Jewish value of . . .

   - The factions in this article are breaking the Jewish law that states . . .

   - Country X and Country Y are at war because they broke the *nedarim* (promises) in the treaty they signed called . . . in which they agreed to . . .

   - Humanitarian workers deliver aid to refugees. In wartime, we must respond to the suffering of innocent people with acts of *rachamim* (compassion).

   - This article discusses the siege of such and such city. If a Jewish army was responsible for the siege, it would need to _____.

5. There are hundreds of war movies and docu-

mentaries, including many with a Jewish angle. Your local Jewish education resource center or Central Agency likely has a selection of videos you can borrow. Discuss your needs or interests with the resource librarian and choose one or more videos (or selections from full-length productions) to share with your group. Keep in mind age appropriateness, length, era, original language (Hebrew, English, other). Possible interests: civilians' experience, refugees, biblical war, the Israeli-Palestinian conflict, the aftermath of war, the Holocaust, resistance movements, experiences in the battlefield/in the trenches, etc.

6. Gather age appropriate books that have a war theme. Work with your synagogue librarian, local town librarian, Jewish bookstore, and/or the librarian at your local Jewish education resource center to help you select suitable books. Look for books that tell stories rather than textbook-like material. Use the books in several ways, such as:

   - Required silent reading during several class sessions (lasting 15 to 30 minutes each).

   - Optional reading during free periods and/or to check out and read at home. (For Day Schools: free-reading selection options for Language Arts.)

   - A "read-aloud."

   If desired, include book reports as part of this activity — either written or oral. Alternatively, the teacher can meet with each student privately after he/she finishes a selection for a brief conversation about the book.

   To take this activity one step further, choose one story to transform into a dramatic retelling — either in storyteller style or in a skit.

Action: Getting Out, Getting Involved

1. Many organizations are trying to offset the terror of war with humanitarian work. Assign individuals or small groups to research and report back on the activities and positions of various organizations. In their reports they should:

   - Summarize what the organization does.

   - Discuss whether it would be appropriate for a committed Jew to become involved in the organization, explaining why or why not.

   - Suggest ways to get involved (assuming the presenters believe in the organization's mission). Mention things to do *now* to help support the organization's work (for example, work on a fund-raiser to help a specific group of refugees, or write members of Congress/Parliament asking them to support an international ban on land mines). Also talk about other potential ways to support the organization (for example, become a doctor and spend a few months working in a war torn country).

   Here are a few suggestions of organizations to research:

   American Jewish World Service: www.ajws.org

   Helping to alleviate poverty, hunger, and disease among the people of the world regardless of race, religion, or nationality.

   CARE: www.care.org

   A humanitarian organization fighting global poverty

   Human Rights Watch: www.hrw.org

   Dedicated to protecting the human rights of people around the world.

   Oxfam America: www.oxfamamerica.org

   Committed to creating lasting solutions to poverty, hunger, and social injustice.

Physicians for Human Rights:
www.phrusa.org

Promotes health by protecting human rights.

Physicians for Global Survival
(Canada): www.pgs.ca

A physician-led organization committed to the abolition of nuclear weapons, the prevention of war, the promotion of non-violent means of conflict resolution and social justice in a sustainable world.

Refugees International:
www.refintl.org

An organization that advocates for refugees of war and victims of humanitarian crisis around the world.

Save the Children USA:
www.savethechildren.org

A nonprofit child-assistance organization to make lasting positive change in the lives of children in need.

You may or may not want to include the following two organizations, which at times have taken actions and promoted ideas that have been controversial in the Jewish community:

Amnesty International:
www.amnesty.org

A worldwide campaigning movement that works to promote internationally recognized human rights.

Doctors without Borders:
www.doctorswithoutborders.org

Delivers emergency aid to victims of armed conflict, epidemics, and natural and man-made disasters, and to others who lack health care due to social or geographical isolation.

2. Find out if there are war refugees living in your area. If possible, invite one of these people to speak with your group. Learn about

the needs of a refugee community or of the needs of those who have remained behind. Plan ways to help out the local community (through English tutoring, becoming a "big brother" or "big sister," babysitting, etc.) and/or ways to help those who live far away (through writing letters, collecting and sending clothing, etc.).

3. Have students investigate the current international debates regarding weapons and warfare. When they have become educated and formed an opinion, they can contact government representatives, write letters to politicians and/or newspapers, create petitions and gather signatures, and so on.

4. Have students write letters or cards to soldiers stationed far away from home who are facing difficult and dangerous circumstances.

5. A key principle of the martial art karate is this: "There is no first strike in karate." That means karate is self defense training (as opposed to "attack training"). Judaism upholds the belief that a just war ethic essentially limits itself to self defense.

    Karate is one way for students to embody some of the use of force concepts they are learning with their minds. Do one of the following: Have your group do some karate training together (arranging for a qualified master to teach); encourage students who are interested to learn karate and to share their feelings about their training with your group; ask students who currently are studying karate (or another martial art) to talk about how their experience compares with what Judaism teaches about self defense.

Wrestling: Engagement with the Issues

1. Stage a debate. Some suggested topics:

    *   Who is responsible for war? The Talmud says that even those released from combat duty could be called to support a war through other means, i.e., by supplying water and food, and repairing roads for

the army (*Sotah* 44a). Is someone who provides backup services in war any less responsible for killing the enemy than someone on the battlefield itself? One side of the debate says yes, the other says no.

- What are our responsibilities to civilians in war? One side of the debate says we simply are obliged not to kill them, we must allow them to escape and that's all. The other side says we must provide greater protections — refugee camps, food, clothing, safety from criminal acts, and so on, plus commit to rebuilding their land, government, and society following the war.

- Is praying to God for victory in war acceptable, or is it a desecration?

- Do we spend too much on the military? One side says yes, the other says no. Keep in mind that we as Jews and as a society as a whole have so many additional responsibilities such as education, health, a clean environment, alleviation of poverty and hunger, and so forth. Teams will have to do some research to participate knowledgeably in this debate. A good resource for looking at American spending priorities is the National Priorities Project, www.natprior.org.

2. Debate the ethics of a current conflict and how it is being fought. To what extent would Judaism accept the battle as being justifiable? Participants should gather articles and do other research to be informed enough to offer reasoned opinions.

3. In pairs, take turns listening to each other talk about fears, feelings, attitudes, and questions about war. The tenor of your listening is all-important. Listeners must be open hearted, nonjudgmental, supportive. In addition, they are not to interrupt the speaker, nor offer any comment or reaction. The speaker should speak for 3-5 minutes (possibly longer for more mature participants).

After one person has had a turn speaking, switch roles, so that the speaker now becomes the listener. You can do this as a journal exercise too — the "listener" being the pages of the journal. After everyone has had an opportunity to "speak" (either to another person or to write in his/her journal), come back together as a group and allow participants to share their reactions to this experience.

4. We might choose these words spoken by the prophet Zechariah as a motto for a Jewish war ethic: "Not by might, nor by power, but by Your spirit . . . " (Zechariah 4:6). Have participants write an essay or a journal entry explaining how Zechariah's words reflect Jewish attitudes toward war.

   Alternatively, choose (or allow participants to choose) a different line or passage from Jewish sacred texts as a war ethic motto to write about.

5. Students create a collage which visually captures the complexity of war. Here are some words, phrases, and images to help trigger your own ideas: killing, self defense, whose blood is redder, weapons, conflict, siege, fear, terror, the king, authorities, soldiers, civilians, suffering, courage, a poisoned environment, injuries, hope, prayer, peace, "They shall beat their swords into plowshares, and their spears into pruning hooks; nation shall not lift sword against nation, they shall never again know war" (Isaiah 2:4), your own ideas.

6. Instead of making a collage, students use various images in the previous activity to create a painting, dance, or poem about war.

7. Invite students to create a series of educational and/or inspirational posters that might be hung at an army base (or at a governmental defense department building, such as the Pentagon). These posters would reinforce ethical guidelines regarding war.

8. Refer to Text Study #5A (p. 204) which dis-

cusses Abram's fears following his participation in the War of the Kings. Have small groups create skits based on one or more of the texts.

Alternatively, everyone imagines he/she is Abram. Each Abram writes a letter to a friend (possibly another biblical character) about what happened in the War of the Kings. He shares what his experience was, his concerns, and fears.

9. Refer to Text Study #5B above (p. 204), Josephus's description of the effects of war. Participants (perhaps divided in small groups) choreograph a creative movement piece based on the passage.

Empathy

1. Students write a prayer for peace. To go one step further, copy the prayer and center it on high quality paper. Students can illuminate the borders. Alternatively, choose a verse about peace from a traditional Jewish source, copy, and illuminate as above.

2. Have students write a prayer a soldier might recite before entering battle. Stage a reading of these prayers, going around in a circle, having each "soldier" read his or her words aloud.

3. Specify a day in which you ask students to do the following: "Live today as if tomorrow you will be at war. Try to be really aware of the decisions you make, how your perspective on things may be different, how you act toward people, how you feel about God . . . "

Afterward, process the experience with the students. For example, what was different about their behavior, what was the same? What did they learn from the experience that might influence their everyday actions and attitudes from now on?

Variation: If a whole day seems too long to focus on this challenge, set aside a morning, then evaluate the experience in the afternoon.

GLOSSARY

Milchemet Chovah:

A compulsory war, sometimes distinguished from a milchemet mitzvah.

Milchemet Mitzvah:

An obligatory or commanded war.

Milchemet Reshut:

An authorized or optional war.

BIBLIOGRAPHY

Books and Articles

Artson, Bradley Shavit. *It's a Mitzvah! Step-by-Step To Jewish Living.* West Orange, NJ: Behrman House and New York: The Rabbinical Assembly, 1995.

Bleich, J. David. "Preemptive War in Jewish Law." In *Contemporary Halakhic Problems,* vol. III, pp. 251-292. New York, NY: KTAV Publishing House, Inc., and Yeshiva University Press, 1989.

Broyde, Michael J. "Fighting the War and the Peace: Battlefield Ethics, Peace Talks, Treaties, and Pacifism in the Jewish Tradition." In *Jewish Law Articles: Examining Halacha, Jewish Issues and Secular Law,* www.jlaw.com, copyright by Ira Kasden, 1997-2001.

Carroll, Andrew, ed. *War Letters.* New York: Scribner, 2001.

Falk, Richard. "Ends and Means: Defining a Just War." *The Nation,* October 29, 2001.

Freeman, Susan. *Teaching Jewish Virtues: Sacred Sources and Arts Activities.* Denver, CO: A.R.E. Publishing, Inc., 1999.

Gendler, Everett E. "War and the Jewish Tradition." In *Contemporary Jewish Ethics,* edited by Menachem Marc Kellner. New York: Sanhedrin Press, 1978.

Henslin, James M. "War, Terrorism, and the Balance of Power." In *Social Problems.* Englewood Cliffs, NJ: Prentice Hall, 1990.

Josephus. *The Jewish War.* Middlesex, England: Penguin, 1984. (Or see the Loeb Classic Library Edition, Cambridge, MA: Harvard University Press, 1978).

Kadden, Barbara Binder, and Bruce Kadden. *Teaching Mitzvot: Concepts, Values, and Activities.* Rev. ed. Denver, CO: A.R.E. Publishing, Inc., 2003.

Lackey, Douglas P. *The Ethics of War and Peace.* Englewood, NJ: Prentice Hall, 1989.

Leadingham, Carrie, et al., eds. *Peace Prayers: Meditations, Affirmations, Invocations, Poems, and Prayers for Peace.* San Francisco, CA: Harper San Francisco, 1992.

Schochet, Elijah J. *A Responsum of Surrender.* Los Angeles, CA: University of Judaism Press, 1973.

Sokolow, Moshe. *The Pursuit of Peace.* New York: CAJE, 1993.

Walzer, Michael. *Just and Unjust Wars: A Moral Argument with Historical Illustrations.* New York: Basic Books, 1977.

Web Sites

See the sites listed in the section, "Action: Getting Out, Getting Involved" above (p. 212-213).

Films

The following commercial films deal with war in an often intense and graphic manner. While certain sections may be valuable for illustrating certain ideas about the realities of war, it may not be appropriate for students to view the entire film. Prescreening is strongly recommended.

Apocalypse Now (1979, 153 minutes, rated R)
Based on Joseph Conrad's *Heart of Darkness.* The story of an army Captain in Vietnam who is sent on a mission to "terminate with extreme prejudice" a renegade Green Beret Colonel who has succumbed to madness and set himself up as God among a remote jungle tribe.

Band of Brothers (2001, 10 episodes at 60 minutes each, not rated)
The HBO miniseries that tells the story of Easy Company of the U.S. Army Airborne Paratrooper division and their mission in France during World War II.

Casualties of War (1989, 113 minutes, rated R)

During the Vietnam war, a girl is taken from her village by five American soldiers. Four of the soldiers rape her, but the fifth refuses. The young girl is killed, and the fifth soldier is determined to see justice done.

Full Metal Jacket (1987, 116 minutes, rated R)

A group of soldiers develop dehumanized personalities in their training and it shows in their tour of duty in Vietnam.

Platoon (1986, 120 minutes, rated R)

A young recruit in Vietnam faces a moral crisis when a sergeant orders the massacre of villagers.

Saving Private Ryan (1998, 170 minutes, rated R)

A World War II drama about a platoon of men sent behind enemy lines to find and send home a soldier whose three brothers have been killed in the war.

PART III

CITIZENS OF THE PLANET

ANIMAL EXPERIMENTATION

CONSUMERISM: HOW MUCH IS TOO MUCH?

CHAPTER 9

ANIMAL EXPERIMENTATION

OVERVIEW

Is it ethical to use animal lives in the hopes of obtaining information that may improve the quality of human life? Many ethicists and activists challenge the morality of using millions of animals each year in medical experiments, as part of cosmetic and household product research, and in classroom instruction (for dissection).

For our study of animal experimentation, we will examine beliefs about animal *welfare* and animal *rights* — what is the basis for these concepts and how far do we go with them. In addition, we will look at the objectives of experiments. Perhaps not all experiments are of equal merit. For instance, is testing mascara as worthy a research goal as investigating a possible cure for cancer? If animals are living, sentient creatures and not disposable objects, do they deserve compassion and do they have the right to be protected from abuse? Just how far can we go in justifying the use of animals' lives for human benefit?

Jewish Perspectives

The *welfare* of animals is a concern that threads through centuries of Jewish literature and culture. *Tza'ar Ba'alay Chayim* is the Jewish term for consideration of the "pain of living creatures." Applying this value helps distinguish the legitimacy of some experiments over others. Even so, what contributes to the toughest decisions concerning animal experimentation is discerning the degree to which animals have independent rights. As we explore our topic, we will look at how various beliefs might influence decisions regarding animal experimentation.

Let's begin with the Bible. First of all, animals are God's creatures. In the story of Creation, all of God's creatures are called "good" (Genesis 1). God causes grass to spring up for cattle, gives food to beasts, satisfies every living thing, and preserves humans and beasts (Psalms 104:14, 147:9, 145:16, 36:7). God's mercy extends to all of God's works (Psalms 145:9). God's concern for animals sets the precedent for what our own attitude should be. Animals, as part of God's sanctified world, are deserving of respectful regard.

Cruelty toward animals is forbidden. There are numerous laws protecting animals from harm and compelling humans to behave mercifully toward them. These include the prohibitions against eating a limb cut off from a living animal, slaughtering an animal and its young on the same day, muzzling an ox as it threshes (which would deprive it of food while it is working), plowing with an ox and an ass together (not able to keep up with the strong ox, the ass would be caused pain), and taking eggs or fledglings from a bird's nest in view of the mother.[1] We are told that if we come across an enemy's ox or ass wandering about, despite our feelings for our enemy, we must return the animal. If an enemy's animal is stuck lying beneath its burden, we must assist in releasing the animal's burden and help get the animal back up (Exodus 23:4-5). Animals are deserving of rest on Shabbat and are included in the privilege of enjoying food that grows in the fields during the sabbatical year (Exodus 20:10, 23:12, Deuteronomy 5:14, Leviticus 25:6-7).

Laws impose restrictions on eating meat and dictate strict guidelines on slaughtering animals

---

[1] Genesis 9:4 and Deuteronomy 12:23, Leviticus 22:28, Deuteronomy 25:4, 22:10, and 22:6-7.

for consumption. (Kosher slaughtering or "*she-chitah*" is a near instantaneous procedure using an exceedingly sharp knife.) It may be permissible to eat meat (Genesis 9:2-3), but moderation is required, and the pain a slaughtered animal might experience must be minimized. In addition, hunting is regarded very negatively. Maimonides expressly states a prohibition against hunting for sport. The first chief Rabbi of Israel, Rabbi Abraham Isaac Kook, discusses whether eating meat is permissible at all. He and many other prominent Jewish leaders have embraced a vegetarian diet as ideal.

Besides laws, there are stories in the Bible which reinforce the expectation of sensitivity for the pain of animals. Rebecca proves she is a worthy wife for Isaac when she brings water not only for Abraham's servant Eliezer, but also for his camels (Genesis 24:14). An angel rebukes Balaam for smiting his ass (Numbers 22:32). God admonishes Jonah for not having pity on the city of Nineveh, for neither seeming to care about the 120,000 people who live there, nor their cattle (Jonah 4:11). The Rabbis asserted that the experience Moses and David had as shepherds contributed to their fitness as leaders (e.g., *Exodus Rabbah* 2:2).

To review thus far, animal welfare is of deep concern for Jews. Jewish requirements for animal experimentation would thus include protecting animals from abuse and unnecessary cruelty. Proper nutrition, sanitary conditions, sufficient physical space for animals, social contact with other animals, the use of anesthesia when necessary, consultations with and supervision by qualified veterinarians — are all factors that need to be taken into account when designing humane experiments.[2] Without question, Judaism would insist that animals be treated with compassion in a laboratory setting.

But the discussion doesn't end here. Certainly, when we know the parameters of an experiment, we should look for ways to maximize the comfort of the animals involved. However, a more essential question precedes analysis of cage size or thermostat settings. That is: are all experiments equally valid? Furthermore, are there instances when the rights of animals supersede the needs or wants of humans? Such rights may override human privileges and desires to run certain experiments in the first place. For instance, an experiment that tests a remedy for a deadly disease might be acceptable, but one that tests make-up products may be considered unjustly indulgent of human desires (the desire for beauty and product variety). When we talk about *rights* of animals, suddenly the ethics of animal experimentation becomes much more complex. If animals have rights, the permissibility of a wider variety of experiments comes into question.

We can open an analysis of animal rights by asking what the relationship is between human beings and the rest of the created world. Three possible Jewish views seem to stand out: (1) human beings are part of a "web" of creation in which everything has a place and purpose, (2) human beings have dominion over the created world, and (3) human beings are earth's caretakers.

Human beings are part of a "web" of creation in which everything has a place and purpose. The creation account asserts that all of God's creatures are good — "God saw all that God had created, and behold, it was good" (Genesis 1). Midrash extends and underscores the notion that there is a place and a purpose for everything: "Even those things that you may regard as completely superfluous to Creation — such as fleas, gnats, and flies — they too were included in Creation; and God's purpose is carried out through everything — even through a snake, a scorpion, a gnat, or a frog" (*Genesis Rabbah* 10:7). The sixteenth century mystic, Rabbi Moses Cordovero, says, "Your compassion should encompass all creatures, not destroying or despising them, for [God who is] Wisdom on High encompasses all created things — minerals, plants, animals, and human beings!" (*Tomer Devorah* or *Deborah's Palm Tree* 3, end).

---

[2]Federal law in the United States has such requirements as discussed in the next section.

Human beings have dominion over the created world. There's an equally compelling but quite different message as well in the account of Creation. That is, humankind has dominion over the created world: "God blessed [the male and female] and said to them, 'Be fertile and increase, fill the earth and master it; and rule the fish of the sea, the birds of the sky, and all the living things that creep on earth'" (Genesis 1:28). The hierarchical idea that humans are master creatures "above" others originates from these verses.

Human beings are earth's caretakers. Being the creatures "on top" does not mean humans may abuse non-human animals. A third way of framing humankind's relationship to nature is as earth's caretakers. Adam is to till and tend the land in which he is placed (Genesis 2:15). Some might claim that if we are responsible for tilling and tending the earth, we're entitled to reap earth's bounty — including the use of its animals. Others might disagree, saying that being a caretaker is more about preserving and protecting the earth. They would be more restrictive in defining what is meant by the legitimate "use" of earth's bounty.

What is interesting here is that there *are* three ways (at least) of viewing humankind's relationship with the earth, just from the first two chapters of Genesis. It is not *only* dominion over the earth that counts. Humans are part of a bigger web in which all "points" (creatures) on the web are valued. And human beings are caretakers. Humans may be endowed with dominion over other creatures, but that dominion is moderated. It exists in tension with our other roles as "members of a web" and caretakers. Understanding this tension helps refine the discussion of animal experimentation. Human animals may be permitted to use non-human animals for some purposes, but certainly not for whatever human benefit might be foreseen.

From the Jewish discussion so far, we might feel more compelled to care, respect, and avoid abuse of animals. We may even decide there are experiments that are not justified because of the compassion we owe animals. But humans are still in the advantageous position when *we decide*, when we judge whether or not to avoid an animal's pain and forego a potential human benefit. A next level challenge is to ask if animals, in and of themselves, have rights that under certain circumstances supersede those of humans? Are there instances in Judaism in which God demands that we take a step down the ladder of creation hierarchy and allow animals' needs to rise above our own?

Humans as well as animals are commanded to rest for a full day each week. The observance of Shabbat restricts humans from participating in a number of activities that are considered work, thus providing the opportunity to enjoy relief from the day-to-day strain of labor. But restrictions are lifted at times for the sake of animals. Shabbat and Jewish holidays may be desecrated in order to alleviate the suffering of an animal.

Here are some examples of how on Shabbat animals' needs are put before certain human benefits (i.e., the human benefit of not having to do physical labor). If an animal falls into a water-filled canal on Shabbat, we are to relieve the animal of its suffering pending its rescue after Shabbat. We are to feed the animal, and if necessary, place pillows or mattresses underneath the animal to enable it to raise itself out of the water and escape from its suffering. Handling pillows and mattresses in such ways on Shabbat normally would be prohibited (*Shabbat* 128b). Maimonides asserts that we must dismount from our animals on Shabbat to prevent the animal from suffering. Similarly, if we return from a journey on Friday night with a laden animal, we are to unload its pack on Shabbat for the same reason. Under no circumstances may we leave an animal laden until after Shabbat, since that would cause the animal to suffer (*Mishneh Torah, Hilchot Shabbat* 21:9-10). Other relaxations of Shabbat and festivals are permitted for the sake of caring for sick animals, such as anointing fresh and painful animal wounds with oil or salve and removing flies that are irritating an animal (Jakobovits).[3]

Earlier in this chapter, consumption of meat was discussed. We might desire meat and are permitted to eat it, but we are not allowed to consume thoughtlessly. There are limits to fulfillment of human desires — some of our cravings must be subdued. On a related topic, we are obliged to delay the satisfaction of our own hunger for the sake of our animals. We are forbidden to eat prior to feeding our animals (*Brachot* 40a and *Gittin* 62a), thus placing animals' needs before our own.

Human activity may have to be modified not only for the sake of animals' physical well-being (unloading an animal's pack on Shabbat or feeding an animal before sitting down to one's own meal), but for their emotional well-being as well. The *feelings* of animals need to be taken into consideration. Jewish sources ascribe sentience to animals and express concern for the emotional pain animals experience. It is forbidden to slaughter an animal "and its young on the same day" (Leviticus 22:28). Maimonides explains that:

> "This prohibition is a precautionary measure in order to avoid slaughtering the young animal in front of its mother. For in these cases, animals feel very great pain, there being no difference regarding this pain between humankind and the other animals. For the love and the tenderness of a mother for her child is not consequent upon reason, but upon the activity of the imaginative faculty, which is found in most animals just as it is found in humans" (*Guide for the Perplexed*, 3:48).

Maimonides gives the same reason — sensitivity for a mother animal's emotional pain — for shooing a mother away before taking her fledglings or eggs from the nest (Deuteronomy 22:6-7):

> "If then the mother is let go and escapes of her own accord, she will not be pained by seeing that the young are taken away" (*Guide for the Perplexed*, 3:48).

Rabbi Judah in the Talmud was condemned for not being sensitive to the fear of a calf being taken to slaughter. The terrified animal tried to hide under Rabbi Judah's robes. Rabbi Judah, however, pushed the animal away, saying, "Go, for this you were created." Rabbi Judah was punished with many physical ailments that didn't go away until years later when he showed mercy to some weasels who were about to be swept away by his servant (*Baba Metzia* 85a).

Our Tradition goes even further — ascribing not only sentience to some animals, but even moral sensibility. Here's one example. In ancient times, an ox known for its temperamental behavior that gored a person to death was itself stoned to death (Exodus 21:28ff). No portion of the ox's body could ever be used. It seems odd. Why *stone* the animal to death? Stoning is a punishment usually reserved for sinful behavior — can an animal be sinful? And why waste the carcass of a perfectly good animal? It is doubtful that the ancient Israelites could afford such waste. The reason would seem to be related to the notion that certain animals are capable of *choosing* to do wrong, of acting morally or immorally. Similar to the fate of the deadly goring ox, an animal that participates in acts of bestiality is killed, as if it bears some responsibility for the aberrant behavior. The bodies of such animals are not used because they are tainted with sin.

In the Talmud there's a discussion about a conflict between two cows concerning right of way on a road. One cow lying in the road prevents another from passing. The cow trying to pass kicks the one blocking its way. While the context of the conflict is more complicated than we need to get into here, there's a comment worthy of note. The cow lying down can say to the kicking cow, "Even if you are entitled to tread upon me, you still have no right to kick me" (*Baba Kamma* 32a). The Rabbis accept that cows have the wherewithal to be devious and that they have some sense of what it means to perpetrate injustices!

---

[3] I. Jakobovits, "The Medical Treatment of Animals in Jewish Law," *Journal of Jewish Studies 7*, 1956, 207-220.

On a different note, being compassionate toward animals helps us to be more caring people in general. Cruelty leads to callousness. Maimonides puts it this way: "If the Torah provides that such grief should not be caused to animals or to birds, how much more careful must we be that we should not cause grief to humans" (*Guide of the Perplexed* 3:48). The commentator Nachmanides suggests, "The reason for the prohibitions [against cruelty to animals] is to teach us the trait of compassion and that we should not be cruel, for cruelty expands in the human soul" (Nachmanides, Commentary on Deuteronomy 22:6). We should not become impervious to the suffering that goes far beyond the animal world.

Though we may understand Judaism's concern for animal welfare, it still is challenging to know how to approach the question of animal experimentation. How do we factor animal sentience and even morality into the discussion — both of which are acknowledged beginning with ancient Jewish texts? It is difficult to answer the philosophical questions satisfactorily. Even so, Jewish sources offer some practical guidelines in evaluating use of animals for human benefit.

For a lenient opinion, the commentator Moses Isserles (Ramah) is often quoted. Remarking on Joseph Karo's *Code of Jewish Law*, Isserles states that anything necessary for medical or other useful purposes is excluded from the prohibition of cruelty to animals (*Shulchan Aruch, Even Ha'ezer*, 5:14). Hence, he adds, "it is permissible to pluck feathers from living geese" in order to obtain quills for writing despite the ban on cruelty to animals. Nevertheless, he concludes that "we refrain from doing so because it is an act of cruelty." It is *permissible,* but we refrain. We may have "dominion" in the world, but we exercise our role as "caretakers." In this way, Isserles resolves the tension between the various roles humans play in the world.

Subsequent permissive Rabbinic rulings on animal experimentation for medical research base themselves on Isserles' statement. Still, scholars have suggested restraint. In the nineteenth century, Jacob Ettlinger proposed limits on Isserles' view that animals could be used for medical and other useful purposes. He said that Isserles' opinion applies only to medical purposes, but not for financial gain (Responsa *Binyan Zion*, no. 108). Another nineteenth century sage, Joseph Saul Nathanson was especially restrictive. He said we may only disregard the prohibition against *tza'ar ba'alay chayim* — causing pain to living animals — if the human benefit gained is proportionate to the pain inflicted on the animal. Should the potential gain for human beings, however, be of a lesser magnitude than the pain inflicted on the animal, Jewish law would forbid it.[4]

The contemporary scholar David Bleich offers a summary of what the Jewish discussion reasonably might conclude about animal experimentation:

> Jewish law clearly forbids any act that causes pain or discomfort to animals unless such act is designed to satisfy a legitimate human need. There is significant authority for the position that animal pain may be sanctioned only for medical purposes, including direct therapeutic benefit, medical experimentation of potential therapeutic benefit and training medical personnel. Those who eschew these positions [and thus are less stringent about the use of animals] would not sanction painful procedures for the purpose of testing or perfecting cosmetics. An even larger body of authority refuses to sanction inflicting pain on animals when the desired benefit can be acquired in an alternative manner ("Judaism and Animal Experimentation," in *Animal Sacrifices*: *Religious Perspectives on the Use of Animals in Science*, as quoted in *Who Renews Creation* by Earl Schwartz and Barry D. Cytron, p. 78).

---

[4]As quoted in *Who Renews Creation* by Earl Schwartz and Barry D. Cytron, 78.

Thus, a majority Jewish opinion probably would allow animal experimentation for medical benefits. However, if the desired benefit can be gained in another way, then the research would not be permitted. This stipulation would apply to both medical research and dissection (for the training of medical personnel). Most Jewish authorities would agree that it is unacceptable to use animals for experiments testing cosmetics or household products.

General Perspectives

In the secular world, there are a number of organizations dedicated to the protection of animals. Some of these focus their energies on sheltering abandoned or unwanted animals and promoting humane education. Others advocate for animal welfare through publicizing wide-ranging abuses, staging protests, promoting boycotts, and working for change through political channels. Others are more activist, making efforts to "liberate" laboratory animals, sometimes justifying illegal tactics (e.g. vandalism or violence) for what they feel are legitimate ends. Of course, using violence to effect change raises its own ethical questions.

Also part of the general discussion are a number of industries, companies, medical organizations, animal dealers, educational institutions, and research facilities that defend animal experimentation. Research institutions themselves are required by law to establish an Institutional Animal Care and Use Committee (IACUC) to oversee their work with animals. Under federal guidelines, IACUC's are to monitor and regulate the use of animals. They are to ensure that animals are used only when necessary, that personnel are trained to avoid mishandling of animals, that a good living environment is provided, and that procedures are used to minimize pain or discomfort experienced by the animals.

The need to treat animals mercifully and with consideration of their pain are near universal concerns in general discussions of the ethics of animal welfare. The Animal Welfare Act (AWA) sets standards for the housing, handling, feeding, and transportation of experimental animals. This Act, first passed in 1966 and subsequently amended several times, reflects efforts to provide more humane treatment of animals. Though there is debate about how effectively the AWA is enforced, the *value* of humane treatment of animals is not the hotly contested issue.

More controversial is the philosophical debate on animal *rights*. Judaism recognizes animal sentience and even acknowledges a version of moral sensibility for certain animals. In the secular world, zoologists and other animal behavior researchers have published numerous findings that would support and extend that Jewish notion. Some of the categories of animal study include levels of consciousness; genetic similarity of animals to humans;[5] ability to "think"; socialization; communication; logic, math, and counting abilities; use of tools, self-awareness, imitation, ability to teach, intentional deception, and empathy.[6]

Once we start down the path of accepting that animals can experience pain and pleasure (and more), and that their welfare deserves *some* consideration, it is difficult to know where to draw the line. Just how much consideration do animals deserve? When do we say concern for animal welfare ends because potential human benefit has overtaken it? The ethical slope — from animal *welfare* to animal *rights* — becomes very slippery very quickly. If we accept that non-human animals have some rights, what's to stop us from admitting them rights equal to human animals? If we are reluctant to grant animals such liberal rights, what is the rationale? How do we justify elevating human benefits above animal needs?

The philosophical questions can be unsettling. Yet, we rely on the discussion of animal

---

[5]I.e. chimpanzees share 99.5% of the same base sequences along every double strand of DNA as human beings. This finding is described by Nicholas Wade in "Human or Chimp? 50 Genes are the Key," *New York Times*, D1, October 20, 1998.

[6]For a thorough treatment of these categories in the context of animal rights, see *Rattling the Cage: Toward Legal Rights for Animals* by Steven M. Wise.

welfare and rights to direct our course of action regarding animal experimentation. Though the philosophical questions may leave us hanging, once we enter the realm of practical issues, the debate comes more into focus.

Animal rights advocates argue that there are viable alternatives to animal experimentation. These alternatives are more humane than conventional use of lab animals. Furthermore, many of these advocates cast doubts on certain justifications given for animal experimentation. Some of the shortcomings they cite are refuted by animal researchers:

1. What animal advocates say: Animals and humans differ in significant ways. Because animals vary in their response to drugs, the results of experiments can be misleading to humans. Drugs thought to be safe on humans — because they were tested on animals — have not necessarily proven to be so. On the other hand, beneficial drugs for humans may be dangerous to animals' lives. For instance, the "miracle drug" penicillin — fatal to guinea pigs — has saved millions of human lives. Thus, depending on animal tests might cause a helpful drug to be overlooked or disregarded. Toxicity and irritancy tests done for cosmetics and household products have been criticized on scientific grounds. Even among closely related species, different animals react in different ways to toxic substances. Thus, extrapolating from non-human animals to human animals is unreliable.

   What animal researchers respond: There are significant medical advances that would not have come about without animal experimentation. For example, without such research chemotherapeutic advances against cancer (including childhood leukemia and breast malignancy), beta-blockers for cardiac patients, and electrolyte infusions for patients with dysfunctional metabolism

would never have been achieved.[7]

2. What animal advocates say: Insistence on animal testing has delayed availability of experimental drugs. Those with debilitating health conditions complain that they don't have the luxury of waiting for time consuming animal tests required by the FDA (Federal Drug Administration).

   What animal researchers and FDA officials argue: Extensive testing of experimental drugs is necessary for the protection of people's health. Earnest testing also may help protect drug and cosmetic companies from lawsuits that might arise if potentially dangerous products are allowed to be distributed.

3. What animal advocates say: The scientific merit of certain experiments can be questionable.

   What animal researchers respond: True, it is important to question the merit of experiments. But such a responsibility should not be left solely to animal defense organizations such as the American Anti-Vivisection Society. Scientists, along with ethicists, animal advocates, doctors, and others should evaluate whether or not certain experiments are justified.

4. Animal advocates warn: Animal experimentation and dissection may desensitize individuals to animals' pain. This hazard is especially problematic for doctors who must strive to develop exquisite sensitivity to suffering.

   Researchers maintain: People can indeed separate their laboratory work from their interactions with human beings. Being a skillful laboratory scientist does not necessarily make you a less sensitive person.

5. Animal advocates urge the use of scientifically reliable alternatives to animals in experiments, involving use of cells, tissue cultures, and computer models. In addition, there are

---

[7]From a reprint of an AMA position paper by Jerod M. Loeb, William R. Hendee, Steven J. Smith, and M. Roy Schwarz, "Human Vs Animal Rights" in *The Journal of the American* *Medical Association* 262:2716-20. N 17, '89. Copyright 1989 by the American Medical Association, in *Animal Rights and Welfare, The Reference Shelf,* 78.

chemical tests that can be conducted for cosmetics and household products.

Animal researchers suggest that such alternative testing methods might be used as adjuncts to animal experiments and sometimes as substitutes. But there are experiments in which such alternatives are inadequate because they do not encompass the physiological complexity that whole animals do.

6. There are suitable alternatives to animal dissection for educational purposes. These include use of films, models, diagrams, computer programs, cadavers, and other demonstrative techniques. Many medical schools do not use animals in the training of medical students.

7. Scientific priorities need to be reevaluated. The cost of animal experimentation is enormous, one of the main reasons being the tremendous amount of resources appropriately allocated to enforcing the Federal guidelines for proper animal care. This expense is acknowledged by taxpayers, scientists, and animal advocates alike. It is far more economical to use alternative testing methods (with cells, tissues, models). In addition, it may be wise to shift some of our research abilities and financial resources toward public health measures and preventive medicine.

8. The scholars Hugh LaFollette and Niall Shanks[8] offer moderate suggestions regarding the volatile and unsettling questions surrounding animal experimentation. A summary of their proposals is an appropriate conclusion to our overview of animal experimentation issues.

Scientific Proposals:

1. We must define more accurately what we mean by "success" when we apply that goal to animal research.

2. We need to improve the methods by which we judge whether or not a practice is "successful."

3. We must determine the worthiness of the contribution of experiment results to human well-being.

Moral Proposals:

1. We must increase our understanding of the nature of non-human animals.

2. We must think more carefully about how to make moral judgments when comparing the worth of different creatures.

3. We must learn how to measure and evaluate animal pain more accurately.

Derivative Proposals:

1. We need stronger public health measures to reduce chronic illness caused by environmental factors.

2. Universities should reconsider the criteria for granting tenure to animal researchers.

3. There should be increased support for developing alternatives to animal research.

4. We should be open to consider and assess evidence offered by theorists on all sides of the debate.

Summary of the Overview

Ethicists and activists question the morality of using millions of animals each year in medical experiments, as part of cosmetic and household product research, and in classroom instruction (for dissection).

1. Through experiments involving animals, we attain helpful information for improving the quality of human life.

2. Animals are living, sentient creatures, not

---

[8]*Brute Science: Dilemmas of Animal Experimentation*, 266-269.

disposable objects. They deserve compassion and have the right to be protected from abuse.

3. All experiments are not necessarily equally legitimate. Some reasons for conducting animal experiments include: for medical information that may save human lives (cancer or AIDS research), for medical reasons that may improve certain health conditions (treatment of acne or mosquito bite itching), for cosmetic purposes (testing mascara for irritability to eyes), for household products (toxicity of floor wax), for psychological information (determining the stress of infant animals raised in isolation from mothers and others), or for general educational purposes (dissection of animals in school science classes).

4. Our challenge is to come up with guidelines that evaluate the legitimacy of human needs and desires, plus take into account animal welfare and animal rights.

SCENARIOS: HOW THINGS HAVE CHANGED

Below are two imaginary scenarios which illustrate the challenging ethical questions concerning the proper treatment of animals that have concerned Jews and non-Jews through the ages. They are intended to raise questions and spark discussion. Read each scenario to or with your students, and engage them in small or large group discussions. Use the "Focus the Discussion" section below to help identify the important issues and facilitate these discussions. Note that additional questions relating to these scenarios are found in the "Stories: Understanding through Listening" section below (p. 237).

Following the discussions, have students continue on to the "Text Study" section to see what Jewish and other sources have to say on the subject. Finally, you may wish to have students discuss the scenarios a second time, to see if their views have changed.

Scenario I: In Ancient Days

Chaya lives with her family on a small farm outside a Jewish village. She has only lived there for a few years. Every summer, Chaya has noticed that certain bushes produce plump pink berries. But just because something looks tantalizing, Chaya knows it still could be poisonous. Therefore, she doesn't dare eat the berries. Last summer, Chaya questioned local villagers about the berries. What did they know about the berries; were they safe to eat? The villagers were non-committal in their opinions. This summer, Chaya has decided to conduct her own berry experiment. It happens that she has a sheep that has become lame and seems to be in increasing amounts of pain. Chaya feels that at some point over the summer, she will have to put the animal to sleep. This is her idea: Why not mix some of the mashed berries into the sheep's food one day and see what happens? If the sheep becomes sick or dies, she will know that the berries could also be poisonous to people and that she should continue to avoid them. And since the sheep is going to need to be put to sleep anyway, she isn't doing anything overly cruel to the animal. If nothing unusual happens to the sheep as a result of ingesting the berries, Chaya would feel that she could safely eat small quantities of the berry until she herself becomes more certain that just as the berries didn't hurt the sheep, neither would they be detrimental to humans.

After completing her "experiment" (in which nothing happens to the sheep), Chaya tells her friend about what she did and what she found out. The friend scolds Chaya, "Didn't God provide enough good fruits and plants for you to eat without having to subject your poor sheep to berries which could have made that sick animal suffer even more?!"

Scenario II: Contemporary Times

Eve is a researcher for a pharmaceutical company. She has been doing research on drugs that would be safe for pregnant women to take (safe for mother and developing fetus). Some pregnant women experience nausea, even to an incapacitating level, particularly in the early stages of their pregnancies. Recently, Eve read a report about a tribe in the Amazon jungle that uses a certain berry to treat nausea. Though within the Amazon tribe, the berry isn't used by pregnant women per se, perhaps there are good prospects for the purposes of interest to Eve.

A preliminary experiment is devised using rats and mice. Eve is scrupulous in following federal regulations concerning care for animals during experiments. After a long wait, the IACUC (Institutional Animal Care and Use Committee) at the University where Eve works approves her experiment proposal. The berry is given to the animals. The rats show no reaction to the berry, whereas mice given very high quantities of the berry show signs of dizziness. More animal experiments are planned — with the goal being to refine the conclusions. The next level of experiments will involve giving animals a nausea-producing substance prior to giving them the berry. This way the effects of the drug can be observed in animals that are suffering from nausea to begin with. Though Eve feels conflicted by the decision to begin her next series of experiments by deliberately making animals feel sick, she believes the potential benefit to humans (in this case, pregnant women) is worth the suffering the animals will go through.

Focus the Discussion

The moral and philosophical questions about human use of animals hasn't changed all that much over the years. Promoting animal welfare and wrestling with animal rights are concerns humans have faced for centuries. Today, we may have more scientific studies and statistics to back up our impressions of animals and extend our knowledge of non-human creatures. Still, even our oldest Jewish sources reveal an impressively nuanced understanding and concern for animals.

What has changed most is the *extent* to which animals are used for human purposes. In ancient days, animals were used primarily for food, clothing, transportation, hauling, agricul-

ture-related activities, and ritual purposes. Nowadays, it is not uncommon for animals to be bred, raised, and kept for the sole purpose of testing substances that potentially may benefit humans. Millions of animals will have no life outside a research laboratory. Medical and pharmaceutical advances have propelled us to seek more sophisticated methods to support our quest to cure, heal, and understand. Perhaps there's even a primal "preservation of the species" urge that drives our quest. But it's not only to cure and to heal that provides the motivation to experiment. There are financial gains to be had by devising desirable household and cosmetic products. There are incentives — not always the most honorable — for developing new drugs, as well. Modern interests demand that we scrutinize the morality of our motives for using animals.

For many reasons, in recent decades pressures have increased to use animals in experiments. Alternative testing methods are not always viable. Nevertheless, it is important and worthwhile to continue seeking alternatives to animal experimentation when possible; to continue to improve the education of researchers and the public in appropriate animal use; and to vigorously enforce and improve existing animal use guidelines.

TEXT STUDY

There are many difficult questions to consider concerning animal welfare, animal rights, and the ethics of animal experimentation. Jewish textual sources provide many answers, but these answers often highlight the tension between seemingly opposing considerations. The chart on the next page poses the questions and offers two opposing points of view. Text sources supporting each of these points of view follow below.

Making an Ethical Decision about Animal Experimentation: Questions to Consider

The Question	On the One Hand	On the Other Hand
1. What is the relationship between human beings and the rest of the created world? (see p. 231)	Human beings have dominion over the earth.	Human beings are part of nature's "web," plus play a role as earth's caretakers.
2. What is the status of human vs. non human animals in the "eyes of God?" (see p. 232)	The special role of human beings in the world is God-given.	All creatures are under God's care.
3. What human uses of animals are acceptable? (see p. 232)	Human beings are allowed to use animals in ways that benefit them.	There are significant restrictions on the use of animals.
4. How much pain is it permissible to cause animals? (see p. 233)	Causing pain to an animal is permitted if it leads to the benefit of human beings.	We try to avoid causing pain to animals — physical or emotional — whenever possible.
5. Which deserves higher priority, human needs or animal rights? (see p. 234)	Taking care of human needs should be our first priority.	Animals have rights that sometimes supersede those of human beings.

1. What is the relationship between human beings and the rest of the created world?

On the One Hand:

Human beings have dominion over the earth.

A. God blessed them and God said to them, "Be fertile and increase, fill the earth and subdue it! Have dominion over the fish of the sea, the birds of the sky, and all the living things that crawl about the earth" (Genesis 1:28).

B. [God said to Adam], "The fear and the dread of you shall be upon all the beasts of the earth and upon all the birds of the sky — everything with which the earth is astir — and upon all the fish of the sea; they are given into your hand. Every creature that lives shall be yours to eat; as with the green grasses, I give you all of these" (Genesis 9:2-3).

On the Other Hand:

Human beings are part of nature's "web," plus play a role as earth's caretakers.

a. And God saw all that God had made, and found it very good (Genesis 1:31).

The following is a commentary on Genesis 1:31:

> Each created thing is "good" in itself; but when combined and united, the totality is proclaimed "very good." Everything in the universe was as the Creator willed it — nothing superfluous, nothing lacking — a harmony. "This harmony bears witness to the unity of God who planned this unity of Nature" (Luzzato) (J.H. Hertz, *The Pentateuch and Haftorahs*, London: Soncino Press, 1979, p. 5).

b. The Eternal God took the man and placed him in the garden of Eden, to till it and tend it (Genesis 2:15).

c. In the hour when the Holy One, Who Is Blessed created the first human being, God took him and let him pass before all the trees of the Garden of Eden and said to him: "See my works, how fine and excellent they are? Now all that I have created, for you have I created them. Think upon this and do not corrupt and desolate My world. For if you corrupt it, there is no one to set it right after you" (*Ecclesiastes Rabbah* 7:28).

Probing: Ideas and Issues

How does Genesis define the relationship of humans with the world? Which human role is most pronounced in our day — master and ruler of nature; harmonious member of nature's unity or "web;" or earth's caretaker and protector? What do humans need to work on most in their relationship with nature?

2. **What is the status of human vs. non human animals in the "eyes of God?"**

On the One Hand:

The special role of human beings in the world is God-given.

A. When I look at Your heavens, the work of Your hands, the moon and work which you have established, what are humans that You are mindful of them, and the children of humans that You care for them? Yet You have made them little less than God, and crown them with glory and honor. You have given them dominion over the works of Your hands; You have put all things under their feet . . . (Psalms 8:4-7).

On the Other Hand:

All creatures are under God's care.

a. The Eternal is good to all, and God's mercy is upon all God's works" (Psalms 145:9).

b. The eyes of all look to You expectantly, and You give them their food when it is due. You give it openhandedly, feeding every creature to its heart's content (Psalms 145:15-16).

Probing: Ideas and Issues

What is unique about our human role in the world? Why might humans have a role different from other creatures? What expectations does God have of us that God doesn't have of other creatures?

3. **What human uses of animals are acceptable?**

On the One Hand:

Human beings are allowed to use animals in ways that serve them.

A. It was taught: Rabbi Simeon ben Eleazar said, "In my whole lifetime I have not seen a deer engaged in gathering fruit, a lion carrying burdens, or a fox as a shopkeeper, yet they are sustained without trouble, though they were created only to serve me, whereas I was created to serve my Maker . . . " (*Kiddushin* 82b).

On the Other Hand:

We are constrained by laws reflecting concern for animals.

a. When you see the ass of your enemy lying under its burden and would refrain from raising it, you must nevertheless raise it with him (Exodus 23:5).

b. Six days you shall do your work, but on the seventh day you shall cease from labor, in order that your ox and your ass may rest and that your bondsman and the stranger may be refreshed (Exodus 23:12).

c. No animal from the herd or from the flock shall be slaughtered on the same day with its young (Leviticus 22:28).

d. I will also provide grass in the fields for your cattle — and thus you shall eat your fill (Deuteronomy 11:15).

The Talmud comments:

> Thus said Rabbi Judah in the name of Rav: It is forbidden for people to taste anything until they have given food to their animal, as it says [first], "I will also provide grass in the fields for your cattle," and then [second], "and thus you shall eat your fill" (*Gittin* 62a).

e. Make sure that you do not partake of the blood; for the blood is the life, and you must not consume the life with the flesh (Deuteronomy 12:23).

The commentator Rambam adds:

> The oral tradition has taught that the biblical verse, "and you must not consume the life with the flesh" is a reference to the prohibition against eating a limb severed from a living animal (Rambam, *Hilchot Ma'achalot Assurot* 5:1).

f. You shall not plow with an ox and an ass together (Deuteronomy 22:10).

g. You shall not muzzle an ox while it is threshing" (Deuteronomy 25:4).

Probing: Ideas and Issues

The gist of these texts is that animals may serve us, but we have responsibilities toward them. Do you agree that the animal world was created for the purpose of serving human beings? Suppose you wanted to add new laws that would address current threats to animals' welfare. What are a few that you would include?

4. Is it permissible to cause animals pain?

On the One Hand:

Causing pain to an animal is permitted if it leads to the benefit of humans.

A. Regarding anything that is needed for healing or for any purpose whatsoever — the prohibition against *Tza'ar Ba'alay Chayim* (causing pain to animals) does not apply. For example, it is permitted to pluck down feathers from live geese. In such a case, you need not be concerned about *Tza'ar Ba'alay Chayim* (Joseph Karo, *Shulchan Aruch, Even haEzer* 5:14).

B. It appears that the prohibition against *tza'ar ba'alay chayim* (causing pain to animals) does not apply if one is using [the animals] for the benefit of humankind, since all creatures were created to serve humankind" (Israel Isserlein, *"Terumat haDeshen," Pesakim u-Ketavim* 105, 15th c. Germany).

On the Other Hand:

We try to avoid causing pain to animals — physical or emotional — whenever possible.

See also the quote by J. David Bleich at the end of the "Jewish Perspectives" section in the Overview, p. 225.

a. This is the crucial gloss to Joseph Karo's comment (see #4A above):

> Nevertheless, people hold back from doing it [plucking down feathers from live geese], since it is indeed cruel [The practice is technically permitted, but it is to be avoided if possible.] (Moshe Isserles, gloss to Joseph Karo's *Shulchan Aruch, Even haEzer* 5:14, 1572).

b. [The nineteenth century scholar] Rabbi Joseph Saul Nathanson says that one may disregard the prohibition against *Tza'ar*

Ba'alay Chayim — "causing pain to living animals" — only if the human benefit gained is *proportionate* to the pain inflicted on the animal. Should the potential gain for human beings, however, be of a lesser magnitude than the pain inflicted on the animal, he claims that Jewish law would forbid it (As quoted in *Who Renews Creation* by Earl Schwartz and Barry D. Cytron, p. 78).

c. The reason for the prohibitions [against cruelty to animals] is to teach us the trait of compassion and that we should not be cruel, for cruelty expands in the human soul (Nachmanides, Commentary on Deuteronomy 22:6).

d. Maimonides instructs us to avoid not only an animal's physical pain, but its emotional pain, as well. See the citations quoted from his *Guide To the Perplexed* in the "Jewish Perspectives" section of the Overview, pp. 221-226.

Probing: Ideas and Issues

Do you agree that causing pain to an animal is acceptable if it leads to the benefit of humans? Are there "benefits" not worthy of the pain that would be caused to animals in order to gain them? Would it be acceptable to you to use a medicine that involved research painful to animals? Would it be acceptable to you to use a cosmetic that involved research painful to animals? How about a household product (such as floor wax)?

5. **Which deserves higher priority, human needs or animal rights?**

On the One Hand:

Taking care of human needs should be our first priority.

See Texts #4A and #4B above.

On the Other Hand:

Animals have rights that sometimes supersede those of humans.

a. A number of relevant texts about animal rights are cited and discussed in the Overview, "Jewish Perspectives," pp. 221-226.

b. Perhaps the ideal for compassion is that it be boundless, whether directed toward human or non-human animals:

> A concern for animal suffering hardly excludes concern for human suffering. There is no limit to human moral concern (Richard H. Schwartz, *Judaism and Vegetarianism*, p. 111).

Probing: Ideas and Issues

How would you define animal rights? Do you think animals deserve rights? Would you say that concern for animals distracts from more pressing human problems? Or, do you believe that increased compassion for animals can only add to the sum benefit of more compassion for all of God's creatures — human and non-human animals alike?

RELATED MIDDOT AND MITZVOT

Practicing these virtues and commandments will help enhance ethical treatment of animals.

Anavah (Humility): Usually we talk about humble individuals, but not about humble species. Perhaps we need to examine how human animals collectively see themselves — as better than non-human animals — and strive for more communal *anavah*.

Bal Tashchit (Preserving the Earth; Not Destroying): Animals are part of God's precious domain. We have a responsibility to ensure that animals are not unnecessarily "wasted" or destroyed.

Histapkut (Contentedness): We must be vigilant about asking what our real *needs* are. For example, if we were more content with the types and varieties of products available to us, perhaps fewer animals would need to give their lives for the purpose of testing products for us.

Kashrut (Dietary Laws): Limiting (or eliminating) meat in our diets, plus requiring humane slaughter, can be ways of increasing sensitivity to animals.

K'vod et Ha-Briyot (Honoring Created Things): Besides refraining from wasteful or destructive environmental practices (*Bal Tashchit*) and recognizing the pain of animals (*Tza'ar Ba'alay Chayim*), we can go one step further. We can cultivate a sense of *honor* and *respect* for all created things.

Tochechah (Rebuking): Abuse or intentional cruelty to animals is as deserving of rebuke as other sinful actions.

Tza'ar Ba'alay Chayim (Compassion for Animals): This literally means concern for the "pain of living creatures." Discussed in great detail in the Overview above.

Yirah (Awe and Reverence): To be in awe of God includes striving for an attitude of reverence toward all of God's creatures.

ACTIVITIES

A First Look: Key Issues and Ideas

1. A good way to begin studying this topic is to "survey" the students about what their relationship with animals is and what they know in terms of Jewish views on the subject. On the board (or pairs of students could do this together), put the following headings:

   - What I do in consideration of animals: (such as, feed my pet, limit meat consumption, volunteer at the animal shelter, etc.)

   - What society does to protect animals: (outlaws the sale of ivory — which comes from poached elephants, protects endangered species, prohibits cock-fighting, establishes wildlife preserves, etc.)

   - Jewish Laws: (some examples are listed in Text Study #3a-g above)

   After completing the above task, ask students if they are satisfied that their own relationship with animals is ethically sound. What about society's relationship with animals — what's working and what's not? What can Jewish teachings on *Tza'ar Ba'alay Chayim* offer in terms of guidance on some of the difficult issues we face today regarding use of animals?

2. Here's another "survey" exercise to raise students' awareness of our relationship to animals. Have students list as many ways as they can that people use animals. Ask students to be specific (e.g., instead of saying "for food," have them list "milk from cows, eggs from chickens, beef, veal, fowl," etc.) and comprehensive (e.g., for companionship, hauling loads, shoes, coats, circus entertainment, whale watching, dissection, testing medicines, testing cosmetics, etc.). After a substantial list has been created, go back and do the following: put a check mark next to each "use" that is felt to be acceptable; put a question mark next to each "use" that is questionable; and put an "X" next to each "use" that is unacceptable. Clearly, not everyone will agree on the acceptability of the various uses. The leader may want to have votes for each "use" and award ratings based on the most votes. Alternatively, the leader can go around the room and allow one person at a time to award a rating. Allow time for stu-

dents to discuss their reaction to the exercise and to listen to each other's reasoning behind differing views.

3. Review with students Jewish and secular material on the topics of animal welfare and animal rights. Then, have students write an "Animal Bill of Rights" that they feel is consistent with Jewish belief and practice. Under the "Animal Bill of Rights," what kinds of experiments using animals would be permitted?

4. Invite to class someone who uses animals for scientific research and someone who works for an animal welfare organization. Ask the guests to describe their work, what they consider to be appropriate use and handling of animals, and what abuses of animals they most believe should be addressed by our society. What parameters should there be for animal experimentation? Who should set these parameters?

   Students should process the experience by comparing their own Jewish knowledge of the topic with the ideas presented by the guests. Note: this activity can be done in conjunction with the one listed below in "Stories" #3.

5. Have your group educate itself on current issues regarding animal research by exploring the content in the web sites mentioned in the Bibliography below. Looking at the web sites and referring to some of the links will give students a sense of the many organizations dedicated to animals.

6. Have students create an imaginary course syllabus on Jewish Ethics for Animal Researchers. For an eight session course, what topics should be included? Some possible subjects for sessions include: Animal Welfare in the Bible, Animal Rights in Ancient Days and in Modern Times, Evaluating Ethical Use of Animals, Are All Experiments Created Equal?, How to Judge the Ethics of Animal Experiments, etc.

   To extend this exercise, add a few key ideas that should be covered under each session heading. A further challenge is to have individuals or pairs prepare one of the topics to teach to the rest of the group.

Applying Middot and Mitzvot

1. Refer to the *middot* and *mitzvot* listed above on pp. 234-235. Have students rank these from what they consider most to least important in terms of developing a proper attitude toward animals. Then, have them discuss and explain their rankings.

2. Ask: Which particular *middah* or *mitzvah* would most contribute to your own personal growth in sensitivity toward animals? What specifically could you do to try to incorporate the virtue or practice? (For example, someone who wants to work on *histapkut,* or contentment, might decide to purchase fewer cosmetics and make sure the ones purchased have not been tested on animals.)

3. Ask: Is there something related to mistreatment of animals you've observed that you believe is deserving of rebuke? Have students strategize about how to give an appropriate rebuke regarding animal abuse. An example might be to write a letter to the newspaper condemning those who taunt squirrels and pigeons in the local park by throwing rocks and other objects at them

4. For more information and activities on:

   Anavah (Humility): see *Teaching Jewish Virtues: Sacred Sources and Arts Activities* by Susan Freeman, pp. 8-25, and *The Jewish Moral Virtues* by Eugene B. Borowitz and Frances Weinman Schwartz, pp. 137-148.

   Bal Tashchit (Preserving the Earth; Not Destroying): see *It's a Mitzvah! Step-by-Step To Jewish Living* by Bradley Shavit Artson, pp. 50-61.

   Histapkut (Contentedness): *Teaching Jewish Virtues: Sacred Sources and Arts Activities* by Susan Freeman, pp. 211-227, and *The Jewish*

Moral Virtues by Eugene B. Borowitz and Frances Weinman Schwartz, pp. 161-172.

Kashrut (Observing Dietary Laws): see *Teaching Mitzvot: Concepts, Values, and Activities* by Barbara Binder Kadden and Bruce Kadden, pp. 83-88, *It's a Mitzvah! Step-by-Step To Jewish Living* by Bradley Shavit Artson, pp. 84-95, and *The Jewish Dietary Laws* by Samuel H. Dresner, Seymour Siegel, and David M. Pollock.

K'vod et Ha-Briyot (Honoring Created Things): see *Teaching Jewish Virtues: Sacred Sources and Arts Activities* by Susan Freeman, pp. 179-194.

Tochechah (Rebuking): see *Teaching Jewish Virtues: Sacred Sources and Arts Activities* by Susan Freeman, pp. 318-331.

Tza'ar Ba'alay Chayim (Being Kind to Animals): see *Teaching Mitzvot: Concepts, Values, and Activities* by Barbara Binder Kadden and Bruce Kadden, pp. 137-141, and *It's a Mitzvah! Step-by-Step To Jewish Living* by Bradley Shavit Artson, pp. 196-215.

Yirah (Awe and Reverence): see *Teaching Jewish Virtues: Sacred Sources and Arts Activities* by Susan Freeman, pp. 332-346.

Stories: Understanding through Listening

1. Have students read over the scenarios found above on pp. 229-230. Discuss with them the following questions:

   - What was Chaya's interest in the berry? What was Eve's?

   - How did each woman go about devising a berry experiment?

   - What similarities and differences were there in each woman's use of animals?

   - What ethical issues did the women face?

   - Did both Chaya and Eve act in a responsible, ethical manner?

   - What are the most difficult ethical decisions regarding animal treatment in our day?

   To go a step further, reenact the scenarios or invent your own. After actors perform, allow audience members to interview actors (still in character), asking questions about the circumstances of their experiment, how they made decisions regarding use of animals, etc.

2. There are a number of traditional stories about animal welfare that lend themselves to skits. Here are a few that students can be asked to perform:

   - Rabbi Judah's lack of compassion for a calf and his regret about it years later. See the Overview, p. 224, or *Baba Metzia* 85a.

   - Moses' attitude toward animals while he was a shepherd that earned him the role of Jewish leader:

     > While our teacher Moses was tending the sheep of Jethro in the wilderness, a kid ran away from him. He ran after it until it reached Hasuah. Upon reaching Hasuah it came upon a pool of water [whereupon] the kid stopped to drink. When Moses reached it, he said, "I did not know that you were running because [you were] thirsty. You must be tired." He placed it on his shoulder and began to walk. The Holy One Who Is Blessed said, "You are compassionate in leading flocks belonging to mortals; I swear you will similarly shepherd my flock, Israel" (*Shemot Rabbah* 2:2).

   - The oxen in the road, one which kicks the other when it won't move out of its way. See the Overview, p. 224, or *Baba Kamma* 32a.

   - The requirement of shooing the mother bird away before taking her eggs or fledglings. See the Overview, p. 224, or Deuteronomy 22:6-7 and Maimonides

Guide for the Perplexed, 3:48.

- All creatures have their purpose in God's creation:

    "Heaven and earth were finished — all their array" (Genesis 2:1). Our Rabbis said: Even those things that you may regard as completely superfluous to creation — such as fleas, gnats, and flies — even they too were included in creation; and God's purpose is carried out through everything — even through a snake, a scorpion, a gnat, or a frog (*Genesis Rabbah* 19:7).

    After presenting the scenarios, the actors (still in character) participate in a "round table" discussion about animal experimentation. They are now experts that have been invited to cross the boundaries of time to form an ethics panel that must come up with ten (or so) guidelines for conducting animal experiments. Panel members should wear name tags so that everyone can keep track of who everyone else is. If all the scenarios above are used, the group of panel members minimally would include:

    Rabbi Judah, the calf on its way to slaughter, some weasels, a maid;
    Moses, God;
    Two oxen;
    An egg/fledgling collector, a mother bird;
    A snake, a scorpion, a gnat, and a frog.

3. There are many stories of people's lives who have been saved or quality of life improved by medical breakthroughs. Some of these breakthroughs have come about as a result of information gained by means of animal research. Inquire around to find someone who has expertise in medical research using animals. Invite the expert to visit your group and discuss the "stories" of people who have been helped because of animal research. You also may wish to ask the guest about what he/she sees as the most challenging struggles and limitations of animal research. That is,

have the guest address the issue of research efforts ("stories") that have not progressed in ways the medical community had hoped they would.

Note: this activity can be done in conjunction with the one listed above in "A First Look: Key Issues and Ideas" #4, p. 236.

Action: Getting Out, Getting Involved

1. Get an up-to-date list of companies that don't test cosmetics or household products on animals. (The American Anti-Vivisection Society publishes a booklet called "Guide To Compassionate Shopping" which you can request on their web site, www.aavs.org.) Check whether or not the products you use are "cruelty-free." Then, make a commitment to purchase only products that have not been tested on animals. Write to companies that still test products on animals and encourage them to use alternative testing procedures.

2. Have students find out what their school's policy is on animal dissection. What does someone do who is opposed to participating in dissection projects? If the school's policy does not permit students to opt out of such activities, have your group make a plan of action to encourage a change in policy that will allow for alternatives to dissection in the classroom.

3. Numerous opportunities to act on behalf of animal welfare exist beyond the realm of animal experimentation. Many excellent suggestions are given by Bradley Shavit Artson in *It's a Mitzvah!*, pp. 204-214. Helpful details are included in Artson's book for each suggestion. This list gives a general sense of his thoughtful recommendations:

    - Buy products that specifically state that they have not been tested on animals.

    - Use cruelty-free products.

- Don't support the fur industry.

- Refuse to buy and to accept ivory products (which come from poached elephants).

- Reduce the number of leather products you use.

- When choosing a pet, go to a nearby pound (many pet store puppies are raised in inhumane conditions).

- Neuter your pets (to help decrease the number of unwanted animals).

- Do not alter an animal's appearance because you think it makes the animal look better.

- Limit the number of animals used in scientific experiments and research.

- Prevent hunting for sport.

- Eliminate thoughtless consumption of animals: e.g., Don't eat veal, buy only "dolphin safe" tuna, eat less meat, or become a vegetarian.

Have your group discuss and learn more about some or all of the above suggestions. Ask students, either individually or in pairs, to come up with a plan of action for increasing their commitment to *Tza'ar Ba'alay Chayim*. How might treatment of research animals and quality of experiments change if people take some of the above steps to increase compassion toward animals?

4. Some of the web sites listed in the Bibliography discuss current animal issues in need of action, including ones related to animal experimentation. Find an issue you would like to research and work on.

Wrestling: Engagement with the Issues

1. Have your group imagine it sits on the equivalent of an IACUC (Institutional Animal Care and Use Committee) for a Jewish animal research facility. Come up with guidelines for appropriate animal use and care which incorporate Jewish values. If possible, acquire existing guidelines prepared by university and other research institutions. These will give you ideas on how you might want to approach the creation of your own document.

2. Refer in the Overview, pp. 222-223, to the discussion of three ways of viewing human's relationship with the world — as dominators, as members of nature's "web," and as caretakers. Also see Text Study #1. Assign individuals (or pairs) to one of the three viewpoints. Have them write a position paper (or prepare an oral statement) on animal experimentation from their perspective. In their paper (or statement) they should address the legitimacy of carrying out animal experiments for:

- Medical information that may save human lives (cancer or AIDS research).

- Medical reasons that may improve certain health conditions (treatment of acne or mosquito bite itching).

- Cosmetic purposes (testing mascara for irritability to eyes) and household products (toxicity of floor wax).

- Psychological information (determining the stress of infant animals raised in isolation from mothers and others).

- General educational purposes (dissection of animals in school science classes).

3. A variation on the above activity is to hold a debate. Divide the group into three debate teams, taking on the viewpoints outlined above. After each group presents its "opening statement," give time for responding to each other's arguments.

4. Create a series of educational and/or inspirational posters that might be hung in an animal research facility. These posters would reinforce ethical rationales for using animals in research and highlight ways of providing quality care.

A variation: Use paint, collage items, or other materials to create artwork appropriate for an animal research facility that depicts our relationship with the created world. Or, choose one of the *middot* included in the "Related Middot and Mitzvot" section above (pp. 232-233) to illustrate, such as *Anavah* (Humility), *Bal Tashchit* (Preserving the Earth, Not Destroying), *Histapkut* (Contentedness), *K'vod et Ha-Briyot* (Honoring Created Things), *Tochechah* (Rebuking), *Tza'ar Ba'alay Chayim* (Compassion for Animals), *Yirah* (Awe and Reverence).

5. Have small groups create and perform skits in which characters must wrestle with ethical issues involving use of animals. Participants can come up with their own ideas or use one of these:

- An 8th grader does not want to participate in the "required" science labs in which students dissect frogs.

- A custodian working for an animal research facility believes animals have not been cared for appropriately.

- A physician must convince a patient who is an animal rights activist that in order for him/her to survive a debilitating illness, the patient will need to take a treatment that was developed by means of research involving extensive animal testing.

- Business executives must decide if they want to test a new artificial sweetener on animals. The new product could prove extremely profitable. The test will include finding out how much of the sweetener various animals can tolerate before it kills them.

Empathy

1. Write a prayer that expresses appreciation for and sensitivity toward all of God's creatures.

2. Write a story or create a play in which animals are imagined to have "voices." Have the animals discuss their questions about human beings and their opinions about human actions and attitudes. Focus on developing an interesting plot, as well.

BIBLIOGRAPHY

Books

The Animal Rights Handbook. Los Angeles, CA: Living Planet Press, 1990.

Artson, Bradley Shavit. *It's a Mitzvah! Step-by-Step To Jewish Living.* Springfield, NJ: Behrman House and New York: The Rabbinical Assembly, 1995, pp. 196-215.

Bernstein, Ellen and Dan Fink. *Let the Earth Teach You Torah.* Wyncote, PA: Shomrei Adamah, 1992, pp. 165-169.

Bleich, J. David. "Judaism and Animal Experimentation." In *Animal Sacrifices: Religious Perspectives on the Use of Animals in Science,* edited by Tom Regan. Philadelphia, PA: Temple University Press, 1986.

Bleich, J. David. "Vegetarianism and Judaism." In *Contemporary Halakhic Problems,* vol. III. Hoboken, NJ: KTAV Publishing House, Inc. and New York: Yeshiva University Press, 1989.

Borowitz, Eugene B., and Frances Weinman Schwartz. *The Jewish Moral Virtues.* Philadelphia, PA: Jewish Publication Society, 1999.

Brestrup, Craig. *Disposable Animals: Ending the Tragedy of Throwaway Pets.* Leander, TX: Camino Bay Books, 1997.

Cooksey, Gloria. *Endangered Species, Must They Disappear?* Information Plus Reference Series. Farmington Hills, MI: Gale Group, 2001.

Dresner, Samuel H.; Seymour Siegel; and David M. Pollock. *The Jewish Dietary Laws.* New York: The Rabbinical Seminary of America, 1982.

Freeman, Susan. *Teaching Jewish Virtues: Sacred Sources and Arts Activities.* Denver, CO: A.R.E. Publishing, Inc., 1999.

Kadden, Barbara Binder, and Bruce Kadden. *Teaching Mitzvot: Concepts, Values, and Activities.* Rev. ed. Denver, CO: A.R.E. Publishing, 2003.

Rosner, Fred. "Animal Experimentation." In *Modern Medicine and Jewish Ethics.* Hoboken, NJ: KTAV Publishing House, Inc. and New York: Yeshiva University Press, 1991.

Isaacs, Ronald. *Animals in Jewish Thought and Tradition.* Northvale, NJ: Jason Aronson Inc., forthcoming.

Kalechovsky, Roberta. *Vegetarian Judaism: A Guide for Everyone.* Marblehead, MA: Micah Publications, Inc., 1998.

Klagsbrun, Francine. *Voices of Wisdom.* New York: Pantheon Books, 1980, pp. 457-461.

LaFollette, Hugh, and Niall Shanks. *Brute Science: Dilemmas of Animal Experimentation.* London: Routledge, 1996.

Shochet, Elijah Judah. *Animal Life in Jewish Tradition: Attitudes and Relationships.* New York: KTAV Publishing House, Inc., 1984.

Schwartz, Earl, and Barry D. Cytron. *Who Renews Creation.* New York: United Synagogue of Conservative Judaism, Department of Youth Activities, 1995.

Schwartz, Richard H. *Judaism and Vegetarianism.* New York: Lantern Books, 2001.

Sequoia, Anna. *67 Ways to Save the Animals.* New York: Harper Perennial, 1990.

Stein, David E. *A Garden of Choice Fruits: 200 Classic Jewish Quotes on Human Beings and the Environment.* Wyncote, PA: Shomrei Adamah, 1991.

Toperoff, Shlomo Pesach. *The Animal Kingdom in Jewish Thought.* Northvale, NJ: Jason Aronson, 1995.

Williams, Jeanne, ed. *Animal Rights and Welfare, The Reference Shelf,* Vol. 63, No. 4. New York: The H.W. Wilson Company, 1991.

Wise, Steven M. *Rattling the Cage: Toward Legal Rights for Animals.* Cambridge, MA: Perseus Books, 2000.

Web Sites

Many of these web sites have clear positions to promote and publicize. Some are supportive of animal research, others are adamantly opposed to it. By surfing through several of the sites, one can get a sense of the range of perspectives, plus a feeling for some of the emotion behind the words.

American Anti-Vivisection Society: www.aavs.org

A non-profit animal advocacy and educational organization dedicated to ending experimentation on animals in research, testing, and education.

CHAI (Concern for Helping Animals in Israel): www.chaionline.org

Assists the Israeli animal protection community in their efforts to improve the condition and treatment of Israel's animals.

Foundation for Bio-Medical Research: www.fbresearch.org

Dedicated to improving human and animal health by promoting public understanding and support for the humane and responsible use of animals in medical and scientific research.

Judaism 101— Treatment of Animals: www.jewfaq.org/animals.htm

An overview of the Jewish view of animal treatment.

Physicians Committee for Responsible Medicine: www.pcrm.org

Promotes preventive medicine, conducts clinical research, and encourages higher standards for ethics and effectiveness in research.

The Schwartz Collection on Judaism, Vegetarianism, and Animal Rights: schwartz.enviroweb.org

A large collection of articles, FAQs, divrei Torah, *and book reviews relating to Judaism and vegetarianism.*

Films:

While the following films may contain specific sections that are valuable for illustrating certain aspects of the topic of animal experimentation, it may not be appropriate for students to view the entire film. Prescreening is strongly advised.

Chicken Run (2000, 84 minutes, rated G)

A claymation adventure about chickens attempting to escape from the cruelty of a sinister chicken farm. Available from video stores.

Project X (1987, 107 minutes, rated PG)

A young inductee into the military is given the task of looking after chimpanzees used in the mysterious "Project X" experiment. Soon he begins to suspect that there is more to the secret project than he is being told. Available from video stores.

The Secret of NIMH (1998, 149 minutes, rated G)

An animated film in which the characters include rats who were freed from a National Institute of Mental Health testing lab, but only after being subjected to mind altering experiments. Available from video stores.

Tools for Research: Questions about Animal Rights (1983, 37 minutes, unrated)

A classic animal rights documentary that raises important questions about the use of animals in laboratories. Available from Bullfrog Films, www.bullfrogfilms.com.

CHAPTER 10

CONSUMERISM: HOW MUCH IS TOO MUCH?

OVERVIEW

Consumerism presents diverse and troubling ethical quandaries. Arguably, consumerism affects more vast and critical realms than other topics dealt with in this book. In exploring the issues, the urgency of the challenges becomes clear. Specifically, our planet — along with our very humanity — is at stake with the consumption choices we make. Consumerism confronts us with spiritual questions, as well. This chapter offers us opportunities to scrutinize our priorities and evaluate what really is important in the end.

A particular wrinkle to this topic is this: If we benefit personally from the consumer practices of our culture; if our standard of living is high compared to the rest of the world, consumption offenses may be the easiest ethical breaches to ignore.

Jewish Perspectives

Regarding Wealth

Judaism is not a religion of denial. We do not applaud poverty. While some religious traditions embrace austerity and asceticism, we do not seek such lifestyles. Judaism teaches that we must accept that suffering is a part of life. However, aside from Yom Kippur and a few other religious observances throughout the year, we do not purposefully invite affliction upon ourselves. Yechiel ben Yekutiel, a thirteenth century Italian scholar and physician, succinctly sums up essential notions of a Jewish view of wealth:

> Wealth that comes to us with justice, trust, and uprightness is one of the desirable eminences . . . For when we have wealth, we can sustain ourselves without suffering, without

great effort, and without great deliberation in the areas of livelihood, economy, and welfare (*Sefer Ma'alot Ha-middot*, pp. 248-249, see Text Study #8A below).

At the other extreme are extravagance and conspicuous consumption. Just as Judaism rejects denial and poverty, it scorns indulgence and wastefulness. Beginning with the Bible, we are warned not to distort the value of money and wealth. In the story of the golden calf (Exodus 32), gold becomes god. That is, people transform gold into an idol, worshiping it. This episode causes the shattering of spiritual values — Moses smashes the tablets that contain God's commandments.

As part of Moses' final address to the Israelite people, he describes how Yeshurun (another name for the Israelites) "grew fat and kicked" (Deuteronomy 32:15). "Growing fat" suggests overindulgence. The phrase implies inflated prosperity, wealth, and success. "Kicking" suggests arrogance and rebellion. Throughout the Prophets and Writings, we discover additional warnings regarding the treacheries of wealth (see Text Study #6a, #7a, #8a, and #8b below). Variations on these warnings continue in Jewish literature through the centuries.

Now, if Judaism is not a religion of denial, and it is not a religion of indulgence, what sort of lifestyle does Judaism embrace?

Moderation and modesty characterize the ideal way of life. Satisfaction with what one has, resisting envy and jealousy, are essential ingredients for contentment and spiritual equilibrium. "Who is rich?" asks Ben Zoma. "One who is happy with what one has" (*Pirke Avot* 4:1, Text Study #8c below).

So far, we have outlined some general parameters regarding Jewish views of wealth. These parameters provide a helpful backdrop to our topic. Besides potential rebelliousness and arrogance ("growing fat and kicking"), what additional challenges to Jewish ethical living do consumer excesses raise? We can separate the issues into these categories: the environment, social justice, quality of life concerns, and spiritual values.

Environment

As we will discuss in some detail in the "General Perspectives" section below, human consumption habits, particularly in Western countries, are a terrible strain on our planet. Two Jewish ideas in particular will help us flesh out an ethical approach to our responsibilities to protect the environment.

The first idea is balancing human dominion on earth with our role as the planet's caretakers. The first two chapters of the Bible delineate essentials of our relationship with the environment. On the one hand, we are to "master the earth, and rule the fish of the sea, the birds of the sky, and all the living things that creep on earth" (Genesis 1:28). On the other hand, the very next chapter identifies our role as earth's caretakers. Adam is to till and tend the Garden in which he is placed (Genesis 2:15). Thus, a tension exists between *dominating* the earth, using it however we see fit, and *preserving and protecting* it. In terms of consumerism, if our consumption is overwhelmingly about dominating the earth, rather than tending it, we have allowed the balance to become skewed. Dominating the earth to the point of devastation violates the balanced relationship to the planet that Judaism requires of us.

Consistent with the first idea is the notion of *Bal Tashchit*, commonly translated as "not wasting" or "not destroying" (see "Related Middot and Mitzvot," p. 262). In recent years, excessive consumption has hit epidemic levels. How should Judaism respond? Throughout the ages, Jewish Sages express concern for environmental devastation. As God warns in a *Midrash*, "Make sure you don't ruin or devastate My world. For if

you do, there will be no one after you to fix it" (*Ecclesiastes Rabbah* 7:28, Text Study #2b below).

Judaism also is sensitive to how individual acts affect the common good of the community. One person's (or community's) use of the world's resources will have an impact on the wider population. Rabbi Shimon ben Yochai offers this parable:

> A group of people sat in a boat. One of them took a drill and began making a hole beneath his seat. His companions said to him, "What are you doing?" He replied, "What do you care? Aren't I drilling beneath *my own* seat?" They answered, "But the waters will rise and drown *all of us*!" (*Vayikra Rabbah* 4:6, see also Text Study #2a below)

The point is that one person's actions (one person's consumption) can have widespread repercussions, possibly very serious ones. How one community uses the planet's resources can in fact harm other communities, even to the point of endangering life. Judaism frowns on wasting, destroying, and polluting. While human survival and basic comforts may require drawing on natural resources, Judaism implores us to minimize the damage and consume only what is truly necessary.

Social Justice

Essentially, these are the justice issues: (1) global distribution of wealth is vastly unequal, and (2) impoverished workers toil in often oppressive conditions as they produce goods for consumers in wealthier nations.

What might Judaism say about these concerns? *Tzedakah* or charity (literally, "righteousness") may be a first response. Perhaps we should give money, or better yet, work with authorities to improve work conditions and wages. That would help; that would be a good Jewish thing to do, yes? Another possibility is to research which companies and corporations are the worst offenders and refuse to buy their goods, so that we avoid being co-conspiring oppressors.

Both responses — *tzedakah* and avoiding "ethically-tainted" goods — are consistent with good Jewish values. However, these responses address primarily the second difficulty, regarding worker conditions and wages. What about the first concern, that global distribution of wealth is vastly unequal? That question is a little trickier.

What makes it tricky is that Judaism does not teach that everyone's income and lifestyle should be completely equal. Even if perfect equality *should* be the ideal, how can we insist on ways of being that are unrealistic for human societies as we know them? Still, we need to object to certain rationalizations for inequality. For example, the Libertarian notion of "I'll mind my business, and you mind your own" is not a Jewish value. Individuals do not live in isolation. Our actions do affect one another. Our lifestyle choices must not cause others to suffer or "drown" (see the text quoted in the "Environment" section above). (For more on Libertarianism, see Text Study #3A and #3B below.)

From a Jewish perspective, what is the problem with the huge gaps that exist between the "haves" and the "have-nots" of the world (or those who have much less)? One way of looking at it begins with the *mitzvah V'ahavta L'rayacha Kamocha (*loving one's fellow person as oneself), a commandment many Jewish Sages call most important. The Rabbis understood the command as including both love and honor (*Avot d'Rabbi Natan*, 26).

Consider these statistics: Large populations across the globe live in poverty while small minorities enjoy immense wealth. The U.S.A., with only 6 percent of the world's population, consumes 30 percent of its resources. Twenty percent of the world's population consumes over 70 percent of its material resources and owns over 80 percent of its wealth.[1]

Such statistics challenge our commitment to *V'ahavta L'rayacha Kamocha*. Can privileged minorities honestly claim to love and honor their fellow human beings when they consume quantities so far beyond what might be considered a fair share? Or, would we call such a claim arrogance? If it is arrogance, then we must consider this: Those who feel they live in the shadow of arrogance likely do not feel "loved and honored." Rather, such global inequality is a humiliation. If we love others as ourselves, we honor them. We conduct our lives so as to preserve, as much as possible, the dignity of others around the globe.

In sum, the Jewish objection to excessive consumption is not that everyone must be forced to be perfectly equal. The objection has more to do with the problem — that the way some consume puts others in a position of shame and dishonor. One possible appropriate Jewish response to global inequality is this: We must share space and resources so that others have more opportunity, better health, a living wage, and a cleaner, safer environment. And to do so, *we curb our own consumer appetites.*

Quality of Life Concerns

With excessive consumerism, pursuit of wealth and material goods can displace other important individual, familial, and societal values. On the one hand, our Sages point out that "Where there is no bread, there is no Torah" (*Pirke Avot* 3:21). That is, without basic sustenance, we will be unable to embrace other important values. On the other hand, the Sages do not suggest that "Where there is no caviar, there is no Torah." To insist on caviar creates a lopsided equation. Insisting on caviar — that is, insisting on earning the kind of money that will afford luxuries — typically means little time or energy left for much else. High ambitions for financial achievement require elevating wealth accumulation to a top priority. Doing so usually requires serious sacrifices in other areas of life. Such sacrifices might include time for learning, worship, exercise, and personal growth, and time with family and for community involvement.

---

[1] "Enough: Anticonsumerism Campaign," http://enough.enviroweb.org/enough02.htm.

Truly, we must be grateful for daily sustenance. Furthermore, Judaism recognizes the importance of work and earning a living: "The Eternal will bless you in all the work of your hands" (Deuteronomy 2:7) . . . "No blessing rests on persons except by the work of their hands" (*Tosefta Brachot* 7,8). But even as we direct energy toward meeting basic needs, we must strive for balance in our lives. We must leave time for Torah, make time for study and personal growth, for family and friends, and for community events and concerns.

Spiritual Values/Wealth Belongs To God

In the first paragraphs of this section, we touched on Jewish views of wealth. From that discussion, we could conclude that a spiritually centered lifestyle embraces the values of modesty, moderation, and contentedness. In contrast, greed, envy, indulgence, and excessiveness corrupt spiritual well-being.

On a practical level, we choose what and how much to consume. Since our choices very much affect the planet and our global community, we must strive to be responsible and respectful. But any freedom we seem to have should not delude us about our role in the world. On a less tangible level, our consumer attitudes reflect our relationship with God.

Previously, we considered the hazards of wealth, the potential arrogance in consuming quantities beyond what might be considered a fair share. Now, we question whether excessive consumption reflects not only arrogance toward people who have less, but toward God, as well. "Yeshurun grew fat, and kicked" (Deuteronomy 32:15) is an expression of contempt and rebellion toward God.

Mastering the traits of modesty, moderation, and contentedness is a challenge! Our culture links happiness with materialism, ownership, and accumulation. It is all too easy to ignore God's role in the world, to lose the sense that something exists beyond ourselves, beyond our needs and desires. Attachment to material achievement can lead to alienation from what is holy and meaningful in the world. It can lead to worshiping entitlement rather than God.

Commonly, people believe that if they work for something, they deserve what they gain. However, awareness of God leads to the understanding that *all wealth belongs to God*. What we own is simply a loan from God: "Riches and honor are Yours [God] to dispense; You have dominion over all . . . All things come from You . . . " (I Chronicles 29:12, 14). "Give God what is God's, for both you and whatever is yours belong to God" (*Pirke Avot* 3:8).

General Perspectives
Regarding Wealth

To some extent, our approach to money reflects philosophical and practical ideas of which we are fully aware. But as we will see, we are not likely aware of all factors influencing our relationship with money.

Here is an example of how one individual might describe his/her views on wealth:

> "It is important to me that I can support myself and my family. I want to have enough to live on, plus some extra for special items, emergencies, travel, and charity. I also want to be able to save money for my children's college education and for retirement. I want to be comfortable, but I don't want money to control my life."

Sounds reasonable enough. Such a philosophy doesn't seem unusual for someone living in America or Canada today. Yet, is this person *fully* aware of how money functions in his/her life? Several phrases are vague and open-ended. Specifically, what are the rational limits for this individual's desires, ambitions, and possessions? Someone in our culture who lives modestly *or* lavishly might make these comments:

- I want some extra [money] for special items.

- I want to be comfortable.

- I don't want money to control my life.

However, such comments can mean vastly different things. For instance, is the "special item" a 100 percent wool blanket for extra warmth on winter nights? Or is it a luxury car? Does "being comfortable" require a 1500 square foot home for a family or a 3500 square foot home? Does resistance to "money controlling my life" mean I will leave a good paying job in which I often feel miserable and take a serious pay cut for a new, less stressful job? That is, would I make a change that would still allow me to make ends meet, but would force me to live much more frugally?

Research shows that attitudes toward money reflect more than philosophy or moral intentions. Cultural conditioning — including media, advertising, and social expectations — is a significant factor influencing human striving for affluence. Also at work are primal motivations that drive competitiveness. Concern about relative position in the social hierarchy is a key element of this competitiveness. Even biology seems involved in our efforts to achieve, purchase, and accumulate. For instance, in males, serotonin and testosterone become elevated with certain successes. Elevated concentrations of testosterone facilitate behaviors that help achieve and maintain high status.

Morally sensitive communities, Judaism included, warn of dangers associated with wealth. Problematic traits include envy, jealousy, greed, anxiety, selfishness, and stinginess. Still, concentrating on personal traits will not necessarily cure a focus on money. Typically, problems of excessive consumption are not solved by labeling indulgent spenders unethical, by accusing them of being selfish and greedy.

Clearly, avoiding excessiveness requires us to examine our values and strive for moral self-discipline. However, for a responsible and healthy relationship to money, we must also be aware of forces that exist under the surface. To control money, rather than have it control us, communities must address the influences of cultural conditioning and increase understanding of human nature.

Environment

The aspiration to hone moral attributes may or may not convince typical consumers to change their consumption habits. In contrast, the impact of consumer wealth on the environment raises urgent and concrete concerns that may be more difficult to ignore. The rate at which human beings are depleting the world's natural resources is alarming. Pollution and other environmental destructions are endangering the health of our planet and its creatures.

"Global demand for many key materials is growing at an unsustainable rate," writes Michael T. Klare in *Resource Wars*. An increase in world population is one factor. But equally important is "the spread of industrialization to more and more areas of the globe." A steady worldwide increase in personal wealth is producing "an insatiable appetite for energy, private automobiles, building materials, household appliances, and other resource-intensive commodities . . ."[2]

Scholars, researchers, ecologists, politicians, and grassroots activists are sounding warnings about unrestrained resource consumption. One potentially catastrophic outcome for the global environment is irreversible damage to the earth's capacity to sustain life. Between 1970 and 1995, the earth lost nearly one-third of its available natural wealth. Already, many species have disappeared. More are destined to do so, too. In 1998, the World Wildlife Fund reported "a significant decline in the availability or quality of many critical resources, including forest cover, marine fisheries, freshwater systems, and fossil fuels . . ."[3]

An anticonsumerism campaign warns that current trends in consumption will eventually lead to collapse, "sudden, uncontrolled decline

---

[2]Michael T. Klare, *Resource Wars*, 15, also Text Study #1c.

[3]This information comes from "Population Growth, Resource Consumption, and a Sustainable World," a statement by the Royal Society and the National Academy of Sciences, 1992, and from Michael T. Klare, *Resource Wars*, 18. See also, Text Study #1d and #2e.

in population and output" and "environmental breakdown." Avoiding such a catastrophe will require a combination of strategies:

- Limiting material production

- Limiting population

- Technologies for increasing efficiency of resource use

- Decreasing pollution

- Controlling erosion

- Increasing land yields[4]

Social Justice

In "Jewish Perspectives: Social Justice" above, we touched on these troublesome challenges: (1) the inequality of global distribution of wealth, and (2) oppressive work conditions for impoverished laborers.

How bad, really, are these injustices? Readings in the "Text Study" section below present a sample of findings regarding distribution of wealth, use of natural resources, and labor-related issues (see Text Study #3b, #3c, #4b, #5b, #5c below). In essence, the citizens of wealthy (industrial) nations (such as the U.S.A.) consume huge amounts in comparison to other citizens around the globe. For their numbers, wealthy nations are responsible for disproportionate amounts of pollution. Regarding disparity of income, the wage gap is enormous between First World and Third World citizens. Two billion workers earn less than two American dollars a day (Text Study #5b below). Low wages and inadequate and unhealthful working conditions plague workers in many poorer countries. For those on the "losing" side of the gap between the haves and the have-nots, the injustices are very real.

For many living in wealthy nations, the injustices may seem far away. Even so, increasing numbers of activists, scholars, and public leaders

warn that concerns about injustices go beyond morality and unfairness. Not addressing economic injustices is extremely unwise. Specifically, the have-nots and their leaders may blame a growing globalization gap for their own economic hardships, joblessness, hunger, and environmental devastation. Escalating resentment has the potential to ignite dangerous conflicts and crises around the world. With declining global stability, insecurity, both on a national and personal level, increases (see Text Study #4c and #5d below).

Yes, ignoring injustices may be unwise. But wisdom aside, do we have a moral responsibility to address economic injustices? We explored a few possible Jewish responses to that question (see "Jewish Perspectives: Social Justice"). Now, from a more general perspective, we look at other ways people may view their responsibilities.

On one side of the responsibility spectrum is Libertarianism. As we mentioned in the "Jewish Perspectives" section above, Libertarians hold that people have a right to make their own decisions, to live the way they choose. Thus, a Libertarian might say:

"If I want to spend my money in extravagant ways, that's my business. True, the whole world may not be able to spend the way I do, but I don't have to assume personal responsibility for that."

On the same side of the spectrum, we could add what we'll call the "Philosophy of Entitlement." The gist of such a philosophy is this:

"If I earned this money (or inherited it), I have a right to spend it the way I want. I'm *entitled* to what I own and what I may choose to buy (or consume)."

Libertarianism and the "Philosophy of Entitlement" are not consistent with cherished Jewish values. (For more on Libertarianism, see Text Study #3A and #3B below.)

On the other side of the responsibility spec-

---

[4]"Enough: Anticonsumerism Campaign," http://enough.enviroweb.org/enough07.htm. See also, Text Study #2f.

trum are individuals who seek to replace what they view as reckless consumerist trends with more responsible alternatives. One consumer activist group describes these options:

- Green Consumerism: This occurs when people purchase goods or participate in services that attempt to replace existing ones with something designed to be "friendlier" and less damaging to ecosystems and natural planetary resources.

- Ethical Consumerism: Going beyond green consumerism, this approach considers a variety of wider issues than just a product's green credentials. For instance, it might look at whether the manufacturer invests in the arms trade or has supported oppressive regimes. Through a comprehensive monitoring of the behavior of modern businesses, ethical consumerism aims to encourage trade to be as responsible as possible within the current economic system.

- Anticonsumerism: This approach challenges many assumptions about what we need in contemporary society. Taking the view that rich nations of the world are fundamentally damaging the planet and themselves in the pursuit of material acquisition, it raises the question, "How much is enough?" Rather than just buying green or ethically produced goods, anticonsumerism advocates different ways of living, trading, and working. The goal is to "live more lightly" on the earth and be less dependent on buying things to feel good about ourselves.[5]

Quality of Life Concerns

An emphasis on consumerism raises quality of

life issues. In essence, critics of consumerism culture make this claim: When pursuit of material things becomes a priority, other values suffer.

Jeremy Brecher and Tim Costello, authors of *Global Village or Global Pillage* argue: "When public policy and social practice seek solely to maximize private profit in the market, they slight other values of great significance."[6] These are some values that may get short-shrifted[7]:

- Democratic decision making

- Environmental protection

- Social caring

- Equality

- Human solidarity

- Community stability

- Individual and family security

- Long-term public and private planning and investment

- Dignity in the work process

- Goods and services consumed collectively

- Cultural diversity

We pay a heavy price for consumption excesses. Robert H. Frank, in *Luxury Fever,*[8] alerts us to problems of rising consumer debt and bankruptcy claims. He discusses the diminishing quality of our work environments. For instance, workers have fewer days off (i.e., more work stress) and operate in smaller work spaces. Workers often must deal with frustrating commuter challenges, such as traveling long distances, traffic congestion, and fewer and smaller parking spaces at their place of employment. Those who work long hours have less time with family and friends.

Research from 1991 reports that employed Americans spent 163 hours more per year on the

[5]These definitions are adapted from "Enough: Anticonsumerism Campaign," http://enough.enviroweb.org/enough01.htm.

[6]*Global Village or Global Pillage: Economic Reconstruction from the Bottom Up,* 72.

[7]Ibid., 72.

[8]*Luxury Fever,* "The Price of Luxury," 45–63.

job than they did in 1969.[9] American parents spent 40 percent less time with their children than they did in 1965.[10] The average working American spent nine hours per week behind the wheel.[11]

Sacrifices take place in the public sphere, as well. When we priortize resources for conspicuous consumption, we have less available to direct toward such things as the following:[12]

- Clean drinking water

- Air quality standards

- Safe agricultural regulations

- Better pay for public school teachers

- Bridge and highway maintenance

- Drug treatment and prevention programs

Shifting Values

We concluded our discussion of the "Jewish Perspectives" by looking at spiritual values. Similarly, from a general perspective, societies must scrutinize their values. How do consumerism patterns need to shift? How much is *too much*? Where do we begin in addressing inequitable use of world resources, environmental devastation, economic injustices, and the distortion of personal and societal priorities?

We might say that positive change begins with each individual. Thus, we could offer the following suggestions:

- Educate yourself about the impact on workers and the energy resources that go into the manufacture of items you want to purchase. As much as possible, avoid buying unethically produced items.

- Besides educating yourself, educate others.

- Acquire only items built to last.

- Buy things only because you want or need them, never because they are cheap.

- Do not own what you rarely use.

- Consume the least processed foods you can find.

- Avoid foods and other products with wasteful packaging.

- Learn to control desire (i.e., recognize "those first consumption stirrings so as to cut them off before they gain a full head of steam.")[13]

- Avoid "retail therapy" (i.e., "consuming as a way to fight the blues, to savor a happy moment, to reward [yourself], to enhance self-esteem, or to escape from boredom.")[14]

- For holidays and other celebrations, impose limits and guidelines for gift giving and parties.

- Set priorities so that pursuing wealth does not displace other important values. (You even may want to consider making a change that means earning less, but having better control of your time and your life.)[15]

Robert Muller, Assistant Secretary-General of the United Nations in the early 1990s, said, "The single most important contribution any of us can make to the planet is a return to frugality." Muller's statement, along with the other suggestions, could be placed under the heading "Voluntary Simplicity." The ideas seem reasonable as a starting point for shifting values. However, to change existing patterns of consumption, voluntary simplicity has serious limits. Robert H. Frank explains:

---

[9]Juliet Schor, *The Overworked American*, 29.

[10]William R. Mattox, Jr., "The Parent Trap," *Policy Review*, no. 55, Winter 1991, 6.

[11]Alan Thein Durning, *How Much Is Too Much? The Consumer Society and the Future of the Earth,* New York: W.W. Norton & Co., Inc., 1992, 84.

[12]*Luxury Fever,* "The Price of Luxury," 45-63.

[13]Juliet B. Schor, *The Overspent American*, 146.

[14]Ibid., 158.

[15]Ibid., 163.

I must not overstate the difficulties associated with voluntary simplicity. Our imbalanced consumption patterns no doubt stem in part from the fact that we are poorly informed, that we fail to anticipate how we will adapt to different experiences, and that we lack the patience and willpower to execute even our well-considered consumption plans. Voluntary simplicity can help mitigate all these problems.

Yet our consumption imbalance would persist even if we were perfectly informed, rational decision makers with limitless patience and willpower. The problem is that many important rewards in life depend on how much we spend relative to others. If we all cut back, we do better; but someone who cuts back unilaterally often does much worse . . . Individual action, by itself, simply won't be enough.[16]

While the "little picture" (voluntary simplicity) has its place, the "big picture" still looms. A theme throughout this Overview has been the importance of addressing wide-ranging factors in scaling back runaway consumer trends. Any proposed agenda for change must seek to improve the lives of the great majority of the world's people over the long run. Besides our personal efforts, science and technology play a crucial role. Furthermore, we urgently need global policies that will do the following:[17]

- Promote responsible economic development throughout the world.

- Help stabilize world population.

- Integrate the interests of people in all parts of the world.

- Provide handles for action at a variety of levels.

- Make it easier, not harder, to protect the environment and preserve natural resources.

---

[16]*Luxury Fever*, 193.

Summary of the Overview

The statements below summarize main points about consumerism as discussed in the Overview.

1. Well-being for individuals and society does not depend on increasing levels of consumption.

2. Current consumption trends are causing environmental devastation.

3. Current consumption trends are causing alarming rates of natural resource depletion.

4. Consumer patterns around the globe reveal deep disparities of wealth and consumption in richer versus poorer populations.

5. The consumer demands of richer populations contribute to economic injustices and instances of worker exploitation in impoverished societies.

6. A focus on money distorts personal and communal priorities.

7. A focus on money distorts spiritual values. God is the source of wealth, and everything belongs to God.

SCENARIOS: COMPARING TYPES OF CONSUMERS

How do we compare the consumer choices people make? Should we pronounce judgments, or should we refrain from doing so? Do we suggest that certain lifestyles are modest and ethical, whereas others are excessively consumerist and overly indulgent? Undoubtedly, a complex combination of factors influences consumer decisions.

Below are two imaginary scenarios, set in two different communities, which illustrate the chal-

---

[17]Some of these policy ideas are adapted from *Global Village or Global Pillage*, 170.

lenging ethical questions that have concerned Jews and non-Jews through the ages. They are intended to raise questions and spark discussion. Read each scenario to or with your students, and engage them in small or large group discussions. Use the "Focus the Discussion" section below to help identify the important issues and facilitate these discussions. Note that additional questions and activities relating to these scenarios are found in the "Stories: Understanding through Listening" section below (pp. 264-265).

Following the discussions, have students continue on to the "Text Study" section to see what Jewish and other sources have to say on the subject. Finally, you may wish to have students discuss the scenarios a second time, to see if their views have changed.

Scenario 1: Long Ago and/or Far Away (from Wealthy Suburban America)

Members of the BenDor household include a father and mother, four sons, and a grandmother and her sister — eight people altogether. Originally, the BenDor home had two bedrooms — one for the parents and one for the sons, a bathroom, and a kitchen/dining area. When the grandmother and her sister moved in, the family built on another small bedroom for the two women to share. The home, at 1400 square feet, is now one of the largest in the village.

Walking is the family's main mode of transportation. In addition, the father helps his brother maintain two work horses, and thus can borrow them and a wagon now and then.

The family barely makes ends meet. There are days when there doesn't seem to be enough to eat. While everyone in the BenDor family contributes however they can toward the family income, they wish they had a little more. With a bigger financial cushion, they would have enough stocks of food, wood for the stove, animals of their own, and money to pay for the education of their sons.

Scenario 2: In a Wealthy American Suburban Community

The Bender household includes a father and mother, two sons, and two golden retrievers — four people and two dogs altogether. Originally, their 1700 square foot ranch home had three bedrooms — one for the parents and one for each son, two bathrooms, an eat-in kitchen, a formal dining room, and a living room.

Since the family had been doing well financially and since the home was beginning to feel a bit cramped, the family decided to remodel. A second and third story to their home added two more bedrooms, two offices, a recreation room, a media entertainment center, and three more bathrooms. The Benders also remodeled the master bedroom and kitchen, and landscaped the backyard anew, adding a swimming pool and large hot tub. The home is now 3600 square feet. Before the remodeling, their home was one of the smaller ones in the neighborhood. Now, it is at least as large as, if not larger than, most of the homes.

For transportation, the family has three cars (though the boys do not drive yet) — a van, a sedan, and a sports car. In addition, the family owns four mountain bikes and two motorized scooters.

The Bender parents work hard and have very little leisure time. With all the pressures they are under, they can barely get involved in their sons' activities, much less in community events and issues at large.

While the parents' salaries are decent, expenses are high. Both sons currently attend private schools, and the family needs to save for their college educations. Black-tie affairs for each boy's Bar Mitzvah required enormous outlays of cash. Besides these expenses, the family will make significant purchases in the next few years. The family has acquired lakefront property two hours away. Currently, bulldozers are clearing trees and shrubbery from the land, to make way for the four-bedroom vacation cottage the Benders plan to build. The family also intends to buy a motor boat and a couple of kayaks.

Focus the Discussion

How do we compare the BenDors and the Benders? Do we judge them? Do we applaud the BenDor's living style as being modest and ethical? Conversely, do we consider the Bender's way of life to be excessively consumerist and overly indulgent?

The problem with judging too harshly is this: If social and cultural circumstances were reversed, quite likely the standard of living of the families would be reversed, as well. That is, the BenDor's living standards might resemble those of wealthy suburbanites, and the Benders might live more modestly, in a smaller home with fewer possessions.

The point is that an individual's cultural and social environment will play a significant role in determining his/her level of consumerism. Undoubtedly, a complex combination of factors influence consumer decisions. Simply focusing on the behaviors of individual consumers is an insufficient strategy for modifying widespread excessive consumption habits.

Ecologists and humanitarians urge human beings to "live lightly on the earth." For this ideal to become reality requires a multi-faceted effort. In short, human beings will need to:

- question moral behavior,

- live modestly,

- reevaluate personal and communal priorities,

- commit to sound and just global policies.

TEXT STUDY

Consumerism raises many difficult questions regarding our attitudes toward wealth, the environment, social justice, and quality of life concerns. Jewish and other textual sources provide many answers, but these answers often highlight tensions between seemingly opposing considerations. The chart on the next page poses the questions and offers two opposing points of view. Text sources supporting each of these points of view follow below.

1. **To what extent are human beings entitled to use of the world's resources?**

On the One Hand:

The world has abundant riches for humans to use and enjoy.

A. God blessed them and God said to them, "Be fertile and increase, fill the earth and subdue it! Have dominion over the fish of the sea, the birds of the sky, and all the living things that crawl about the earth" (Genesis 1:28).

B. You have given [humans] dominion over the works of Your hands; You have put all things under their feet . . . (Psalms 8:7).

C. . . . If destruction is necessary for a higher and more worthy aim, then it ceases to be destruction and itself becomes wise creating. [For example] cutting down a fruit tree which is doing harm to other more valuable plants, [and] burning a vessel when there is a scarcity of wood in order to protect one's weakened self from catching cold . . . (Samson Raphael Hirsch, *Horeb: A Philosophy of Jewish Laws and Observance*, p. 281).

On the Other Hand:

Our consumption practices are contributing to alarming rates of depletion of the earth's resources.

a. "And have dominion over the fish of the ocean" (Genesis 1:28). Rabbi Chanina said: "Humanity will rule over if they deserve to; if they do not deserve to, then they will go under" (*Genesis Rabbah* 8:12).

b. Do not believe that all things exist for the sake of humanity. On the contrary, one must believe that . . . everything

Consumerism: How Much Is Too Much? Questions to Consider

The Question	On the One Hand	On the Other Hand
1. To what extent are human beings entitled to use of the world's resources? (see p. 253)	The world has abundant riches for humans to use and enjoy.	Our consumption practices are contributing to alarming rates of depletion of the earth's resources.
2. Must we take personal responsibility for the environmental repercussions of consumer choices? (see p. 255)	We must live for today. Let politicians, scientists, and technology experts worry about clean and efficient production.	Our level of production and consumption exacerbates — often to dangerous degrees — pollution and other environmental damage.
3. How should we respond to global inequalities in wealth? (see p. 256)	If I work hard (or legitimately inherit what my loved ones worked hard for), I am entitled to my wealth.	Regardless of how hard a particular individual works, global distribution of wealth is indefensibly unequal.
4. What are our responsibilities to workers around the globe? (see p. 257)	In capitalist democracies (like America) everyone has opportunities to prosper. Don't deny me, and I won't deny you.	In feeding consumption appetites, wealthy industrialized nations are responsible for exploiting poor workers across the globe.
5. What economic benefits do individuals and societies derive from consumption? (see p. 258)	Our consumption creates needed jobs for poor people.	Serving the consumption of wealthy nations is not always the best way for developing nations to improve their lot.
6. How might money factor into my personal happiness and well-being? (see p. 259)	Spending money and acquiring possessions give me pleasure.	Beyond a moderate level, more consumption does not make for increased well-being.
7. What value should I attach to wealth? (see p. 260)	Wealth and owning certain things will make me feel good about myself.	Dedication to materialism and financial competitiveness divert attention away from more important values, both individual and societal.
8. How much is reasonable for us to consume? (see p. 261)	Judaism is not a religion of denial.	Materialism and indulgent consumption alienate us from essential Jewish/spiritual qualities.

exists for its own sake and not for anything or anyone else (Maimonides, *Guide of the Perplexed* 3:14).

c. See also the two passages from Michael T. Klare's *Resource Wars*, cited in the "General Perspectives" section of the Overview, pp. 246-251.

Probing: Ideas and Issues

What guidance can we glean from these texts regarding ethical use of the world's natural resources? What restrictions should Jews impose upon themselves regarding use of earth's resources? Should the rate of depletion of natural resources alarm us?

2. **Must we take personal responsibility for the environmental repercussions of consumer choices?**

On the One Hand:

We must live for today. Let politicians, scientists, and technology experts worry about clean and efficient production.

Jewish sources would not advocate this position. We must reach to find any published opinion favoring such a view.

A. "I have affixed to me the dirt and dust of countless ages. Who am I to disturb history?" (Bob Herbert, quoting Pig-Pen, the filthy and proud-of-it character from the "Peanuts" cartoon, in "Fouling Our Own Nest" Op-Ed, *The New York Times*, July 4, 2002, p. A).

B. We've been trashing, soiling, even destroying the wonders of nature for countless ages . . . Oh, the skies may once have been clear and the waters sparkling and clean. But you can't have that and progress, too. Can you? (Bob Herbert, making a sarcastic remark, in "Fouling Our Own Nest" Op-Ed, *The New York Times*, July 4, 2002, p. A).

On the Other Hand:

Our level of production and consumption exacerbates — often to dangerous degrees — pollution and other environmental damage.

a. See the Overview, p. 244, for Rabbi Shimon ben Yochai's parable on how individual actions make an impact on the greater community.

b. Upon creating the first human being, God took him around the Garden of Eden . . . saying: "Look at my creations! See how beautiful and perfect they are? I created everything for you. Make sure you don't ruin or devastate My world. For if you do, there will be no one after you to fix it" (*Ecclesiastes Rabbah* 7:28).

c. Destruction [includes] making use of more things and more valuable things when fewer and less valuable ones would suffice; or if this aim is not really worth the means expended for its attainment. [For example] kindling something which is still fit for other purposes for the sake of light; . . . wearing down something more than is necessary . . . consuming more than is necessary . . . (Samson Raphael Hirsch, *Horeb: A Philosophy of Jewish Laws and Observance*, p. 281).

d. The use of property for the creation of wealth, in ways which disturb or damage the property, health, or aesthetic pleasure of others, creates ethical and economical problems. This is true even where legal possession is undisputed and the actions are performed solely within the confines of the private domain of the user (Meir Tamari, *In the Marketplace: Jewish Business Ethics*, p. 129, drawing on *Mishnah, Baba Batra* 2:7 and 2:9).

e. Unrestrained resource consumption for energy production and other uses, especially if the developing world strives to achieve living standards based on the same levels of consumption as the developed world, could lead to catastrophic outcomes for the global environment . . . Some of the environmental changes may produce irreversible damage to the earth's capacity to sustain life. Many species have already disappeared, and many more are destined to do so ("Population Growth, Resource Consumption, and a Sustainable World," statement by the Royal Society and the National Academy of Sciences, 1992).

f. If the majority of the world's citizens are also to achieve a consumerist standard of living . . . , then all of the present levels of global pollution and waste are going to more than quadruple . . . No amount of technology would be capable of bringing environmental damage under control if all of the world's citizens were to achieve a standard of living even remotely comparable to that of the consumer class ("Enough: Anticonsumerism Campaign," http://enough.enviroweb.org/enough02.htm).

Probing: Ideas and Issues

What are the problems with the "On the One Hand" position? What are our responsibilities to the environment according to the "On the Other Hand" texts? Do your personal consumption habits reflect the "On the One Hand" or the "On the Other Hand" position?

3. **How should we respond to global inequalities in wealth?**

On the One Hand:

If I work hard (or legitimately inherit what my loved ones worked hard for), I am entitled to my wealth.

The following two passages illustrate the Libertarian position.

A. The Libertarian objects that Tom's unhappiness about Bill's increased consumption simply does not constitute legitimate grounds for curbing Bill's consumption. Tom may be unhappy, but it is nonetheless Tom's responsibility to simply mind his own business. The Libertarian argues that to restrict Bill's consumption because it makes Tom unhappy is essentially no different from telling Bill he can't wear a purple shirt because Tom doesn't like the color purple. Tough luck, Tom! Bill has a *right* to wear a purple shirt, and those who don't like it had just better get used to it (*Luxury Fever*, p. 195-196).

B. I have no right to decide how you should spend your time or your money. I can make that decision for myself, but not for you, my neighbor. I may deplore your choice of lifestyle, and I may talk with you about it provided you are willing to listen to me. But I have no right to use force to change it . . . Where do my rights end? Where yours begin. I may do anything I wish with my own life, liberty, and property without your consent, but I may do nothing with your life, liberty, and property without your consent. If we recognize the principle of [human's] rights, it follows that the individual is sovereign of the domain of [his/her] own life and property, and is sovereign of no other domain (John Hospers, "What Libertarianism Is," in *The Libertarian Alternative,* edited by Tibor R. Machan. Chicago, IL: Nelson-Hall company, 1974, p. 6).

On the Other Hand:

Regardless of how hard a particular individual works, global distribution of wealth is indefensibly unequal.

a. There are factors in the world over and above the right to property and the creation of economic wealth . . . Morally, economic growth of the individual and of society should be limited to the provision of necessities alone, however these may be defined (Meir Tamari, *In the Marketplace: Jewish Business Ethics*, p. 130).

b. The U.S.A. alone, with only six percent of the world's population, consumes 30 percent of its resources . . . What causes global hunger is not a shortage of resources, but the unequal distribution of those resources in favour of the rich . . . 20 percent of the world's population, (in other words its wealthy consumer class), is responsible for over 50 percent of its "greenhouse effect" atmospheric pollutants, 90 percent of its ozone-depleting CFC gases, 96 percent of its radioactive waste . . . and so on ("Enough: Anticonsumerism Campaign," http://enough.enviroweb.org/enough02.htm).

c. If you are a member of an average American college-grad household, you are richer than 99.9 percent of the human beings who have ever lived. You are stinking rich (David Brooks, *The New York Times Magazine*, June 9, 2002, p. 91).

Probing: Ideas and Issues

Would Judaism support a Libertarian attitude? Explain. What would Meir Tamari (Text #3a above) say about Libertarianism? Do you agree that "global distribution of wealth is indefensibly unequal?" Explain.

4. What are our responsibilities to workers around the globe?

On the One Hand:

In capitalist democracies everyone has opportunities to prosper. Don't deny me, and I won't deny you.

Also see the Libertarian position presented in Text Study #3B above.

A. The environment of abundance accounts for the energy, creativity, and dynamism that marks national life. The lure of plenty, pervading the landscape, encourages risk and adventure (David Brooks, "Why the U.S. Will Always Be Rich," *The New York Times Magazine*, June 9, 2002, p. 91).

On the Other Hand:

In feeding consumption appetites, wealthy industrialized nations are responsible for exploiting poor workers across the globe.

a. Jewish law recognizes that the community, whether seen as neighbors in a courtyard, citizens in a town, or a people in a larger community, has rights which have to be protected against injury from the action of individuals. These express themselves in the communal right to taxation — which, in effect, takes property from individuals to finance communal needs — but also in the right to limit activities of individuals which damage the environment or detract from the community's scenic beauty. These rights are the basis of Jewish zoning laws and of communal action to protect even a non-physical aspect of property rights (Meir Tamari, *In the Marketplace: Jewish Business Ethics*, p. 130).

b. Today, young, mostly female workers in Bangladesh, a Muslim country that is the fourth largest garment producer for the United States market, are paid an average of 1.6 cents for each baseball cap with a Harvard logo that they sew. The caps retail at the Harvard bookstore for $17, which means the garment workers, who often are younger than the Harvard students, are being paid a tenth of 1 percent of the cap's price in the market. Also in Bangladesh, women receive five cents for each $17.99 Disney shirt they sew. Wages like these are not enough to get ahead (Tom Hayden and Charles Kernaghan,

"Pennies an Hour, and No Way Up," *The New York Times*, Op-Ed, July 6, 2002, p. A27).

c. If we choose to continue consuming more than our share of the world's resources, we are placing ourselves in danger. Those who are left without are unlikely to passively tolerate the situation. Conflicts will arise, producing a more policed, more governed, more insecure world. Some argue that this has already begun, and yet few commentators point to correcting these disparities as a solution ("Enough: Anticonsumerism Campaign," http://enough.enviroweb.org/enough11.htm).

Probing: Ideas and Issues

Though some may argue otherwise, let's assume that wealthy nations' consumptive habits compromise the living conditions and environment of poor workers across the globe. To what extent would Judaism suggest we restrict individual freedom for the sake of the well-being of others? What would a Jewish response be to Text #4A above?

5. **What economic benefits do individuals and societies derive from consumption?**

On the One Hand:

Our consumption creates needed jobs for poor people.

A. The value of preventing damage or promoting the ecological welfare of society has to be gauged against the potential benefits to be earned from economic activity. The individual corporation has to consider the ecological costs suffered by the community, or by individuals, as part of its production of goods or services. Given the jobs created, the goods or services provided, and even the tax payments paid by the corporation, society

must weigh these against the cost of, for example, pollution to air, or a lower quality of life (Meir Tamari, *In the Marketplace: Jewish Business Ethics*, p. 130).

B. Some economists argue that even the most exploited and impoverished workers are better off than those who are unemployed or trapped in slave labor (Tom Hayden and Charles Kernaghan, "Pennies an Hour, and No Way Up," *The New York Times*, Op-Ed, July 6, 2002, p. A27).

On the Other Hand:

Serving the consumption of wealthy nations is not always the best way for developing nations to improve their lot.

a. The Eternal is good to all, and God's mercy is upon all God's works" (Psalms 145:9).

b. About two billion of the world's six billion people live on less than $2 (American) a day. More than 60 countries have a lower per capita income now than they did in 1990 (Barbara Crossette, "U.N. Report Says New Democracies Falter," *The New York Times*, July 24, 2002, p. A8).

c. Women in Bangladesh say they could care for their children if their wages rose to 34 cents an hour, two-tenths of 1 percent of the retail price of the Harvard hat (Tom Hayden and Charles Kernaghan, "Pennies an Hour, and No Way Up," *The New York Times*, Op-Ed, July 6, 2002, p. A27).

d. The distribution of [economic] competitiveness is now uneven . . . This pattern raises the disturbing prospect of a "globalization gap" between the winners and the losers . . . Leaders of the losers often blame outsiders or unpopular insiders for economic hardship. Some foment crises to distract domestic attention from joblessness and hunger (Institute for

National Security Studies, 1999, quoted by Michael Klare, *Resource Wars*, p. 24).

e. Refer to Text #5B above. That comment seems open to the claim that consumption in wealthy countries creates needed jobs. However, the commentators immediately add:

> But that argument is not about offering anyone a ladder up, but about which ring of Dante's inferno people in developing nations are consigned to (Tom Hayden and Charles Kernaghan, "Pennies an Hour, and No Way Up," *The New York Times*, Op-Ed, July 6, 2002, p. A27).

Probing: Ideas and Issues

Jews believe the Eternal is good to all, and that God's mercy is upon all God's works. We also believe we are to strive to be like God (*halachta bidrachav*). That is, we must try to be "good to all." What does "being good to all" require of us regarding our responsibilities toward workers around the world?

6. **How might money factor into my personal happiness and well-being?**

On the One Hand:

Spending money and acquiring possessions give me pleasure.

A. The noblest, most creative and fullest life is not to be found by the backwaters of Walden Pond, but in the rushing mainstream of life, in the office parks and the malls and the Times Squares twinkling with lights, screens, and money (David Brooks, "Why the U.S. Will Always Be Rich," *The New York Times Magazine*, June 9, 2002, p. 124).

B. The culture [is] no longer concerned with how to work and achieve, but with how to spend and enjoy (Daniel Bell in a 1970 study called "The Cultural Contradictions of Capitalism," quoted by Patricia Cohen, *The New York Times*, July 7, 2002, section 9, p. 2).

On the Other Hand:

Beyond a moderate level, more consumption does not make for increased well-being.

a. Those who love money never have their fill of money, nor do those who love wealth have their fill of income (Ecclesiastes 5:9).

b. It is characteristic of wealth, that when one has little, one desires more, and when one attains more, one desires double of what already has been acquired, and so on *ad infinitum*. Thus, a *midrash* teaches, "No person leaves this world with even half of his or her desires attained. If one has one hundred, one desires two hundred . . . " (*Ecclesiastes Rabbah* 1:13). Wealth is like a fire: the more wood one adds, the more the flame increases and the fire blazes (Bahya ben Asher, as quoted in *Creating an Ethical Jewish Life*, p. 127).

c. Once one passionately seeks wealth, one discovers that it entails immense efforts of thought and exertion, keeping one awake at night and plagued by responsibilities by day so that even when one has acquired what one desires, one can't sleep properly . . . When people make money, the object of all their strivings, and devote themselves to it with mad ambition and avidity . . . then the love of money becomes for them like a consuming fire, like a wilderness, like death or barrenness that are never sated (Saadiah Gaon, *The Book of Beliefs and Opinions*, Book 10, Chapter 8).

d. When we subordinate other desires to money, we lose our ability to recognize "enough." Those goals and desires that are capable of satisfaction have been co-opted by money, and the desire for money *has no natural limit.* Since it cannot in itself satisfy anything, we can *never* have enough. A number of rich men have acknowledged that they could satisfy all their material needs — and even whims — with a fraction of what they hold, yet are unable to stop trying to make more. Once money is given priority there is no longer any basis for deciding when and where to stop accumulating (*Wealth Addiction,* p. 43).

e. Behavioral scientists find that once a threshold level of affluence is reached, the average level of human well-being in a country is almost completely independent of its stock of material consumption goods (*Luxury Fever,* p. 65).

Probing: Ideas and Issues

From a Jewish perspective, what would make the viewpoints expressed in Texts #6A and #6B problematic? Does wealth contribute to well-being? Explain. When does spending become excessive?

7. What value should I attach to wealth?

On the One Hand:

Wealth and owning certain things will make me feel good about myself.

A. Consumer culture in one sense is "democracy's highest achievement, giving meaning and dignity to people when workplace participation, ethnic solidarity, and even representative democracy have failed" (Patricia Cohen, quoting Gary Cross in "In Defense of Our Wicked, Wicked Ways," *The New York Times,* July 7, 2002, section 9, p. 2).

B. A house may be large or small; as long as the surrounding houses are equally small, it satisfies all social demands for a dwelling. But if a palace rises beside the little house, the little house shrinks into a hut" (Karl Marx as quoted in *Luxury Fever,* p. 137).

C. Compelling evidence [exists] that concern about relative position is a deep-rooted and ineradicable element of human nature (*Luxury Fever,* p. 145).

On the Other Hand:

Dedication to materialism and financial competitiveness divert attention away from more important values, both individual and societal.

a. Don't exhaust yourself trying to make money. You see it and then it's gone. It grows wings and flies away (Proverbs 23:4-5).

b. When told of a man who had acquired great wealth, a Sage replied, "Has he also acquired the days in which to spend it?" (Ibn Gabirol, *Choice of Pearls,* in *Leo Rosten's Treasury of Jewish Quotations* NY: Jewish Publication Society of America and McGraw-Hill Book Company, 1972, p. 536).

c. An across-the-board reduction in the rate of growth in conspicuous consumption would, in time, free up literally trillions of dollars worth of resources annually . . . These resources could be used to support more time with family and friends, more freedom from congestion and pollution, greater autonomy and flexibility in the workplace, and increases in a variety of other forms of inconspicuous consumption that would enhance the quality of our lives (*Luxury Fever,* p. 194).

Probing: Ideas and Issues

What is the relationship between competitiveness and excessive consumption? What benefits might come from shifting our spending away from conspicuous consumption, and toward other values? What values do you think suffer most in our society from an overemphasis on consumption? How would your own life be different if you focused less on accumulating material possessions?

8. **How much is reasonable for us to consume?**

On the One Hand:

Judaism is not a religion of denial.

A. Wealth which comes to us with justice, trust, and uprightness is one of the desirable eminences . . . For when we have wealth we can sustain ourselves without suffering, without great effort, and without great deliberation in the areas of livelihood, economy, and welfare (Yechiel ben Yekutiel, *Sefer Ma'alot Ha-middot*, pp. 248-249).

B. In passing from this world and then confronting ultimate judgment, one will be obliged to explain, among other penetrating questions, why one abstained from enjoying the pleasures and delights of this world (Jerusalem Talmud, *Kiddushin* 4:12, as explained by Reuven Bulka in *Judaism on Pleasure*, p. 4).

C. [O]n balance, it can be safely stated that Judaism rejects the notion of denial for denial's sake, even as it recognizes special situations calling for denial. And those special situations do not negate the general affirmation of the obligation to taste the appealing things of this world (*Judaism on Pleasure*, p. 4).

On the Other Hand:

Materialism and indulgent consumption alienate us from essential Jewish/spiritual qualities.

a. Give me neither poverty nor riches, but provide me with my daily bread, lest being sated, I renounce, saying "Who is the Eternal?" Or, being impoverished, I take to theft and profane the name of my God (Proverbs 30:8-9).

b. Why do you spend money for what is not bread,
Your earnings for what does not satisfy? (Isaiah 55:2).

c. Ben Zoma said: Who is rich? One who is happy with what one has (*Pirke Avot* 4:1).

d. Envy, lust, and pursuit of honor will ruin a person's life (*Pirke Avot* 4:30).

e. [We condemn] the deterioration in the character of the Bar Mitzvah "affair." The extravagant consumption, the conspicuous waste, and the crudity of many of these affairs are rapidly becoming a public Jewish scandal. The lowering of standards as reflected in many Bar Mitzvah celebrations is in direct violation of the teaching of the Torah. The trend toward the abandonment of aesthetic standards can lead to the abandonment of ethical standards as well (The Central Conference of Reform Rabbis, 1964).

f. In a certain community, Orthodox Rabbinical authorities created guidelines to curtail extravagant spending on weddings. One of the authorities, Rabbi Shafran, explained:

> The rationale for the guidelines . . . is not only social and economic but also religious. The concept of modesty, not only in dress but in behavior and expression is central to the Torah . . . Limiting excess, whether in general lifestyle or celebrations, is an inherently Jewish ideal" (Francine Parnes, "A Big Wedding with a Smaller Bill," *The New York Times*, May 25, 2002, p. A13).

Probing: Ideas and Issues

Compose a Jewish response to this question: Is rejecting extravagance equivalent to denial? Should communities (Jewish and general) impose spending restrictions on members/citizens? Do you feel materialism and indulgent consumption alienate us from essential values? Explain.

RELATED MIDDOT AND MITZVOT

Practicing these virtues and commandments enhances efforts to keep consumer habits in check.

Bal Tashchit (Not Destroying; Protecting the Environment): Rampant consumerism takes an enormous toll on the environment. Minimizing consumption to meet only essential needs will help preserve the earth and its resources.

Emet (Truth): Luxurious lifestyles and material abundance have hidden costs. Corporations, merchants, advertisers, and some politicians have an interest in shielding consumers from certain uncomfortable truths regarding environmental destruction and worker exploitation.

Lo Tachmod (Not Coveting): Jealousy, envy, wanting what others have — these sentiments intensify consumer appetites.

Lo Titeyn Michshol (Not Placing a Stumbling Block): Production of many goods today involves worker exploitation or results in devastating environmental damage. Merchants who sell such goods might be accused of placing a stumbling block before the blind. That is, they might be accused of involving unsuspecting consumers in unethical business practices.

Ometz Layv (Courage): It takes a special kind of strength and discipline to live simply in the face of pressures to achieve wealth and accumulate. One needs resolve to resist social expectations and media assaults that extol materialism.

Samayach Be'Chelko (Contentment with Your Lot): Habituating yourself to satisfaction with what you have helps you avoid succumbing to materialistic excesses.

Simchah (Joy and Happiness): Beyond a modest standard of living, having more wealth and owning more things do not bestow greater happiness.

Tochechah (Rebuking): Speaking out against consumer excesses presents especially delicate challenges. Our culture generally sees wealth as a private matter. If you criticize others' consumer habits, they may accuse you of being judgmental, jealous, self-righteous, and simply out of line (i.e., "my spending habits are none of your business!").

Tzeniyut (Modesty): A modest lifestyle discourages indulgence and extravagance.

V'ahavta L'rayacha Kamocha (Loving One's Fellow Person as Oneself): If we love others as ourselves, we do not exploit them for our gain. Rather, we live in ways in which it is possible for all people to enjoy living wages, safe work conditions, and a healthy environment.

ACTIVITIES

A First Look: Key Issues and Ideas

1. As an opening activity, write the title of this chapter on the board, "Consumerism: How Much Is Too Much?" Ask students some or all of the following questions:

   - What do you think this topic is going to deal with?

   - Why might consumerism be a "hot topic"?

   - What ethical quandaries do you expect this issue to raise?

   - Is this a topic you've thought about

much in the past? Explain.

- What do you suppose you will learn by studying this issue?

- Is it important to learn about this issue?

Consider returning to a variation of this activity as a closing exercise. In this case, you might phrase questions such as these:

- Why did we study the topic of "Consumerism: How Much Is Too Much?"

- Would you *now* label consumerism a "hot topic"? Explain.

- What ethical quandaries did this topic raise?

- How did our study of consumerism match your expectations for this unit?

- What did you learn or think about that you wouldn't have expected to?

- How will what you learned influence you in the future?

- What was most valuable about studying this issue?

2. Another opening activity: Write the word "Wealth" on the board. Have participants "free associate" words and ideas that come to mind when they think of that word. After a round of free associating, invite students to elaborate on their feelings and attitudes toward wealth. Continue with an overview of Jewish and general perspectives of wealth (see pages 243 to 251). Another useful resource for this activity is the chapter on wealth or *osher* in *The Jewish Moral Virtues* by Eugene B. Borowitz and Frances Weidman Schwartz, pp. 105-118.

3. Refer to the Summary of the Overview, p. 251. In preparing to give students an overview of this topic, be sure to include details that exemplify each of the summary points.

4. Individually, students rank order the 16 "On

the One Hand/On the Other Hand" points included in the "Text Study" section on pages 253-262. Rank as number "1" the most important consideration, and the least important as "16." Reconvene and have group members compare and explain their ratings. Ask: What do your results reflect about your attitude toward consumerism? What was most challenging about completing this exercise?

5. Have your group educate itself on current issues regarding consumerism by exploring the content in the web sites mentioned in the Bibliography below (p. 268). Looking at the web sites and referring to some of the links will give students a sense of the breadth of discussion related to this topic.

Applying Middot and Mitzvot

1. Refer to the "Related Middot and Mitzvot" section above (p. 262). Ask participants to answer and explain their responses to the following questions:

- Which *middah* or *mitzvah* do you think is most important to cultivate in order to avoid unethical consumerism?

- Are there *middot* or *mitzvot* you would add to this list?

- Are there any you would leave off?

- Which *middah* or *mitzvah* would *you* most like to work on, that you believe would most help you avoid the pitfalls of excessive consumerism?

- How would you go about working on the chosen *middah* or *mitzvah*?

2. Plan an exhibit of inspirational posters designed by students on avoiding excessive consumerism. The poster designers should focus on a particular *middah* or *mitzvah*, including words and/or drawings to convey their message.

3. It is possible to see wealth or *osher* as a virtue. Hold a discussion on how wealth

might be considered a virtue. Then, ask for examples of when wealth crosses the line from virtue to vice. One example might begin this way: "Rejoicing with bride and groom is a *mitzvah,* and might include celebrating with a party and banquet. However, wedding extravagance crosses the line when _____." A useful resource for this activity is the chapter on wealth or *osher* in *The Jewish Moral Virtues* by Eugene B. Borowitz and Frances Weidman Schwartz, pages 105-118.

4. For more information and activities on:

   Bal Tashchit (Not Destroying; Protecting the Environment): see *Teaching Mitzvot: Concepts, Values, and Activities* by Barbara Binder Kadden and Bruce Kadden, pp. 199-203, and *Let the Earth Teach You Torah* by Ellen Bernstein and Dan Fink.

   Emet (Truth): see *Teaching Jewish Virtues* by Susan Freeman, pp. 69-84.

   Lo Tachmod (Not Coveting): see *Teaching Jewish Virtues* by Susan Freeman, pp. 211-227.

   Lo Titayn Michshol (Not Placing a Stumbling Block): see *Teaching Mitzvot* by Barbara Binder Kadden and Bruce Kadden, pp. 193-198.

   Ometz Layv (Courage): see *Teaching Jewish Virtues* by Susan Freeman, pp. 195-210.

   Samayach Be'Chelko (Contentment with Your Lot): see *Teaching Jewish Virtues* by Susan Freeman, pp. 211-227, and *The Jewish Moral Virtues* by Eugene B. Borowitz and Frances Weidman Schwartz, pp. 161-172.

   Simchah (Joy and Happiness): see *Teaching Jewish Virtues* by Susan Freeman, pp. 283-298.

   Tochechah (Rebuking): see *Teaching Jewish Virtues* by Susan Freeman, pp. 318-331.

   Tzeniyut (Modesty): see *The Jewish Moral Virtues* by Eugene B. Borowitz and Frances Weidman Schwartz, pp. 149-160.

   V'ahavta L'rayacha Kamocha (Loving One's Neighbor): see *Teaching Mitzvot* by Barbara

Binder Kadden and Bruce Kadden, pp. 223-228.

Stories: Understanding through Listening

1. Read over the scenarios in "Scenarios: Comparing Types of Consumers" section above (pp. 251-253). Discuss the following:

   • Describe the BenDor's standard of living.

   • Describe the Bender's standard of living.

   • What do we know about the BenDor family's values?

   • What do we know about the Bender family's values?

   • What similarities and differences are there between the two families?

   • Do you think the BenDor's are ethical consumers? Explain.

   • Do you think the Bender's are ethical consumers? Explain.

   • What would you like these two families to know about consumerism issues?

   • Would you suggest either of the families change their habits in any way? Explain.

2. Again, refer to the scenarios (pp. 251-253). Set up a mock television-style panel interview. The guests are members of the BenDor and the Bender families. The interviewer should probe family members in an effort to learn about their views on wealth, consumerism, personal and communal priorities, and "how much is *too much.*"

3. Identify one or more individuals in your community who have committed to a lifestyle of "voluntary simplicity." Invite the person or persons to visit your group to share thoughts and feelings about lifestyle choices they have made. Why have they chosen to live the way they do? What are their views on consumerist trends around the globe?

4. Have students compose their own stories that

will explore benefits and potential pitfalls of wealth. Ask them to choose one of the passages below (also included in the "Text Study" section above) as a theme, moral, or plot motivator for their stories:

- Don't exhaust yourself trying to make money. You see it and then it's gone. It grows wings and flies away (Proverbs 23:4-5).

- When told of a man who had acquired great wealth, a Sage replied, "Has he also acquired the days in which to spend it?" (Ibn Gabirol, *Choice of Pearls*, in *Leo Rosten's Treasury of Jewish Quotations* NY: Jewish Publication Society of America and McGraw-Hill Book Company, 1972, p. 536).

- Give me neither poverty nor riches, but provide me with my daily bread, lest being sated, I renounce, saying "Who is the Eternal?" Or, being impoverished, I take to theft and profane the name of my God (Proverbs 30:8-9).

- Why do you spend money for what is not bread,
  Your earnings for what does not satisfy? (Isaiah 55:2).

- Ben Zoma said: Who is rich? One who is happy with what one has (*Pirke Avot* 4:1).

- Envy, lust, and pursuit of honor will ruin a person's life (*Pirke Avot* 4:30).

(For a related activity, see "Wrestling: Engagement with the Issues" #2, below.)

Action: Getting Out, Getting Involved

1. Many people are trying to address consumerism issues through involvement in environmental and consumer awareness organizations. Assign individuals or small groups to research and report back on various organizations. (Some suggestions for organizations to research are those listed under "Web Sites" in the Bibliography, p. 269.) In their reports students should:

- Summarize what the organization does.

- Discuss whether it would be appropriate for a committed Jew to become involved in the organization, explaining why or why not.

- Suggest ways to get involved. Mention things individuals can do *now* to support the organizations' work. Also, explain efforts the organization is making to try to influence problems on a more global level.

2. "Global Exchange" is an international human rights organization. One of its areas of concern is economic justice in the marketplace through fair trade. Fair trade criteria include:

- Paying a fair wage in the local context

- Offering employees opportunities for advancement

- Providing equal employment opportunities for all people

- Engaging in environmentally sustainable practices

- Being open to public accountability

- Building long-term trade relationships

- Providing healthy and safe working conditions within the local context

- Providing financial and technical assistance to producers whenever possible

- Ensuring that there is no abuse of child labor

Ask participants to discuss how fair trade is compatible with Jewish values. Then, have your group research one or more of these topics:

- Companies dedicated to fair trade

- Current campaigns to promote fair trade

(e.g., in coffee, cocoa, athletic shoes, or rugs)

- Political policies that either support or hinder fair trade

Using their findings, students outline a plan of action to help promote and support fair trade. They should come up with five or so specific things that they (and others) can do.

Here is one example of how students might complete this exercise. First, students may discover information, such as the following about the coffee trade:

> Coffee is the second largest U.S. import after oil, and the U.S. consumes one-fifth of all the world's coffee, making it the largest consumer in the world. But few Americans realize that agriculture workers in the coffee industry often toil in what can be described as "sweatshops in the fields." Many small coffee farmers receive prices for their coffee that are less than the costs of production, forcing them into a cycle of poverty and debt (www.globalexchange.org/economy/coffee/index.html).

After doing more research, suppose students decide to focus on fair trade in coffee. They may come up with suggestions such as the following:

- Commit to having their own household purchase only fair trade coffee.

- Write a letter to the synagogue board, asking them to serve only fair trade coffee at events. Better yet, write to synagogues and churches all around the area with this request.

- Write letters to coffee shops, urging them to brew fair trade coffee.

- Plan a publicity campaign with flyers and posters urging people to purchase only fair trade coffee.

- If the local supermarket carries fair trade coffee, speak to the manager of the store, thank him/her, and let him/her know how important you think this is.

3. A great deal of advertising exacerbates the worst consumer tendencies. The organization "Adbusters" seeks to undermine manipulative advertising. Check out some of the spoof ads displayed on the web site www.adbusters.org and print out a few choice ones to share with the group. Alternately, have students check out the web site on their own (though note that if some of the spoof ads were "rated," they would be PG-13, at least). After the Adbuster orientation, have students create their own spoof ad campaign. Then, display the ads, adding labels describing the ads' dangers to consumers (and possibly the earth and its creatures).

4. Refer to the section "Shifting Values" in the Overview under "General Perspectives," p. 250. Have students illustrate one suggestion of things individuals can do to contribute toward positive change in consumption trends. Display the illustrations as part of a consumer (or consumerism) awareness campaign.

Wrestling: Engagement with the Issues

1. Refer to the "Shifting Values" section of the Overview under "General Perspectives," pages 250. Listed there are 11 specific suggestions of things individuals can do to contribute toward positive change in consumption trends. Have students assign each suggestion one of these ratings:

- "Y" for "YES, I already do that."

- "T" for "I don't do this, but I want to TRY."

- "N" for "NO, I don't think I can take this one on."

In small groups have students explain their ratings to each other. That is, why did they assign each particular rating the way they did?

2. Refer to "Stories: Understanding through Listening" #4 above. In that activity, students write stories based on suggested texts. For this activity, have students use art or creative movement to illustrate one of the texts.

3. Stage a debate. Refer to the "On the One Hand/On the Other Hand" points found in the "Text Study" section above (pp. 253-262) for eight debate topic ideas.

4. Facilitate a stream of consciousness writing exercise. Give the students the opening words: "Wealth is _____." Then, ask them to write for five (or so) minutes without stopping on this topic. They should write down whatever comes to mind, without worrying about making sense, and without judging their words. When the time is up, invite students to share anything they want from the process — either something they wrote, or their reactions to participating in this exercise.

5. This exercise would make an appropriate follow-up from the previous one, or it can stand on its own. After students study Jewish texts on wealth, have them compose their own "Philosophy of Wealth." For passages on wealth included in this chapter, see Text Study #3a, #4A, #4a, #5a, #6a-c, #7a, #7b, #8A-C, #8a-d. Other passages in Text Study will be relevant, as well.

   A variation: Have students compose a "Prescription for Consumer Fitness."

6. Over the course of a week or two, have students pay special attention to newspaper and magazine stories and advertisements. Alternately, bring in a stack of newspapers and magazines. Ask students to cut out any items that they feel exemplify excessiveness or indulgent consumption. Once they have collected a pile, have them create collages that express "Consumerism: This Much Is *Too Much*." You may want to give them the option of adding other touches to their collages — words, texts, drawings, etc.

7. Ask students to draw on more abstract artistic expression to create a piece of artwork, or a creative movement or music piece. Suggest one of these themes or have them choose one of their own:

   Indulgence, Greed, Materialism, Excessiveness, Conspicuous Consumption, The Globalization Gap, Exploitation, Environmental Devastation.

   When their projects are complete, have participants share their art and respond to questions others may have about their work.

Empathy

1. Refer to Text Study #4b above (p. 257). Ask participants to imagine they are one of these Bangladeshi workers. Have them write about their work life: what day to day work consists of, how they feel about their work, what their hopes and dreams are.

2. Refer to Text Study #6c above (p. 259). Ask students to write an imaginary first person account of someone who "passionately seeks wealth," so that eventually "love of money becomes for them like a consuming fire, like a wilderness, like death or barrenness that are never sated . . . "

   Alternately: Give students the option of completing this exercise through another medium — creative movement, film, photos, or a series of drawings.

3. Individually or in small groups, have participants write a play using the voices of animals. The animals are experiencing devastation of their surroundings because of the seemingly insatiable human demand for the resources in their environment. When the script is completed, rehearse and perform the play.

BIBLIOGRAPHY

Books and Articles

Bernstein, Ellen, and Dan Fink. *Let the Earth Teach You Torah*. Wyncote, PA: Shomrei Adamah, 1992.

Borowitz, Eugene B., and Frances Weidman Schwartz. *The Jewish Moral Virtues*. Philadelphia, PA: The Jewish Publication Society, 1999.

Brecher, Jeremy, and Tim Costello. *Global Village or Global Pillage: Economic Reconstruction from the Bottom Up*. Boston, MA: South End Press, 1994.

Brooks, David. *Bobos* in Paradise: The New Upper Class and How They Got There*. NY: Simon and Schuster, 2000. (* = Bourgeois Bohemians)

Brooks, David. "Why the U.S. Will Always Be Rich," *The New York Times Magazine*, June 9, 2002, p. 124.

Bulka, Reuben P. *Judaism on Pleasure*. Northvale, NJ: Jason Aronson Inc., 1995.

Cross, Gary. *An All-Consuming Century: Why Commercialism Won in Modern America*. New York: Columbia University Press, 2000.

D'Souza, Dinesh. *The Virtue of Prosperity*. New York: Simon and Schuster, 2000.

Folbre, Nancy. *The Invisible Heart: Economics and Family Values*. New York: The New Press, 2001.

Frank, Robert H. *Luxury Fever: Why Money Fails to Satisfy in an Era of Excess*. New York: The Free Press, 1999.

Freeman, Susan. *Teaching Jewish Virtues: Sacred Sources and Arts Activities*. Denver, CO: A.R.E. Publishing, Inc., 1999.

Galbraith, John Kenneth. *The Affluent Society*. Boston, MA: Houghton Mifflin Co., 1998.

Gaon, Saadiah, *The Book of Beliefs and Opinions*. Samuel Rosenblatt, trans. New Haven, CT: Yale University Press, 1948.

Henslin, James M. "Economic Justice." In *Social Problems*, Englewood Cliffs, NJ: Prentice Hall, 1990.

Hirsch, Samson Raphael Hirsch. *Horeb: A Philosophy of Jewish Laws and Observances*, I. Grunfeld, trans. New York: Soncino Press, 1981.

Kadden, Barbara Binder, and Bruce Kadden. *Teaching Mitzvot: Concepts, Values, and Activities*. Rev. ed. Denver, CO: A.R.E. Publishing, Inc., 2003.

Klare, Michael T. *Resource Wars: The New Landscape of Global Conflict*. New York: Metropolitan Books, Henry Holt and Company, LLC, 2001.

Myers, David G. *The American Paradox: Spiritual Hunger in an Age of Plenty*. New Haven, CT: Yale University Press, 2000.

Nathanson, Stephen. *Economic Justice*. Upper Saddle River, NJ: Prentice Hall, 1998.

Salkin, Jeffrey K. *Putting God on the Guest List: How to Reclaim the Spiritual Meaning of Your Child's Bar or Bat Mitzvah*. Woodstock, VT: Jewish Lights Publishing, 1996.

Schor, Juliet B. *The Overspent American: Upscaling, Downshifting, and the New Consumer*. New York: Basic Books, 1998.

———. *The Overworked American*. New York: Basic Books, 1991.

Schor, Juliet B., and Douglas B. Holt, eds. *The Consumer Society Reader*. New York: The New Press, 2000.

Sherwin, Byron L., and Seymour J. Cohen. *Creating an Ethical Jewish Life: A Practical Introduction To Classic Teachings on How to Be a Jew*. Woodstock, VT: Jewish Lights Publishing, 2001.

Siegel, Seymour. "A Jewish View of Economic Justice." In *Contemporary Jewish Ethics and Morality*, ed. by Elliot N. Dorff and Louis E. Newman. New York: Oxford University Press, 1995.

Slater, Philip. *Wealth Addiction*. New York: E.P. Dutton, 1980.

Tamari, Meir. *In the Marketplace: Jewish Business Ethics*. Southfield, MI: Targum Press, Inc., 1991.

Yekutiel of Rome, Yechiel ben. *Sefer Ma'alot Ha-middot*. Jerusalem: Eshkol, 1978. (This thirteenth century Italian author's ideas were first published in Istanbul in 1512.)

Twitchell, James B. *Living It Up: Our Love Affair with Luxury*. New York: Columbia University Press, 2002.

Web Sites

Adbusters: www.adbusters.org

Campaigns and spoof ads (some outrageous and risque) seek to undermine manipulative advertising.

Earthscan . . . delivering sustainability: www.earthscan.co.uk

Earthscan describes itself as the "world's leading publisher on environmentally sustainable development."

Never Enough? Anticonsumerism campaign: http://enough.enviroweb.org

This "critical look at consumerism, poverty, and the planet" presents powerful information and arguments.

Envirolink — The Online Environmental Community: www.envirolink.org

Clearinghouse for environmental information on the Internet.

Global Exchange: www.globalexchange.org

An international human rights organization dedicated to promoting political, social, and environmental justice globally.

The Center for a New American Dream: www.newdream.org

An organization with the mission of "helping Americans consume responsibly to protect the environment, enhance quality of life, and promote social justice."

The New Road Map Foundation: www.newroadmap.org

Claims to provide "people with practical tools and innovative approaches for managing and mastering basic life challenges," including personal finances, how we relate to money, and how to live more simply. "People need new ways to navigate the road of life — ways based on a vision of a cooperative human community in a diverse yet interconnected world."

The Northwest Earth Institute: www.nwei.org

Offers discussion courses on "sustainability, deep ecology, living in place, and the practice of simplicity."

TV Turn-Off Network: www.tvturnoff.org

Sponsors of TV Turn-Off Week, the goal of which is to direct energy away from values inherent in TV viewing (e.g., consumerism) and toward more worthwhile priorities and activities.

Films

The Cost of Cool: Youth, Consumerism, and the Environment (2001, 26 minutes, grades 6-12).

Looks at everyday items, from t-shirts to sneakers, and tracks the effect of their manufacture on the world's resources and environments. Teenagers examine their learned buying patterns, recognizing that much of the stuff they acquire is not needed. (Available from The Video Project, 1-800-4PLANET/ 1-800-475-2638 or www. videoproject.net)

Erasable You (1998, 85 minutes, unrated).

A dark comedy about a woman, hooked on incontrollable consumerism, who plots to rob her ex-husband and his nice new wife of all their earnings. Available from video stores or from amazon.com (www.amazon.com).

PART IV

SEXUALITY

FOUNDATIONS OF SEXUAL ETHICS

MASTURBATION

BIRTH CONTROL

HOMOSEXUALITY

SEX OUTSIDE OF MARRIAGE

CHAPTER 11

FOUNDATIONS OF SEXUAL ETHICS

OVERVIEW

Jewish Perspectives

Appreciating Our Bodies

We are part of God's creation. In Judaism we believe in the goodness of God and the purposefulness of God's work. In the Genesis story, God calls the creation of human beings "very good." Human bodies consist of hundreds of parts. That we are "very good" implies that all of our body parts are good. Whereas some belief systems and the language of the streets may attach shamefulness and crudity to the sex organs, Judaism stresses that we must treat our whole selves with honor and gratitude.

Jews serve God by living according to the values and teachings of our tradition. Every limb and organ — created for good — can be a vehicle for holiness. As we chant in the *"Nishmat"* prayer on Shabbat morning, each limb and organ (*ayvareem*) God molded for us is to give thanks, bless, praise, glorify, exalt, admire, sanctify, and declare the sovereign power of God's name . . . Every fiber of our being is to praise God's holy name.

Our bodies and our sexuality indeed can be vehicles for holiness while serving very tangible purposes, as well. These include procreation — "to be fruitful and multiply" — (Genesis 1:28), companionship, and pleasure. Not all these purposes are as straightforward as they may at first seem.

Procreation

Judaism considers it a *mitzvah* to have children, unless there are physical reasons why a person is unable to do so. Children are a source of joy.

Through children, we pass along traditions and values. Raising children can help us to become better people — less self-focused, more generous, patient, and caring. Children teach us about love. A specific Jewish concern is sustaining our small population, especially in the face of the losses we suffered through the Holocaust and the more recent strains of assimilation.

Having children may be a prevailing value in Judaism. However, it comes with a few significant challenges. As early as the Talmud, a most basic objection is raised. What if a person doesn't want children? What if a person would prefer to spend time pursuing other things besides raising a family? In a Talmudic discussion, Ben Azzai says he prefers to focus his energy on Torah study. He suggests that not everyone has to fulfill the commandment of procreation (see Text Study #2a below). Today, in many childless households, the adults choose to channel their energy into their careers or other endeavors. What should our Jewish response be to those who choose not to raise children? While some might say these adults are neglecting their responsibilities, others might say it is wrong to judge the personal choices others make.

Another challenge to our value of having children is the worry about overpopulation in the world. Many Jewish leaders acknowledge the concern, but feel that because of Jewish demographics today, we can't afford to see our population diminish any more than it has in the last 100 years or so. We discuss this issue in more depth in Chapter 13, "Birth Control," p. 301.

In a broader context, we should touch upon one other area concerning Jewish attitudes toward children and definitions of family. Many adult Jews never marry and have no children. Single Jews may raise children on their own.

There are couples who struggle with infertility. Defining the ideal Jewish family — what it should look like, how many children it should have — can be a painful subject for some of us. Because of the needs and realities of individual Jews, it is not always appropriate to stress the commandment to "be fruitful and multiply." Some Jewish communities are very conscious about being supportive and inclusive of all Jews, whether single, married, with children or without. However, we could do better. Whether a community is more traditional or less so, sensitivity concerning the needs of all our "families" is something to strive for.

Companionship

The value of an intimate partnership first appears in Genesis: "It is not good for the human to be alone. I will make a fitting companion (*ezer k'neg-do*) for him" (Genesis 2:18; see Text Study #3A below). Interestingly, the literal meaning of "*ezer*" is "helper," and "*k'neg-do*" is "opposite or against him." Thus, essentially, the ideal partner is a helper and a support, but also someone who challenges you, pushes you, and helps you grow. The partners together complement each other and create a greater "whole."

Many years after the Genesis account, the Jewish wedding ceremony became standardized. In this ceremony we call the two companions, the bride and groom, "*ray-eem ahooveem*" or "loving friends." Judaism considers love to be an integral, important facet of a Jewish partnership. Friends who share love on the most intimate level care deeply about each other. They spend time together, they are interested in the thoughts, feelings, and activities of each other, and they consider the other's needs and desires with as much concern as they do their own.

Pleasure

"Loving friends" want to please each other. This includes giving each other sexual pleasure. Many explicit Jewish sources describe ways in which sex should be pleasurable. Traditional Jewish sources predominantly address men's obligations in the sexual relationship. Men are instructed to be sensitive to a woman's desires, to arouse her lovingly and patiently, and to allow her to climax before they do.

"Black and White" and "Gray" Areas of Sexuality

Judaism widely accepts certain "black and white" views of sexual relationships. For instance, Judaism clearly upholds marriage as the ideal adult partnership. In a marital partnership, a couple may have children, enjoy loving companionship, and share sexual pleasure. On the other hand, Judaism explicitly prohibits various sexual relationships, such as incestuous or adulterous ones. Judaism always forbids use of force as part of any sexual contact. Beyond the endorsed relationship of marriage and specified forbidden relationships, the issues get more challenging. Masturbation, homosexuality, and sex outside of marriage are three subjects fraught with complicated feelings and mixed attitudes. Overwhelmingly, Orthodox Jewish authorities would not place these sexual experiences within the "gray areas." That is, the tendency is to denounce these practices. In contrast, outside Orthodoxy, there is greater reluctance to dismiss these sexual experiences as wholly invalid. Liberal Jews are more likely to reconsider traditional views of masturbation, homosexuality, and sex outside of marriage, taking into account modern sources of information and life experiences. (For more on masturbation, homosexuality, and sex outside of marriage, refer to those chapters themselves.)

Obviously, not everyone will agree on what belongs in the "gray areas" of acceptable and unacceptable sexual relationships. Yet, societal pressures direct us to try to find ways to address sexuality that doesn't fit into clear-cut categories. A few decades ago, innovative Jewish thinkers suggested a "*sliding scale* of sexual values" — with marriage at the uppermost point. (For a more detailed explanation of this idea, see "Sex Outside of Marriage," Text Study #1a, pp. 335-336.)

Holiness

Let's return now to the idea of holiness. So far, in this chapter we've mentioned holiness several times. Judaism sees the sexual relationship within marriage as a vehicle for *holiness*. But what is holiness? One possible explanation is this: To make something holy is to transform a mundane, everyday kind of experience into something special.

For example, we can seize upon a plate of food and gobble it up, or we can transform it into something special, which recognizes God's role in the experience. That is, we can wash and bless before eating, and offer gratitude following the meal.

Similarly, we can have a casual sexual encounter with a near-stranger, perhaps while numbed from having a few drinks. A euphemism for this kind of intercourse is "hopping into bed" — something that brings to mind rabbits rather than human beings. Unlike rabbits (or other animals), human beings can express love and enduring commitment, enjoy companionship, and care about each other's pleasure during sex. These elements help transform a physical urge into something special or holy.

To sanctify an act requires discipline — we cannot always have exactly what we want, when we want it. Instant gratification is devoid of meaning. To gain anything meaningful requires discipline. Disciplining ourselves to pursue deep, caring relationships will be more fulfilling in the end.

The Hebrew word for the marriage ceremony is *"Kiddushin,"* related to the word *"kedushah,"* meaning "holiness." When something is *"kadosh,"* it is set apart. A bride and groom "separate" each other from all others. The exclusivity of the relationship contributes to its holiness.

Holiness in sexual intimacy implies a deep "knowing" of the other, an experience of union and oneness. Rabbis throughout the ages suggest that when two married people unite sexually, so, too, does a deeper bonding with God take place (see Text Study #7A-F below).

Modesty/Tzeniyut

The opportunities for holiness in sexual behavior are not limited to experiences between married people. In fact, a person does not have to be involved in a relationship at all. From a Jewish perspective, holiness in sexuality begins with modesty or *tzeniyut*. *Tzeniyut* has to do with privacy and concealment. To be modest means you are respectful and humble, that you don't show off. When you casually reveal your body and allow easy access to it by others, you are like an object, not a "vehicle for holiness."

In a broader context, modesty stands in contrast to the "overexposure" associated with pornography, Internet sex, and elaborate body decoration (such as tattoos). Without modesty, people become "used" rather than "loved." God created us for higher purposes.

Revealing Ourselves

Judaism refers to illicit sexual liaisons (such as incest) as *gilui arayot*, or uncovering nakedness. In essence, *gilui arayot* are improper revelations of self. Today, we might include casual sex, anonymous sex, and sex for the sole purpose of relieving physical urges as *gilui arayot*. Judaism sees such "self-exposures" as destructive and painful. In contrast, we refer to trusting, loving revelations of self as "knowing" another. Being modest helps us consistently to nurture holiness in our sexual behavior. Revealing ourselves only with great care and in an appropriate relationship allows us to remain on the path of holiness. Modesty can help us be mindful of what God ultimately wants for us. We are not objects; we are not merely animals. Instead, we are human beings, striving to live lives of holiness.

General Perspectives

The society in which people live defines what is acceptable sexual behavior. Jews generally live in a society within a society. For committed Jews, their Jewish community will have significant influence on their actions. However, those who live in open societies, are also influenced by the "norms" of the sexual behaviors around them. Within those "norms," many secular thinkers have tried to come up with ethical guidelines for sexual behavior. Holiness is not a concern of secular thinkers — that is something we need to learn and ponder from our own tradition. However, ideas from the secular world can complement Jewish strategies for ethical behavior.

Linda and Richard Eyre, in their book *Teaching Your Children Values*, offer a very straightforward guideline in determining moral behavior. Their values formula directs individuals to *help* and not to *hurt*. They discuss sex in terms of "how and who is *helped* by being careful about sex and how and who is *hurt* when people are not careful about sex" (p. 126).

Sol and Judith Gordon, in their book *Raising a Child Conservatively in a Sexually Permissive World,* offer more details regarding moral sexual behavior. They list seven deadly sins of immoral sex (p. 41):

1. Rape, molestation, and sexual assault

2. Hurting, forcing, deceiving, exploiting, and corrupting

3. Sexually irresponsible behavior (such as a man abandoning a pregnant woman)

4. Perpetuating the double standard

5. Sex stereotyping

6. Sexual harassment of women

7. Lying to young children about the facts of life.

A Planned Parenthood brochure suggests that a healthy relationship must have seven basic qualities: respect, honesty, equality, good communication, trust, fairness, and responsibility.[1]

The same brochure offers "Guidelines for Sex Partners":

- Have each other's consent.

- Never use pressure to get consent.

- Be honest with each other.

- Treat each other as equals.

- Be attentive to each other's pleasure.

- Protect each other against physical and emotional harm.

- Guard against unintended pregnancy and sexually transmitted infection.

- Be clear with each other about what you want to do and don't want to do.

- Respect each other's limits.

- Accept responsibility for your actions.[2]

Judaism certainly encompasses many of the above values. Our tradition teaches us in Leviticus 19:18 to love one another ("love your neighbor as yourself"), to honor and respect each other, to be truthful and fair, and to take responsibility for our actions. We are to strive to be kind and helpful in our relationships. As Rabbi Michael Gold puts it, "Human beings are created in God's image, and anything that hurts or diminishes the dignity of a human being is an affront to God."[3]

Sometimes the phrasing of secular sources will remind us of the rich teachings in our own tradition. Sexual issues are often confusing these days. Judaism gives us enormous insights and inspiration for sorting through the confusion. But if ideas from general sources will enhance our efforts to live ethically, we would be wise to draw on those as well.

Summary of the Overview

- God created our bodies and our sexuality for good.

---

[1]Planned Parenthood Federation of America, "Responsible Choices" series, *"Is This Love: How to Tell If Your Relationship Is Good for You,"* 2000.

[2]Ibid.

[3]Gold, *Does God Belong in the Bedroom*, p. 40.

- Important values in a sexual relationship include: Procreation (when it is physically possible), loving and enduring companionship, and pleasure.

- Values, such as the above, can help transform a physical act into an experience of holiness.

SCENARIOS: HOW THINGS HAVE CHANGED

Love and sex have always been complicated — touching on our deepest hopes, desires, and vulnerabilities. From the beginning of our written history, Jewish texts have commented on the subject. Below are two imaginary scenarios, one set in an earlier era and one set in contemporary times, intended to raise questions and spark discussion. Read each scenario to or with your students, and engage them in small or large group discussions. Use the "Focus the Discussion" section below to help you identify the important issues and facilitate these discussions. Note that additional questions and activities relating to these scenarios are found in the "Stories: Understanding through Listening: section below (pp. 290-291).

Following the discussions, have students continue on to the "Text Study" section to see what Jewish and other sources have to say about our topic. Finally, you may wish to have students discuss the scenarios a second time to see if their views have changed.

Scenario 1: A "Simpler Time and Place" (If It Ever Really Existed)

Moshe and Leah's parents introduced them a few months ago. Moshe is 18 years old, and Leah is 16. They have visited together several times at Leah's home. Moshe has joined the family for dinner on occasion. Leah's parents have asked her if she would like to marry Moshe. Leah sees Moshe as a kind, considerate person who takes an interest in her. She agrees to the marriage. A wedding ceremony is arranged to take place in a few months.

On their wedding night, the bride and groom spend time embracing and touching each other. They tentatively begin to explore each other's bodies. Leah feels nervous about sexual intercourse. Moshe, knowing that it is wrong to force his wife to have sex, suggests they take their time in getting to know each other's bodies. When they both feel ready, they will engage in sexual intercourse. In the meantime, in the privacy of their bedroom, they continue to be physically loving with one another. After a few weeks, they feel trusting enough to reveal themselves fully to one another in their lovemaking. Over the years, the pleasure of their sexual relationship grows as they learn more about what pleases the other, and as they feel love and friendship deepen between them.

Scenario 2: Nowadays

Marc and Liana meet for the first time at a high school basketball game. Liana is playing in the game, and Marc is there watching. He is dating a student on the opposing team. It turns out that Marc's girlfriend is someone Liana knows from her elementary school, but hasn't seen for years. After the game, they all decide to go out and get a bite to eat. At the restaurant, the "chemistry" shifts. Marc is charmed by Liana, and Liana is quite intrigued with Marc. They are pleased to find that each other is Jewish, as well. Marc calls Liana the next day, and they begin dating each other exclusively. Marc is 18 years old and Liana is 16. Though they are young, they are physically mature. After a few months of dating, they feel they want to spend the rest of their lives together.

Focus the Discussion

To continue the second scenario in a way that parallels the traditional Jewish values in the first scenario, we might say:

" . . . Marc and Liana plan a wedding that will take place in a few months (though some legal hurdles will need to be dealt with because of the age of the bride). After they marry, they begin a sexual relationship. Their love deepens over the years, and they stay together for the rest of their lives."

We might nod our heads with understanding and acceptance, reacting to Moshe and Leah's experience in the first scenario: "That's how things used to be . . . " However, if Marc and Liana — like other young high schoolers we know — were to marry nowadays, we likely would consider them unwise.

About Marc and Liana, we might say: "They are making a big mistake. They're too young. They can't be sure of what they ultimately will want in a life partner. They will have a hard time continuing with their educations and pursuing their careers, especially if she becomes pregnant. And they are far too immature to handle the responsibilities of parenthood . . . They'll probably get divorced. They could be emotionally scarred for life . . . ," etc. (We also might have a hard time believing that Liana's parents, who would legally need to give the underage Liana permission to wed, would actually do so.)

The Jewish path of love and marriage as framed hundreds of years ago is not a ready fit for the realities of our present culture and lifestyles. Love and sex have always been complicated — touching on our deepest hopes, desires, and vulnerabilities. As things have changed over the years, love and sex have become more complicated, as well. How should we express our sexuality in Jewishly ethical ways when the blueprint we refer to does not match the situation(s) in which we discover ourselves? Finding our way in love, sex, and marriage is a great challenge that most every Jew wrestles with intently during his/her lifetime.

(Note: For a continuation of Marc and Liana's scenario, see Chapter 15, "Sex Outside of Marriage," p. 329.)

TEXT STUDY

Note: Many of the following texts are appropriate for all ages, commenting on Jewish values of love, marriage, and having children. Others are more explicit in referring to sexual relations. Gauge which texts are most fitting to include in study by considering the age, maturity, and needs of the participants.

In many ways, the Jewish path of love and marriage as framed hundreds of years ago sets the stage for the ideal sexual relationship. However, our present culture and lifestyles have introduced new questions and complexities into love, sex, and marriage. Jewish textual sources provide many important guidelines, but these guidelines often highlight the tension between seemingly opposing considerations. The chart on the next page poses the questions and offers two opposing points of view. Text sources supporting each of these points of view follow below.

1. **How do our physical bodies and our sexuality fit into the framework of Creation?**

   On the One Hand:

   God created everything for good — including all our body parts and our sexuality.

   A. God saw everything God had made and behold it was very good (Genesis 1:31).

   B. A comment on the above verse states:

      Nothing in the human organs are created flawed or ugly. Everything is created with divine wisdom and is therefore complete, exalted, good, and pleasant (*The Holy Letter,* attributed to Nachmanides, pp. 45, 48).

   C. For in the image of God, did God make humankind (Genesis 9:6).

   On the Other Hand:

   We must do our part in protecting and honoring God's creation.

   a. Take good care of yourselves (Deuteronomy 2:4).

TEACHING HOT TOPICS

Foundations of Sexual Ethics: Questions to Consider

The Question	On the One Hand	On the Other Hand
1. How do our physical bodies and our sexuality fit into the framework of Creation? (see p. 278)	God created everything for good — including all our body parts and our sexuality.	We must do *our* part in protecting and honoring God's creation.
2. Is procreation a necessary function of sexuality? (see p. 280)	One purpose of sexuality is procreation.	Not everyone is able to procreate; some choose not to.
3. What does sexuality contribute to our emotional lives? (see p. 281)	A key facet of sexuality is companionship and the expression of love.	Opportunities for anonymous sex, casual sex, sex that provides physical release, variety, and/or excitement are readily available in secular culture.
4. To what extent should pursuit of pleasure be a contributing factor to a healthy sexual relationship? (see p. 283)	There are duties and responsibilities regarding sex.	Sex should be a source of pleasure.
5. Is the context of the relationship important in evaluating the validity of engaging in sex? (see p. 284)	Judaism consistently affirms and approves of sex in certain contexts.	Judaism consistently disapproves of sex in other contexts.
6. Should we embrace modesty as a worthy value in our day? (see p. 285)	Modesty (*tzeniyut*) is a value for all Jews.	While all Jews should embrace modesty, not everyone accepts the same "code" of behavior.
7. What role might sexuality play in our spiritual lives? (see p. 287)	Sexual intimacy can be an expression of holiness.	Misusing our sexuality can lead to alienation from what God ultimately wants for us (i.e., love, companionship, pleasure).

b. A blessing we are to include in daily worship:

Blessed are You, our Eternal God, Sovereign of the Universe, Who has made our bodies with wisdom, combining openings and closings — arteries, glands, and organs — into a finely balanced network . . .

c. I praise You, for I am awesomely, wondrously made. Your work is wonderful; I know it very well (Psalms 139:14).

d. Judaism does not despise the carnal. It does not urge us to desert the flesh but to control and to counsel it; to please the natural needs of the flesh so that the spirit should not be molested by unnatural frustrations . . . Judaism teaches us how even the gratification of animal needs can be an act of sanctification (Abraham Joshua Heschel, *Man Is Not Alone: A Philosophy of Religion*, New York: Farrar, Straus and Giroux, 1972, p. 263).

Probing: Ideas and Issues

Would you describe sexuality as a gift? Explain your answer. What would a Jewish response be to comments such as, "I hate the way I look" or "I can't stand my body"? What might "taking good care of yourself" mean in regard to one's sexuality? Should a person offer a prayer of thanks prior to or following sexual relations?

2. Is procreation a necessary function of sexuality?

On the One Hand:

One purpose of sexuality is procreation.

Note: Texts in Chapter 13, "Birth Control," (p. 301) have relevance here, too.

A. God blessed them and said to them, "Be fruitful and multiply, fill the earth and master it; and rule over the fish of the sea, and the birds of the sky, and every living thing that moves on the earth" (Genesis 1:28).

B. A man may not refrain from fulfilling the commandment "Be fruitful and multiply" unless he already has children. The School of Shammai ruled he must have two sons. The School of Hillel ruled: a son and a daughter, for it is written, "Male and female God created them" (Genesis 5:2) (*Yevamot* 6:6).

C. Ben Azzai said: those who do not engage in propagation of the race act as though they shed blood and diminish the divine image in the world . . . " (*Yevamot* 63b).

D. We Jews numbered approximately 18 million before the Holocaust, and we lost a third of our numbers during those terrible years. Even if we forget about replenishing the numbers we lost, we are not replacing ourselves as we are now . . . [Statistics show] we are endangering ourselves demographically as a people. The world's overpopulation problem is real, but Jews are only 0.2% of the world's population, and so even if the reproductive rate of Jews increased to the replacement rate, the impact upon the world's population problem would be minimal. That would still be true even if the Jewish people increased to replenish the six million lost in the Holocaust. Sacrificing the existence of the Jewish people is neither an effective solution nor a warranted one to reduce the world's problems of overpopulation and limited resources. These important concerns are better addressed by increasing the availability and usage of contraception worldwide and by fostering the responsible use of resources. The contemporary, demographic problem of the Jewish people, then, must also be a factor which figures into the thinking of Jews using contraception (Rabbi Elliot N. Dorff, *This Is My Beloved, This Is My Friend: A Rabbinic Letter on Intimate Relations*, p. 27-28).

E. Reform Judaism approves birth control, but we also recognize our obligation to maintain a viable and stable Jewish population. Therefore, couples are encouraged to have at least two or three children (Resolution by the Central Conference of American Rabbis, 1978).

On the Other Hand:

Not everyone is able to procreate; some choose not to.

a. In the discussion that continues from Text #2C above, the bachelor Ben Azzai is called to account for his failure to have children.

> They said to Ben Azzai: Some preach well and act well, others act well but do not preach well; you, however, preach well but do not act well!
> Ben Azzai replied: But what shall I do, seeing that my soul is in love with the Torah? The world can be carried on by others (*Yevamot* 63b).

b. Intercourse with a woman incapable at all of childbearing is permissible, and the prohibition of *hash-hatat zera* [improper emission of seed] is not involved so long as the intercourse is in the manner of procreation; for the Rabbis have in every case permitted marriage with women too young or too old for childbearing. No prohibition is involved with a barren or sterile woman, except that the *mitzvah* of procreation is not thus being fulfilled (*Nimmukei Yosef*, early 15th century, commentary to Rabbi Isaac Al Fasi's Code to *Yevamot*, chapter 5).

c. It is not amiss that the reason why women are exempt from the obligation of procreation is grounded in the reasonableness of the judgments of the Eternal and the Eternal's ways. The Torah did not impose upon Israel burdens too difficult for a person to bear . . . Women, whose lives are jeopardized by conception and birth, were not enjoined (*Meshekh Chochmah* to Genesis 9:7, quoted by David S. Shapiro in *Jewish Bioethics*, p. 65).

Probing: Ideas and Issues

Why do you think the Torah instructs human beings to "be fruitful and multiply"? What is Ben Azzai's dilemma concerning this commandment (as described in #2a above)? Is Ben Azzai's explanation for not fulfilling the commandment legitimate? What are good reasons to have children in our time? What might be good reasons not to have children? Are we *obligated* to have children? Should guidelines for procreation be different for Jews as opposed to non-Jews?

3. **What does sexuality contribute to our emotional lives?**

On the One Hand:

A key facet of sexuality is companionship and the expression of love.

A. It is not good for the human to be alone. I will make a fitting companion (*ezer k'neg-do*) for him (Genesis 2:18).

B. Therefore a man leaves his father and mother and clings to his wife, so that they become one flesh (Genesis 2:24).

C. Oh, give me of the kisses of your mouth,
For your love is sweeter than wine . . .
My beloved is mine
And I am his . . .
You have captured my heart,
My own, my bride,
You have captured my heart . . .
I am my beloved's,
And his desire is for me . . .
Let me be a seal upon your heart,
Like the seal upon your hand.
For love is fierce as death,
Passion is mighty as Sheol;
Its darts are darts of fire,
A blazing flame.

Vast floods cannot quench love,
Nor rivers drown it . . .
(Song of Songs 1:2; 2:16; 4:9; 7:11; 8:6-7).

D. This blessing chanted during the wedding ritual refers to the bride and groom as *"ray-eem ahuveem"* or "loving companions":

We praise You, Eternal God, who causes bride and groom to rejoice. May these loving companions rejoice as have Your creatures since the days of creation.

E. In a right and perfect union, the love of a man and a woman is, and should be, inseparable from sexual experience. The emotion of love, which is spiritual, expresses itself in sexual acts, which are physical, so as to create total human participation. The sex-love relationship is not complete unless it is accompanied by a feeling of permanence. It is not an act of deception or even honest hyperbole that impels lovers to swear that their love will endure forever. What is deep and all-inclusive will not be satisfied without the conviction that it will endure.

The love of a man and a woman expresses itself not only in a physical desire for each other, but also by a sense of concern for one another, a desire to make the partner happy at any cost, even a major sacrifice (Robert Gordis, *Love and Sex: A Modern Jewish Perspective*, p. 105).

F. Before sex he should speak sweet words to her, according to his ability . . . and he should soothe her and make her happy, so that they will feel love for each other (*Sefer Kedushah v'Tzniyut*, p. 26b, #22).

On the Other Hand:

Opportunities for anonymous sex, casual sex, sex that provides physical release, variety, and/or excitement are readily available in secular culture.

a. It is part of human nature for a people to emulate the conduct of their immediate society (Maimonides, *Mishneh Torah, Hilchot De'ot* 6:1).

b. David G. Myers, a professor of psychology, explains what can happen as a result of succumbing too readily to sexual opportunities:

Early promiscuity helps predict an individual's statistical risk of sexually transmitted disease, sexual coercion and rape, extramarital sex, nonmarital pregnancy, cohabitation — and, for some of these reasons, the risk of future marital unhappiness and divorce (*An American Paradox*, p. 18).

c. This comment was made by the feminist Sally Cline. She refers to the sexual revolution, in retrospect, as the "Genital Appropriation Era":

What the Genital Appropriation Era actually permitted was more access to women's bodies by more men; what it actually achieved was not a great deal of liberation for women but a great deal of legitimacy for male promiscuity; what it actually passed on to women was the male fragmentation of emotion from body, and the easily internalized schism between genital sex and responsible loving (Cline, 1993 as quoted in *A Return To Modesty: Discovering the Lost Virtue*, p. 192).

Probing: Ideas and Issues

God makes a fitting companion or *"ezer k'neg-do"* for Adam (Text #3A above). In the Hebrew *"ezer k'neg-do"* literally means "a helper opposite or against him." Explain what you think this means — that is, what is the significance of choosing such a phrase for characterizing an appropriate mate?

In Text #3D above, the wedding blessing speaks of *ray-eem ahuveem* or loving companions.

Elaborate on what specifically this might mean (e.g., sharing thoughts and feelings, spending time together pursuing common interests, traveling together, etc.).

Text #3E above says an important aspect of an intimate, loving relationship is that it is *enduring*, that the partners are committed to it lasting a lifetime. Song of Songs gives the same impression (Text #3C above). Do you believe intimate companionship should include the feeling that the relationship will be permanent?

What would be Jewish objections to anonymous or casual sex?

4. **To what extent should pursuit of pleasure be a contributing factor to a healthy sexual relationship?**

On the One Hand:

There are duties and responsibilities regarding sex.

A. The times for conjugal duty prescribed in the Torah are: for men of independent means, every day; for laborers, twice a week; for donkey drivers [who travel about during the week], once a week; for camel drivers [who travel for long periods], once in 30 days; for sailors [who may travel for months], once in six months (*Ketubot* 61b).

. . . Suppose a man wants to change occupations from a donkey driver to camel driver [which pays more but keeps him from home for longer periods]? The answer: a woman prefers less money with enjoyment to more money with abstinence . . . (*Ketubot* 62b).

B. A man is forbidden to compel his wife to have marital relations . . . Rabbi Joshua ben Levi similarly stated: One who compels his wife to have marital relations will have unworthy children (*Eruvin* 100b).

C. Rabbi Joshua ben Levi said: One who knows his wife to be a God-fearing woman and does not duly visit her is

called a sinner (*Yevamot* 62b).

D. The husband and the wife are equal partners in marriage, and they are likewise equal partners in the sexual union. It is true that biologically the sexual act seems to incline toward the man as the initiator and the woman as cooperator with the initiating male. This is true merely in biological fact, but not to the extent of designating the man as the active partner and the woman as the passive partner. Talmudic tradition is very clear about the fact that the woman is not merely a passive partner, and, in many instances, her active role is even greater than that of the man (Rabbi Reuven P. Bulka, *Judaism on Pleasure*, p. 145).

On the Other Hand:

Sex should be a source of pleasure.

a. His left hand was under my head,
His right hand caressed me.
I adjure you, O maidens of Jerusalem:
Do not wake or rouse
Love until it please!
(Song of Songs 8:3-4).

b. People will have to render an account [to God] for all the good things that their eyes beheld, but that they refused to enjoy (*Talmud Yerushalmi*, *Kiddushin* 2:65).

c. Sensual pleasure is unlike other pleasures in two main respects. First . . . for sensual pleasure to approach ultimate bliss, it takes the cooperation of the two involved . . . Second, the sensual experience, if improperly approached, can be very painful, physically and emotionally, for either or both of the individuals. There is thus an implicit challenge in the sensual experience, to each of the partners, to approach the situation properly and to thus assure that it is a pleasurable rather than a painful event (Rabbi Reuven P. Bulka, *Judaism on Pleasure*, p. 132).

d. This text and the one that follows simultaneously address both responsibility and pleasure:

> There must be close bodily contact during sex . . . Rav Huna ruled that a husband who says, "I will not perform my marital duties unless she wears her clothes and I mine," must divorce her and give her also her *ketubah* (marriage contract) settlement (*Ketubot* 48a).

e. When you are ready for sexual union, see that your wife's intentions combine with yours. Do not hurry to arouse her until she is receptive. Be calm, and as you enter the path of love and will, let her insemination (i.e., orgasm) come first . . . (*The Holy Letter,* attributed to Nachmanides).

Probing: Ideas and Issues

What responsibilities do lovers have according to these texts? What additional responsibilities are addressed in other texts you have studied? In Text #3c, Rabbi Reuven Bulka says that sensual pleasure can turn painful. What could this mean? In an intimate relationship, what are the most important things for people to work on to avoid causing pain to each other?

5. **Is the context of the relationship important in evaluating the validity of engaging in sex?**

On the One Hand:

Judaism consistently affirms and approves of sex in certain contexts.

A. Betrothal (*Erusin*) used to take place a year before the actual wedding ceremony (*Kiddushin*) under the canopy (*chupah*). Today, a couple undergoes *Erusin* and *Kiddushin* in one ceremony. This *Erusin* blessing introduces the first step in the formal Jewish sanctioning of sexual relations.

> Praised are You, Eternal our God, Ruler of the Universe, who has sanctified us with Your commandments and commanded us regarding forbidden relations, forbidding sexual relations with our betrothed, permitting marital relations following *chupah* and *Kiddushin*. Praised are You, who sanctifies Your people Israel by *chupah* and *Kiddushin*.

B. Maimonides includes exceptions to the following "rule." Nevertheless, the fundamental principle is quite openminded. Note that Maimonides' permissive attitude toward a man's sexual behavior with his wife presupposes her interest and willingness to receive his advances.

> A man's wife is permitted to him. Therefore a man may do whatever he wishes with his wife. He may have intercourse with her at any time he wishes and kiss her on whatever limb of her body he wants. He may have natural or unnatural sex, as long as he does not bring forth seed in vain (Maimonides, *Mishneh Torah, Hilchot Isuray Biah* 21:10).

On the Other Hand:

Judaism consistently disapproves of sex in other contexts.

a. You shall not commit adultery (Exodus 20:13).

b. If a man is found lying with another man's wife, both of them — the man and the woman with whom he lay — shall die. Thus you will sweep away evil from Israel (Deuteronomy 22:22).

c. The Bible specifies forbidden sexual relations for a man (a comparable list would apply for a woman):

- His mother (Leviticus 18:7).

- His stepmother (Leviticus 18:7).

- His sister, including his half-sister (Leviticus 18:9).

- His daughter (Leviticus 18:10 refers to granddaughter; but daughter is inferred, too).

- His biological aunt (Leviticus 18:12, 13).

- His uncle's wife (Leviticus 18:14).

- His son's wife (Leviticus 18:15).

- His brother's wife (Leviticus 18:16).

- His stepdaughter or mother-in-law (Leviticus 18:17).

- Two sisters (Leviticus 18:18. He may marry a second sister after the first dies).

d. For all transgressions in the Torah, if a person is told "transgress and do not die," that person should transgress and not die. (For example, better to break Shabbat than be killed or eat non-kosher food than be killed, etc.) The exceptions are for idolatry, incest-adultery, and murder. (For example, if someone says, "Have sex with that man's wife or I'll kill you" or "Have sex with your father or I'll kill you," you still should not do it.) (*Sanhedrin* 74a)

e. "I will clear you of those who rebel and transgress against Me" (Ezekiel 20:38). Rabbi Levi said: These [rebels and transgressors] are the offspring which result from nine types [of objectionable sexual relations] (*Nedarim* 20b):

- Children of a man who makes his wife afraid and forces her to have intercourse

- Or who dislikes his wife and thinks of another woman during relations

- Or who is forbidden to have sexual relations by Rabbinic decree

- Or who was not sure which of his wives was with him

- Or who had intercourse when angry at his wife after a quarrel

- Or who was drunk

- Or who had already made up his mind to divorce his wife

- Or children of a woman who had intercourse promiscuously with many men

- Or a woman who demands sexual relations with her husband in an immodest way.

Probing: Ideas and Issues

The above texts draw out black and white areas of permitted and forbidden sexual relationships. From ancient days through our day, Judaism consistently approves of sexual intercourse within marriage. On the other hand, incest and adultery have always been considered wrong. For texts that deal more with the gray areas in sexual relationships, see the "Text Study" section in Chapter 15, "Sex Outside of Marriage," (p. 329). Can you think of other types of objectionable sexual relations besides the ones Rabbi Levi mentions in Text #5e?

6. **Should we embrace modesty as a worthy value in our day?**

On the One Hand:

Modesty (*tzeniyut*) is a value for all Jews.

A. It has been told to you what is good, and what the Eternal requires of you; only to do justly, to love mercy, and to walk modestly (*hatzne'a*) with your God (Micah 6:8).

B. Standing around naked inevitably decreases a person's dignity (*Tosefta, Brachot* 2:14).

C. The Rabbis asked why Balaam, sent to curse the Jews, blessed them instead. They answered:

> Each tent was arranged so that no doorway faced another doorway. No one could ever easily look into another's tent. Balaam was so impressed that Israel valued privacy and modesty that he changed his curse into a blessing (Rashi on Numbers 24:5).

D. Marital intercourse should be modest and holy, carried on in a spirit of restraint and delicacy, in reverence and silence (Eliezer b. Samuel of Mainz, *Hebrew Ethical Wills,* as quoted in *The Jewish Moral Virtues*, p. 155).

On the Other Hand:

While all Jews should embrace modesty, not everyone accepts the same "code" of behavior.

a. The text below and others like it has led the most traditional Jewish communities to embrace restrictive codes of dress and behavior. Not every Orthodox community interprets the standards in the same way. However, at their strictest, the standards may include: requiring women to keep most of their bodies and all their hair covered, disallowing women to sing in front of men who are not close relatives, and not permitting men to listen to women on radio, television, or recordings, nor attend opera or theater.

> Rav Hisda said: A woman's leg is *ervah* (sexually suggestive) . . . Shmuel said: A woman's voice is *ervah* . . . Rav Sheshet said: A woman's hair is suggestive (*Brachot* 24a).

b. Elliot Dorff, a Conservative Rabbi, offers his take on modesty for our times:

> The privacy (*tzniut*, modesty) that Judaism requires of sex affects our clothing, our speech, and our public activities. We may dress in accord with the styles of the times, but never should our apparel accentuate the sexually arousing parts of our bodies. Thus sexually suggestive or revealing clothes for either men or women are not in keeping with Jewish law or sensibilities.
>
> Similarly, our speech patterns should manifest respect for our bodies as creations of God, and this includes the generative parts of our bodies. Sexual language which is crass or violent bespeaks discomfort with one's body and disrespect for its divine value. It also cheapens the level of discourse, thereby diminishing the stature of everyone concerned, including especially the speaker.
>
> Judaism's expectations of modesty also affect our behavior in public. Sexual activity should be reserved for private quarters. This is not to demean sex as something sordid which one must hide; quite the contrary, it is to sanctify it as the intense, intimate, mutual expression of love that it should be. Such love is understood within Jewish sources to be a great good, but a private one (*This Is My Beloved, This Is My Friend: A Rabbinic Letter on Intimate Relations*, pp. 9-10).

c. A Reform statement on modesty:

> The classic *Iggeret Ha-Kodesh*, "The Holy Letter," sets forth the Jewish view that the Holy One did not create anything that is not beautiful and potentially good. The human body in itself is never to be considered an object of shame or embarrassment. Instead, " . . . it is the manner and context in which it is utilized, the ends to which it is used, which determine condemnation or praise." Our

behavior should never reduce the human body to an object. Dress, language and behavior should reflect a sensitivity to the Jewish respect for modesty and privacy. As Jews we acknowledge and celebrate the differences between public, private and holy places as well as the differences between public, private and holy time (*Ad Hoc Committee On Human Sexuality, Report to the CCAR Convention,* June 1998).

Probing: Ideas and Issues

What is the connection between "walking modestly with God" (Text #6A) and being a modest person in dress and behavior? What does a person gain by being modest? What does a person lose by being immodest? Do you feel there should be a higher standard of modesty in our culture? Explain. Should there be a higher standard of modesty in your own social group?

7. **What role might sexuality play in our spiritual lives?**

On the One Hand:

Sexual intimacy can be an expression of holiness.

A. You shall be holy, for I, the Eternal your God, am holy (Leviticus 19:2).

B. What is that small verse on which hangs all the critical principles of the Torah? "In all your ways, know God" (Proverbs 3:6) (*Brachot* 63a).

C. [A man and woman] should have the same intentions in sex, and when they are thus united, the two are one in body and soul. In soul — for they cleave to one another with one will and desire, and in body — for a person who is unmarried is only half a body. When male and female unite sexually they become one body. So there is then one soul and one body, and

together they are called "one person," and the Holy One, Who Is Blessed comes to rest on that one (*Reshit Chochmah, Sh'ar ha-Kedushah*, chapter 16, #3, quoted in *Sefer Kedushah v'Tzniyut,* and by Yitzhak Buxbaum, *Jewish Spiritual Practices,* p. 593).

D. "From my flesh, I shall see God . . . " The sexual organ is the seat of one's greatest physical pleasure. This pleasure comes about when man and woman unite, and it thus results from unification. From the physical, we perceive the spiritual (Baal Shem Tov, quoted by Jacob Joseph of Polnoye, *Toledot Yaakov Yosef,* Jerusalem, 1960, volume 1, p. 57).

E. There is no sexual intercourse without embracing and kissing preceding it. And there are two kinds of kissing: the first is before sexual intercourse, where the purpose of kissing is that the man soothe the woman and arouse the love between them; the other kind is during intercourse itself, where the purpose is to accomplish the two kinds of union, the lower one and the supernal one together (*Siddur Yabetz* quoted in *Sefer Kedushah v'Tzniyut* p. 29, #28, and by Yitzhak Buxbaum, *Jewish Spiritual Practices,* p. 604).

F. Physically, one sexual relationship looks pretty much like another. Biologically the process is the same, whether the relationship is a casual pickup at a bar, an adulterous liaison at a hotel, a couple in love but not ready for the commitment of marriage, or a married couple sharing a bed as they build a home together. Yet in Judaism only the last relationship is called *kiddushin*, marriage — literally, holiness . . .

Our task as Jews is to connect ourselves to the realm of the holy by making *kedushah* part of our lives . . .

Holiness is achieved by walking a middle road between asceticism and hedonism. It comes through discipline, through the understanding that pleasure comes through observing the commandments, and through making an act special and set apart. Judaism claims that sex attains this level of holiness only within the context of marriage . . . (Michael Gold, *Does God Belong in the Bedroom*, p. 20-21, 25).

On the Other Hand:

Misusing our sexuality can lead to alienation from what God ultimately wants for us (i.e., love, companionship, pleasure).

a. Sin diminishes the Image of God (*Yevamot* 63b).

b. "God saw everything God had made and behold it was very good" (Genesis 1:31).

    Nothing in the human organs is created flawed or ugly. Everything is created with divine wisdom and is therefore complete, exalted, good, and pleasant. But when one sins, ugliness becomes attached to these matters (Attributed to Nachmanides, *The Holy Letter*, p. 45, 48).

c. Sex, as understood in the Jewish tradition, can distance one from God if one violates some of Judaism's norms relevant to it, but sex can also bring human lives closer to God as one fulfills the divine purposes of companionship and procreation (Elliot N. Dorff, *This Is My Beloved, This Is My Friend*, p. 13).

Probing: Ideas and Issues

What makes a relationship holy? Why is holiness important in a sexual relationship? How will you or do you conduct yourself so that you pursue holiness in an intimate relationship?

RELATED MIDDOT AND MITZVOT

These *middot* (virtues) and *mitzvot* (commandments) help infuse decisions about sex with Jewish values. They are applicable to all five chapters on issues of sexuality found in Part IV of this book.

Emet (Truthfulness): Lovers must be able to trust one another (see *Emunah*, below). Being truthful is a necessary element of building trust.

Emunah (Trustworthiness): In sexual relationships, partners make themselves vulnerable as they reveal themselves to each other. This requires the individuals to trust each other deeply.

Lo Levayesh (Not Embarrassing): A person's body and sexuality are private. What happens between two people as part of their intimate life is private as well. It is wrong to tease or embarrass others about personal matters.

Ma'akeh (Preventing Accidents): Unwanted pregnancies and sexually transmitted diseases can occur when people do not take the necessary precautions. Those who engage in sex must be responsible for preventing "accidents."

Mechabayd Zeh et Zeh (Honoring Others): Honor and care about others' dignity. Do not treat people as objects (i.e., physical machines), but respect them as full, complex human beings.

Ohev Zeh et Zeh (Loving Others): At some time in our lives, we may have a special love for one person. Along the way, as we encounter potential partners, love for our fellow human beings requires that we not cause hurt.

Shmirat HaGuf (Taking Care of Your Body): In terms of sexuality, this includes: getting regular physical checkups, being responsible about birth control, keeping clean, avoiding circumstances that might lead to getting or giving a sexually transmitted disease, and getting help when a relationship feels dangerous or has become violent.

Simchah (Joy and Happiness): We celebrate the pleasures of sexual relationship.

Tzeniyut (Modesty): This includes being respectful and humble, not showing off. Casually revealing your body and allowing easy access to it by others makes you more like an object than a "vehicle for holiness."

ACTIVITIES

A First Look: Key Issues and Ideas

1. A set induction: Survey students about what they know about Jewish sexual ethics and what they would like to learn about the topic.

2. After some initial study, with the whole group or in pairs, list some of the foundations of Jewish sexual ethics (for example, "companionship" and "modesty").

3. Refer back to Text Study #1. Lead a discussion on the importance of self-esteem and a positive body image for ethical sexual behavior.

Applying Middot and Mitzvot

1. Refer to the "Related Middot and Mitzvot" section above. Have students rank the values and commandments from most to least important in terms of developing a proper attitude toward sexuality. Discuss and explain their rankings. Then ask them to answer these questions and explain their responses:

- Which *middah* or *mitzvah* is most difficult?

- Which comes most easily to people? How about to *you* personally?

- Are there other *middot* and *mitzvot* you would add to the list?

- Do you know "role models" — that is, people who model the *middot* and *mitzvot* in their relationship? Explain.

- If you are in a committed relationship, how well do you and your partner model the *middot* and *mitzvot*?

- What is the relationship between these *middot* and *mitzvot* and "holiness"?

2. Have the group (perhaps in pairs) come up with examples or imaginary scenarios of when each *middah* or *mitzvah* (or select ones) does and does not happen. Here are sample ideas participants could expand upon:

- A couple honors each other when _____.

- A couple doesn't honor each other when _____.

- Trust builds in a relationship when _____.

- Trust is destroyed in a relationship because _____.

3. Modern Jewish perspectives have emphasized the importance of equality and mutuality in relationships (more so than do traditional Jewish sources). After initial study of the foundations of Jewish sexuality (including text study), look up the dictionary definitions for "equality" and "mutuality." Then, ask students:

- How are the values of equality and mutuality reflected in Jewish tradition?

- Do you think the dictionary definitions of equality and mutuality should apply in dating relationships? In marriage?

- To what degree are the values of equality and mutuality upheld in the dating relationships you witness in your community? In the marriages?

- What do you believe are your personal obligations in bringing equality and mutuality to an intimate relationship?

4. For more information and activities on:

Emet (Truthfulness): see *Teaching Jewish Virtues* by Susan Freeman, pp. 69-84.

Emunah (Trustworthiness): see *The Jewish Moral Virtues* by Eugene B. Borowitz and Frances Weinman Schwartz, pp. 27-39.

Lo Levayesh (Not Embarrassing): see *Teaching Jewish Virtues* by Susan Freeman, pp. 119-135.

Ma'akeh (Preventing Accidents): see *Teaching Mitzvot* by Barbara Binder Kadden and Bruce Kadden, pp. 205-208. For an Instant Lesson that focuses on "safe sex," see "Prevention Is a Mitzvah" by Joel Lurie Grishaver.

Mechabayd Zeh et Zeh (Honoring Others): see *Teaching Jewish Virtues* by Susan Freeman, pp. 179-194.

Ohev Zeh et Zeh (Loving Others): see *Teaching Jewish Virtues* by Susan Freeman, pp. 179-194.

Shmirat HaGuf (Taking Care of Your Body): see *Teaching Jewish Virtues* by Susan Freeman, pp. 269-282.

Simchah (Joy and Happiness): see *Teaching Jewish Virtues* by Susan Freeman, pp. 283-298.

Tzeniyut (Modesty): see *The Jewish Moral Virtues* by Eugene B. Borowitz and Frances Weinman Schwartz, pp. 149-160. For an excellent full unit on modesty, see the Instant Lesson "Body Ethics: Modesty" by Kerry M. Olitzky and Joel Lurie Grishaver.

Stories: Understanding through Listening

1. Ask a married couple(s) whose relationship you admire to visit your class. Have them share what they feel makes their relationship work. You may want to prepare a list of appropriate questions to ask the visitors beforehand. A few possible sample questions:

- How did you meet?

- What attracted you to each other?

- What made you realize that you wanted to get to know each other better?

- How did you decide to get married?

- What kind of advice did the Rabbi give you before you were married?

- What was the best advice you were given about marriage?

- Have you followed the advice?

- What is the most difficult thing about marriage?

- Etc.

A variation: Instead of inviting visitors, have participants conduct interviews on their own, outside of class. Then, have them report back to the group on their findings.

2. Invite a Rabbi to speak with your group. Ask him/her to share what happens during pre-marital counseling sessions. What kind of advice does he/she give? Have the Rabbi share stories about marriages he/she has witnessed (disguising the actual people's identities). Specifically, here are some suggestions on what to ask:

- What problems do you see most often with married couples?

- How do people deal with the problems most effectively?

- What do you believe makes for a strong marriage?

- What are the worst things you've observed in marriages?

- What are the best things?

- How would you define a good sexual relationship?

- Why is a good sexual relationship important in a marriage?

- Have you ever refused to perform a wedding ceremony for a Jewish couple? For what reasons did you refuse?

- How would you respond to a couple that says they never want to have children?

- How would you respond to a couple that says they want to get married, they love each other, but don't believe they're sexually compatible?

3. Invite a guest to class to speak about *taharat ha-mishpachah* (the laws of family purity) and *mikvah* (ritual immersion). For many Jews, these practices are an important part of the rhythms of their sex life. If possible, include an actual visit to a *mikvah*.

4. Refer to the "Scenarios: How Things Have Changed" section above (pp. 277-278). Review the stories and ask these questions:

- What are some of the positive aspects of Moshe and Leah's relationship?

- What challenges might Moshe and Leah face in their relationship?

- What might we learn and apply from their experience to relationships today?

- What are some of the positive aspects of Marc and Liana's story?

- What do you think about their plans to marry?

Now, ask participants (perhaps in pairs) to write a scenario with a continuation to the Marc and Liana story that they think would be ideal. When everyone completes the task, have them share their work with the whole group. For one possible continuation of Marc and Liana's story, see the "Scenario Update" in Chapter 15, "Sex Outside of Marriage," beginning on p. 329.

Action: Getting Out, Getting Involved

1. What is the sex or health education curriculum in your school (or your child's school)? Is it adequate? appropriate? Does it address the necessary issues effectively? Are sexual ethics part of the curriculum? Where does the curriculum seem to succeed? What doesn't seem to be working as well, and why? Give feedback about this area of education to the appropriate authorities.

2. This activity is for a group in which there is a good level of trust. Ask: Are the lines of communication sufficiently open in your family regarding issues of sexuality? What is easy to talk about? What is more difficult? How might family members improve communication on this topic? Have group members plan steps to make improvements in this area, then report back to the group.

3. Planned Parenthood has a brochure called *"Is This Love?: How to Tell If Your Relationship Is Good for You."* Try to obtain a copy of this brochure, though it is not necessary for this activity. Ask students to write their own version of such a brochure that would be appropriate to make available to Jewish high school (or possibly middle school) students.

   Aim to have the group produce a high quality version that can be printed up and actually made available.

Wrestling: Engagement with the Issues

1. Refer to the "General Perspectives" section of the Overview. Go over with your group Sol and Judith Gordon's list of the seven deadly sins of immoral sex (p. 276). Then ask group members to come up with seven additional sins, which they specifically derive from their studies of Jewish sexual ethics.

   Make torn paper collages for one or more of the "deadly sins."

2. Have participants choose a preferred art medium — drawing/painting, sculpture, collage, dance, poetry, prose, etc. Ask them to express their ideas and feelings in a creative, artistic way about love, companionship, pleasure, and holiness.

   A variation: use an art form to express ideas about modesty (*tzeniyut*).

3. Gather a stack of popular health, beauty, and/or fashion magazines. Have participants flip through them and find stories and articles related to sexuality. Have them summarize the point of view of each piece and what values underlie it. Then, have them comment on whether or not the message conveyed is consistent with Jewish values. Explain why or why not.

4. Refer to the "Scenarios: How Things Have Changed" section above (pp. 277-278). Review the stories. Then, ask participants to compose a love advice letter (i.e., "Dear Abby" style) from one of the four characters: Moshe, Leah, Marc, or Liana. The letter response should be from a Jewish perspective. That means instead of "Dear Abby," the letter will be "Dear Rabbi" (or other Jewish expert).

5. Rabbi Michael Gold, in his book *Does God Belong in the Bedroom*, pp. 169-170, poses 18 sexuality-related dilemmas teens especially might encounter. These are excellent! Use them as discussion starters or adapt them for role-playing. After students come up with their responses, offer what might be Jewish responses (or invite in a Rabbi to do so). Note that some of the dilemmas would fit more precisely under the headings of the other chapters which follow.

   a. Luann, a high school senior, has a boyfriend who says: "If you love me, you will sleep with me."

   b. Jack and Jill decide to live together to see if they are really compatible before marriage.

   c. A public high school wants to establish a clinic which will provide birth control for students.

   d. Sally is sexually abused by her stepfather, who tells her not to tell anyone.

   e. Fred discovers that his wife Sheila has carried on an extramarital affair.

   f. Howard and Kate decide to have an open marriage, with permission to seek other sexual partners.

   g. Barry decides to remain a virgin until marriage although other boys make fun of him.

   h. Janet, 15 years old, is pregnant after sleeping with her boyfriend.

   i. A Jewish high school decides to hold a special sex education class taught by a nurse and a Rabbi.

   j. Jeff wants his wife Debbie to go to the *mikvah* each month.

   k. Steve and Judy tell the Rabbi before their wedding that they plan not to have children.

   l. A new gay synagogue wants to advertise in the local Jewish newspaper.

   m. Rhonda, married with a child, wants to leave her husband for a lesbian lover.

   n. George's parents have told him that masturbation is a sin that leads to disease.

   o. A pornographic theater opens in a local Jewish neighborhood.

   p. Jon likes to brag about his sexual conquests.

   q. A youth group is having an overnight trip and wants boys and girls to sleep in the same room.

   r. Bob and Laurie, married ten years with no children, decide to have a baby using in vitro fertilization.

6. *Love in Your Life* by Roland B. Gittelsohn is another excellent resource for dilemmas to discuss. At the end of each chapter, under the heading "What Do You Think?," is a several paragraph predicament, including discussion questions.

Empathy

1. Assure participants that wrestling with issues of love and sex is a challenge for everyone. Because of the personal nature of sexuality, it can be difficult both to offer support to others and/or solicit support for yourself when you need it. Hold a discussion about ways to get help when you have problems, when you are confused or upset regarding love and sex issues. Who might you turn to? How might they help?

Consider parents, Rabbi, teacher, school counselor or nurse, doctor, close friend, an organization such as Planned Parenthood, etc. Perhaps suggest resources, such as those mentioned in the Bibliography of this chapter or recommend that students visit the local library for appropriate books. Many find prayer and/or meditation to be helpful tools as they try to make sense of a difficult situation. Also, discuss the usefulness of diaries and journals for sorting through dilemmas. You may want to read excerpts of published journals, diaries, or memoirs that deal with this subject.

BIBLIOGRAPHY

Note: The sources listed here are relevant for all five chapters dealing with issues of sexuality found in Part IV of Teaching Hot Topics.

Jewish Sources

Balka, Christine, and Andy Rose. *Twice Blessed: On Being Lesbian, Gay, and Jewish.* Boston, MA: Beacon Press, 1989.

Borowitz, Eugene B. *Choosing a Sex Ethic: A Jewish Inquiry.* New York: Schocken Books for B'nai B'rith Hillel Foundation, 1969.

Borowitz, Eugene B., and Francine Weinman Schwartz. Chapters on *Tzeniyut* (Modesty) and *Emunah* (Trustworthiness). In *The Jewish Moral Virtues.* Philadelphia, PA: The Jewish Publication Society, 1999.

Bulka, Reuven P. *Judaism on Pleasure.* Northvale, NJ: Jason Aronson Inc., 1995.

Buxbaum, Yitzhak. *Jewish Spiritual Practices.* Northvale, NJ: Jason Aronson Inc., 1990.

Cohen, J. Seymour, trans. *The Holy Letter.* New York: KTAV Publishing House, Inc., 1996. (Traditionally attributed to Nachmanides, but actual authorship unknown. First published in Rome in 1546.)

Dorff, Elliot N. *Matters of Life and Death: A Jewish Approach To Modern Medical Ethics.* Philadelphia, PA and Jerusalem: The Jewish Publication Society, 1998.

———. *"This Is My Beloved, This Is My Friend"* (Song of Songs 5:16): A Rabbinic Letter on Intimate Relations.* New York: The Rabbinical Assembly, 1996.

Eisen, Efraim, and Rosalie Eisen. *To Meet Your Soul Mate, You Must Meet Your Soul.* (Part of the "LifeLights" series) Woodstock, VT: Jewish Lights Publishing, 2002.

Feldman, David M. *Marital Relations, Birth Control, and Abortion in Jewish Law.* New York: New York University Press, 1968. Republished by New York: Schocken Books, 1974.

Freeman, Susan. *Teaching Jewish Virtues: Sacred Sources and Arts Activities.* Denver, CO: A.R.E. Publishing, Inc., 1999.

Gittelsohn, Roland B. *Love in Your Life.* New York: UAHC Press, 1991.

Gold, Michael. *Does God Belong in the Bedroom?* Philadelphia, PA: The Jewish Publication Society, 1992.

Gordis, Robert. *Love & Sex: A Modern Jewish Perspective.* New York: Farrar, Straus and Giroux, 1978.

Jacob, Walter, ed. *American Reform Responsa.* New York: Central Conference of American Rabbis, 1983.

Kadden, Barbara Binder, and Bruce Kadden. *Teaching Mitzvot: Concepts, Values, and Activities.* Rev. ed. Denver, CO: A.R.E. Publishing, Inc., 2003.

Lamm, Maurice. *The Jewish Way in Love and Marriage.* San Francisco, CA: Harper & Row, 1980.

Lamm, Norman. "Judaism and the Modern Attitude toward Homosexuality," *Encyclopaedia Judaica Yearbook.* Jerusalem: Keter Publishing House, 1974.

Levine, Judith. "Thinking about Sex." In *Tikkun, an Anthology,* ed. by Michael Lerner. Oakland, CA and Jerusalem: Tikkun Books, 1992.

Marder, Janet. "Jewish and Gay." In *Keeping Posted* 32, 2; November 1986.

Olitzky, Kerry M., and Joel Lurie Grishaver. *Body Ethics: Modesty* (Instant Lesson). Los Angeles, CA: Torah Aura Productions.

Orenstein, Debra. *Life Cycles: Volume 1: Jewish Women on Life Passages and Personal Milestones.* Woodstock, VT: Jewish Lights Publishing, 1994.

Parent Education for Parents of Adolescents: Teacher's Manual. New York: United Synagogue Commission on Jewish Education, Family Education Committee, 1981.

Polish, Daniel F., Daniel B. Syme, and Bernard M. Zlotowitz. *Drugs, Sex, and Integrity.* New York: The UAHC Press, 1991.

Prevention Is a Mitzvah (Instant Lesson). Los Angeles, CA: Torah Aura Productions, 1992.

Rosner, Fred, and J. David Bleich. *Jewish Bioethics.* New York: Sanhedrin Press, 1979.

Sherwin, Byron L., and Seymour J. Cohen. *Creating an Ethical Jewish Life: A Practical Introduction To Classic Teachings on How to Be a Jew.* Woodstock, VT: Jewish Lights Publishing, 2001.

Strassfeld, Sharon, and Michael Strassfeld, eds. *The Second Jewish Catalogue.* Philadelphia, PA and Jerusalem: The Jewish Publication Society, 1976, Ch. 1, pp. 10-150.

Tendler, Moshe. *Pardes Rimonim.* New York: The Judaica Press, 1979.

Waskow, Arthur. *Down-To-Earth Judaism: Food, Money, Sex, and the Rest of Life.* New York: William Morrow & Co., 1995.

Yedwab, Paul. *Sex in the Texts.* New York: The UAHC Press, 2001.

General Sources:

Calderone, Mary, and Eric Johnson. *The Family Book about Sexuality.* New York: Harper and Row, 1989.

Eyre, Linda and Richard. *Teaching Your Children Values.* New York: Simon and Schuster, 1993.

Gordon, Sol and Judith. *Raising a Child Conservatively in a Sexually Permissive World.* New York: Simon and Schuster, 1983.

Gravelle, Karen. *What's Going on Down There? Answers To Questions Boys Find Hard to Ask.* New York: Walker and Company, 1998.

Maguire, Daniel C. *Sacred Choices: The Right To Contraception and Abortion in Ten World Religions.* Minneapolis, MN: Fortress Press, 2001.

McCoy, Kathy, and Charles Wibbelsman, M.D. *Growing and Changing: A Handbook for Preteens.* New York: The Berkley Publishing Group, 1986.

Madaras, Lynda. *The What's Happening To My Body? Book for Boys.* New York: Newmarket Press, 1988.

Madaras, Lynda. *The What's Happening To My Body? Book for Girls.* New York: Newmarket Press, 1988.

Mayle, Peter. *"What's Happening To Me?"* Secaucus, NJ: Lyle Stuart Inc., 1975.

Myers, David G. *The American Paradox: Spiritual Hunger in an Age of Plenty.* New Haven, CT and London: Yale University Press, 2000.

Palardy, Debra J. *Sweetie, Here's the Best Reason on the Planet to Say No To Your Boyfriend: Even If You've Already Said Yes.* Pittsburgh, PA: Dorrance Publishing Co., Inc., 2000.

Pollack, Rachel, and Cheryl Schwartz. *The Journey Out: A Guide for and about Lesbian, Gay, and Bisexual Teens.* New York: Puffin Books, 1995.

Shalit, Wendy. *A Return To Modesty: Discovering the Lost Virtue.* New York: Touchstone, 1999.

Web Sites:

Human Rights Campaign Fund: www.hrc.org

> *Advocates for lesbian, gay, bisexual, and transgender equal rights. Also, click on "Links" to see numerous links to other relevant organizations.*

Parents, Families and Friends of Lesbians and Gays (PFLAG): www.pflag.org

> *Promotes the health and well-being of gay, lesbian, bisexual and transgendered persons, their families and friends through support, education, and advocacy.*

Planned Parenthood:
www.plannedparenthood.org

Advocates for the fundamental right of each individual, throughout the world, to reproductive self-determination.

Religious Coalition for Reproductive Choice:
www.rcrc.org

Works to ensure reproductive choice through the moral power of religious communities.

Spiritual Youth for Reproductive Freedom:
www.syrf.org

Pro-choice, pro-faith education and advocacy.

United Nations Population Fund:
www.unfpa.org

The world's largest international source of funding for population and reproductive health programs.

World Congress of Gay, Lesbian, Bisexual, and Transgender Jews (Keshet Ga'avah):
www.wcgljo.org

Representing the interests of lesbian, gay, and bisexual Jews around the world.

Population Connection (formerly Zero Population Growth):
www.populationconnection.org

A national grassroots population organization that educates young people and advocates progressive action to stabilize world population at a level that can be sustained by Earth's resources.

CHAPTER 12

MASTURBATION

OVERVIEW

Jewish Perspectives

Often, Judaism expresses a range of views on a topic. That is, in each era of discussion, some Sages will give restrictive opinions and others more lenient ones. For most of its history, this exchange of ideas was not part of masturbation discussions. Traditional Jewish sources denounced (male) masturbation unequivocally, often in strong language. They focused on male masturbation. Female masturbation was not considered a serious concern. In recent decades, views of masturbation have opened up considerably (though less so in Orthodoxy).

There are several reasons why Jews today might reconsider masturbation in a more lenient light. One is that medical experts have discounted the detrimental physical concerns associated with male masturbation. Traditional Jewish texts express concern regarding "wasting the seed," as if men are endowed with a limited, irreplaceable supply. We now know that men continually produce sperm throughout their lives, and that the "extra" ejaculations (of typical masturbation) will not damage a man's fertility.

Some express concerns that masturbation turns a sexual experience into a selfish one, rather than one shared with a partner. In contrast, others say that to enjoy *one's own* body does not cancel out a person's ability to enjoy sex with a partner. Masturbation helps relieve a physical urge — an ethically neutral event. With a partner, sex is a completely different experience. Ideally, sex with a partner involves emotional bonds of love, caring, and commitment.

Some might say that masturbation is "indecent" or "immodest." Others might respond that masturbation should be a private matter. That is, if masturbation remains private, modesty is not compromised. However, most Jewish authorities would agree that a group of teenage boys or girls (or men or women) masturbating together would be "indecent."

Our culture places new demands on sexual ethics in many ways. A central one is that, though young men and women are physically mature and have sexual urges by their mid-teens, they often do not marry for another ten to 20 years. Forbidding sexual release for that amount of time is difficult to expect of people. Some communities might respond by urging young people to marry earlier. Earlier marriages will diminish the temptations of masturbation and premarital sex. Others call for rethinking Jewish guidelines for sexual behavior. As far as masturbation goes, it does not have the potential consequences of sex with a partner (i.e., pregnancy or sexually transmitted diseases). Most agree that younger teens do not have the maturity to handle a sexual relationship (marriage or otherwise). Therefore, masturbation actually can be an appropriate and helpful way to deal with sexual urges.

General Perspectives

While masturbation can be an embarrassing topic, sex educators generally try to remove the stigma from it. They see masturbation as a normal activity, something most people experience at some point or even continually throughout their lives. They may point out positive benefits of masturbation, such as getting to know your body better and learning what gives you pleasure. As stated above, medical experts overwhelmingly dismiss physical dangers of masturbation. As long as thoughts and experiences of masturbation don't infringe on living a healthy life, there is no (general) reason to worry if it is something one enjoys doing.

Summary of the Overview

- While traditional Jewish sources denounce masturbation, lenient Jewish attitudes have become more prevalent.

- Key elements influencing opinions on masturbation include: traditional Jewish views, modern medical expertise, modesty and privacy, questions of the validity of pleasing oneself, and the need to respond to young people's lifestyles today.

- Sex researchers generally see masturbation as normal, not something to be ashamed about, having some practical benefits, as well.

SCENARIOS: HOW THINGS HAVE CHANGED

Jewish thinkers are reevaluating traditional attitudes toward masturbation. The two scenarios below reflect the trends of Jewish opinion about masturbation. These scenarios, one set in ancient days and one in contemporary times, are intended to raise questions and spark discussion. Read each scenario to or with your students, and engage them in small or large group discussions. Use the "Focus the Discussion" section below to help you identify the important issues and facilitate these discussions. Then continue on to the "Text Study" section to see what Jewish and other sources have to say about our topic. Finally, you may wish to have students discuss the scenarios a second time to see if their views have changed.

Scenario 1: In Days of the Talmud

Shimon and Reuven are 16 years old. Both feel tremendous sexual tension, thinking about sex all the time, imagining themselves having intercourse, and often unexpectedly having erections. They, of course, have never spoken about this private matter. Both boys know that Judaism teaches that they shouldn't masturbate. Shimon

resists the urge, though it is uncomfortable, even painful to do so. Reuven does masturbate and enjoys great relief and pleasure in this activity. However, he feels guilty about his actions, and often feels depressed because he worries that he is a sinner.

Scenario 2: Nowadays

Simon and Richard are 16 years old. Both feel tremendous sexual tension, thinking about sex all the time, imagining themselves having intercourse, and often unexpectedly having erections. Each has masturbated privately for a couple of years. They have never spoken about this personal matter with anybody but each other. It helps to have at least one person to confide in. In their sex education class and from their reading, the boys feel assured that masturbation is a normal and acceptable way to relieve sexual tension. When they begin to study recent Jewish teachings on the matter, they remain comfortable with their choice to masturbate. They enjoy great relief and pleasure from this activity. They feel they are not ready for intercourse with their girlfriends. Masturbation has helped them resist pressuring their girlfriends to have sex.

Focus the Discussion

The scenarios reflect the trends of Jewish opinion about masturbation. Traditional Jewish opinion — then and now — has opposed it. Liberal Jews today express more lenient attitudes. They generally accept research that sees masturbation as a normal and healthy behavior, and rules of the past as outdated and irrelevant.

TEXT STUDY

Though historically Judaism has taken an unequivocal stance on the question of masturbation, in modern times that attitude has begun to change. Jewish texts and other sources express varying viewpoints which highlight the

Masturbation: A Question to Consider

The Question	On the One Hand	On the Other Hand
1. What is Jewish opinion on masturbation? (see this page below)	Historically, Judaism has frowned on masturbation.	Modern liberal attitudes tend to be more accepting of masturbation.

tension between seemingly opposing considerations. The chart above highlights the key Jewish question about masturbation. Text sources supporting the two opposing points of view follow.

1. What is Jewish opinion on masturbation?

On the One Hand:

Historically, Judaism has opposed masturbation.

A. Although it is difficult to isolate a biblical sanction against masturbation, David M. Feldman summarizes some of the negativity expressed in various Rabbinic texts:

> With or without literal biblical sanctions, the sin, in the Rabbinic view, is serious enough. He who destroys his generative seed commits murder, acts like a beast which takes no heed of what it does, cannot receive the *Sh'khinah* [Presence of God], stands "under the ban" [akin to excommunication], and is guilty of autoerotic indecency (*Marital Relations, Birth Control, and Abortion in Jewish Law*, p. 114).

B. Though not referring to masturbation, Maimonides offers his opinion about medical consequences of ejaculation:

> Semen constitutes the strength of the body, its life, and the light of the eyes. Its emission to excess causes physical decay, debility, and diminished vitality . . . Whoever indulges in sexual dissipation becomes prematurely aged; his strength fails; his eyes become dim; a foul odor proceeds from his mouth and armpits; the hair of his head, eyebrows, and eyelashes drop out; the hair of his beard, armpits, and legs grow abnormally; his teeth fall out; and besides these, he becomes subject to numerous other diseases . . . (Maimonides, *Mishneh Torah, Laws of Ethics* 4:19).

On the Other Hand:

Modern liberal attitudes tend to be more accepting of masturbation.

Note: Text Study #1a in Chapter 13, "Birth Control" (p. 306) concisely explains historical attitudes regarding "wasting the seed" — an issue relevant to masturbation, as well.

a. In modern times, many Orthodox Jews retain [restrictive] beliefs and prohibitions [concerning masturbation], but Conservative, Reform, and unaffiliated Jews largely do not. The grounds for this change are largely medical: neither physicians nor laypeople believe that masturbation has the medical consequences described by Maimonides. Moreover, few believe the mystical tradition's depiction of the dire results of masturbation. To date, none of the three movements has taken an official position validating masturbation, but in practice the tradition's abhorrence of masturbation is largely ignored (Elliot N. Dorff, *Matters of Life and Death*, p. 119).

b. While, in Rabbinic, and especially post-Rabbinic literature . . . there is editorial comment denouncing the practice, no punishment is set down. Evidently, it was realized (even then) that the practice was common and had certain "natural" advantages so that, while it warranted denouncing, the denunciation was (evidently) intended as a control factor to diminish rather than eliminate (*Parent Education for Parents of Adolescents: Teacher's Manual*, p. 48, quoted by Michael Gold, p. 175-176).

c. If teen sexual activity is to be discouraged, what can teenagers do to relieve the very real sexual tension they feel? With the onset of puberty, the hormones are raging and the sexual drive is immense. The only realistic solution is that perhaps it is time for Rabbis to rethink the Jewish prohibition against masturbation (Michael Gold, *Does God Belong in the Bedroom?*, p. 175).

d. Masturbation is a risk-free sexual activity because no body fluids are shared with a partner. Some people are embarrassed to talk about it, but most people enjoy masturbation throughout their lives (*Sexual Health Series:* "A Young Woman's Guide To Sexuality," Planned Parenthood Federation of America, 2001).

Probing: Ideas and Issues

What are some traditional reasons for the disapproval of masturbation? Why do many modern Jewish thinkers take issue with "tradition" on this topic? Do you feel the reasons for taking issue are valid? Explain.

RELATED MIDDOT AND MITZVOT

A complete list of *middot* and *mitzvot* that relate to issues of sexuality appears in Chapter 11, "Foundations of Sexual Ethics," on pages 288-289.

ACTIVITIES

A First Look: Key Issues and Ideas

1. Work with students to list traditional objections to masturbation and what might be a lenient response to each. Discuss how your orientation to Jewish practice in general might influence your attitude toward masturbation.

Applying Middot and Mitzvot

1. Discuss the relevancy of these *middot* and *mitzvot* to masturbation:

Tzeniyut (Modesty): For example, masturbation is a personal matter, engaged in only in private.

Lo Levayesh (Not Embarrassing): For example, taunting and teasing others about masturbation is wrong.

Ma'akeh (Preventing Accidents): For example, masturbation may alleviate sexual tension. This in turn may help young couples resist engaging in intercourse prematurely, and therefore prevent risks of unwanted pregnancy and/or sexually transmitted disease.

Shmirat HaGuf (Taking Care of Your Body): For example, depending on your perspective, this might mean masturbating or refraining from masturbation.

BIBLIOGRAPHY

A complete Bibliography for the five chapters dealing with issues of sexuality (Chapters 11-15) appears at the end of Chapter 11, "Foundations of Sexual Ethics," on pages 294-296.

CHAPTER 13

BIRTH CONTROL

OVERVIEW

Jewish Perspectives

One reason to have sex is to make babies. Procreation is an integral component of Jewish sexual ethics. Yet, according to Jewish texts, other worthy elements of a sexual relationship include expressing love, and giving and receiving pleasure. For many reasons, having children could present problems to a couple. Jewish ethics on birth control must address the tensions between competing values. When childbearing is not reasonable or practical, love and pleasure should not be off limits. The difficulty is this: How are we to decide what grounds are reasonable and practical for refraining from the *mitzvah* of procreation? This question underlies our discussion of birth control.

We addressed the *mitzvah* of procreation in some detail in Chapter 11, "Foundations of Sexual Ethics" (see that section's "Jewish Perspectives," pp. 273-275 and Text Study #2, p. 280). Briefly we discussed the commandment to "be fruitful and multiply" (Genesis 1:28). Through children, we have the opportunity to ensure the continuity of generations, and experience a special kind of love and joy. Concerns of overpopulation in the world may be legitimate. Yet, most Jewish authorities argue that the worthiness of having children overcomes these concerns, especially in light of our small numbers and the great loss of life sustained by our people over the years. Of course, if people cannot physically bear children, the *mitzvah* does not apply.

Traditional Jewish sources assign the *mitzvah* of procreation to men, but not to women. One reason is that you cannot force upon people something which may be overly burdensome. Specifically, bearing children may be such a painful experience for some women that expecting or insisting that they give birth is unreasonable. Thus, we have one area of birth control most authorities consider legitimate. That is, a woman may use birth control if a pregnancy would endanger her life or cause her unbearable suffering.

The dangers of pregnancy are behind a classic Rabbinic text affecting birth control for women. It deals with minors, pregnant women, and nursing mothers. Because of pregnancy concerns, birth control was permitted, some say required, for these women (see Text Study #1B below).

Today, eleven and twelve-year-old young women do not get married; medical experts are not concerned about pregnant women having "unprotected sex"; and there are mixed views about whether pregnancy for nursing mothers is inadvisable. Nevertheless, Rabbis and scholars derive insights and guidelines concerning the permissibility of birth control from the Rabbinic text about minors, pregnant women, and nursing mothers. The ideas have had significant influence on the development of Jewish birth control ethics.

"Spilling the seed" or "wasting the seed" is an issue that affects birth control (as it does masturbation and homosexuality). Jewish sources seem to view a man's "seed" (semen) as his very life force and of limited supply. Such a belief has framed attitudes regarding birth control (see Text Study #1a below). *Coitus interruptus* means that ejaculation happens outside a woman's body. The "seed," in effect, is for naught; it is "wasted." A condom stops the natural flow of semen, as well. Orthodox authorities disapprove of *coitus interruptus* and condoms as forms of birth control. Liberal Judaism usually is reluctant to denounce explicitly these methods of birth control. Most liberal Jews tend to dismiss concerns of "spilling the seed" as irrelevant to present lifestyles, knowledge, and beliefs.

For reasons similar to those above, Orthodox and other traditional authorities do not approve of vasectomy (a surgical procedure that causes male sterility). Furthermore, since vasectomy is a nearly irreversible decision, many liberal Jewish ethicists object to this procedure, too.

When *halachic* authorities do authorize use of birth control, they give preference to some forms of birth control over others.[1] Liberal Jews feel less concerned, if at all, about using the "right" kind of birth control.

Sociological reasons may account for the negative attitudes toward birth control throughout Jewish history. When people didn't know how many of their children would survive, having large families made sense. As early as the days of the Bible (e.g., Sarah, Rachel, Hannah), people have struggled with infertility. The need to have large families and fears of infertility likely influenced attitudes toward birth control. For most of our history, the use of birth control probably did not fit into most people's worldview of necessary conveniences. Such sociological analysis may be relevant to liberal Jews. But it is less so to traditionally observant Jews. They are more likely to reject the shifts of sociology as a legitimate force in affecting such important values as having children.

A sensitive birth control issue involves single people. Of course, some traditional Jewish authorities say that single people should not be having sex in the first place. Therefore, talk of birth control is beside the point. Other Jewish thinkers may be more understanding of non-marital sex. Regardless, the reality is unmarried people *are* having sex. Many liberal Jews choose to address this issue in a couple of notable ways. One is to urge couples to use birth control. The consequences of an unwanted pregnancy are inevitably problematic (see Text Study #2e and

#2f below). Second is to emphasize the importance of using condoms since sexually transmitted disease is always a threat. Unprotected (condom-less) sex can lead to irritating, lifetime problems involving the sex organs (and other body parts). Worse, sexually transmitted disease can be deadly.

What if a married couple does not *want* to have children? Perhaps they want to focus on learning, a career, or other pursuits. Perhaps they don't feel they would be good parents, or that they have no interest in rearing children. Similarly, what if a couple wants to limit the size of their family? Perhaps they feel they can only provide adequately for a specific number of children. Perhaps their interests or their work limits the amount of time and energy they have for a family. What does Judaism have to say about birth control in these situations?

In the most traditionally observant communities, arguments such as not *wanting* children would not be considered worthy. In modern Orthodox communities, it is difficult to assess how couples reconcile other personal needs and values with traditional Jewish birth control guidelines. Birth control is such a personal issue. Still, if modern Orthodox couples do use birth control, they may limit it to methods that authorities determine as acceptable.[2] In addition, they may choose to consult a competent *halachic* authority regarding their personal situation.

Ben Azzai in the Talmud preferred to study Torah than marry and have children (see "Foundations of Sexual Ethics," Text Study #2C and #2a, pp. 280-281). The Rabbis express disapproval about Ben Azzai's preference, though the text seems to give some credence to his feelings. Ben Azzai defends his way of life, saying that not everyone has to fulfill the commandment of procreation. The issue in the text is not specifically about birth control. Nevertheless, the text brings to light the fact that there *are* competing values when it comes to raising a family.

---

[1] For example, from an Orthodox perspective, the "rhythm method" is not as controversial as other methods. However, with the "rhythm method," observance of the laws of *nidah* would limit sexual intercourse to just a few days each month.

Oral contraceptives are preferred to the diaphragm, and the diaphragm is preferred to condoms.

[2] See footnote #1 above.

Jewish communities are more or less liberal according to the degree to which they believe in personal autonomy. Specifically, should a person make ethical decisions on his/her own; should a person depend on a knowledgeable or legal authority to make some or all decisions? Orthodox Jews put more trust in the interpretations of authorities, whereas Reform Jews tend to rely on making their own educated choices. Conservative and Reconstructionist Judaism also put special emphasis on the role of history and contemporary community standards.

Suppose we apply the above theological aside to the birth control debate. If you are more traditional, you will take your cues for personal ethical decisions largely from what you understand Judaism — God, law, and your community — demands or expects of you. If this means having a large family and shunning birth control, this is what you most likely will do. The more liberal you are, the more natural it will be for you to entertain choices for yourself. While you may choose to marry and have children, you also may feel perfectly legitimate in deciding to go with a "competing value." For example, the competing value of "my aspirations as an artist" might outweigh the expectation to raise a family.

Besides competing "personal" values, some Jews feel it is appropriate to limit fertility because of competing Jewish values. For instance, they may point out that justice is a primary value in Judaism. We mentioned problems of overpopulation earlier. One might say these problems lead to injustices. Justice is compromised when there are too many people in the world — with some nations consuming more than their fair share. Overpopulation in many parts of the world exacerbates poverty. Alleviating poverty and promoting fair distribution of the world's resources begins with limiting the size of families. We promote justice when we work for reproductive freedom all around the world, especially through education and making birth control widely available. (For more on the ethics of consuming our fair share, see Chapter 10, "Consumerism: How Much Is Too Much?," p. 243.)

Being more observant or more liberal does not determine the ease of your path. Relying strictly on *halachic* authorities, on Jewish law, is challenging, but so is relying on your own conscience and learning to make informed, ethical decisions. Whether you choose to raise a large family, a small family, or contribute to the community in other ways, ideally your chosen path will be an honorable and meaningful reflection of Jewish values.

General Perspectives

In his book, *Sacred Choices: The Right To Contraception and Abortion in Ten World Religions*, Daniel C. Maguire writes: *"Ethics is simply the systematic effort to study what is good for people and for this generous host of an earth"* (p. 19, italics are the author's).

Historically, Jews were not the only ones concerned with infant mortality, fertility, and simply having *enough* people. This concern likely influenced attitudes about birth control the world over. Individual religions and philosophies bear influences of history and sociological realities. We need to understand that laws and customs around fertility and family issues bear the weight of hundreds and even thousands of years of beliefs. Nevertheless, we have today's reality to worry about.

Religious leaders representing a variety of traditions are finding ways to recognize the value of reproductive freedom. In *Sacred Choices*, the author finds some openness to birth control in ten major world religions (including, Judaism, Catholicism, Protestantism, Islam, and several Eastern religions). But, like Judaism, most religions have practitioners who are very conservative in interpreting their tradition. They may rely on the authority of one designated leader or one strand of their religious tradition. So, for example, many Catholics will continue to disapprove of artificial contraception, if they understand it to be the official teaching of the Church, from the Pope down. They will do so even if new thinkers suggest innovative ways of reframing familiar teachings to allow for more reproductive freedom of choice.

But it is not only religion that influences birth control decisions, especially in democratic societies. Belief in individual choice and personal autonomy often trumps traditional religious beliefs. That is, people decide for themselves. Religious heritage may provide interesting and important issues to consider, but ultimately believers in autonomy will see reproductive choice as a personal matter. In fact, they may find it offensive for any authority (religious or political) to seek to impose rules that obstruct reproductive freedom. They view it as wrong for authorities to impose *their* values on others. Believers in individual choice suggest that obstructive rules are "oppressive," especially to women. That is, women usually bear the brunt of the consequences of not being able to control their fertility.

Individuals may wrestle with a variety of personal issues, some of which were raised in the "Jewish Perspectives" section above. Generally, family planning is the most significant issue affecting birth control decisions. Some common considerations include: how to balance family and career, ability to provide adequately for a specific number of children, interest in parenting, feeling too young or too old to parent, health issues, and stability of a couple's relationship.

Overpopulation is a serious world problem. Some people feel they must respond personally to this concern by limiting the number of children they bear. (For more about population control issues, see the web site for Population Connection [formerly Zero Population Growth]: www.populationconnection.org.)

A few more areas may affect birth control, some of which we touched on in the "Jewish Perspectives" section above. In this culture, the prevailing view is that minors or teens should not be having children, or for that matter even be having sex. However, if they do have sex, they should use birth control. Though Hollywood couples may have us think otherwise, it seems the generally accepted perspective still is that marriage should precede childbearing (not the other way around). In other words, any unmarried couples of childbearing age should use contraception.

Adequate sex education involves teaching about birth control. This topic raises difficult and controversial questions. For instance, does sex education include telling teens that they can freely obtain condoms from the school nurse? Does making birth control available make sex more enticing to young people who would otherwise postpone the experience? There are many views on how, when, and who should teach about sex. Whether parents, clergy, and/or schools teach about sex; whatever age the children are; and whatever resources are used — birth control must be addressed.

Summary of the Overview

- Judaism teaches that procreation is a *mitzvah* (commandment).

- While *halachic* authorities may shun certain methods of birth control, there are traditional Jewish reasons for applying leniency in fulfilling the *mitzvah* of procreation.

- Personal circumstances, feelings, beliefs, and needs also may affect birth control decisions.

- One's general orientation to Jewish observance likely will influence one's attitude toward birth control.

SCENARIOS: HOW THINGS HAVE CHANGED

The two scenarios below reflect the trends of Jewish opinion about birth control. These scenarios, one set in ancient days and one in contemporary times, are intended to raise questions and spark discussion. Read each scenario to or with your students, and engage them in small or large group discussions. Use the "Focus the Discussion" section below to help you identify the important issues and facilitate these discussions. Note that an additional activity relating to these scenarios is found in the "Stories:

Understanding through Listening" section below (p. 309).

Following the discussions, have students continue on to the "Text Study" section to see what Jewish and other sources have to say about our topic. Finally, you may wish to have students discuss the scenarios a second time to see if their views have changed.

Scenario 1: In Ancient Days

Yoni and Rivka have known tragedy. Prior to giving birth to their son Uziel, Rivka suffered three miscarriages and a stillbirth. After Uziel was born, Rivka had two more miscarriages before giving birth to Sarah. When Sarah was 18 months old, she became ill with a respiratory ailment and died. Two years later, Rivka gave birth to another girl, Devorah. Uziel and Devorah both seem to be thriving well.

After a couple of more years, with another pregnancy ending in stillbirth, a friend comes to comfort Rivka. The friend says, "Rivka, why don't you take the potion that Judith, Rabbi Chiyya's wife, took to prevent her from ever becoming pregnant again? You wouldn't have to suffer anymore from such terrible pregnancies" (see Text Study #1C below). But Rivka worries. Who knows if Uziel and Devorah will make it past childhood? She and Yoni love children. They would like children to be part of and develop the family trade. They want sons who will be able to become Torah scholars and enrich Jewish learning in the community. They want daughters who will perpetuate family traditions. No, she would not consider intentionally making herself sterile.

Scenario 2: Nowadays

Jon and Risa have struggled with fertility issues for two years. After three miscarriages, Risa undergoes medical tests to find out if there is anything clearly wrong. The tests detect a health condition that can be treated with a prescription medicine. The condition had made her susceptible to miscarriages. The doctors assure her that she should be able to have as many children as she would like, now that she is taking the medicine. During the next four years, Risa gives birth to two healthy children. For a variety of reasons, Jon and Risa then decide that they don't want more children. Besides, they feel they have fulfilled the Jewish value of procreation by having two children. During the years that follow, Risa and Jon are diligent about using contraception.

Focus the Discussion

Pregnancy and giving birth do not pose the risks they once did. Babies and children are not as susceptible to fatal illnesses as they once were. Medical procedures and treatments can address many fertility problems. Overpopulation is at a crisis point now in the world. In other words, people don't worry the way they used to, either as individuals or as a society, about having *enough* children.

Many birth control methods are available now. In modern, democratic countries, responsible individuals are taking charge of their family planning. They may seek to place their individual situation within the framework of a religious tradition, or religious considerations may play less of a significant role. In any case, people have more options for controlling their fertility. Whether to bring children into the world is a very personal decision. Those who defend reproductive freedom see choice as essential.

TEXT STUDY

The attitude that contemporary Jews hold in regards to birth control can vary depending on a variety of factors: level of observance, community affiliation, sociological factors, and personal values. Jewish texts and other sources express varying viewpoints which highlight the tension between seemingly opposing considerations. The chart below highlights the key Jewish question about birth control. Text sources supporting the two opposing points of view follow.

Birth Control: A Question to Consider

The Question	On the One Hand	On the Other Hand
1. What are Jewish views on birth control? (see this page, below)	Traditional Jewish sources restrict the use of birth control devices.	For many Jews, personal needs and modern science play a central role in influencing birth control choices.

Note: Beliefs regarding the *mitzvah* of procreation are also relevant here. See Question #2 in the "Text Study" section of Chapter 11, "Foundations of Jewish Sexual Ethics," p. 280.

1. **What are Jewish views on birth control?**

On the One Hand:

Traditional Jewish sources restrict the use of birth control devices.

A. It is forbidden to destroy [improperly emit] seed. Therefore, a man may not practice coitus interruptus (Maimonides, *Mishneh Torah, Isuray Biah* 21:18).

B. Commentators differ as to whether the following three types of women *may* use birth control (and others may not), or whether they *must* do so (and others may).

> Three types of women use an absorbent [contraceptive device, called a *mokh*]: a minor, a pregnant woman, and a nursing mother.
>
> The minor [from 11 years and one day to 12 years and one day], lest she become pregnant and die; a pregnant woman, lest she cause her fetus to become a *sandal* [a flat, fish-shaped fetus]; and a nursing woman [otherwise], she might have to wean her child too soon and the child would die (*Yevamot* 12b). (For an extensive discussion of this text, see *Marital Relations, Birth Control, and Abortion in Jewish Law* by David M. Feldman.)

C. Judah and Hezekiah were twins. One was completely developed at the end of nine months, and the other at the beginning of the seventh month [the implication being that they were born three months apart].

> Their mother Judith, wife of Rabbi Chiyya, suffered agonizing pains during childbirth. When she recovered, she disguised herself and appeared before Rabbi Chiyya.
>
> "Is a woman commanded to propagate the race? she asked.
>
> "No," he answered.
>
> As a result of that conversation, she drank a sterilizing potion so that she would have no more children.
>
> When her action finally became known, he exclaimed, "Would that you bore me only one more issue of the womb" (*Yevamot* 65b).
>
> Thus, the Rabbis ruled:
>
> A man is not permitted to drink a cup of roots, but a woman is permitted to drink a cup of roots so that she does not give birth (*Tosefta Yevamot* 8:2).

D. Only the most competent Torah authority, whose piety, erudition, and sensitivity to family and social problems are well established, can advise on the complex issue of family planning. In general, only the health requirements of the wife, both physical and psychological, can modify the *halakhic* disapproval of all contraceptive techniques (Rabbi Moshe Tendler, *Pardes Rimonim*, p. 17).

TEACHING HOT TOPICS

On the Other Hand:

For many Jews, personal needs and modern science play a central role in influencing birth control choices.

a. The chapter in this book on masturbation also refers to an idea similar to that below. (That is, today, people understand semen differently from how they once did — see the "Text Study" section in Chapter 12, "Masturbation," pp. 298-300.)

> At the time of the birth of Jesus, Jews and most other people believed that it was the man and his semen who provides the actual life, the "seed," and that the woman was merely the soil, so to speak, in which the seed grew to maturity to be born. It was considered almost like murder to allow the "seed" to be "wasted" through masturbation, homosexuality, or sexual intercourse without intent to procreate. It was also erroneously believed . . . that semen, "the precious fluid," was limited in quantity so that if it was "wasted" the energy and strength of the man would thereby be reduced (Mary Calderone and Eric Johnson, *The Family Book about Sexuality,* p. 158, quoted by Rabbi Michael Gold, p. 107).

b. Jewish sources from as early as the second century C.E. describe methods of contraception and prescribe when they may or should be used. Until the later half of the twentieth century, though, Jews never contemplated using contraceptives for purposes of family planning. Judaism, after all, values large families. Moreover, if one wanted even two children to survive to adulthood, one had to try to have children continually, for many such attempts would be frustrated in miscarriages or in stillbirths, and many of the children who survived birth would die of childhood diseases or infections before being ready to propagate themselves. In addition, many Jews would find that they could not beget or bear children, as the stories of the difficulties endured by Abraham and Sarah and by Jacob and Rachel so poignantly describe.

In judging the permissibility of contraceptives, then, we must recognize that we are asking an entirely new question. Not only have the techniques of contraception improved considerably, but the very purpose for which Jewish couples use them has changed. Thus, although the use of contraceptives in our time may bear some formal resemblance to their use in times past, these changes in method and purpose must be kept clearly in mind as we examine traditional sources on contraception (Rabbi Elliot N. Dorff, *Matters of Life and Death,* p. 121).

c. As Jews, we take pride in our historic emphasis upon the values of family life. We believe that it is the sacred duty of married couples to "be fruitful and multiply," unless childbearing is likely to impair the health of the mother or the offspring . . . We believe, moreover, that a righteous God does not require the unlimited birth of children who may, by unfavorable social and economic circumstances, be denied a chance for a decent and wholesome life. Therefore, we declare that parents have the right to determine the number, and to space the births of their children in accordance with what they believe to be the best interests of their families (Commission on Justice and Peace of the Central Conference of American Rabbis, *Yearbook* 1960).

d. Condoms are problematic from the perspective of traditional Jewish law and are not always effective:

> Nevertheless, condoms must be used if unprotected sexual intercourse

poses a medical risk to either spouse, for condoms do offer some measure of protection against the spread of some diseases, and the duty to maintain health and life supersedes the positive duty of the male to propagate (*This Is My Beloved, This Is My Friend: A Rabbinic Letter on Intimate Relations* by Rabbi Elliot N. Dorff, p. 27).

e. Year after year a large number of supposedly intelligent people continue to get involved in extramarital pregnancy . . . Careful, effective contraception is an ethical necessity if there is to be any legitimization of premarital sexual intercourse (Eugene B. Borowitz, *Choosing a Sex Ethic*, p. 21).

f. For single people who are sexually active, it is patently irresponsible not to use birth control . . . For a single woman, an unplanned pregnancy raises numerous difficult issues of Jewish law and morality. Abortion as a form of birth control is a serious violation of Jewish law. Single parenting, although not uncommon, is recognized as less than ideal for imparting Jewish values to children. Rushing into a marriage on account of pregnancy is hardly an auspicious start for a healthy, lifelong relationship. Placing a baby for adoption, an option rarely practiced by Jewish women, is a wrenching emotional decision (Rabbi Michael Gold, *Does God Belong in the Bedroom*, p. 110).

Probing: Ideas and Issues

Summarize what you understand to be the traditional Jewish attitude toward contraception according to the first group of texts (#1A to #1D). Summarize how a liberal Jewish community might view contraception, referring to the second group of texts (#1a to #1f). Which text do you find most challenging to understand or challenging to your current views? Are you surprised by what any of the texts say? Explain.

What do texts #1d, #1e, and #1f suggest should be the role of contraception for unmarried couples? Do you agree or disagree? Explain.

RELATED MIDDOT AND MITZVOT

A complete list of *middot* and *mitzvot* that relate to issues of sexuality appears in Chapter 11, "Foundations of Sexual Ethics," on pages 288-289.

ACTIVITIES

A First Look: Key Issues and Ideas

1. With participants, list all the factors that you can that seem to affect Jewish attitudes toward birth control.

    Here are a few examples:

    *   The *mitzvah* of procreation.

    *   The prohibition against "wasting the seed."

    *   If pregnancy would be dangerous to the woman.

    *   Condoms provide protection from sexually transmitted disease.

    *   Etc . . .

    Go back through the list with the group, and mark a small "t" (for "traditional") next to factors that are concerns that originate in traditional Jewish sources. Then use a small "m" (for "modern") to mark those factors that are more of a modern concern. You may end up assigning both a "t" and an "m" to some factors.

Lead a discussion exploring the difficulties of reconciling traditional Jewish concerns with modern issues. What traditional belief is hardest to reconcile with a modern concern? Where is there most consistency between beliefs "back then" and now? Depending on your community of learners (whether more traditional or more liberal), this discussion could go in many different directions.

2. Ask: On a scale of one to ten, how would you rate Judaism in terms of its openness to contraception (one is least open, ten is most)? How would you rate your country? Your community? Have participants explain their ratings.

Applying Middot and Mitzvot

1. Ask how the following virtues might affect issues of birth control:

   Mechabayd Zeh et Zeh (Honoring Others)

   Ma'akeh (Preventing Accidents)

   Shmirat HaGuf (Taking Care of Your Body)

Stories: Understanding through Listening

1. After reviewing Text Study #1C, have group members write four journal entries in the imagined voices of Rabbi Chiyya and Judith. These are the general parameters of the entries:

   - Judith:

     Reflecting on her personal situation and the recent birth of her children.

     Coming to the decision that she wants to prevent another pregnancy.

     Thinking through how to do so.

   - Rabbi Chiyya:

     Sorting through his feelings about fatherhood.

     Reflecting on and recording his observations of Judith's physical health and emotional state.

   - Judith:

     Writing about her feelings after taking the sterilizing potion and giving the news to her husband.

   - Rabbi Chiyya:

     Expressing his reactions to what Judith has done.

     When group members finish the writing exercise, have volunteers share some of their "journal entries."

2. Conduct interviews of the characters in the imaginary situations in the "Scenarios" section above, pp. 304-305. Assign students to be the actors and the interviewers. There are different ways to carry out this activity: One is to interview each character separately. Alter-natively, gather all the actors and conduct interviews in a panel discussion style. Depending on the improvisational abilities of the group, you may want to do some preparation before bringing on the actors. That is, work with participants to list appropriate possible interview questions.

Action: Getting Out, Getting Involved

1. Group members imagine that Planned Parenthood Federation of America (PPFA) has assembled "feedback and brainstorming" committees across the country. These committees are to discuss one of PPFA's policy statements. PPFA is interested in soliciting ideas from all kinds of groups, representing various religions, socioeconomic groups, educational backgrounds, etc. Your committee is to share ideas that draw on Jewish values.

Your specific job is to supply PPFA with a list of concrete action suggestions for carrying out their mission. Here is the statement:

> It is the policy of Planned Parenthood Federation of America to assure that all individuals have the freedom to make reproductive decisions. In order to enable the individual to make and implement a responsible decision, there should be access to information and services related to sexuality, reproduction, methods of contraception, fertility control, and parenthood. Furthermore, Planned Parenthood asserts that both parenthood and nonparenthood are valid personal decisions (*Mission and Policy Statements*, adopted 1984).

2. Refer back to the previous exercise and policy statement. Now your committee has been asked to design a series of posters for publicizing their ideas. Get to work.

3. Have small groups research and report back on these five organizations: United Nations Population Fund (www.unfpa.org), Population Connection (formerly Zero Population Growth - www.populationconnection.com), Religious Coalition for Reproductive Choice (www.rcrc.org), Spiritual Youth for Reproductive Freedom (www.syrf.org), and Planned Parenthood (www.plannedparenthood.org). Here are a few questions "researchers" should answer in their reports:

   • What does the organization believe?

   • What does the organization do?

   • Is the organization's work consistent with Jewish values? Explain.

   • Are there projects or efforts that you would like to get involved in? If so, what good might result from "getting out and getting involved?"

   • Do you believe the organization is doing important work? Explain.

Another worthwhile web site is www.sacredchoices.org. It suggests interesting links to check out.

Wrestling: Engagement with the Issues

1. Have participants imagine they are Rabbis. Say: A couple has come to see you prior to getting married. They wish to discuss issues of family planning with you. How would you advise this couple? What Jewish ideas would you want them to know relevant to their situation? Below are a few possible scenarios to discuss. After the group has had a chance to share their ideas, you may want to invite a Rabbi to class to solicit his/her views.

   • One partner wants a large family, the other wants a small family.

   • One partner wants children, the other isn't sure.

   • One partner wants children, the other clearly does not.

   • Both partners agree that after they have two children (assuming they are able to), the man will get a vasectomy.

   • Both partners agree that after they have two children (assuming they are able to), the woman will undergo an operation that will make her permanently infertile.

   • Both partners agree that after they have one child, they will use contraception.

   • Both partners agree that they won't be able to provide for children adequately for at least ten years. After that, they will make the decision whether to have children. They will use birth control until then.

   • A pregnancy would endanger the woman's life. For health reasons, oral contraceptives are not an option. The couple prefers to use condoms (with spermicide) to prevent pregnancy. Researchers consider this contraceptive effective in preventing pregnancy.

- The couple is concerned about overpopulation. Therefore they want to adopt children who would otherwise face a life of poverty, rather than have biological children.

- The bride-to-be's previous marriage ended in divorce. She experienced severe postpartum depression following the birth of a child from that marriage. She does not want to risk that experience again and wishes to use birth control. The groom-to-be has no children of his own.

2. Have the group discuss or role-play this scenario: A 17-year-old young woman tells her mother that she wants an appointment with a gynecologist. The young woman has a steady boyfriend, and the mother wonders if her daughter is or intends to become sexually involved with the young man. She confronts her daughter, and the daughter admits that she and her boyfriend are becoming more physically involved and that she wants to be "prepared" (with contraceptives). The daughter tells her mother that nothing her mother says will change her mind, that she will make her own decisions about her love life. Where do the mother and daughter go from here?

    A variation: Adapt this scenario for a father and son. Begin with the father finding a box of condoms under his son's bed while vacuuming the house.

3. Stage a debate on the topic "Does Judaism Permit the Use of Birth Control?" One side are the followers of Rabbi Moshe Tendler (see Text Study #1D above). The other side are the followers of Rabbi Elliot Dorff (see Text Study #1b above). Alternatively, the other

side could be Reform Rabbis as represented in Text Study #1c above.

Empathy

1. Lead a discussion on making the decision to become a parent. Those who are not parents might share:

    - how they feel about parenthood

    - how they think they will decide whether to have children

    - what they might find exciting about parenthood

    - what they would worry about as parents

    - etc.

    Those who are parents might share:

    - their feelings about parenthood

    - what they like about it

    - what they find most challenging

    - how they decided to become parents

    - how they decided on the number of children to have

    - etc.

BIBLIOGRAPHY

A complete Bibliography for the five chapters dealing with issues of sexuality (Chapters 11-15) appears at the end of Chapter 11, "Foundations of Sexual Ethics," on pages 294-296.

CHAPTER 14

HOMOSEXUALITY

OVERVIEW

Note: Generally accepted studies show that somewhere between three and ten percent of the general population is homosexual.[1] The leader may want to remind the group that some of the participants may be gay or lesbian, and that everyone needs to be sensitive to this possibility as they engage in study of the topic.

Jewish and General Perspectives

Homosexuality is perhaps the most emotional sub-topic of sexuality. The sexual orientation of gays, lesbians, and bisexuals influences their life on many levels: physical attractions and desires, social connections, emotional relationships, and cultural experience. In short, homosexuality is an essential part of their identity.

Some cultures and communities are growing in their acceptance of homosexuality. However, discrimination is still widespread, with denial, ambivalence, and even hostility toward homosexuality. Where do these sentiments come from? A few responses are clear. Other theories are more speculative.

From a Jewish perspective, traditional texts undeniably convey negative attitudes toward homosexuality. A thorough study of the Bible, Talmud, Medieval Codes, and Responsa literature would turn up statements severely disapproving of homosexual acts. In response, modern liberal scholars are taking a hard look at traditional perceptions of homosexuality. They are doing so in light of historical and scientific findings (see Text Study #1a and #5a-c below). That is, they feel we need to have a sense of who wrote the

statements, why they wrote them, what the context was, what people didn't understand about homosexuality (in the past) that we now do, and so on.

Probably the most significant modern finding is the widely accepted conclusion that most gays and lesbians have *no choice* about their sexual identity. It is a "fixed," organic, and authentic part of their beings (for instance, see Text Study #5a below). Another concern is that male homosexual acts "waste" precious "seed." Modern scholarship addresses this issue by explaining the context of this concern (see Text Study #1a in Chapter 13, "Birth Control," p. 307).

Historical and scientific insights are deflating some of the opposition toward homosexuality. Those who "allow" modern insights to influence traditional attitudes are "re-envisioning" tradition. Whereas liberal Jews are more open to this re-envisioning process, more traditionally observant Jews hold to stricter interpretations of Jewish law.

We sometimes attach the word "homophobic" to those who feel antagonism toward homosexuals. To be homophobic is to have fears regarding homosexuality. Though we associate "homophobia" with modern lingo, Jewish sources clearly express some "fears" about this way of life.

The fears seem to involve expectations of the Jewish community's social order. Historically at least, community members viewed homosexuality as a threat to key institutions in the society. Perhaps condoning homosexuality would lead to the devaluing and disintegration of marriage and

---

[1]Kinsey, Pomeroy, & Martin, 1948; Kinsey, Pomeroy, Martin, & Gebhard, 1953; Fay, Turner, Klassen, & Gagnon, 1989; Hatfield, 1989; Laumann, Gagnon, Michael, & Michaels, 1994; Lever & Kanouse, 1996; Rogers & Turner, 1991.

family life (see Text Study #3A, #4A, and #6A below). Jewish concerns regarding these threats are not especially different from those voiced in many other communities and religions.

Advocates for homosexual issues today willingly respond to such concerns. They point out that homosexuals also can and do uphold institutions so dearly cherished by Judaism and others. That is, many homosexuals commit to long-term, monogamous relationships similiar to marriage. Furthermore, many homosexuals raise children in loving homes (see Text Study #4a and #6a-c below).

Not all who sanction gay and lesbian commitment ceremonies are comfortable using the traditional Jewish wedding format and terminology (*Erusin* and *Kiddushin*). Others, however, feel strongly that it is wrong to discriminate against gays and lesbians on any level. The latter individuals support homosexual marriage fully.

Endorsing and even encouraging homosexuals to commit to a long-term monogamous relationship includes other "equal opportunity" repercussions. Just as Judaism deplores promiscuous or anonymous sex among heterosexuals, the same must apply to homosexuals. Pornography and prostitution, whether involving homosexuals or heterosexuals, offends Jewish sensibilities.

Certain fears about homosexuality have led some people to hatred, bigotry, harassment, and violence. We might speculate about why individuals would act in such cruel ways, but it is hard to know for sure. Whatever the case, ignorance and misinformation are undoubtedly factors. In their book *The Journey Out*, Rachel Pollack and Cheryl Schwartz discuss "myths" and "facts" about homosexuality.[2] We will summarize these:

- To the charge that homosexuality is sick and unnatural, Pollack and Schwartz respond that medical and psychiatric opinion does not support this belief. (For example, see Text Study #5a below.)

- To the fear that homosexuals are child molesters, the authors explain that most child abuse happens in families, with a father or uncle violating a female child. Furthermore, recent studies show that outside the family, 95 percent of child molesters are heterosexual males, with girls being victims twice as often as boys.

- To the allegation that homosexuals recruit, Pollack and Schwartz write: "'Recruiting' is impossible. There is no social or scientific evidence that anyone can change your sexual orientation. In fact, if recruiting were possible, everyone would probably be heterosexual, given the pressure from the media, religious institutions, family, and society to be straight."[3]

- Regarding the belief that homosexuals and bisexuals choose to be this way, Pollack and Schwartz point out that people do not *choose* their sexual orientation (see Text Study #5a-c below). Researchers believe sexual orientation is fixed at a very young age. It may even be determined before birth.

- To the suggestion that homosexuals and bisexuals are unfit teachers, Pollack and Schwartz say, "We know that *no one* can change a person's sexual orientation and that a homosexual teacher is no more likely to molest students or try to 'recruit' them than a heterosexual one."[4] Nevertheless, this matter continues to stir up agitated feeling and even provoke court debates. Even so, in 1974, The National Education Association — the largest organization representing public school teachers and employees — added "sexual orientation" to its list of nondiscriminatory policies.

---

[2]See *The Journey Out: A Guide for and about Lesbian, Gay, and Bisexual Teens* by Rachel Pollack and Cheryl Schwartz, 71-73.

[3]*Ibid.*, 72.
[4]*Ibid.*, 73.

There may be other emotional/psychological reasons that contribute to why some homophobic people turn to cruel acts. Fully unraveling such reasons is beyond the scope of this chapter. Still, we can make some important Jewish comments about such behaviors. Judaism teaches: all people are created in the image of God; you must "love your neighbor as yourself" (Leviticus 19:18); and we can make the world a better place by living righteously and doing good works (*Tikkun Olam*). The essential thrust of general moral perspectives is that we must *help* and *not hurt* others.[5]

Hatred, harassment, violence, and cruelty are wrong. They are wrong from a Jewish perspective, and they are wrong from a general moral perspective. With regard to homosexuality, our primary Jewish responsibilities are to be humble in the face of things we don't fully understand (and no one fully understands homosexuality), and to be compassionate, loving, and respectful of other human beings. Even leading Orthodox scholars accept the "compelling" nature of a gay or lesbian person's sexual orientation (see Text Study #5A below). Those who are homosexual will perhaps need to make extra efforts in fulfilling these additional challenges: to be true to themselves and to be honest and unashamed about who they are in the world.

Summary of the Overview

- Historically, for Jews and others, predominant attitudes toward homosexuality have been negative.

- Modern Jews are re-envisioning historical attitudes about homosexuality in light of current findings and beliefs.

- The majority of today's Jewish community falls somewhere along this spectrum regarding homosexuality:

  - Those on one end may suggest greater compassion and understanding toward

gays and lesbians, but still maintain disapproval of homosexual acts.

  - On the other end are those who emphasize fully equal and non-discriminatory treatment in all realms of life for gays and lesbians. This includes equal treatment as Jews.

SCENARIOS: HOW THINGS HAVE CHANGED

The two scenarios below reflect the trends of Jewish opinion toward homosexuality. These scenarios, one set in ancient days and one in contemporary times, are intended to raise questions and spark discussion. Read each scenario to or with your students, and engage them in small or large group discussions. Use the "Focus the Discussion" section below to help you identify the important issues and facilitate these discussions. Note that additional questions relating to these scenarios are found in the "Stories: Understanding through Listening" section below (p. 325).

Following the discussions, have students continue on to the "Text Study" section to see what Jewish and other sources have to say about our topic. Finally, you may wish to have students discuss the scenarios a second time to see if their views have changed.

Scenario 1: In the Days of the Talmud

Rabbi Noam Mordecai always felt attracted to men. He remembers having homosexual feelings since he was a child. Of course, he never spoke about this with anyone. As he became a teenager, his homosexual feelings became more intense. Despite his secret, talk of an appropriate wife for him began in his household. Already, he was a diligent student at the *Yeshivah*. As talk of

---

[5]See *Teaching Your Children Values* by Linda and Richard Eyre, 15.

a "match" intensified, the young Noam Mordecai spent more and more time studying. When he was seventeen, he told his mother and father that he wanted to delay marriage. He begged his parents to help him in his efforts to study in Pumpedita, 150 miles from his home. His plan was to spend a year or so in a village between his hometown and Pumpedita. There he would earn some money as a day laborer, then continue to Pumpedita. His parents gave their support, and Noam Mordecai was off on his own.

Shortly after arriving in the village, Noam Mordecai and another man befriended each other. Their relationship slowly evolved into a sexual affair. Noam Mordecai was overjoyed to be so in love, to be so physically and emotionally fulfilled. But he was also torn apart. It was impossible that the relationship could continue. He knew that his sexual behavior was considered sinful. After a torrentially emotional year, Noam Mordecai broke off the affair, then continued on, by himself, to Pumpedita. There he became one of the finest scholars of his day.

Rabbi Noam Mordecai never married, insisting that his love of Torah (study) was all-consuming — leaving no time for family. But he never forgot the happiness he experienced in the village on the way to Pumpedita. It seemed strange to repent for the happiness he felt. However, that is what he did. Throughout his life, though he felt something central was missing, he never loved another man again.

Scenario 2: New York City, 2003

Noam always felt attracted to men. He remembers having homosexual feelings since he was a child. Of course, he never spoke about this in his early years, because kids teased boys who showed interest in other boys. Still, he knew that it wasn't so unusual that people of the same sex might get together as couples. There were several kids in his school with two moms or two dads.

As Noam entered his teenage years, his homosexual feelings became more intense. Sex education classes gave him some sense that his feelings were not so unusual. Yet, he felt he needed to understand more about himself, more about his sexual feelings. Over the years, he had noticed a bookstore focused on gay, lesbian, and bisexual interests in Greenwich Village (a neighborhood in New York City). One day, he visited. Besides picking up a book about teens and homosexuality, he spent time looking at the bulletin board. He noticed there was a support group for gay, lesbian, and bisexual teens held at a local synagogue. This particular synagogue had a special interest in outreach to gays, lesbians, and bisexuals. Through attending the support group, Noam was able to work through conflicted feelings regarding his sexuality. He also met other teenagers like him.

At first, Noam was secretive with his family about attending the group. After a few months however, he felt he wanted to be honest with them. While his parents weren't openly critical of Noam, it did take several months for them to accept that Noam wasn't "just going through a phase." Even during this rough period, Noam always knew his parents loved him. Eventually, they became accepting of his homosexuality.

By the time he was in college, Noam felt very comfortable with and clear about his sexuality. He enjoyed learning in a wide variety of areas, including Jewish studies. During his senior year of college, Noam was weighing whether he should continue his studies in biology or apply to Rabbinical school. Whatever the decision, he felt strongly that he wanted to remain close to Daniel, the man he had been dating for the past two years, the man he loved.

Focus the Discussion

The two scenarios are not necessarily typical. What they show are two individuals adjusting to living with their sexual orientation in ways that *could* reflect their reality. But, they are closer to "best case" scenarios for *their time and place* than they are typical.

While Rabbi Noam Mordecai leads a celibate life (something that does not sound like "best case"), things could have turned out much worse for him. Homosexuals commit suicide at a much higher rate than do heterosexuals. Less extreme is turning to substance abuse or suffering depression as a result of trying to cope with the implications of homosexual identity. Rabbi Noam Mordecai immersed himself in studies to distract himself from homosexual desires (and distract others from trying to marry him off). But people like him have committed suicide because of the shame they feel, because they believe they are "sinners," or because they feel trapped by their sexuality, unable to live openly and happily with their true sexual identity. The American Psychiatric Association reported in its April 1993 *Fact Sheet* that " . . . gay men and lesbians who have accepted their sexual orientation positively are better adjusted than those who have not done so" (see Text Study #5a below).

The story of Noam, the New Yorker, represents one possible outcome for a gay teen living in America. Again, we can't say Noam's experience is typical for American youth today. The truth is that considerable discrimination and hatred toward homosexuals still exists. As far as the Jewish community goes, while openness to gays and lesbians is increasing, there is prejudice, as well — in some communities more than others. Living in a modern, open society doesn't mean a homosexual person will find full acceptance and community support for his/her lifestyle. Many gays and lesbians are plagued with feelings of isolation, shame, humiliation, and even suicidal thoughts. Some are subjected to severe taunts and physical violence. The *potential* for changed attitudes is here. And in many communities, changed attitudes *are* in effect. But many others have a long way to go to overcome fear, hostility, and bigotry.

TEXT STUDY

As we have seen, homosexuality is an emotional and complex topic. While some cultures and communities have grown in their acceptance of homosexuality, others maintain strong disapproval. Jewish texts and other sources express varying viewpoints which highlight the tension between seemingly opposing considerations. The chart on the next page poses the questions and offers two opposing points of view. Text sources supporting each of these points of view follow below.

Note: Text Study #1a in Chapter 13, "Birth Control," (p. 307) concisely explains historical attitudes regarding "wasting the seed" — an issue relevant to homosexuality, as well.

1. **Must we accept traditional Jewish beliefs about homosexuality?**

   On the One Hand:

   Beliefs that male homosexuality is an abhorrence (toe-ay-vah) and lesbianism is licentious or obscene (p'ree-tzoo-ta) are rooted in the Bible and Talmud.

   A. Do not lie with a male as one lies with a woman: it is an abhorrence (*toe-ay-vah*) (Leviticus 18:22).

   B. [Concerning] women who practice lewdness with one another . . . the action is regarded as mere obscenity (*p'ree-tzoo-ta*) (*Yevamot* 76a).

   On the Other Hand:

   In light of the context in which our ancestors formed their beliefs, it is legitimate to challenge their views about homosexuality.

   a. In the Talmud, a deaf-mute was considered to be retarded, mentally incompetent, an imbecile not able to serve as a witness, or to be counted in the *minyan*, or to effect marriage or divorce. But that ruling was based on empirically false data. On a visit to the Vienna Institute for the Deaf and Dumb, Rabbi Simchah Sofer saw that their impaired speech and hearing had nothing to do with their intelligence and accountability, and

Homosexuality: Questions to Consider

The Question	On the One Hand	On the Other Hand
1. Must we accept traditional Jewish beliefs about homosexuality? (see p. 317)	Beliefs that male homosexuality is an abhorrence (*toe-ay-vah*) and lesbianism is licentious or obscene (*p'ree-tzoo-ta*) are rooted in the Bible and Talmud.	In light of the context in which our ancestors formed their beliefs, it is legitimate to challenge their views about homosexuality.
2. Might it be best simply to ignore homosexuality? (see p. 319)	Denial is one way traditional Jewish sources deal with homosexuality.	That Jews are not involved in homosexuality is empirically inaccurate. We need to deal with reality.
3. Does being accepting of homosexuality deny "the natural order of things"? (see p. 320)	Homosexuality is "unnatural."	God created all kinds of people, both heterosexuals and homosexuals.
4. Does homosexuality threaten "family values"? (see p. 320)	Homosexuality violates family values.	There are many ways to contribute to the Jewish community. One is establishing a loving home and raising children — something many homosexuals choose to do.
5. What is the range of responses to homosexuality in the Jewish community? (see p. 320)	Mainstream Orthodoxy today generally condemns homosexual acts, though may encourage compassion for individual "sufferers."	Scientific, social, and moral concerns have propelled many Jewish communities to reexamine homosexuality with increasing openness.
6. Does homosexuality threaten the cherished institution of marriage? (see p. 322)	Homosexuality can destroy marriages.	A homosexual person's constitution prevents him/her from finding happiness and fulfillment in marriage with someone of the opposite sex. Sanctifying same-sex partnerships promotes the Jewish values of long-term, monogamous relationships.

urged altering the older Rabbinic judgment. The law and its legal interpretation are rooted in history. Every text has its context . . .

The Rabbis of the Talmud assumed that homosexual acts were acts of free will, even ideological. They did not know of "constitutional" gay and lesbians who had no control over their sexual orientation. Moreover it is far from clear what the biblical term *toe-ay-vah,* translated as "abomination," means or to what it refers. Some biblical scholars maintain that *toe-ay-vah* refers not to homosexuality, but more likely to cultic prostitution; and that what the Bible inveighed against was the pagan tradition that paid obeisance to pagan gods by all forms of illicit sexual behavior (Rabbi Harold M. Schulweis, "Morality, Legality and Homosexuality," Rosh HaShanah sermon, 1992).

Probing: Ideas and Issues

Why does Rabbi Schulweis make the comparison between deaf-mutes and homosexuals? Is his point a legitimate one? What problems does he find in applying the term *toe-ay-vah* to homosexuals today? Suppose we assume that the Bible actually does consider homosexuality a sin. Do you believe changing historical contexts and beliefs should allow us to discount what is written in the Bible?

2. **Might it be best simply to ignore homosexuality?**

On the One Hand:

Denial is one way traditional Jewish sources deal with homosexuality.

A. Rabbi Judah said an unmarried man must not tend cattle nor may two unmarried men sleep together under the same cover. But the sages permit it . . . They said to

Rabbi Judah: Israel is suspected of neither homosexuality nor bestiality (Mishnah *Kiddushin* 4:14 and *Kiddushin* 82a; see also Maimonides, *Issuray Bi-ah* 22:2; Rabbi Joseph Karo, *Even Ha-Ezer* 24; and Rabbi Joel Sirkes, *Bayit Chadash* to *Tur, Even Ha-Ezer* 24).

On the Other Hand:

That Jews are not involved in homosexuality is empirically inaccurate. We need to deal with reality.

a. The following passage is included in a longer citation (see Text Study #4b below):

> I, for one, cannot believe that the God who created us all produced a certain percentage of us to have sexual drives that cannot be legally expressed under any circumstances. That is simply mind-boggling — and, frankly, un-Jewish . . . (Rabbi Elliot Dorff, *Matters of Life and Death*, p. 145).

Probing: Ideas and Issues

The Sages maintain that Jews are not (or were not) homosexuals. What reasons might there be for saying such a thing? (I.e., (1) That is really what the Sages believed. (2) The sages didn't really believe this. Yet, such a statement would allow them to turn their eyes from something that was happening that they knew they couldn't or didn't want to try to control. Perhaps they felt that punishing homosexuals as "abominators" was not helpful or justifiable. Since the Sages would not simply disregard a statement in Torah, they "covered" themselves by saying "Jews don't do these things . . . ") Should we in our day, claim as the Sages did that Jews are "not suspected of homosexuality"? Explain.

Does Rabbi Dorff make a valid point? Do you agree with his point? Explain.

3. **Does being accepting of homosexuality deny "the natural order of things?"**

On the One Hand:

Homosexuality is "unnatural."

A. You are going astray from the foundations of the creation (Rabbi Aruch Halevi Epstein, *Torah Temimah* to Leviticus 18:22).

On the Other Hand:

God created all kinds of people, both heterosexuals and homosexuals.

a. See Text Study #2a above.

Probing: Ideas and Issues

What difficulties might someone have in defining the word "natural"? How do *you* define "natural"? What do you think Rabbi Epstein means by the phrase: "going astray from the foundations of the creation"? Is there more than one way to understand what are the foundations of creation? If we say, "yes, but one way is *more legitimate* than other ways," by what authority do we do so?

4. **Does homosexuality threaten "family values"?**

On the One Hand:

Homosexuality violates family values.

A. At the root of the precept [against homosexuality] lies the reason that the Eternal Who Is Blessed desires the settlement of the world God created. Therefore God commanded us that human seed should not be destroyed by carnal relations with males: for this is indeed destruction, since there can be no fruitful benefit of offspring from it, nor the fulfillment of the religious duty of conjugal rights [due one's wife] . . . (*Sefer Ha-Chinuch*, no. 209).

On the Other Hand:

There are many ways to contribute to the Jewish community. One is by establishing a loving home and raising children — something many homosexuals choose to do.

a. What grounds could there be, Jewishly speaking, for a more permissive stand [concerning homosexuality]?

> There are other ways . . . of contributing to the survival of the Jewish people, aside from physically begetting or bearing children: many Jewish homosexuals support worthy Jewish causes and institutions . . . some make their contributions as teachers of Judaism . . .
>
> As to the crucial importance of the family for providing a nurturing, loving, and caring relationship, many homosexuals establish a home in which mutual love, genuine sharing, responsiveness and responsibility and lifelong faithfulness are a reality: many are prepared, when society allows, to serve as adoptive or foster parents: and some homosexuals lovingly rear children that they themselves have begotten or borne in a previously heterosexual marriage (Rabbi Herschel Matt, *Conservative Judaism*, Spring 1987).

Probing: Ideas and Issues

Why might someone suggest that homosexuality violates family values? What would Rabbi Matt's arguments be for contesting such a suggestion?

5. **What is the range of responses to homosexuality in the Jewish community?**

On the One Hand:

Mainstream Orthodoxy today generally condemns homosexual acts, though may encourage compassion for individual "sufferers."

A. Clearly, while Judaism needs no defense or apology in regard to its esteem for neighborly love and compassion for the individual sufferer, it cannot possibly abide a wholesale dismissal of its most basic moral principles on the grounds that those subject to its judgments find them repressive . . .

Homosexuality is no different from any other anti-social or anti-*halakhic* act, where it is legitimate to distinguish between the objective act itself, including its social and moral consequences, and the mentality and inner development of the person who perpetuates the act . . . To use *halachic* terminology, the objective crime remains a *ma'aseh avayrah* (a forbidden act) whereas the person who transgresses is considered innocent on the grounds of ["*oh-ness*"] (force beyond one's control) (Rabbi Norman Lamm, "Judaism and the Modern Attitude toward Homosexuality," *Encyclopaedia Judaica Yearbook*, 1974).

On the Other Hand:

Scientific, social, and moral concerns have propelled many Jewish communities to reexamine homosexuality with increasing openness.

a. The American Psychiatric Association, in its April 1993 *Fact Sheet* (p. 1) states:

There is no evidence that any treatment can change a homosexual person's deep-seated sexual feelings for others of the same sex. Clinical experience suggests that any person who seeks conversion therapy may be doing so because of social bias that has resulted in internalized homophobia, and that gay men and lesbians who have accepted their sexual orientation positively are better adjusted than those who have not

done so.

b. Rabbi Elliot N. Dorff presents numerous sources, including the previous one, indicating that homosexuals cannot alter their sexual orientation.

It seems to me, [there is a necessity for] a rethinking and recasting of the law, *for if anything is clear about the tradition, it is that it assumed that gay behavior is a matter of choice.* Otherwise, a commandment forbidding it would logically make no sense — any more than would a commandment that prohibited breathing for any but the shortest periods of time.

Now, of course, it is logically possible to say to gays and lesbians, as some Rabbis writing on the subject have said, that if they cannot change their homosexual orientation, they should remain celibate all their lives. That result, however, is downright cruel.

Moreover, I find such a position theologically untenable. I, for one, cannot believe that the God who created us all produced a certain percentage of us to have sexual drives that cannot be legally expressed under any circumstances. That is simply mind-boggling — and, frankly, un-Jewish . . .

Furthermore, it seems to me that to ask gays and lesbians to remain celibate all their lives is not halakhically required. If gays and lesbians are right in asserting that they have no choice in being homosexual . . . then they are as forced to be gay as straights are forced to be straight . . .

Putting the matter theologically, as the texts on compulsion do, if human beings can never reasonably require a person to do what is impossible for him or her, one would surely expect that to be even more true of God, who presumably knows the nature of each of us and therefore commands only what is appropriate to the various groups of us . . . (Elliot Dorff, *Matters of Life and Death*, pp. 144-147).

c. . . . [The] basic choice [for homosexuals] is not whether "to be homosexual" but whether to live openly and with integrity what they truly are — men and women, who, for reasons not of their own making or choosing, are able to know the blessing of true sexual fulfillment primarily or exclusively through relationship with someone of their own sex . . .

   As for the Torah's condemnation of homosexuality, we follow those teachers who have taught us that though the Torah contains God's word, it is not identical with God's word; it is both divine and human. Insofar as the Torah reflects the divine intent, its prohibition of homosexuality could not have had in mind the kind of homosexuality we have been speaking of: insofar as it reflects mere human attempts to grasp the divine intent, it reflects also a human misunderstanding of the kind of homosexuality that is forbidden . . . (Rabbi Herschel Matt, *Conservative Judaism*, Spring 1987).

Probing: Ideas and Issues

Rabbi Norman Lamm uses these *halachic* terms: *ma'aseh avayrah* (a forbidden act) and *oh-ness* (force beyond one's control). How does he apply the terms to homosexuality? In what ways is his statement consistent with views expressed in traditional Jewish texts? In what ways does his statement reflect modern attitudes regarding homosexuality? Do you feel Rabbi Lamm succeeds in balancing traditional beliefs with modern concerns? Why or why not?

What are some reasons why many Jewish

communities are reexamining homosexuality with increasing openness? If you were (are) homosexual and felt you wanted to talk to someone about personal issues regarding your sexual identity, who would you go to: Rabbi Lamm, Rabbi Dorff, or Rabbi Matt? Explain your choice.

6. **Does homosexuality threaten the cherished institution of marriage?**

On the One Hand:

Homosexuality can destroy marriages.

A. *Toe-ay atah bah*, "you are going astray" is regarding . . . those who abandon their wives and indulge in homosexuality (Rabbi Asher ben Jehiel).

On the Other Hand:

A homosexual person's constitution prevents him/her from finding happiness and fulfillment in marriage with someone of the opposite sex. Sanctifying same-sex partnerships promotes the Jewish values of long-term, monogamous relationships.

a. The Jewish values and principles which I regard as eternal, transcendent and divinely ordained do not condemn homosexuality. The Judaism I cherish and affirm teaches love of humanity, respect for the spark of divinity in every person and the human right to live with dignity. The God I worship endorses loving, responsible and committed human relationships, regardless of the sex of the persons involved (Janet Marder, "Jewish and Gay," *Keeping Posted* 32, 2; November 1986).

b. The Jewish tradition sanctifies monogamous, loving sex among heterosexuals as marriage, and, the argument goes, we should do the same in our time for homosexuals (Elliot Dorff, *Matters of Life and Death*, p. 149).

c. A statement from the Reform Movement's Central Conference of American Rabbis (CCAR):

> WHEREAS justice and human dignity are cherished Jewish values, and
>
> WHEREAS, the institutions of Reform Judaism have a long history of support for civil and equal rights for gays and lesbians, and
>
> WHEREAS, North American organizations of the Reform Movement have passed resolutions in support of civil marriage for gays and lesbians, therefore
>
> WE DO HEREBY RESOLVE, that the relationship of a Jewish, same-gender couple is worthy of affirmation through appropriate Jewish ritual, and
>
> FURTHER RESOLVED, that we recognize the diversity of opinions within our ranks on this issue. We support the decision of those who choose to officiate at rituals of union for same-gender couples, and we support the decision of those who do not, and
>
> FURTHER RESOLVED, that we call upon the CCAR to support all colleagues in their choices in this matter, and
>
> FURTHER RESOLVED, that we also call upon the CCAR to develop both educational and liturgical resources in this area (Ad Hoc Committee on Human Sexuality, CCAR, 1998).

Probing: Ideas and Issues

What might be an objection(s) to Jewish commitment ceremonies or same-sex marriages? What are reasons to endorse them?

RELATED MIDDOT AND MITZVOT

A complete list of *middot* and *mitzvot* that relate to issues of sexuality appears in Chapter 11, "Foundations of Sexual Ethics," on pages 288-289.

ACTIVITIES

A First Look: Key Issues and Ideas

1. A set induction: As presented in the "Overview" and "Text Study" sections above, the issue of homosexuality often elicits strong reaction from people. To establish an atmosphere of openness about this topic, canvass the group's preconceptions about homosexuality. Make two lists on the board: Entitle one "What We (Think We) Know about Homo-sexuality," and the other "Things We've Heard about Homosexuality (that may or may not be true)." At this point don't correct students by saying, "Actually, we don't know that for sure," or "That happens to be a myth." Allow students simply to get their ideas out there for everyone to look at. Here are some examples of what a group might come up with for each of the categories.

What We (Think We) Know about Homosexuality:

- Homosexuals are born that way.

- The Torah says you aren't supposed to be gay.

- Some people who are homosexual try to hide it.

- There are gays and lesbians who adopt children.

- There are gay/lesbian synagogues.

- You can get A.I.D.S. from gay sex.

- Etc.

Things We've Heard about Homosexuality (that may or may not be true):

- Gay men like to meet at bars.

- People from other religions often decide to lead celibate lives because they're homosexual.

- People are less prejudiced toward lesbians than gay men.

- Parents who treat their sons like sissies can make them turn gay.

- In communities that strongly oppose homosexuality, some gay people will get married, but then go to same-sex prostitutes on the side.

- Etc.

Following this exercise, you can go in one of several directions:

One option: Simply put the lists aside for now and continue with an overview of the topic, text study, and discussion of the scenarios (as outlined above). Afterwards, as an exercise to conclude study of the topic, come back to the lists and have students reexamine them. Ask students to comment on what they now believe is true and what they think is myth, and why.

Another possibility: Invite to class a Rabbi, or better, a whole panel of guests to discuss their views of the comments on the lists. Include in a panel: a Rabbi (or two Rabbis who represent different perspectives), a psychologist (or other mental health professional), and one or more well-adjusted gay or lesbian adults.

A third possibility: Use the list as a basis for student research. Divide the comments among the students or small groups of students. Ask them to research responses to the comments, then report back to the group. Brainstorm ways to do the research. For example, students might look at Jewish texts, talk to Rabbis and other educated Jewish teachers, talk with gay and lesbian individuals, do research in the library, and/or do research on the Internet.

2. Explain the comment below by drawing on the material in the "Overview" and "Text Study" sections above (the statement is the "On the Other Hand" answer to Text Study question # 5 above):

> Scientific, social, and moral concerns have propelled many Jewish communities to reexamine homosexuality with increasing openness.

Address: (1) What specifically are the concerns, and (2) how some Jewish leaders (representing "communities" of thought) are responding.

Applying Middot and Mitzvot

1. Discuss the relevance of these *middot, mitzvot,* and Jewish concepts to the topic of homosexuality:

- Being created in the Image of God

- *Anavah* (Humility)

- *Emet* (Truthfulness)

- *Emunah* (Trustworthiness)

- *Lo Levayesh* (Not Embarrassing)

- *Ma'akeh* (Preventing Accidents)

- *Mechabayd Zeh et Zeh* (Honoring Others)

- *Ohev Zeh et Zeh* and *"V'ahavta L'rayacha Kamocha"* (Loving Others; "Love your neighbor as yourself")

- *Simchah* (Joy and Happiness)

- *Tikkun Olam* (Repairing the World)

Note that some of the above ideas are mentioned in the last two paragraphs of the Overview above, p. 315. Others can be found in the "Related *Middot* and *Mitzvot*" section of Chapter 11, "Foundations of Sexual Ethics," on pp. 288-289. This list serves as a general list for all issues of sexuality in Chapters 11 through 15. Chapter 11 also contains suggestions about where to find more information about several of the *middot* and *mitzvot* — see "Activities: Applying *Middot* and *Mitzvot*," pp. 289-290. For more on *Anavah* (Humility), see *Teaching Jewish Virtues: Sacred Sources and Arts Activities* by Susan Freeman, pp. 8-25.

Stories: Understanding through Listening

1. With the group, read over the situations in the "Scenarios: How Things Have Changed" section above (pp. 315-317). Ask two volunteers to play the main characters, Rabbi Noam Mordecai and Noam from New York. Have group members "interview" the characters. Remind participants to be respectful of *tzeniyut* or modesty — that is, no sexually explicit questions. Appropriate sample questions are:

   - When did you first think you might be gay?

   - How did you feel when you thought you were gay?

   - Were you worried about what other teenagers would think about your homosexuality?

   - Were you worried about what your parents would think?

   - What is (or was) the most difficult thing about being gay?

   - Would you do anything different regarding your lifestyle if you had to do it over again?

   - Etc.

2. Conduct an interview, similar to the one outlined above. Instead of interviewing imaginary characters, invite gay or lesbian individuals from the community to talk with your group. Ask them to share their stories about coming to understand their sexual identity; their relationship with Judaism and the Jewish community; how they do and do not feel accepted in their sexual identity; and what Jewish family means to them. You may want to incorporate the suggested interview questions from the previous exercise.

3. Suggestions for further reading:

   - Visit a bookstore that features gay, lesbian, and bisexual interests. Browse and/or speak with a salesperson about your interests. Many large bookstores also have a special section featuring this topic.

   - Browse on your local library's computer, entering a "search" for your particular interest (for example, "gay teens").

   - Browse one of the on-line book stores, entering a "search" for your particular interest. Bookstores to check out include: Amazon.com (www.amazon.com), Barnes and Noble (www.barnesandnoble.com), and Books-A-Million (www. booksamillioninc.com).

   - For an excellent bibliography that includes both fiction and nonfiction, see the one published in *The Journey Out: A Guide for and about Lesbian, Gay, and Bisexual Teens* by Rachel Pollack and Cheryl Schwartz, pp. 134-139.

Action: Getting Out, Getting Involved

1. Many organizations exist that address issues pertinent to gays, lesbians, and bisexuals. The organizations may focus on education, advocacy, political lobbying, religious concerns, providing emotional support, and/or health issues. Assign individuals or small groups to research and report back on the activities and positions of various organizations. In their reports they should:

   - Summarize what the organization does.

   - Discuss why (or why not) a committed Jew might want to become involved in the organization.

   - Investigate ways the organization suggests interested individuals might get involved with their agenda.

Here are a few suggestions of organizations to research:

World Congress of Gay, Lesbian, Bisexual, and Transgender Jews (Keshet Ga'avah): www.wcgljo.org.

Human Rights Campaign Fund: www.hrc.org.

Parents, Families and Friends of Lesbians and Gays (PFLAG): www.pflag.org.

For additional suggestions, visit the Human Rights Campaign Fund's web site (www.hrc.org) and click on "links."

2. Find out if your synagogue has a support, interest, or concerns group for gays, lesbians, and bisexuals. If not, and your group feels there would be interest in such a group, have them help plan and organize one.

3. Lead a discussion: Does your city have a Gay/ Lesbian/Bisexual Pride march? If not, imagine that it did. Should the Jewish community be represented in such a march? Who should go? What should their banner or sign boards say?

4. Have your group create a series of posters opposing bigotry and promoting tolerance and compassion. Fold large pieces of paper in half. On one half, write at the top in large letters the heading: "What Bigotry Leads To . . . " On the other half, write: "Showing Tolerance Means . . . " (or "Showing Compassion Means . . . "). Students provide illustrations reflecting the statements. Display the posters in a public place.

Wrestling: Engagement with the Issues

1. In the 1990s, an artist put together a photograph exhibit featuring various families, entitled "Love Makes a Family." Ask participants to envision a photograph exhibit showing families with:

- Two adults of the opposite sex and children.

- A single adult and children.

- Adults and children spanning several generations.

- Members of different colors or races.

- Members who have physical disabilities.

- Two adults of the same sex and children.

- Two adults and no children.

- An older man and a much younger woman with children.

- An older woman and a much younger man with children.

- Etc.

The group imagines they are members of the synagogue exhibit committee. They must come up with a recommendation: Should the synagogue feature this exhibit in their gallery?

2. Refer to the previous exercise. Have the group actually create their own exhibit called "Jewish Families." They might use photographs (old and new), drawings, sculpture, etc. As part of the exhibit planning and preparing, they must make a decision about how they will incorporate gay and/or lesbian headed households.

Empathy

1. Have participants talk about how it might feel to be a homosexual. How might it feel to be the target of bigotry, hatred, or violence because of your sexual orientation? Read and discuss this passage by Reverend Martin Niemöller, a German Lutheran pastor who was arrested by the Gestapo and sent to Dachau in 1938. He was freed by the Allied Forces in 1945:

First They Came For . . .

In Germany, the Nazis first came for the Communists,
and I didn't speak up because I wasn't a Communist.

Then they came for the Jews,
and I didn't speak up because I wasn't a Jew.
Then they came for the trade unionists,
and I didn't speak up because I wasn't a trade unionist.
Then they came for the Catholics,
but I didn't speak up because I was a Protestant.
Then they came for me,
and by that time there was no one left to speak up.

Ask: What happens in this piece by Reverend Niemöller? What point is he trying to get across? What might this passage suggest are our obligations to people who are different from us? What if the difference between "us" and "them" (or "me" and "you") is our sexual identity — that is, what obligations do we have to stand up for those who are victimized because of their sexual orientation? Have you witnessed others stand up against such bigotry? Have you yourself ever done so? Will you do so in the future if the opportunity presents itself?

2. Have participants write an empathetic letter to an imaginary friend who has just revealed to you that he is gay or that she is lesbian.

BIBLIOGRAPHY

A complete Bibliography for the five chapters dealing with issues of sexuality (Chapters 11-15) appears at the end of Chapter 11, "Foundations of Sexual Ethics," on pages 294-296.

CHAPTER 15

SEX OUTSIDE OF MARRIAGE

OVERVIEW

Judaism, like many other religions and cultures, highly values marriage. Sex between spouses does involve ethical considerations. Still, the marital relationship provides well-established boundaries for appropriate sexual intimacy. In comparison, once we consider sex outside of marriage, ethical dilemmas multiply.

A significant reason for increased dilemmas is that responsibilities of unmarried sex partners are poorly defined. Even so, ethics challenge us to maintain *some* standards in nonmarital sexual relationships. Is it logical to think we can do so? That is, can we expect love, even if we don't require long-term commitment? Can we insist on mutual respect, even if we don't require love? If mutual respect is a sufficient standard for intercourse, why draw the line there? Why not condone anonymous, casual sex? And if casual sex is okay, who are we to say that promiscuity and pornography are "out-of-bounds"? These questions illustrate the ethical "slippery slope" regarding nonmarital sex.

In effect, the slippery slope warns: Suppose we allow for some exceptions to the sex-only-in-marriage rule. What is to prevent us from justifying different sex partners, some of them strangers, every night of the week? In short, how can we legitimately draw *any* boundaries for appropriate sex, once we remove the boundary of marriage?

Pondering *how* to draw up appropriate guidelines assumes we accept that this is something we *should* do. Thus, we must ask: why, with all the concerns of the slippery slope, would we consider challenging the boundary of marriage? The primary reason is that we face new cultural and sociological realities in our day. Especially

significant is the fact that most sexually mature individuals spend a significant portion of their lives not married. Many people never marry. Specifically, young people may delay marriage in order to realize professional and/or educational goals. Young people may delay marriage because they do not feel emotionally ready for that commitment. They may want more life experience in order to clarify what they seek in a life partner. For divorced individuals or for widows/widowers, remarriage raises complicated issues of its own.

Rushing marriage so as to have sex "legally" is not particularly wise. If two unmarried adults consent to have intercourse, we cannot accuse them of being *unethical*. They are not hurting anyone. But would such individuals be violating standards of Jewish ethics? Can a Jewish viewpoint legitimately relax its traditional presumptions regarding single people? That is, should Judaism insist on celibacy for never married, divorced, or widowed individuals? What is Judaism's responsibility in responding to the challenges of our time? What innovative guidelines can our tradition offer that will both recognize the realities of our circumstances, yet respect cherished values? Finally, how should community adults guide youth through the confusing landscape of sexual expectations today?

Jewish Perspectives

Background

This discussion of "Sex Outside of Marriage" from a Jewish perspective begins with a review of a few important themes first covered in Chapter 11, "Foundations of Sexual Ethics" (pp. 273-296). The following ideas directly apply to our present topic:

- "Black and White" and "Gray" Areas of Sexuality

- Holiness

- Modesty (*Tzeniyut*)

- Revealing Ourselves

"Black and White" and "Gray" Areas of Sexuality

Sex outside of marriage can imply various sexual interactions, from monogamous "living together" situations to orgies. Some sexual behaviors are never acceptable from a Jewish point of view. These "black and white" cases include forbidden sexual relations such as incest and adultery.

Putting these examples aside, modern Jews recognize the commonplace occurrence of intercourse outside of marriage. If we turn to Judaism to help us apply ethical guidelines to relationships that aren't forbidden, but aren't marriage either, we navigate a "gray area." An example "gray area" relationship might be two 20-year-old individuals who have dated steadily, love each other, and enjoy sexual intimacy with each other. But for personal and professional reasons, these individuals are not ready to commit to marriage.

The Rabbi and theologian Eugene B. Borowitz presents a nuanced understanding of sexual relationships in his book *Choosing a Sex Ethic: A Jewish Inquiry*. The ethics he examines include: (1) healthy orgasm, (2) mutual consent, (3) love, and (4) marriage.

Borowitz first examines the ethics of the healthy orgasm. He finds its criterion for sex to be ethically defective primarily because it makes "possible the subordination of one person's rights to that of the other."[1]

The mutual consent criterion for sex is an ethical advance over intercourse that may involve coercion or exploitation. But because mutual consent is interested only in two aspects of a person — his/her will and his/her sexuality — it is unsatisfactory as well. A person's moral function becomes something separate from the rest of him/her. Mutual consent may not be *unethical,* but it compromises essential aspects of what it is to be a human being. Meaningful relationships ask individuals to embrace the *fullness* of who the other is.[2]

What about love? A sexual relationship that is born of love and is an expression of love is not unethical. As Borowitz writes, "Any love-making which is true to the love between us, even if we are unmarried, is right."[3] Love and friendship are highly esteemed values in a relationship. A sexual relationship that grows out of love and friendship can be a source of great pleasure and an expression of deeply felt emotion.

Still, Borowitz would view an "ordinary" love relationship on a continuum of values. Love may be wonderful in the present moment, and perhaps carry past meaning as well. However, the future, too, is integral to the wholeness of a person's identity.

> "The integrity of self . . . carries on from birth to death . . . Every ordinary love takes on great joy at its inception because of the hope that it will be what we have always known we wanted, a lifelong love, one that will fill our lives not merely in the present but in all the future . . . As the Song of Songs [8:6] puts it, 'Love is stronger than death.' This is less a romantic exaggeration than the acknowledgment of the most meaningful possible human situation."[4]

Rabbi Arthur Green suggests another innovative way to frame sexuality. He proposes a *"sliding scale* of sexual values" (see Text Study #1a below). Suppose we place Borowitz's four ethics on this sliding scale. A fully loving, committed relationship — that is, marriage — would stand at the top of the scale. Love (without commitment) would be a little lower. Mutual consent

---

[1]*Choosing a Sex Ethic*, 104.

[2]*Ibid.,* 105.

[3]*Ibid.,* 109-110.

[4]*Ibid.,* 109.

would be lower still. And below that would be healthy orgasm.

Holiness

See Chapter 11, "Foundations of Sexual Ethics" (pp. 273-296) for a fuller exploration of this value. Here, our intention is to connect the discussion immediately above to holiness. Judaism advocates marriage as the ideal vehicle for attaining holiness in a relationship. Likewise, marriage is at the top of a Jewish "sliding scale of sexual values."

Judaism guides us to aspire to holiness in our lives. If we become involved in a sexual relationship outside of marriage, we are not to lose sight of Jewish aspirations. We can incorporate holy values into our intimate lives, however defined. Judaism expects this of us. Honesty, integrity, respect, humility, love, and modesty elevate our relationships. These qualities raise us higher on the "sliding scale."

Modesty (Tzeniyut)

Refer to Chapter 11, "Foundations of Sexual Ethics," pp. 273-296.

Revealing Ourselves

Besides reviewing the ideas in Chapter 11, "Foundations of Sexual Ethics" (pp. 273-296), consider this: An accomplished sex researcher was asked to reflect on his work. What was most surprising to him in his years of research? The researcher responded that he had underestimated how great an impact a person's first intercourse had on him/her.

In meaningful sexual encounters, two people who reveal themselves sexually to each other, reveal vulnerability, as well. We'll come back to this idea. But before focusing on it, we take a closer look at the significance of self-exposure.

Suppose we were "caught" unawares in our physical nakedness. Most likely, we would feel embarrassed or slightly humiliated. To use a blunt example, walking in on someone while he/she is using the bathroom will make him/her feel improperly *exposed*. Most of us get over these fumbles easily enough. Physical "uncoverings" that are more purposeful feel worse. For instance, perhaps we find out that for months a "peeping Tom" (or "Tammy") has been watching us shower. Or, a brother's friends have been reading our diary, including romantic thoughts and fantasies. When privacy is violated in such ways, the tendency is to feel sickened with humiliation.

Unlike what happens when someone walks in on a naked person, a sexual relationship reveals a deeper vulnerability. That is, sexual sharing involves more than a physical revelation of self. True, some individuals so detach their emotional selves from their physical selves that sex becomes hardly different from an animal act (as in the healthy orgasm "ethic"). But for those who seek a holier way of relating, a higher level on the "sliding scale," sexual intimacy will expose our most sensitive spots. In making love, we reveal body, heart, and soul.

A healthy sexual relationship requires the emotional maturity and self-confidence to endure the impact of full self-revelation. Thus, we return to two important ideas mentioned above: (1) the influence of a person's first intercourse; and (2) that in meaningful sexual encounters, in revealing ourselves to one another, we reveal vulnerabilities, as well. Suppose a person exposes too much of him/herself too soon in a relationship. Possible reasons might be because of peer pressure, pressure from a partner, low self-worth, or a desire for the partner to feel more committed to a shaky relationship. Whatever the case, suppose this individual prematurely engages in intercourse. When the relationship inevitably falls apart, the result can be extraordinarily painful. Feelings of humiliation and perhaps violation can be intense. These feelings will go well beyond those associated with inappropriately catching a glimpse of another's nakedness. Carelessly revealing our emotional and spiritual vulnerability can cause suffering lasting longer than we might ever imagine.

Ready for Sex, but Not Ready for Marriage: Some Practical Guidelines

To review so far: We won't find a Jewish ethic urging unmarried individuals to "go out and have sex." Judaism considers marriage to be the ideal relationship for sexual intercourse. Yet, given our modern reality, we understand people will engage in intercourse outside of marriage. We can and should bring Jewish values into our relationships even if they are not marriages. Still, nonmarital sexual relationships are not all equal. We mentioned the "defects" of the ethics of "healthy orgasm" and "mutual consent," and also the benefits and limits of "ordinary love." We suggested the goal of aiming to place ourselves on the higher end of the "sliding scale of Jewish sexual values."

Certainly it can be helpful to have an awareness of some philosophical underpinnings involved in making decisions regarding nonmarital sex. But such awareness doesn't mean making a decision of "should I?" or "shouldn't I?" will be easy. When emotions and ethics are involved, feeling absolutely confident about a decision is rare. Even so, we can add a few more practical insights regarding nonmarital sex to the general guidelines presented thus far.

Making Decisions

The most important guideline is that *we* must take responsibility for making decisions. We are not passive players in a life that unfolds around us. Specifically, we should never fall into bed with someone because passion overtakes us. Simply *allowing* sexual intercourse to happen is equivalent to accepting no guidelines. At its very foundation, Judaism teaches that we have choices, and that we make choices. Therefore, a *desire* for intercourse should only become an *act* of intercourse after conscious and conscientious consideration. In other words, we choose and plan to make love because we have thought about it, because we have discussed it with our partner, and because we have come to a reasoned and ethical decision regarding this significant step.

Choosing Influences

Choosing influences is related to the idea above. We not only decide, but we decide *how to decide*. What ideas and values do we want to employ in making our sexual decisions?

Sexual images and trends saturate our modern world. Media culture often presents sex overly casually and superficially. Pornography turns human bodies into sex objects. There is no shortage of frivolous and even harmful attitudes toward sex in our society. The mode of influence might be a billboard on an urban boulevard. Or, it might be the implicit "everyone's-doing-it" culture of a suburban high school. In essence, we must ask ourselves these two questions regarding what should influence our sexual behavior: Do we believe that (1) sex should be a sacred encounter of two individuals who love and trust each other; or (2) sex is a response to passions, urges, and social pressures? Given these two choices, Judaism clearly would embrace the former.

Questions to Ask, Values to Consider

As stated before, it is important for individuals not to engage in sex prematurely. But what does "prematurely" mean? Outside of marriage, what criteria might we use to figure out when taking the step to engage in sexual intercourse is appropriate in a given relationship? For some specific ideas, see "General Perspectives" in Chapter 11, "Foundations of Sexual Ethics," pp. 275-276. Also see the following paragraphs and Text Study #1B below.

Fleeting vs. Enduring Values

One way to distinguish marriage from other sexual relationships is by singling out the value of commitment. Nonmarital sexual relationships do not presume the enduring commitment that marital relationships do. Nevertheless, the value of commitment can teach us something even about "uncommitted" relationships.

When faced with decisions regarding nonmarital sex, we weigh competing considerations.

Some values may conflict with others. Judaism guides us to embrace enduring values. While pleasure, fun, excitement, and heeding social pressures may be values, they are fleeting ones. Enduring values include trust, respect, honesty, love, modesty, and responsibility. Abiding by fleeting values *in isolation* from enduring ones is an insufficient standard for sex.

Of course, Judaism allows us to enjoy fleeting values, but within the broader framework of enduring values. We may experience sensual pleasure (and savor tasty foods and enjoy the beauty of nature), but must aim for standards that transcend instant or fleeting gratification.

Teen Sex

Our discussion of ethics pertaining to nonmarital sex assumes it happens between adults (18 or older). As Rabbi Michael Gold writes, "Teens are physically ready to have sex long before they are emotionally ready . . . " See Text Study #1c for a fuller exploration of teen sex issues.

Masturbation

This subject relates to teens and others. If, as Rabbi Gold puts it, "teens are physically ready to have sex long before they are emotionally ready . . . ," they need safe and appropriate ways to relieve the sexual tension they feel. Perhaps a relaxation of Judaism's traditional disapproval of masturbation is in order (see Text Study #1c and #1d in Chapter 12, "Masturbation," p. 300, and also "Scenarios: How Things Have Changed" in that chapter, pp. 333-334).

Birth Control

In Chapter 13, "Birth Control," we discuss the responsibility of those who engage in sex outside of marriage to use contraception. As Eugene B. Borowitz puts it, "Careful, effective contraception is an ethical necessity if there is to be any legitimation of premarital sexual intercourse" (see Text Study #1e and #1f in Chapter 13, "Birth Control," p. 308).

General Perspectives

Refer to the information in Chapter 11, "Foundations of Sexual Ethics," in the "General Perspectives" section, pp. 275-276. The notions of ethical sexual behavior outlined there apply to our topic here, as well.

Summary of the Overview

- Marriage is Judaism's ideal relationship for sexual intercourse.

- Yet, current trends suggest that some people will engage in intercourse outside of marriage.

- To remain relevant, Judaism must respond meaningfully to these trends rather than ignore or deny them.

- A meaningful response begins by teaching the importance of bringing enduring Jewish values into intimate nonmarital relationships.

SCENARIOS: HOW THINGS HAVE CHANGED

The "Scenarios: How Things Have Changed" section in Chapter 11, "Foundations of Jewish Sexual Ethics" address the tensions between physical *readiness for sex* and emotional and practical *unpreparedness for marriage* (see pp. 277-278).

In that chapter's "Scenario 2," we met the high school sweethearts Marc and Liana. Marc is 18 years old, and Liana is 16. What we add here is this:

> Marc and Liana continue to date exclusively and continue to feel they want to be together the rest of their lives. But they also are clear that they won't be ready for marriage at least until both are in their mid-twenties. Their physical relationship progresses from kissing to intimate touching over the course of two years. When Liana is 18, they begin to bring each other to orgasm

manually. During those months of more intense sexual intimacy, they also start to talk about having sexual intercourse with each other. After discussing birth control, they agree that Liana will take oral contraceptives. Marc and Liana now are enjoying sexual intercourse with each other. They have been making love for a few months now. When Liana goes to study abroad next year, they wonder what will happen to their relationship. Meanwhile, they feel that, for now, they are relating to each other in a meaningful and worthy way.

How Things Have Changed

Marc and Liana decide to have sex, but remain unmarried. Their decision process is similar to those many young people will engage in. While Marc and Liana have few concrete signposts to guide them in their choices, we sense that they try to anchor their decision using some important standards. Here are some of them:

- They deliberately make a decision rather than "let it happen."

- Their decision seems to be based on their authentic needs and desires, rather than on broader, indirect social pressures.

- Mutuality and equality are evident in their relationship.

- They seem to communicate well with each other.

- They respect each other.

- They trust each other.

- They love each other.

- They enjoy and care about each other's sexual pleasure, but anchor fleeting experiences in more enduring values.

- They use birth control.

- They wait to have intercourse until both are over 18 years old.

These are all significant values. They reflect efforts to live and relate ethically to a lover. Marc and Liana's standards reflect many Jewish ethical values, as well. Clearly, some communities will accept only marriage as the appropriate place for sexual expression. But for those who venture outside traditional standards, Jewish wisdom can provide relevant, meaningful, and supportive guidance.

TEXT STUDY

The question of sex outside of marriage is fraught with ethical dilemmas. Jewish textual sources provide many insights, but these often highlight the tension between seemingly opposing considerations. The chart below poses the central question and offers two opposing points of view. Text sources supporting each argument follow.

Note: For other relevant texts, see Text Study #2E, #3B, #5A, #5a, and #5b in Chapter 11, "Foundations of Sexual Ethics," pp. 273-296, and Text Study #1c and #1d, in Chapter 12, "Masturbation," p. 300.

Sex Outside of Marriage: A Question to Consider

The Question	On the One Hand	On the Other Hand
1. Is sex outside of marriage permissible? (see p. 335)	Sexual relations belong only within the confines of marriage.	Recognizing the realities of modern life, Rabbis and others are rethinking guidelines for sexual relations between unmarried, consenting adults.

1. Is sex outside of marriage permissible?

On the One Hand:

Sexual relations belong only within the confines of marriage.

A. The following passage summarizes the traditional attitude regarding sex outside of marriage:

> Chastity before marriage has been considered an obvious requirement for all and was taken for granted by the tradition . . . There are many statements that support this point of view and demand that an unmarried person refrain from sexual intercourse. The references deal particularly with males (*Pesachim* 113a, b; *Shabbat* 152a). A statement of Rabbi Yochanan makes this very clear: "There is a small organ in man; he who satisfies it goes hungry and he who allows it to go hungry is satisfied" (*Sanhedrin* 107a) . . . All females were expected to be virgins at the time of their first marriage. The dowry of a nonvirgin was less than that of a virgin, and anyone falsely claiming virginity was subject to severe punishment (*American Reform Responsa,* p. 477).

B. Elliot N. Dorff, a Conservative Rabbi and theologian, writes:

> Marriage (*Kiddushin*) is holy precisely because a man and woman set each other apart from all others to live their lives together, taking responsibility for the children they bear. The willingness to assume these responsibilities is critical both for their own pleasure and growth and for the perpetuation of the Jewish community and the Jewish tradition. Marriage is also important in Judaism because it provides a structure for achieving core Jewish values in our intimate lives —

values like honesty, modesty, love, health and safety, and holiness. Marriage is no guarantee that we will succeed in this, but it does help us attain those values. Thus Judaism is not being irrational, prudish, old-fashioned, unrealistic, or mean in demanding that we limit our sexual intercourse to the context of marriage; it is rather responding to concerns that are at least as real and important in the fragmented society of today as they were in the more stable society of times past (*Matters of Life and Death*, p. 136).

C. Eugene B. Borowitz, a Reform Rabbi and theologian, writes:

> The most ethical form of human relationship I know is love-for-life. Its appropriate social and religious structure is the monogamous marriage. This being so, marriage is, if I may use the strange formulation of ethical pluralism, the most right context, that is, the best criterion for the validity of sexual intercourse. And I think every human being should try to reach the highest possible level of ethical behavior (*Choosing a Sex Ethic*, pp. 113-114).

On the Other Hand:

Recognizing the realities of modern life, Rabbis and others are rethinking guidelines for sexual relations between unmarried, consenting adults.

a. Living in a world where we cannot advocate either ideal sex or no sex as the alternatives, what we must begin to evolve is a *sliding scale* of sexual values . . . At the top of this scale would stand the fully knowing and loving relationship . . . , while rape — fully unconsenting and anonymous sexuality — would stand at the bottom. Somewhere near the middle of the scale, neither glorified nor condemned, would be the relationship of two consenting persons, treating one another with decency, fulfilling the biological aspects of one another's love-needs, while making no pretense at deeper intimacy. Given such a scale, a Jew might begin to judge his/her own sexual behavior in terms of a series of challenges which s/he might want to address (Arthur Green, "A Contemporary Approach To Jewish Sexuality," in *The Second Jewish Catalog*, p. 99).

(Please note: This passage makes important points for Jews to ponder today. However, most current thinking would object to including "rape" on any scale of sexual values, even if we call rape a "sexual *sin*." Although rape does involve a sex act, it more fittingly belongs in the category of violent crime.)

b. Those values that lead Judaism to advocate marriage — honesty, modesty, health and safety, love, and holiness — still apply to sexual relations outside marriage; they are just harder to achieve in that context. Indeed, precisely because unmarried couples cannot rely on the support of a marital bond to foster those values, it is all the more critical that if they engage in sexual intercourse, they must consciously strive to live by them. Even though their behavior will not be ideal by Jewish standards, to the extent that they can make those values real in their lives, they will be preserving their own humanity, their Jewishness, and their own mental and physical health, as well as that of their partner (Elliot N. Dorff, *Matters of Life and Death*, p. 137). (For a fuller treatment of these issues, see Dorff, *This Is My Beloved, This Is My Friend*, pp. 30-36.)

c. Regarding sexual relations between *unmarried, consenting adults*, Michael

Gold, a Conservative Rabbi, writes in *Does God Belong in the Bedroom?*:

Each of these three words is important. If one of the adults is married, the relationship becomes adulterous. If one of the adults is nonconsenting, it is a case of rape. If one of the partners is not an adult (18 or older), the relationship involves another dimension — teenage sex . . . (p. 58).

d. About teenage sex, Rabbi Gold writes:

Teens are physically ready to have sex long before they are emotionally ready . . . Teens, however, lack the emotional maturity necessary for a sexual relationship. They usually have neither the self-esteem nor the self-confidence to be truly consenting when confronted with sexual choices . . . Teens are especially susceptible to powerful peer pressure as well as to pressure from the media. They all too easily confuse lust or physical infatuation with love . . . Often teens are involved in reckless behavior [which can lead to pregnancy or the contraction of venereal diseases, including AIDS] . . . Too late, teens discover that they are vulnerable, for people who engage in sex open themselves to another in a very intimate way. An irresponsible sex partner can leave a young person emotionally if not physically scarred. Because of this risk and its serious repercussions, I believe teens are too young to be sexually active . . .

Of course, youngsters do not leap from no sex to full genital intercourse in one step; they move through various levels of sexual experimentation, from rather tentative kissing, to heavy petting with clothes, to genital contact and mutual masturbation. Traditional Judaism forbids all such physical activity between unmarried partners because of fear of the "slippery slope" — that any of these activities will lead to improper sexual intercourse. However, most young people in our society do not and will not abide by a prohibition against all physical contact between members of the opposite sex. Flirting and physical experimentation are part of growing up in today's society.

Recognizing this reality, parents can tell their children that they may draw boundaries within this continuum of physical activity. As we learn in the fourth blessing of the *"Amidah," chochmah* (wisdom) is the ability to distinguish boundaries and to abide by them. Thus we can teach our children that kissing is acceptable at a certain age, whereas genital manipulation is not. Parents can help their children set reasonable boundaries for themselves and their partners (pp. 173, 178-179).

e. About sex education:

Nobody should make assumptions about what kids know about sex. Research shows that while they're highly aware of sex generally, they're often pretty ignorant about the details. Good sex education is safe sex education, too. Helping kids to be aware of their bodies — of health and contraception, masturbation, sensual touching, and fantasy as well as intercourse — and of their feelings about sexuality can only make them better able to practice safe and egalitarian sex in what could be history's most honest chapter of sexual relations (Judith Levine, "Thinking about Sex" in *Tikkun, An Anthology*, edited by Michael Lerner, Oakland, CA and Jerusalem: Tikkun Books, 1992, p. 211).

Probing: Ideas and Issues

Why does Judaism view sex in the context of marriage as the ideal?

In Text #1a above Rabbi Green describes a "sliding scale of sexual values." What does he mean by this? What are the advantages of such a scale? What are the disadvantages? Does the "sliding scale of sexual values" make sense to you?

What is Rabbi Dorff's main point in Text Study #1b above? What advice would he have for a couple that chooses to engage in sexual relations outside of marriage?

In Text Study #1c above, why does Rabbi Gold say these three words — "unmarried," "consenting," and "adults" — are so important in discussing sex outside of marriage? Why should a committed Jew agree with him? What are Rabbi Gold's concerns about teen sex? Are his concerns valid? Do you believe his advice for teens (and their parents) is worthwhile? Explain.

RELATED MIDDOT AND MITZVOT

A complete list of *middot* and *mitzvot* that relate to issues of sexuality appears in Chapter 11, "Foundations of Sexual Ethics," on pages 288-289.

ACTIVITIES

See Chapter 11, "Foundations of Sexual Ethics," pp. 273-296, for a number of activities related to the issues in this chapter. Here are a few additional suggestions.

A First Look: Key Issues and Ideas

1. Below is a checklist of subtopics to cover in an overview of "Sex Outside of Marriage." A teacher should plan to touch on the follow-

ing themes:

- "Black and White" and "Gray" Areas of Sexuality
- Holiness
- Modesty (*Tzeniyut*)
- Revealing Ourselves
- Ready for Sex, but Not Ready for Marriage: Some Practical Guidelines

Guidelines include:

- Making Decisions
- Choosing Influences
- Questions to Ask, Values to Consider
- Fleeting versus Enduring Values
- Teen Sex
- Masturbation
- Birth Control

Stories: Understanding through Listening

1. Marc and Liana's "Scenario Update" is presented above. For a specific activity related to their story, refer to activity #4 in the "Stories:

Understanding through Listening" section of Chapter 11, "Foundations of Sexual Ethics," p. 291.

Wrestling: Engagement with the Issues

1. Have participants define their own sexual values. What standards do they feel must be met before they will engage in sexual intercourse? For those who might say marriage is their standard, ask them to be more specific — that is, what qualities would they seek in a lover who is a life partner? It may be best for participants to write their responses to the questions. If you feel the group is mature enough, have participants share and discuss what they wrote.

BIBLIOGRAPHY

A complete Bibliography for the five chapters dealing with issues of sexuality (Chapters 11-15) appears at the end of Chapter 11, "Foundations of Sexual Ethics," on pages 294-296.